Inside
CorelVENTURA 5

Ken Reeder
June Kanai Reeder
Ed Brown
Lee Musick
Rachel Daeger

NEW RIDERS PUBLISHING

New Riders Publishing, Indianapolis, Indiana

Inside CorelVENTURA 5

By Ken Reeder, June Kanai Reeder, Ed Brown, Lee Musick, Rachel Daeger

Published by:
New Riders Publishing
201 West 103rd Street
Indianapolis, IN 46290 USA

Printed in the United States of America 1 2 3 4 5 6 7 8 9 0

```
Inside CorelVENTURA 5/E.J. Brown…[et al.].
      p.   cm.
   Includes index.
   ISBN 1-56205-341-8
   1. Computer graphics.  2. CorelVENTURA.  3. Desktop Publishing.
   I. Brown, E. J. (Edward J.), 1959-    .
   T385.I4767  1995
   686.2'25445369--dc20                            95-4076
                                                       CIP
```

Warning and Disclaimer

Publisher	Don Fowley
Associate Publisher	Tim Huddleston
Product Development Manager	Rob Tidrow
Marketing Manager	Ray Robinson
Director of Special Projects	Cheri Robinson
Managing Editor	Tad Ringo

About the Author

Ken Reeder is co-owner with his wife, June, of Ideas to Images, a graphics training and consulting business. Ken has been a writer and trainer for the past four years. He also has traveled nationwide giving printing and publishing seminars. Ken has worked in advertising and as a communications manager.

June Kanai Reeder is co-owner with her husband, Ken, of Ideas to Images, a graphics training and consulting business. She has been a writer and trainer for the past six years. June has traveled nationwide giving printing and publishing seminars and worked as a product development specialist, writing, directing, and producing computer training videos.

Lee Musick is marketing coordinator for Indianapolis-based INTEC & Company, Inc., the largest computer supplies marketing group in the country. His main focus is database publishing of INTEC's product offerings, producing a 128-page, four-color catalog, all done with CorelVENTURA. He also develops other marketing materials for the thirty-four-member organization, including newsletters, brochures, sales flyers, product specification sheets, and product presentation materials. Prior to his five-year tenure at INTEC, Musick worked for ten years at a non-profit agricultural organization in Indianapolis, serving as managing editor of a bimonthly tabloid, associate editor of a quarterly four-color magazine, and the sole internal graphic artist and PC trouble-shooter.

A native Hoosier, **Rachel Deager** is a graduate of Indiana University School of Journalism. She joined the staff of The Columbia Magazine, the monthly publication of the Columbia Club of Indianapolis, following graduation. In 1994, she began a new business venture, KDB Press, with an associate, Ken D. Berry. KDB Press is involved with the production of magazines, newsletters, and other publications. Daeger is married and has a son, Aaron. She currently lives in Prince's Lake, Indiana.

Ed Brown graduated from the Hatfield Polytechnic (University of Hertfordshire) with a BSC in Computer Science. He followed a varied career as a programmer, software designer, QA, and support and training person before starting his own consulting business in 1988. He specializes in multinational work for a variety of companies. His company is responsible for the production of TAGLINE, a newsletter for VENTURA Publisher users around the world. Since forming Data & Documents in 1988, Ed has been successful in spreading multinational computing to every continent and is in demand as a speaker at events all over the world. He recently returned to school to study for an MSC in Marine Environmental Protection and is now applying his computer skills and diving skills to assist the environment. He is married to Jane and has a baby son, Joshua Samuel.

Trademark Acknowledgments

All terms mentioned in this book that are known to be trademarks or service marks have been appropriately capitalized. New Riders Publishing cannot attest to the accuracy of this information. Use of a term in this book should not be regarded as affecting the validity of any trademark or service mark. CorelVENTURA is a registered trademark of Corel Systems Corporation.

Product Director
Cheri Robinson

Acquisitions Editor
Stacey Beheler

Production Editor
Cliff Shubs

Copy Editors
Fran Blauw
Gail Burlakoff
Peter Kuhns
Steve Weiss

Technical Editor
John Shanely

Marketing Copywriter
Tamara Apple

Acquisitions Coordinator
Tracey Turgeson

Publisher's Assistant
Karen Opal

Cover Designer
Dan Armstrong

Cover Illustrator
Roger Morgan

Book Designer
Kim Scott

Production Team Supervisor
Katy Bodenmiller

Graphics Image Specialists
Dennis Sheehan
Clint Lahnen

Production Analysts
Dennis Clay Hager
Angela Bannan
Bobbi Satterfield

Production Team
Jama Carter, Charlotte Clapp
MaryAnn Cosby, Donna Harbin
Mike Henry, Judy Everly
Louisa Klucznik, Kevin Laseau
Donna Martin, Casey Price
Brian-Kent Proffitt
Erich Richter, SA Springer
Mary Beth Wakefield
Jeff Weissenberger
Dennis Wesner
Michelle Worthington

Indexer
Greg Eldred

Contents at a Glance

Table of Contents

INTRODUCTION

Introduction

CorelVENTURA 5, the latest addition to Corel's suite of graphics products, is an incredibly robust page layout and document design application. Using VENTURA, you can combine text, graphics, and photography to produce high quality professional publications. The power and flexibility of VENTURA enable you to create easily everything from smaller publications, such as brochures or newsletters, to complex manuals and multi-chapter books.

VENTURA has its origins in VENTURA Publisher, created by the Xerox Corporation. One of the earliest desktop publishing applications on the market, VENTURA has been a respected leader in the world of desktop publishing and part of the phenomenal rise of the use of personal computers. In 1993, the Corel Corporation acquired the rights to sell and distribute VENTURA, and it has gone on to enhance the product in many ways.

Because of its broad range of features, VENTURA Publisher has long been an industry favorite for publishing professionals. Many of the magazines, books, and other publications you have read over the years have been produced with VENTURA Publisher. Acquisition by Corel has given the world of desktop publishing a tool it has long awaited—a full-featured page composition program that is easy to use.

One of the great strengths of VENTURA is its belonging to the Corel suite of products. When you combine the design power of VENTURA with the graphics capabilities available in CorelDRAW, CorelPHOTO-PAINT, and CorelCHART, you will find all the tools necessary to produce creative, professional publications.

Who Should Read This Book

In a large sense, everyone is brand new to CorelVENTURA. Though there are similarities between VENTURA and versions of VENTURA Publisher, previous users will find many differences that require definition and explanation. This book is intended for all users of VENTURA. Newcomers to VENTURA will find that this book offers a solid foundation for becoming proficient in designing and producing a variety of publications, ranging from single-page brochures to multi-chapter books. For those who have used previous versions of VENTURA Publisher, this book will be an extremely useful reference tool. You will want to examine it thoroughly to identify and understand the ways that Corel has changed and improved upon VENTURA Publisher.

How This Book is Organized

This book is divided into four main parts, each intended to cover fully the progressive levels of VENTURA.

Part 1: Understanding How VENTURA "Thinks"

This part familiarizes you with fundamental VENTURA concepts such as publication structure, chapter organization, paragraph tags, and frames. To give you a feel for how documents are built, you will also explore a VENTURA publication file.

Part 2: Building a VENTURA Document

Here you will learn how to set up and create new documents. This section examines the structure of your page layout by adding and manipulating frames, loading text and graphics files, entering and formatting text, and working with graphics. Printing your document is detailed thoroughly, as well.

Part 3: Advanced VENTURA Options and Techniques

Part 3 discusses features of VENTURA designed for longer and more complex documents. You will learn about adding headers and footers and inserting footnotes. The generation of tables of contents and indexes is covered, too.

Part 4: Real-World VENTURA Project Exercises

To provide you an opportunity to build a document from the ground up, two exercises are included. Step-by-step instructions are provided to help you understand the process you will follow to take a publication from concept to printed product.

Using This Book

Inside CorelVENTURA 5 is part tutorial and part reference in nature. If you are new to the product, you will find this book an indispensable teaching tool. As you sit at your computer with CorelVENTURA, use the book to work through various features and steps. After you gain basic proficiency with the product, this book will become an invaluable reference tool. Users of previous versions of VENTURA Publisher will appreciate this aspect of the book, as well. The book is logically organized and thoroughly indexed and referenced for the quick location of portions of the program you need to review.

This book should not be considered a substitute for, nor a restatement of, the program's documentation. It was written as a learning and reference tool intended to enhance your growth as you use the product. The documentation that accompanies the software and online help are as necessary as this book.

Part I

Understanding How VENTURA "Thinks"

Chapter Snapshot

Never before has the Corel package offered so many great tools. With the inclusion of VENTURA, Corel now offers the complete desktop publishing solution. This chapter introduces this powerful desktop publishing package. In this chapter, you learn the following:

VENTURA is a powerful page design program designed to help you produce professional quality documents. This chapter teaches you the basics and gets you started creating your own documents.

CHAPTER

Introducing CorelVENTURA

Welcome to CorelVENTURA, one of the most popular, respected, and powerful desktop publishing applications in the world. In VENTURA, you will find all the tools you need to produce any printed piece. You can design sales brochures sure to dazzle the marketing department, magazines the graphic design department will applaud, training manuals both the instructors and students will appreciate, and stockholder reports that make the VIPs smile at you in the elevator. With CorelVENTURA, you have the power to design professional-looking documents quickly and easily. You will find this book an indispensible aid in discovering how to operate CorelVENTURA quickly and easily.

This chapter is designed to introduce you to CorelVENTURA. It begins with an overview of desktop publishing and moves on to discuss how VENTURA builds documents using style sheet, chapter, and publication files. Understanding how VENTURA builds documents is perhaps the most important step to operating the program quickly and efficiently. In this section, you will learn how to select the best style sheet, how chapter files manage text and graphics, and about the long document features available with publication files. The last section includes the steps for starting CorelVENTURA and a thorough examination of the VENTURA screen to help you get acquainted with the program.

What Is CorelVENTURA?

The whole concept of desktop publishing caused quite a stir in the graphic design and printing industries a few years ago. The term desktop publishing refers to the ability to use a computer to combine text and graphics on a page to produce printed materials. Desktop publishing has all but done away with the days of copyfitting and setting type, using a proportion wheel and a cropping tool to size and position graphics, and cutting and pasting everything together to produce the page layout.

Desktop publishing lets you enter and set type as you write, scale graphics on-the-fly, then piece it all together on the computer screen. Gone also is much of the waiting that accompanied the traditional print process. To produce a print project mechanically, you *waited* for the type to be re-set because it was needed in 11 point instead of 10 point; and *waited* for a graphic to be enlarged 112%, not 110%, and *waited* for your thumb to heal after you stabbed it again with the Exacto knife. With desktop publishing, you can change type faces and type sizes in a few seconds, scale and move text and graphics around the page quickly, even totally redesign the project. And through it all, you can take comfort in the fact that its pretty tough to stab yourself with a mouse (though in this business, its surely been tried a time or two).

CorelVENTURA Is a Welcome Addition

One of the earliest desktop publishing applications on the market, VENTURA has been a respected leader in the world of desktop publishing and part of the phenomenal rise of the use of personal computers. CorelVENTURA 5.0 is an application included in the CorelDRAW 5.0 suite of products. CorelDRAW is a powerful collection of graphics and publishing applications, with Corel-VENTURA being the latest addition. VENTURA is the perfect accompaniment to the Corel suite of products, nicely complimenting the drawing, charting, photo-manipulation, animation, and presentation applications already at your finger-tips.

CorelVENTURA is also sold as a separate product. Obviously, if you bought VENTURA separately, you might not have CorelDRAW and the other Corel applications.

VENTURA's Role in the Corel Suite

It's important to realize how VENTURA fits with the other Corel products. Corel's flagship product, CorelDRAW, is the perfect companion to VENTURA for desktop publishing. CorelDRAW's publishing features, though limited compared to VENTURA, are ideal for small brochures, flyers, and other short documents heavy on graphics, but limited on text. VENTURA, on the other hand, is a robust publishing program, perfectly suited for longer, more complex documents.

Of course you can also use the unparalleled graphics tools in CorelDRAW to create logos, technical drawings, and other illustrations to add to your VENTURA documents. CorelCHART can produce the charts, graphs, and tables your VENTURA documents require to communicate statistical messages. With CorelPHOTO-PAINT, the photographs used in your documents can be manipulated to create amazing special effects. Corel has made it easy to place these elements in a VENTURA document because VENTURA can directly accept files created in other Corel applications. VENTURA can load DRAW, CHART, and PHOTO-PAINT files directly, which means you won't have to export your drawings, charts, and photos into some other graphic format.

How VENTURA Builds Documents

When discussing how VENTURA builds documents, it helps to use the analogy of building a book. As you prepare to assemble a book, you would want to gather all of the elements that go into the book and establish some type of organizational process. First, you might gather all of the text and graphics, such as maps, illustrations and charts, intended for the book. In desktop publishing, the text and graphics are generally stored in separate computer files. For instance, you might want your book to include a logo created in CorelDRAW and a table created in Word for Windows.

The next step involves establishing a consistent look for laying out and formatting the book—often referred to as a *style sheet* in journalism circles. The style sheet determines formatting information such as the page margins and the font used for the book's headings. VENTURA uses a style sheet file in this same manner.

To keep things organized, the book would be built in chapters. The text and graphics for each chapter could be positioned and formatted using the style sheet as a guide. In VENTURA, each individual chapter is saved as a *chapter file.* The chapters are then assembled into the book. The book is what VENTURA calls the *publication file.* The publication file lets you work with all the chapters as one unit to control page numbering for the entire book, set up a table of contents, create an index, and affect other global changes. The concept of using style sheets, and chapter and publication files to build documents is fundamental to how VENTURA operates. Even if you are producing one-page flyers and newsletters, you will still be working with publication, chapter, and style sheet files.

By description, this process sounds relatively straightforward. But you know that organizing this type of project can be a nightmare. Fortunately, VENTURA does most of the really tedious work for you, leaving you charged with the part you are best at—the creative stuff. As you read on, you will discover that VENTURA is a dream for helping you organize complex publications.

Understanding Style Sheets

The concept of style sheets originated with the newspaper business. Style sheets provide a set of rules for everyone to follow in the writing and production of the newspaper. VENTURA's style sheets give you a set of rules for formatting your documents. The style sheet determines page layout information, such as margins and page numbering, as well as typographic information, such as font and paragraph formatting.

Style sheets are separate files that use the .STY extension. Because style sheets are separate files, you can use the same style sheet with several chapters (see fig. 1.1). Every chapter that uses a specific style sheet follows the exact same guidelines. This helps you to maintain consistency in your document designs. For instance, when building a book with multiple chapters, you might want each chapter to have the same page margins and number of columns. You would probably want each chapter heading to appear in the same type face and type size. All of this adds to the consistency and cohesiveness of your book design.

When using the same style sheet in multiple documents, its important to remember that changes made to the style sheet in one chapter file affect all other chapter files using that style sheet. This is great, for example, if all the chapters in your book used the same style sheet, and you need to make a change affecting the whole book. You simply make the changes in one chapter, knowing that all the others are automatically changed. As you will learn in Chapter 3, if you do not want changes to occur to every chapter using a certain style sheet, you must change the name of the style sheet so it has no connection to other chapters.

The steps for applying style sheets to chapter files are covered in Chapter 3, "Creating and Setting Up New Documents."

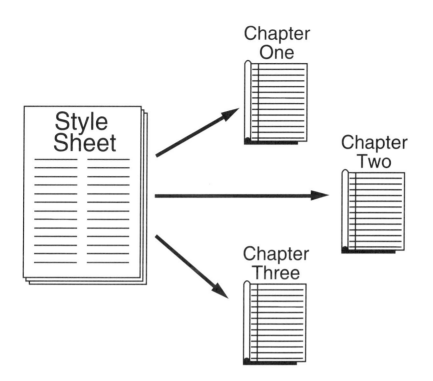

Figure 1.1
One style sheet can be used with all of the chapter files in a publication.

VENTURA's Predesigned Style Sheets

Not everyone is an expert in page layout; therefore, VENTURA supplies predesigned style sheets that provide a head start to producing documents such as magazines, brochures, books, and reports. When you begin a new document in VENTURA, you are asked to select a style sheet. If you are producing a book, use one of the book style sheets to set up a common page layout for books. Use a magazine style sheet to establish a layout ideal for designing magazine spreads. Rather than setting all the margins, columns, and text attributes manually, let an existing style sheet do the work for you.

VENTURA made the predesigned style sheets all the more useful by allowing you to modify and alter them as necessary. If the style sheet establishes a two-column layout, you can easily change it to a three-column layout. Every time you create a new file in VENTURA, you are asked to select a style sheet. The trick is to pick a predesigned style sheet that meets *most* of your requirements. You can then change those attributes that aren't exactly what you had in mind to create your own custom style sheet.

Tip

For a preview of the formatting and text attributes for each style sheet, refer to the Corel clip-art book under the section CorelVENTURA Templates.

When you install VENTURA, you are given the option of which style sheets you want to load and where you want to store them. Unless you specify otherwise, the predesigned style sheets are placed in the TYPESET and VPSTYLE directories. For instance, a style sheet for building books appears in the C:\VENTURA\TYPESET directory, and a style sheet for a tri-fold brochure appears in the C:\VENTURA\VPSTYLE directory.

Table 1.1 explains the predesigned style sheets included with CorelVENTURA.

Table 1.1
VENTURA's Predesigned Style Sheets

Style Sheet Name	Page Layout	Directory Stored In
_book_p1.sty	Book, 1 column	Typeset
_book_p2.sty	Book, 2 column	Typeset
_book_l2.sty	Brochure, landscape, 2 column	Typeset
_bro_p3.sty	Brochure, portrait, 3 column	Typeset
capabili.sty	Printer capabilities page	Typeset
_inv_p1.sty	Invoice form with line items	Typeset
_lstg_p2.sty	Product listing	Typeset
_ltr_p1.sty	Letter	Typeset
_mag_p3	Magazine	Typeset
_news_p2.sty	Newsletter, 2 column	Typeset
_news_p3.sty	Newsletter, 3 column	Typeset
_phone_p2.sty	Phone listing	Typeset
planadoc.sty	Planning form	Typeset
_prel-p1.sty	Press release	Typeset

Style Sheet Name	Page Layout	Directory Stored In
_prpt_p1.sty	Proposal/Report, 1 column	Typeset
_prpt_p2.sty	Proposal/Report, 2 column	Typeset
scoop2.sty	Newsletter	Typeset
_tbl2_l1.sty	Columnar table	Typeset
_tbl_p1.sty	Tabular financial table	Typeset
_tchd_p1.sty	Technical manual	Typeset
_tdoc_p1.sty	Technical manual	Typeset
_vwgf_l1.sty	Viewgraph, landscape	Typeset
_vwgf_p1.sty	Viewgraph, portrait	Typeset
10Kreport.sty	10Kreport	VPstyle
Ad.sty	Single-page ad	VPstyle
Award.sty	Award certificate	VPstyle
B_cards.sty	Business cards	VPstyle
balsheet.sty	Balance sheet	VPstyle
book.sty	Book layout	VPstyle
book.sty	Book layout	VPstyle
brochure.sty	Tri-fold brochure	VPstyle
calendar.sty	Monthly calendar	VPstyle
catalog.sty	Product catalog	VPstyle
contract.sty	Sample contract	VPstyle
depositn.sty	Deposition	VPstyle
envelope.sty	Company envelope	VPstyle
fax.sty	FAX cover sheet	VPstyle
flyer.sty	Three-fold flyer	VPstyle

continues

Table 1.1, Continued
VENTURA's Predesigned Style Sheets

Style Sheet Name	Page Layout	Directory Stored In
index.sty	Index layout	VPstyle
inspolicy.sty	Insurance policy	VPstyle
invite.sty	Invitation	VPstyle
invoice.sty	Company invoice	VPstyle
journal.sty	Multi-page journal	VPstyle
label.sty	Avery labels	VPstyle
legalbrf.sty	Legal brief	VPstyle
letter.sty	Company letterhead	VPstyle
magartcl.sty	Magazine article	VPstyle
manual.sty	Technical manual	VPstyle
memo.sty	Inter-office memo	VPstyle
milspec.sty	Miltary specification document	VPstyle
nletter.sty	Four-page newsletter	VPstyle
nwslttr.sty	Four-page journal/periodical	VPstyle
orgchart.sty	Organization chart	VPstyle
partslst.sty	Parts list	VPstyle
phonelst.sty	Address/phone directory	VPstyle
policy.sty	Policy and procedure manual	VPstyle
preslan.sty	Landscape presentation package	VPstyle
presport.sty	Portrait presentation package	VPstyle
pricelst.sty	Price list	VPstyle
proposal.sty	Report/proposal	VPstyle
purchord.sty	Company purchase order	VPstyle

Style Sheet Name	Page Layout	Directory Stored In
q_a_ad.sty	Single-page ad	VPstyle
qtrrpt.sty	Four-page quarterly report	VPstyle
release.sty	Press release	VPstyle
resume.sty	Resume	VPstyle
scoop.sty	Newsletter	VPstyle
sign.sty	Landscape sign	VPstyle
spec.sty	Specification sheet	VPstyle
tabloid.sty	Tabloid newspaper	VPstyle
techdoc.sty	Technical documentation	VPstyle
thesis.sty	Thesis/Dissertation	VPstyle
time_man.sty	Time management form	VPstyle
toc.sty	Table of contents	VPstyle
toc_2.sty	Table of contents	VPstyle
txtbook.sty	Textbook	VPstyle

Style Sheets Manage Paragraph Tags and Page Layout Information

Style sheets guide the look of your documents by managing two main elements of design—page layout and text formatting. Every chapter file within a publication file uses a style sheet, and that style sheet determines everything from the page numbering to the font used in footnotes.

Paragraph Tags

Style sheets manage a list of paragraph tags, a key element in text formatting. *Paragraph tags* are basically a collection of text attributes that control how individual text blocks or paragraphs are formatted. Rather than applying each of the attributes individually to a text block (choosing the font, setting the spacing, setting the alignment), you can apply a tag with all the desired formatting in one quick step.

For instance, as displayed in figure 1.2, a magazine article might use a tag named subheading. That tag could be applied to each subhead in the article. The tag specifies every element of text formatting, such as type face, type size, line spacing, alignment, indents—even special attributes such as bullets or drop caps. The tags are assigned descriptive names, such as chapter title, footnote, or bullet, to help you remember the specific formatting attributes. As you will discover in Chapter 7, "Formatting Tagged and Freeform Text," applying a tag is as simple as selecting the tag name from a list.

Figure 1.2

Using the same paragraph tags on similar text blocks helps you achieve consistency in document design.

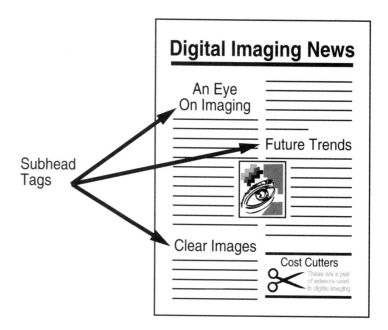

In VENTURA, every paragraph of text has a paragraph tag. A paragraph is defined by paragraph marks, which are created when you press the Enter key. For example, when you press Enter, everything you type until you press Enter again is part of a single paragraph. Paragraphs can range in size from a single word to many lengthy sentences. All that is needed to define a paragraph is one press of the Enter key. Paragraphs with the same tag name use the same formatting attributes. For instance, a tag called subheading could specify that text be 24-point Avant Garde. Thus, each paragraph with the paragraph tag subheading would be formatted with 24-point Avant Garde.

As you can see, paragraph tags make it easy to be consistent throughout documents by applying the same formatting to all similarly tagged text blocks. The paragraph tags also make it easy to modify the text formatting. You can change the attributes of any single text block that has been assigned a specific tag, and all other text blocks using that tag are also changed. Imagine you have created a 50-page training manual with numerous bulleted lists using the tag bullet. As you near the end of the project, suppose you decide to use a smaller type size for the lists. With VENTURA, you can simply redefine the tag definition to reduce the type size for the bullet tag and every other paragraph where that tag is applied is also adjusted to display the smaller type size.

Each style sheet provides a set of paragraph tags. The predesigned style sheets supplied with VENTURA contain paragraph tags intended to work with a specific type of document. For instance, tag names such as Date, Week, and Month are provided in the Calendar style sheet, while tags such as Customer and Line Item appear in the Invoice style sheet. The paragraph tags supplied with these existing style sheets are just another reason to use the predesigned style sheets as you build new documents.

In Chapter 7, you will discover how to apply paragraph tags to text, modify existing tags, and make new ones. As a reference, Table 1.2 itemizes the text attributes that paragraph tags control.

Table 1.2
Controlling Text Attributes with Paragraph Tags

Attribute	What Is Affected
Character Attributes	Typeface, type size, type style (bold, italic, underline, etc.), text color, bullets, drop caps
Alignment Attributes	Vertical position on the page, text justification (left, center, right, full, and decimal), tab settings, text position in multi-column settings, line page, and column breaks
Spacing Attributes	Paragraph spacing, line spacing, paragraph and line indents, text rotation, automatic adjustments when text is enlarged
Default Attributes	Default settings for underlines, superscript and subscript settings, automatic
Typography Attributes	Inter-word spacing, inter-character spacing, automatic kerning, tracking, hyphenation, vertical justification spacing

Page Layout Information

When you create a new file in VENTURA, you select a style sheet that specifies how the page will be set up. For instance, a style sheet for a magazine might use a three-column layout with three-quarter-inch margins. A style sheet for a book might use a one-column layout with a two-inch top and bottom margin, and one-inch left and right margin. Style sheets also control some of the more complex elements of page layout, such as headers and footers, page numbering, and footnotes.

The following list itemizes the page layout information the style sheet controls:

✔ Paper size and orientation

✔ Single-/double-sided printing

✔ Headers and footers

✔ Footnotes

✔ Chapter and page numbering

✔ Widows and orphans

✔ Column balance

✔ Page frame margins

✔ Page frame column layout

Working with Publication and Chapter Files

VENTURA documents are stored in publication files with the file extension .PUB. Every publication file includes at least one chapter file, which uses the file extension .CHP. As discussed earlier in the book-building analogy, you can have several chapter files within one publication file.

Figure 1.3 illustrates a book created in VENTURA with seven chapter files saved in one publication file. To keep them separate, each chapter file is given a different file name. The capability to set up individual chapter files within one publication is essential to producing longer documents because it enables you to save valuable time that would be wasted trying to manipulate large multi-chapter

files. In VENTURA, you can build and format each chapter separately, applying different style sheets to each chapter if desired. The publication file links the chapters so you can work with them all as one unit or as an entire book.

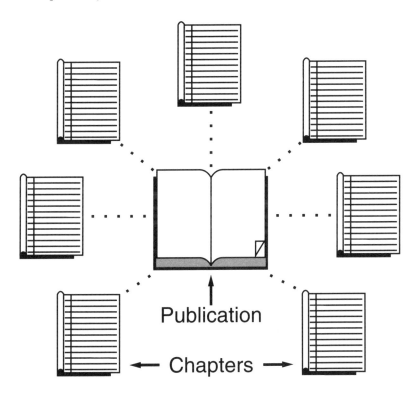

Figure 1.3
A Ventura publication can contain multiple chapters.

Publication

◄— Chapters —►

Now that you are familar with the file structure used to build VENTURA documents, it's important to discuss how VENTURA manages all the elements that go into building a document—publication and chapter files, style sheets, and text and graphic files. The next section discusses VENTURA's unique method for saving publication, chapter, and style sheet files.

How VENTURA Manages Files

As previously discussed, VENTURA documents are saved in publication files that include one or more chapter files. The publication file does not include the contents of each chapter file; instead, it has *pointers* that record the location of the chapters that compose the publication. These pointers go to the drive and directories where the chapter files are stored and open those chapters. Figure 1.4 illustrates how pointers are used to retrieve chapter files when the publication file is opened.

Figure 1.4
When you open a
publication file,
pointers are sent
out to retrieve the
chapter files.

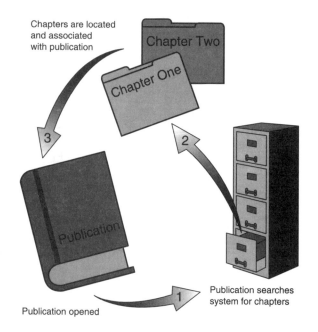

The pointer system is really a two-step process. The first step takes place when the publication sends out pointers to locate the chapter files. Step two occurs as each chapter file sends out pointers to locate and retrieve the style sheets, text, and graphic files used in that chapter (see fig. 1.5). VENTURA's use of pointers means that it does not integrate all of the files into one big publication file. Instead, the publication files are filled with pointers for locating chapter files, and chapter files are filled with pointers for locating the style sheet, text, and graphic files.

This process is different than other Corel applications, such as CorelDRAW. If you import a piece of clip art into a CorelDRAW file, for example, the clip art becomes part of the file. If you load a piece of clip art into VENTURA, the clip art is not saved with the chapter file. Rather, a pointer is saved that indicates on which disk drive and directory the clip art file is located and where it should be placed in the document.

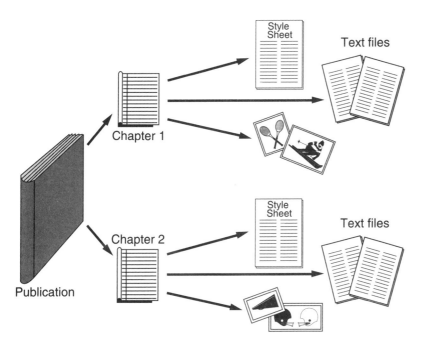

Figure 1.5
When you open a publication file, pointers locate the chapter files, which, in turn, point to style sheets, graphics, and text files.

Benefits of VENTURA's Document Management

There are several benefits to keeping the style sheets, text, and graphics files separate. First, other documents can share the same text and graphics. For instance, you might want to place a logo created in CorelDRAW in several different manuals, or use the same text file in a newsletter and a brochure. Second, because the files do not become part of the VENTURA file, you can continue to edit them in the program they were originally created in.

For example, you could use CorelDRAW to change the colors in the logo, or edit the text file in Word for Windows. The real bonus is that because the files are separate, changes you make to the files automatically appear in your VENTURA documents. This means the changes made to the logo automatically appear in all the manuals, and editing changes made to the text file are reflected in both the newsletter and brochure.

Of course, you must be careful to cooperate with this pointer system. If you delete a style sheet file, the pointer will obviously not be able to find it. In this case, a message appears informing you the style sheet could not be found. Likewise, if you move a text file from one directory to another, the pointer will not find it. In these instances, you would have to reload the style sheet and text file so the pointer can determine the new location. You will learn more about loading style sheets and placing text and graphics in later chapters.

Starting VENTURA

By default, VENTURA is installed in the Windows Program Manager in the Corel group along with CorelDRAW. To start VENTURA, open the Corel group window and double-click on the CorelVENTURA icon. The VENTURA icon appears as shown in figure 1.6.

Figure 1.6
The Corel 5.0
Program Group
opens to
display the
CorelVENTURA
icon.

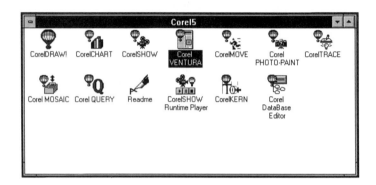

The Panose Font Matching dialog box might appear when you start VENTURA. This occurs when VENTURA is trying to use a font that you do not have installed on your system. A similar font will be substitued. Just click on the OK button to bypass the dialog box. For more information on Panose Font Matching, refer to your VENTURA software documentation.

When you first start VENTURA, a new document appears in the document area (see fig. 1.7). This is a one-page document using the default style sheet. By default, the style sheet, publication, and chapter files are all called "untitled." File names are assigned when you save the publication, chapter, and style sheet files. Chapter 3 will take you through the steps for creating and saving new documents.

Exploring the VENTURA Screen

At the top of the screen is the *title bar*, which displays the name of the currently open publication. Beneath the title bar is the *menu bar*, which contains a selection of commands and functions for operating VENTURA. The menus work just as they do in other Windows applications; you simply click on the menu title and a drop-down list of menu commands appears.

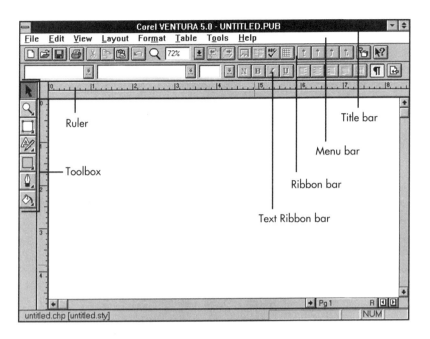

Figure 1.7
The
CorelVENTURA
workspace screen.

Understanding How VENTURA "Thinks"

The ribbon bars appear just under the menu bar. The ribbon bars contain many buttons that provide quick access to VENTURA's most frequently used commands. As a Windows user, you will recognize several of the buttons available on the top ribbon bar, such Open, Save, and Print. The lower ribbon bar, the *text ribbon*, might also be familar; it contains many of the buttons, such as Bold, Italic and Underline, you will find in the more popular word processing applications. Certain buttons might appear grayed out at various times depending on whether they relate to the task at hand. If you forget what a button does, simply hover your mouse cursor over a button, and a *tool tip* appears indicating the button's function.

Working with Rulers

The document area in the center of the screen is where you build and format your documents. Rulers appear along the top and left side of the page area. You'll find the rulers helpful for sizing and positioning elements in your documents. Notice as you move the mouse, small hairlines appear in the ruler to indicate the exact position of the mouse on your document. This is helpful for aligning elements to specific points on the page. You can turn the rulers on and off by choosing **R**ulers from the **V**iew menu.

Changing the Unit of Measure

By default, the measurement system used in the rulers is inches. However, you can change this setting to picas, centimeters, or ciceros. The following steps describe how to change the rulers to measure in picas. (Note: *picas* are a unit of measurement used by printers. There are six picas in one inch.)

1. Select the **R**uler Setup command from the T**o**ols menu. The Set Ruler dialog box appears as displayed in figure 1.8.

2. You can adjust the horizontal and vertical rulers to use the same measurement system or different systems if desired. Click on the down arrow by **H**orizontal Units and choose picas. Click on the down arrow by **V**ertical Units and choose picas.

3. Click on OK. Both rulers now display picas as the measurement system.

Figure 1.8
The Set Ruler
dialog box.

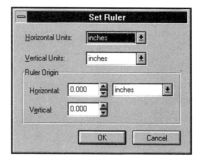

Holding the mouse button down on the box where the rulers meet and dragging on the page brings out a set of crosshairs. This allows you to relocate the zero points anywhere on the page. Double-clicking on the box where the rulers meet resets the zero point to the original location.

Working with the Toolbox

The gray bar directly below the top ruler is the tab bar. The *tab bar* is used to set and display tab stops. You will learn more about setting tabs in Chapter 8, "Managing Paragraph Tags." Running vertically on the left of the screen is the toolbox. As with most Corel 5.0 applications, this toolbox contains many tools for editing your document. Notice that some of the tools display little triangles in the right corner. You can press and hold on these tools to display a flyout menu with additional tools. Table 1.3 provides an overview of each tool.

Table 1.3
The Corel Ventura Toolbox

Tool		Function
Pick tool		Use to select, size, and change the attributes of tables, frames, and graphics.
Zoom tool		Press and hold on the tool to display a set of tools for increasing or decreasing the viewing magnification on a document.
Frame tool		Press and hold on the tool to display the Frame tool for drawing free frames on your document, and the Node Edit tool, which allows you to shape the boundaries of graphics.
Text tool		Press and hold on the tool to display the Freeform and Tagged Text tools. Both let you enter and format text. The Tagged Text tool lets you apply paragraph tags to text. The Freeform tool lets you apply formatting that overrides the paragraph tags.
Drawing tool		Press and hold on the tool to display a flyout that includes five tools for creating graphic objects directly in CorelVENTURA.
Outline tool		Press and hold on the tool to display the Outline tool flyout, which is used to define the outline attributes for frames and graphic objects created with the Drawing tool.
Fill tool		Press and hold on the tool to display the Fill tool flyout, which is used to define the fill attributes for frames and graphic objects created with the Drawing tool.

Using the Quick Format Roll-Up

When you first start VENTURA, a Quick Format Roll-up appears. As displayed in figure 1.9, the Quick Format Roll-up includes collections of ready-made formats to apply to various elements in your chapter. The format categories include: tables, paragraphs, ruling lines, columns and page layout, headers and footers. You will learn more about using the Quick Format Roll-up in later chapters.

To move the roll-up, simply press and hold on the roll-up's title bar and drag it to a new location. To close the roll-up, double-click on the control box at the top left corner of the dialog box. You can "rollup" the roll-up without removing it from the screen by clicking once on the up arrow on the top right corner of the roll-up. Click on the down arrow to redisplay the full roll-up.

Figure 1.9
The Quick Format
Roll-up.

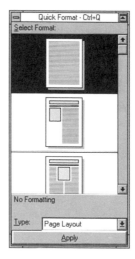

Using the Status Line

The status line at the bottom of the VENTURA screen displays the current name of the chapter and style sheet files. The status line also indicates the presence of special items, such as frame anchors, index markers, and cross-references. As you work with VENTURA, the status line changes to provide you with detail about the current task. For instance, as you edit text, the status line displays information about the paragraph you are currently editing.

You can hide the status line from your screen display by selecting Preferences from the Tools menu. Select the View tab and click on the Status Line option.

Above the status line on the right is the page counter. The page counter indicates the current page number and whether it is a right (R) or left (L) page. When you are working in Facing Pages view, the page numbers of both pages are displayed. Click on the scroll buttons to move to the next or previous page within the current chapter.

Chapter Snapshot

You might have several years of experience with CorelDRAW, but VENTURA might be entirely new to you. Maneuvering through any new program might seem intimidating at first, but this chapter helps you get started. In this chapter, you learn to do the following:

Exploring a document created in VENTURA is a great way to get comfortable with how the program operates. The goal of this chapter is to let you preview some of the components and concepts of VENTURA before you actually start building a document.

CHAPTER

Exploring a VENTURA Document

Before diving in and creating your own documents in CorelVENTURA, it's a good idea to "get your toes wet" by opening a few sample publication files. The sample files give you a feel for how VENTURA documents look, and how to manuever through them. If you are new to desktop publishing and VENTURA, it's especially important to see how all the text and graphics, style sheets, paragraph tags, and frames come together to build a document.

In this chapter, you will explore a sample VENTURA publication file containing several chapters, and a lot of text and graphics. You will learn how to move between chapters, change page views, and select frames and paragraph tags. This chapter also acquaints you with many of the basics of running VENTURA, such as opening files, using the Zoom tool, and saving files.

Opening Publication Files

Publication files link all of the chapters in a document so that you can work with all of the chapters as one unit or book. Previous discussions established that when a publication file is opened, "pointers" are followed to locate and open all associated chapter files. Remember, even less complex publication files, such as one-page brochures, have at least one chapter. When you open a publication file with more than one chapter, you are asked to select which chapter you want to work with first.

In this section, the sample publication file academic.pub is opened and examined. If you installed the publication template files during installation, you can find this file in the VPSTYLE directory. If you did not install the sample files, refer to a following section, "Installing Sample Files." This section also covers installing the publication templates provided by VENTURA. Not only will these sample files be helpful for this exercise, but you may find that you can use them later as templates and style sheets.

The following steps illustrate opening the sample file academic.pub:

1. Select **O**pen from the **F**ile menu, or click on the Open button in the ribbon bar. The File Open dialog box appears as displayed in figure 2.1.

Figure 2.1
The File Open
dialog box.

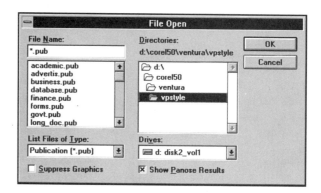

2. Change to the drive where CorelVENTURA is loaded, and open the VENTURA\VPSTYLE directory. The sample publication files appear on the left side of the dialog box under File **N**ame. Select the file name academic.pub and click on OK. You can also double-click on the file name to open it.

New Riders Publishing
INSIDE
SERIES

3. Because the file academic.pub contains several chapters, the Go to Chapter dialog box appears, as displayed in figure 2.2. The <u>C</u>hapter List on the left indicates there are three chapters in the academic.pub file.

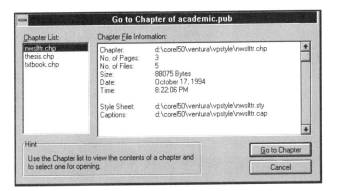

Figure 2.2
The Go to Chapter dialog box.

4. Information about the selected chapter is displayed under Chapter <u>F</u>ile Information. In figure 2.2, the first chapter, nwslttr.chp, is selected. The Chapter <u>F</u>ile Information informs you where the file is stored, the number of pages in the file, and the number of text and graphic files used in the chapter. Click on the <u>G</u>o To Chapter button to open the newsletter chapter of the academic publication file.

When you open a file, the first page of the chapter is displayed. When you place your mouse in the document area, the status line at the bottom of the screen indicates the chapter name, nwslttr.chp, and the style sheet name nwslttr.sty. The title bar at the top of the screen displays the name of the publication file academic.pub.

Publication files with numerous graphics take longer to open and manage. When you want to edit and print only the text elements of a document, you can click on the Suppress Graphics check box in the File Open dialog box to load the publication without graphics. When the publication is opened, the graphics will be hidden from view, while remaining linked to the publication. Instead of the graphics, you will see blank boxes.

Opening Files from Previous Versions of VENTURA

In previous versions of VENTURA, documents were saved as chapter files. You can open chapter files from versions 3 and 4 of VENTURA, including all interim releases, such as 3.3 and 4.2. Basically, the steps are the same as opening

VENTURA 5.0 publication files. Select **O**pen from the **F**ile menu. In the File Open dialog box, change to the drive and directory where the chapter files are stored. Next, click on the down arrow by List Files of **T**ype in the bottom left corner of the dialog box, and select 3.*x*, 4.*x* Chapters (*.chp). The chapter files stored in the current drive and directory appear in the File **N**ame list box. Select the name of the chapter file you want to open and click on OK.

If you used Ami Pro to create text files in VENTURA 4.2, an error message appears when you open a 4.2 chapter file. The solution is to open the text files in Ami Pro, save them again, then reopen the chapter in CorelVENTURA 5.

Installing Sample Files

To install VENTURA's sample files and publication templates, you will need to exit all applications so that only the Windows Program Manager is running. Next, place disk one of the Corel 5.0 installation disks or the CD-ROM in the drive from which you will install. From the **F**ile menu, choose **R**un to open the Run dialog box. In the text box, type the drive where the installation disk is located, then type **Setup**. For example, if your CD-ROM drive is E, and you are loading from CD-ROM, type **E:\Setup**.

If you are installing VENTURA to run from the CD-ROM, you should enter the name of the installation drive and **SETUP2** in the Run dialog box. For more information on installing CorelVENTURA, refer to your documentation.

Follow the instructions on-screen to enter your serial number. As the installation proceeds you are asked where you want to install Corel 5.0. If you have already installed a copy of Corel or CorelVENTURA on your system, the installation process automatically identifes where your Corel files are located. At this point, simply click on OK to confirm the location of your Corel files.

Choose to perform a Minimum/Custom install. The Customize Applications dialog box is displayed. To install only the sample files and publication templates, disable every install option except VENTURA. For example, as displayed in figure 2.3, all the options except CorelVENTURA are disabled.

Click on the Customize button next to VENTURA. The CorelVENTURA Options dialog box appears as displayed in figure 2.4. Click to place an *X* by the Samples and Publication Templates options. You can disable any of the remaining options that are selected. For instance, uncheck Program Files and Online Help.

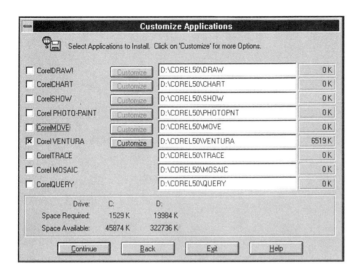

Figure 2.3
The Customize
Applications
dialog box with
only VENTURA
selected.

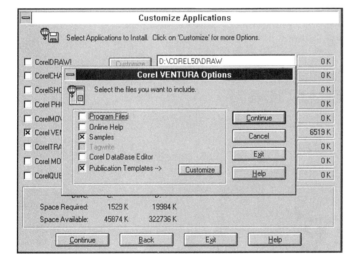

Figure 2.4
The
CorelVENTURA
Options dialog
box.

After selecting the publication templates option, click on the Customize button. The VENTURA Template Selection dialog box appears as displayed in figure 2.5. Select the templates you want to install and click on the **C**ontinue button to return to the CorelVENTURA Options dialog box. Click **C**ontinue again to proceed with the installation. Uncheck any other install options that follow. For example, uncheck the option to install filters. Leaving these checked will only re-install these options.

Figure 2.5
The VENTURA
Template Selection
dialog box.

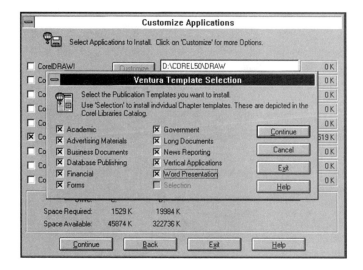

Figure 2.5
The VENTURA
Template Selection
dialog box.

Follow the directions on-screen to continue the installation procedure. After the installation is complete, VENTURA will reboot your system, and the sample files will be available for selection.

Viewing Documents

As you design and produce documents, you will need to control how large or small a document appears on the screen. When editing text or drawing graphics, for instance, you can zoom in on the page to make it easier to read. When adjusting page margins and columns, you might want to zoom out to view the entire page. VENTURA also provides the option for viewing two pages, the left and right pages, at one time.

Using the Zoom Tool

The Zoom tool, the second tool in the toolbox (the magnifying lens), provides an easy way to zoom in and out of the page. For instance, in figure 2.6, the view is set to display the whole first page of the newsletter chapter. The second image shows an up-close view of the top of the same page. When you click on the Zoom tool, a flyout menu appears displaying six tools. The following list explores how to use each Zoom tool.

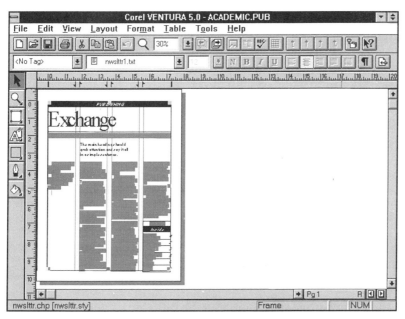

Figure 2.6
You have several ways to view your documents in CorelVENTURA.

Use the Zoom In tool to magnify specific parts of your page. Simply select the first button and move into the page. The shape of the mouse cursor changes to a magnifying lens with a plus sign. Draw a box around the area you want to magnify. When you release the mouse button, VENTURA zooms to that part of the page.

 Select the Zoom Out tool to return to the previous magnification level. If there was not a previous zoom in, the Zoom Out tool zooms out by a factor of two.

 Select the Actual Size tool to display the page at the size it will print. You will find the Actual Size page view handy when you need a "reality check" to determine how big your graphics and text will appear on the printed page.

 Select the Fit in Window tool to zoom out and display the full page. Use this tool when you want to preview the overall page design of your document.

 Select the Full Width tool to zoom into the full width of the page. As displayed in the second image in figure 2.3, this is a great way to see the top or bottom half of the page.

 Select the Full Height tool to zoom out and display the full height of the page.

Viewing Facing Pages

The Facing Pages command lets you view both the left and right pages of your documents at the same time. To understand the concept of left and right pages, think of a four-page book. As illustrated in figure 2.7, page one is a right page, page two is a left page, page three is a right page, and page four is a left page. The Facing Pages command lets you see left and right pages at the same time. Keep in mind that you will only see one page at a time when viewing the first and last page because the first page is a right page and has no left-facing page, and the last page is a left page with no right-facing page.

The ability to view facing pages at the same time lets you create page layouts that consider facing pages as a single unit called a *double-page spread.* When the document is printed and bound, your reader sees two facing pages at once, not a left page, then a right. Designing facing pages as a double-page spread gives your documents a more professional appeal.

 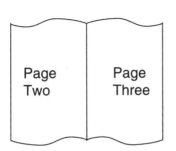 

Page One

Page Two

Page Three

Page Four

Figure 2.7
A four-page document illustrating the concept of left and right pages.

Understanding How VENTURA "Thinks"

To view both the left and right pages, select **F**acing Pages Preview from the **V**iew menu. A check mark appears by the command indicating the feature is turned on. The first page of your document displays on the right side of the screen because it is a right page. Subsequent pages display both the left and right pages. The last page displays on the left side of the screen because it is a left page. Figure 2.8 shows the three pages of the newsletter chapter in Facing Pages view. To return to single-page view, select **F**acing Pages Preview from the **V**iew menu to disable the feature.

 It's important to note that you must be viewing single pages and not facing pages to access the Zoom tool.

Moving Through Pages

When you open a file, the first page of the chapter is displayed. In the bottom right corner of the screen, the page counter displays the page number (see fig. 2.9).

Using the Go To Buttons

To display the next page, click on the arrow pointing to the right—the Go to Next Page button. Continue clicking on this button to view all of the pages in the document. The newsletter chapter has three pages. To display the previous pages, click on the arrow pointing to the left—the Go to Previous Page button.

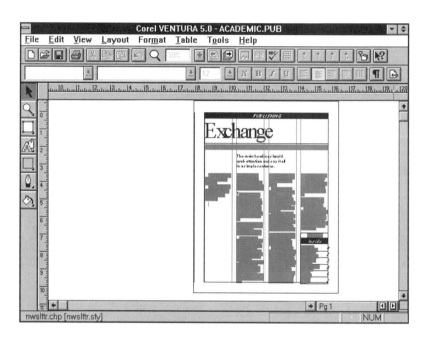

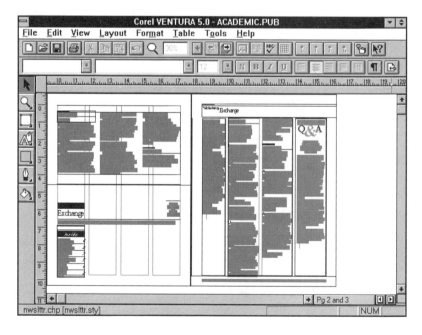

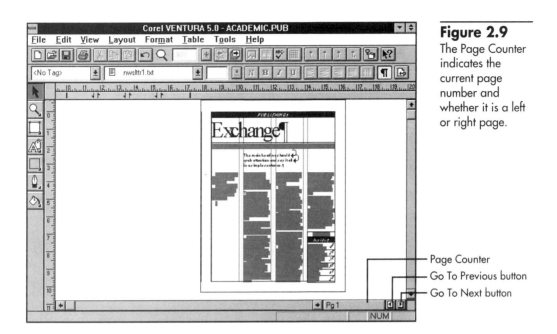

Figure 2.9
The Page Counter indicates the current page number and whether it is a left or right page.

Page Counter
Go To Previous button
Go To Next button

Understanding How VENTURA "Thinks"

Using Keyboard Shortcuts

Another quick way to move through the pages in a chapter file is to use the keyboard shortcuts identified in table 2.1.

Table 2.1
Shortcuts for Moving Through Pages

Key Combination	Action
Ctrl+Home	Go to the first page of the chapter.
Ctrl+End	Go to last page of the chapter.
PgDn	Go to next page.
PgUp	Go to previous page.
Ctrl+G	To access the Go to Page dialog box, covered in the next section.

Using the Go to Page Command

When you are working in a chapter with numerous pages, the Go to Page command provides a quick way to move to a specific page. From the **V**iew menu, select **G**o to Page to display the dialog box in figure 2.10. Enter the number of the page you want to view in the **P**age box, and click on the Go to Page button.

For instance, you could enter 55 to display page 55 of your chapter. (This is much better than pressing the right arrow 54 times!) Because it's hard to remember exact page numbers in lengthy documents, the Go to Page dialog box stays on-screen so you can enter other page numbers until the exact page you want is displayed. To close the dialog box, double-click on the Control box (the gray box with the white bar in the top left of the dialog box).

Figure 2.10
The Go to Page dialog box.

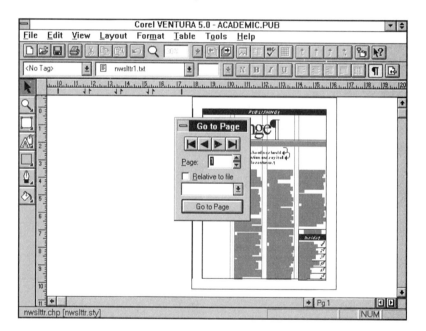

As discussed in Chapter 1, chapter files are composed of text and graphic files. The Go to Page dialog box can also be used to locate the first page of a specific text file. This is convenient for moving through long documents, when you want to move to a certain section but don't remember the page number. The following steps illustrate how to move to the page where the text file nwslttr3.txt first appears in the newsletter chapter:

1. Move to the first page of the newsletter chapter. Select **G**o to Page from the **V**iew menu.

2. In the Go to Page dialog box, select the **R**elative to File option (see fig. 2.11). A list box underneath the option displays the text files placed in the chapter. Click on the down arrow by the list box and select nwslttr3.txt.

3. Click on either the left or right arrows at the top of the dialog box to move to the page where the text file is placed. Remember, the file may flow across several pages; this command takes you to the first page where the file appears. When ready, close the dialog box.

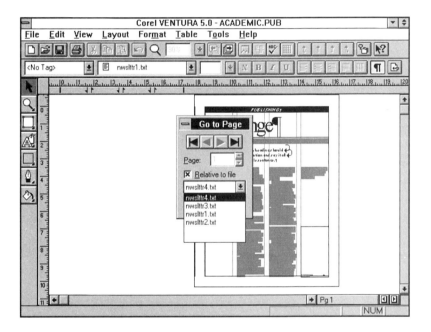

Figure 2.11

The Go to Page dialog box with the Relative to file option selected.

Moving Between Chapters

Chapters are the different sections or units of a publication file. Although the Open command opens a publication file (.PUB file), you actually work on a chapter level—one chapter at a time. The G**o** to Chapter command in the **V**iew menu lets you select which chapter to display. As you will see, this command offers more than a way to move between chapters; it also provides an overview of valuable chapter information, such as the style sheet used and the file size.

Don't forget about this command when you want to verify which style sheet is used in a chapter, or perhaps to perform a quick page count of all of the chapter files. The following exercise illustrates how to display the other chapters in the academic publication (academic.pub) file:

1. Select G**o** to Chapter from the **V**iew menu. The Go to Chapter dialog box appears as displayed in figure 2.12. This is the same dialog box used to select a chapter when initially opening a publication file.

Figure 2.12
The Go to Chapter
dialog box with
thesis.chp
selected.

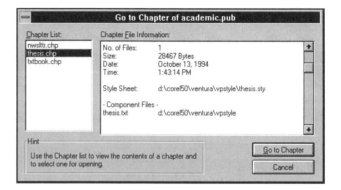

2. Under **C**hapter List, select the second chapter, thesis.chp. The Chapter **F**ile Information box indicates this is a six-page file. Under Component Files, notice only thesis.txt is listed, indicating only one text file is placed in this chapter. To display the thesis chapter, click on the **G**o to Chapter button. The thesis chapter is displayed.

3. To view the last chapter of the publication file, select G**o** to Chapter from the **V**iew menu. Click on txtbook.chp under the **C**hapter List. This chapter has nine pages and uses the txtbook.sty style sheet file. Click on the **G**o to Chapter button to display the textbook chapter.

Table 2.2 displays two keyboard shortcuts for moving through chapters in a publication file. These shortcuts are great when you need to move quickly through your chapters. However, with keyboard shortcuts, the Go to Page dialog box does not appear, so you will not see any chapter information.

Table 2.2
Shortcuts for Moving through Chapters

Key Combination	Action
Alt+PgDn	Go to the next chapter in a publication file
Alt+PgUp	Go to previous chapter in a publication file

Selecting and Examining Frames

VENTURA uses *frames* to hold the text and graphics placed on the pages in a chapter file. A page frame, which is the size of a full page, is automatically placed on each page of a document. You can draw additional frames, called *free frames*, with the Frame tool. Think of free frames as rectangular boxes that "float" on top of the page frame. Unlike the page frame, free frames can be moved anywhere on the page. Free frames can be used to flow articles across several pages in a newsletter or magazine. As an example, text placed in a free frame on page one can be flowed to another free frame on page three.

The size of a frame determines how big a graphic will appear on the page, or how much text fits in the frame. As displayed in figure 2.13, two of the frames contain graphics, and the other frames contain body text. As you can see in the frames holding text, each frame can have different column settings so you can quickly and easily create multi-column layouts.

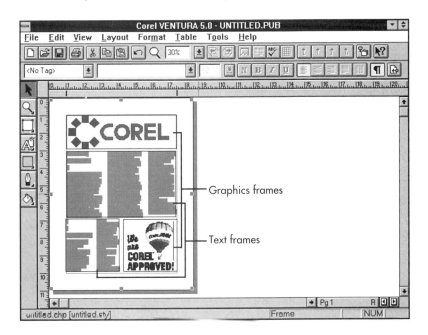

Figure 2.13
Frames hold the text and graphics in your documents.

Graphics frames

Text frames

This section will aquaint you with the basic concept of selecting frames and determining whether the contents of the frame are text or graphics. Refer to Chapter 4, "Working with Frames," for more information about building layouts by creating and positioning frames. The following exercise examines the frames used to build the newletter chapter of the academic publication file:

1. Use the G**o** to Chapter command in the **V**iew menu to display the nwslttr.chp chapter file. Use the Zoom tool to display the whole first page.

2. Select the Pick tool, which is the first tool in the toolbox.

3. To select the page frame, move the mouse into the right margin of the page and click. Eight small gray selection handles appear around the outside edges of the whole page.

4. To select a free frame, move the mouse to the middle of the page and click. Again, selection handles appear around the large frame indicating it is selected. When a frame is selected, the Files list at the top of the page displays the name of the file loaded into the frame. As displayed in figure 2.14. the files list indicates the text file, nwslttr1.txt, was loaded into this free frame.

Figure 2.14

The Files list displays the name of the file loaded in the selected frame.

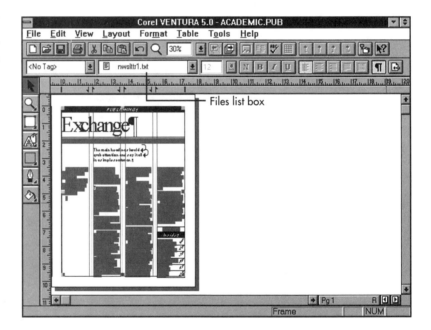

5. Another free frame is located in the bottom right corner of the page. Move inside the frame (by the word "Inside"), and click to select it. The Files list indicates the text file nwslttr2.txt was placed in this frame.

6. Use the G**o** to Chapter command in the **V**iew menu to display the txtbook.chp chapter file. The first page of the textbook displays two free

frames. The top frame holds a graphic file, and the bottom frame holds a text file. Select the top frame, and the Files list indicates the graphic file log45.tif is loaded into this frame.

The goal of this exercise was to familiarize you with how frames work in VENTURA. Learning how to select and examine frames in this sample document should give you a better understanding for how frames are used to build documents. The next section examines another important aspect of creating documents in VENTURA—using paragraph tags.

Selecting and Examining Paragraph Tags

VENTURA uses paragraph tags to format the text in your documents. *Paragraph tags* are a collection of formatting attributes such as font, alignment, and spacing that are saved with a style sheet. You can use the tags supplied by the style sheet or create your own. This section is intended to give you a feel for how paragraph tags are used by selecting paragraphs to see which tags are associated with them.

The following exercise examines the paragraph tags used in the newsletter chapter of the academic publication file. Refer to Chapter 7, "Formatting Tagged and Freeform Text," for more detailed information on working with paragraph tags.

1. Use the Go to Chapter command in the **V**iew menu to display the nwslttr.chp chapter file. Use the Zoom tool to display the full width of the page (the fifth button on the flyout). This view enables you to see the top portion of the page up close.

2. Press and hold on the Text tool (the fourth tool in the toolbox) to display a flyout menu with two text buttons. Select the second button in the flyout—the Tagged Text tool.

3. Before viewing the tag name for a paragraph, you must first click in the paragraph with the Tagged Text tool. Click in the word "Exchange" at the top of the document. A blinking line called an *insertion point* appears where you clicked in the text. As displayed in figure 2.15, the Tag list at the top left of the screen indicates the tag Head 90 was used to format the text. The tag name infers that the tag is for headings displayed in 90-point type.

Understanding How VENTURA "Thinks"

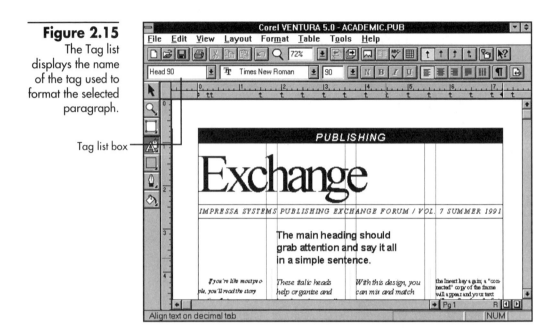

Figure 2.15

The Tag list displays the name of the tag used to format the selected paragraph.

Tag list box

4. Click in the heading that begins with "The main heading...". The Tag list indicates the Head 18 tag is applied to this paragraph of text. Click in the word "Publishing" at the top of the document. The Tag list indicates this paragraph uses the tag Reverse 18.

5. To see a listing of all of the available paragraph tags for this chapter, click on the down arrow by the Tag list. Remember that the tags are saved with the style sheet, so if another style sheet is loaded, a new set of paragraph tags appears.

The purpose of examining the paragraph tags in the newsletter chapter was to familiarize you with some of the formatting aspects of producing documents. In later chapters you can learn how to apply paragraph tags, modify their attributes, and how to create new tags.

Exploring VENTURA's Page Views

Producing and designing documents in VENTURA requires that you perform a variety of tasks to get the job done. One big job is entering, editing, and formatting text. Also important is setting up the page layout by determining page margins and columns, and creating frames. Another task is working with graphics, including manipulating imported graphics and drawing graphics with VENTURA's drawing tools.

In the course of producing your VENTURA documents, you will often find yourself jumping back and forth between these important tasks. Sometimes you will need to get in close for fine-tuning, and other times you will want to step back from your work for a "big picture" view. Because this is how you will work, VENTURA provides three different ways to view your documents. These page views are called the Page Layout view, Draft view and Copy Editor view.

To determine which view is currently being used to display the document, select the **V**iew menu. As displayed in figure 2.16, the three view options appear at the top of the menu list. A small black diamond shape appears by the current page view. In figure 2.16, the current view is Page Layout view.

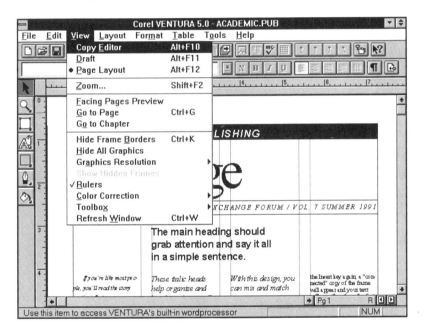

Figure 2.16
A small diamond shape appears by the current page view in the View menu.

Understanding How VENTURA "Thinks"

Page Layout View

The default view, Page Layout view, lets you see your documents as they will appear when printed. The page margins and columns are shown, headers and footers are in place, and text formatting, such as fonts and styles, is displayed. Unlike the other views, the Page Layout view also displays all graphics in the document. Figure 2.17 displays the first page of the textbook chapter in Page Layout view. To switch to Page Layout view, select **P**age Layout from the **V**iew menu, or use the keyboard shortcut Alt+F12.

Figure 2.17

Graphics and text formatting appear when pages are displayed in Page Layout view.

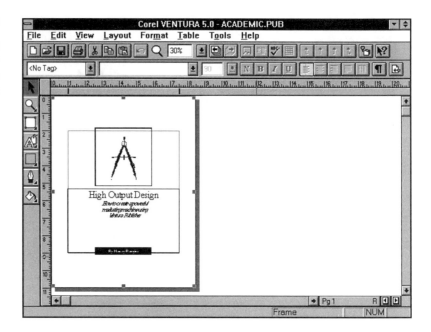

Use the Page Layout view when formatting text and working with graphics. It is always a good idea to switch to the Page Layout view before printing for a quick check of the overall design. Because Page Layout view displays graphics, it is the slowest view for text editing. The graphics must be redrawn on the screen whenever you move the page. Depending on the number of graphics and their complexity, waiting for graphics to redraw can be very time-consuming. This is where the Draft view comes in handy.

Using the Draft View

The Draft view enables you to see the overall page layout, including columns and text formatting such as bold and underline. However, the graphics are not visible; instead, large *X*s appear in the frames holding the graphics. Although the graphic files are still associated with the frames, they are just hidden in Draft view. Figure 2.18 displays the first page of the textbook chapter in Draft view. To switch to Draft view, select **D**raft from the **V**iew menu. Another way to switch to it is the keyboard shortcut, Alt+F11.

Because you do not have to wait for the graphics to redraw on the screen, the Draft view speeds up text editing. When a full page is displayed in Draft view, the text appears as rows of small boxes. The first image in figure 2.19 shows page six of the textbook chapter file. All of the text except the heading appears as small boxes. However, when you zoom in on the page, all the text is visible as displayed in the second image of figure 2.19. When you want to enter and edit text quickly, yet still see the text formatting, the Draft view is your best bet.

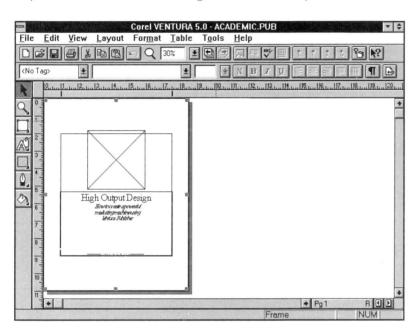

Figure 2.18
While the Page Layout and text formatting appear, graphics are hidden in the draft view.

Using the Copy Editor View

Although each of the page views enables you to enter text, the Copy Editor view is designed solely for entering and editing text. More than a page view, the Copy Editor is a text editor designed to make working with text faster and easier by providing many of features found in popular word processing applications.

Figure 2.20 shows the first page of the textbook chapter in Copy Editor view. Notice that the Copy Editor view displays only text, not page layout and graphics. Formatting codes may also be visible; these instruct VENTURA how to format text. The toolbox is also hidden and is replaced by a column showing the paragraph tags used for each paragraph of text. To switch to Copy Editor view, select Copy **E**ditor from the **V**iew menu, or use the keyboard shortcut, Alt+F10.

Figure 2.19
In the Full page
magnification of
Draft view, text is
represented by
small boxes. When
you zoom in, text
is visible.

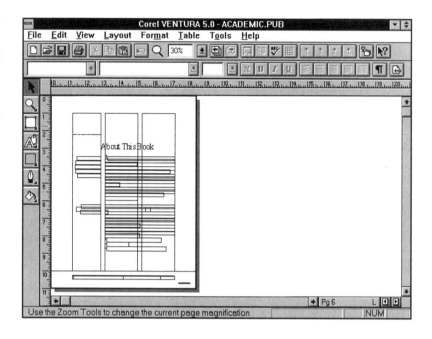

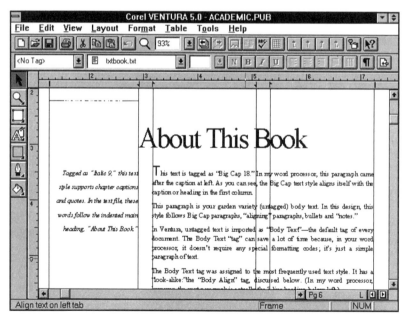

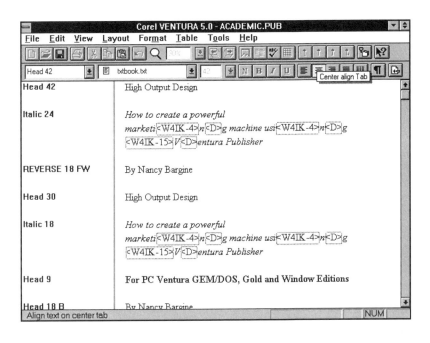

Figure 2.20
The Copy Editor lets you focus on entering and editing text without waiting for graphics to redraw on the screen.

The Copy Editor view displays limited text formatting. One font is used to display all text, though bold, italic, and underline attributes are visible. When you switch from the Copy Editor to Page Layout or Draft view, text will display with its formatting. Use the Copy Editor view to enter and edit large amounts of text. You cannot open or print files while working in the Copy Editor view. Refer to Chapter 6, "Entering and Editing Text," for more information on working with the Copy Editor.

Showing Column Guides

Column guides determine the way text flows in the frame. For instance, text can flow in one big column across the frame or in three smaller columns. Although hidden by default, you can show the column guides on the page frame. The benefit of showing the column guides is that you can see the number of columns set up on the page frame. For instance, the first image in figure 2.21 shows a frame without the column guides displayed, making it difficult to see the column layout in the frame.

The same frame is shown in the second image with the column guides displayed. You can see that the frame is set up for three columns. Keep in mind that though the column guides are displayed, they will not print. Column guides display only on page frames, not on free frames. However, if you have applied columns to a free frame, you can select it and refer to the marks on the horizontal ruler to determine the width of each column. The following steps illustrate how to show the column guides:

Figure 2.21
Displaying column guides lets you see the number of columns specified in a page frame.

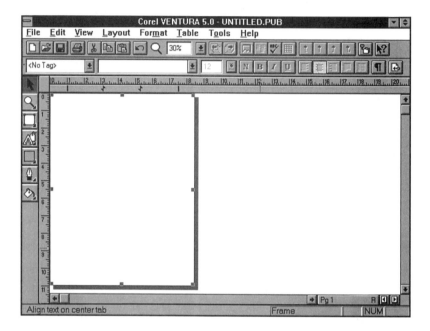

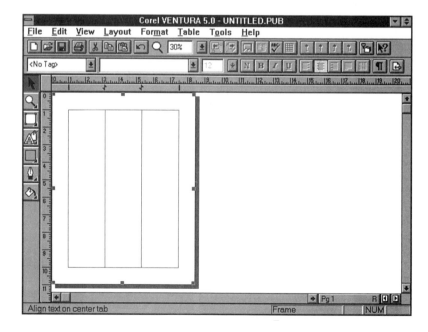

1. Use the G**o** to Chapter command in the **V**iew menu to display the nwslttr.chp chapter file. Use the Zoom tool to display the full page (the fourth button on the flyout).

2. Select Pre**f**erences from the T**o**ols menu. The Preferences dialog box appears as displayed in figure 2.22. Click on the View tab.

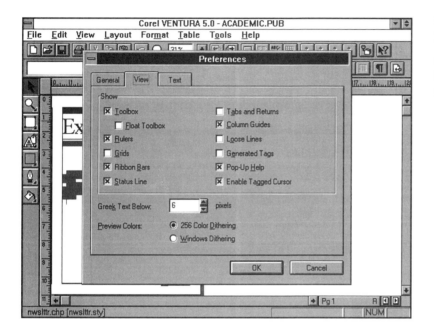

Figure 2.22
The Preferences dialog box with the View tab selected.

3. Click on **C**olumn Guides to place an *X* by the option. The *X* indicates the feature is turned on. Click on OK. Column guides are displayed on the page, indicating a four-column layout was used in the first page of the newsletter chapter.

Remember that turning on the column guides is independent of the publication file. When you turn on the column guides, they remain on until you repeat the preceding steps to turn them off. If the column guides are displayed while you are working with one chapter file, for example, they will also be visible when you go to another chapter file or open another publication file.

Use the keyboard shortcut Ctrl+Alt+G to quickly turn the display of the column guides on and off.

Showing Tabs and Returns

As you edit text, you might find it convenient to be able to recognize where paragraphs begin and end, where line breaks appear, and when the tab key was used. Turning on the Tabs and Returns option displays these symbols to aid you in editing and formatting text. For example, because the formatting attributes of paragraph tags are applied to paragraphs of text, it can be valuable to see symbols indicating the end of a paragraph.

To turn on the Tabs and Returns option, click on the Show/Hide Returns button on the text ribbon (second-to-last button). In figure 2.23, the Tabs and Returns feature is enabled, with symbols appearing on the first page of the newsletter chapter. The meaning of each symbol is detailed in table 2.3.

Figure 2.23
Formatting your document is often easier with Tabs and Returns enabled.

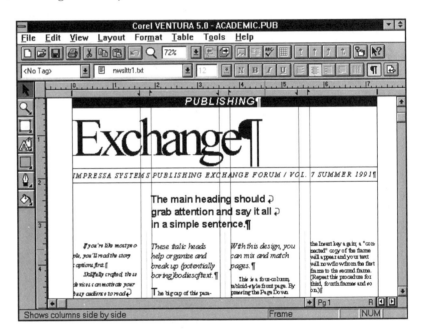

Table 2.3
Tabs and Returns Symbols

Symbol	Definition
Paragraph mark	The paragraph mark (resembling a reversed letter "P") indicates the Enter key was pressed to end one paragraph and begin another. In figure 2.23, the paragraph marks after each of the headings indicates they separate paragraphs. There is a paragraph mark at the end of the

Symbol	Definition
	third line in the text block that begins with "The main heading...", indicating that all three lines of text are considered one paragraph.
Line break	The line break symbol (a curved arrow) indicates when the combination Ctrl+Enter was pressed to start a new line in the text block without starting a new paragraph. In figure 2.23, the heading that begins with "The main heading..." is stacked into three lines with the use of line breaks. Using line breaks is discussed in Chapter 6.
Tab	The Tab symbol indicates when the Tab key was pressed to move the text to the nearest tab stop. You will learn more about setting tabs in Chapter 9, "Advanced Text Formatting Options."

Although the symbols appear on the page, they never print. They can, however, affect how the text is displayed on screen. The symbols take up space in the text blocks, which can distort the positioning and spacing of text on screen. The symbols do not affect the text formatting when the document is printed. It is a good idea to turn off the display of the tabs and rulers before printing so your screen accurately displays what will be printed.

Part II

Building a VENTURA Document

Chapter Snapshot

Creating documents with VENTURA is a simple task when you use the predesigned style sheets that accompany the program. If these style sheets don't quite fit your needs, you can modify them as you like. In this chapter, you learn to do the following:

This chapter provides the information you need to create a new document. Understand and working with style sheets is very important to becoming proficient in VENTURA.

CHAPTER

Creating and Setting Up New Documents

Creating documents is easy with VENTURA's wide assortment of predesigned style sheets. Style sheets are included for all types of business documents, ranging from books to balance sheets to business cards. You will even find style sheets for calendars, memos, and fax sheets. No matter what kind of document you are producing, VENTURA has a style sheet to help you get started.

Don't worry about handing over control of the page design to a predesigned style sheet, however. You can manipulate and modify every setting in the style sheet to fit your exact needs. If you don't like the way the margins are set up, for example, you can change them. Style sheets are designed to enhance and speed up your work, not make you feel tied to a particular page layout. If you are unsure about the concept of style sheets, refer to the section in Chapter 1 titled "Understanding Style Sheets."

This chapter focuses on creating new documents. You will learn to create a new document by selecting an appropriate style sheet. Then you will learn to save the publication, chapter, and style sheet files associated with the new document. This chapter also covers the steps for adding chapter files to a publication file and applying style sheets to those chapters. The last section focuses on setting up the document to fit your exact needs. Here you will learn how to set the page size and orientation, control the page margins, and specify the number of columns.

Selecting a Style Sheet

Before creating a new document, you must select a style sheet for formatting the new document. Remember, the style sheet determines the new document's page orientation, the size of the page margins, and other important formatting information. All new documents consist of a single blank page, which means you're in charge of inserting additional pages and chapters. In essence, you are building a document from the ground up: adding frames, loading text and graphics into the frames, and formatting the text.

Because style sheets are such an integral part of creating new documents, it's essential that you know how to select the right style sheet. As discussed in Chapter 1, a style sheet contains paragraph tags for formatting text, and page layout information, such as the number of columns used and the page numbering style.

Selecting Predesigned Style Sheets

VENTURA provides a variety of predesigned style sheets to choose from. The key to selecting a style sheet is to choose one that best represents the document you are producing. For instance, if you are producing a book, you would find two style sheets available for books (see fig. 3.1). You could then select the design that is closest to what you had in mind for your book and later modify it for your exact needs. The templates section of the Corel clip-art book includes a section on the CorelVENTURA style sheets. Here you can preview the different style sheets to select the best one for your document.

Figure 3.1
VENTURA provides a wide variety of style sheets to choose from, including two designed for books.

Selecting an Existing Style Sheet

In addition to the predesigned style sheets, you can also select one of your own style sheets—a style sheet designed for a previous document you created. For example, imagine you had produced a training manual and worked hard to set up a style sheet that perfectly matched your formatting requirements for the manual. When it came time to produce a second manual, you could save tons of time by selecting the style sheet used with the first manual to format the second manual. The capability to share style sheets between similar documents is an area in which VENTURA particularly excels.

Selecting the Default Style Sheet

VENTURA also offers a default style sheet that includes a few basic paragraph tags. You might use the default style sheet to create a quick document requiring little formatting, such as a letter to mom. In most cases, however, you can probably find a predesigned style sheet that will suit your needs better than the default style sheet.

Creating a New Document

After selecting a style sheet to create a new document, a single blank page is displayed. Actually, this new document is a publication file, containing one chapter file that consists of one page. The chapter file uses the selected style sheet to format the page. In the process of creating a new document, you will have linked the three files required to build documents in VENTURA—the publication file, chapter file, and style sheet file.

In the following exercise, you create a new document by selecting a predesigned style sheet. The style sheet book_p1.sty is used as an example. Substitute whatever style sheet fits the needs of your publication.

1. Select **N**ew from the **F**ile menu or click on the New button in the ribbon bar. The New Publication dialog box in figure 3.2 appears.

2. Click on the Load **S**tyle button. (To load the default style sheet, click on the **D**efault Style button.) The Open Style Sheet dialog box appears, as displayed in figure 3.3. Change to the drive and directory where the style sheet you want to use is stored. The book_p1.sty style sheet is located in the VENTURA\TYPESET directory.

Figure 3.2
The New
Publication
dialog box.

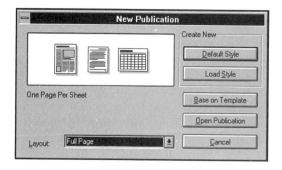

Figure 3.3
The Open Style
Sheet dialog box.

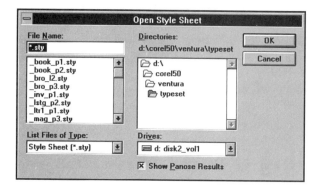

3. Select the book_p1.sty style sheet and click on OK. A new publication is displayed containing one chapter file with one page (see fig. 3.4). Because you have not yet saved the file, the title bar displays untitled.pub for the publication file name. The status line displays untitled.chp for the chapter file name and book_p1.sty for the style sheet name.

You are now ready to begin building your document. The next section discusses the steps for saving the document. The last section discusses changing the page layout information, such as setting the page size and orientation. Remember, changing the page layout settings alters the style sheet file. It is important to read the following section on saving style sheets to understand how this can affect your work.

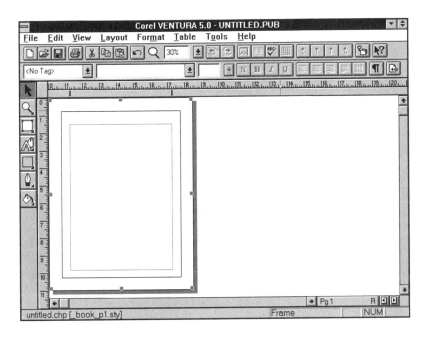

II

Building a VENTURA Document

Figure 3.4
A single blank page is displayed after you have created the new document.

Saving Your Work

Publication, chapter, and style sheet files are the building blocks of all VENTURA documents. Some publication files use multiple chapter and style sheet files, but others require only one chapter and style sheet file. Publication files are saved with the file name extension .PUB. The individual chapter files that build the publication are saved with the file name extension .CHP. Every chapter file is associated or *linked* to a style sheet file. Style sheet files are saved with the file name extension .STY.

Saving the publication file saves any changes made to the files used to build the document, such as the chapter and style sheet files. However, because the chapter and style sheet files are separate, you have the option of renaming and saving them individually. For instance, you might want to specify certain file names for the chapters in your publication. This section discusses the options for saving publication, chapter, and style sheet files.

Saving Publication Files

As discussed in Chapter 1, the publication file does not save the actual information used to build the chapter files. Instead, the publication file saves pointers that retrieve the chapter files when the publication is opened. The contents of a publication file are similar to a map, with directions for locating particular chapter files and the style sheets associated to them. Refer to Chapter 1 for more information on how VENTURA uses pointers to manage the files required to create a document.

To save a publication file, you must enter a file name. For instance, you might enter airsafe.pub as the publication file name for a brochure on air safety. By default, VENTURA applies the file name to the publication file *and* the first chapter file in the publication. For example, the first chapter in the airsafe.pub file would be named airsafe.chp.

Using the same name for both the publication and chapter files works great for single-chapter documents, such as newsletters and resumes. Because they share the same file name, you can quickly identify which publication and chapter files belong together. However, for publications with multiple chapters, such as books and manuals, you need to specify a unique file name for each chapter.

The style sheet file name is not affected when you save a publication. For instance, if the style sheet named brochure.sty was used with the air safety brochure, the name would not be altered when you saved the publication file. The steps for saving style sheets are covered later in this section.

Saving a Document for the First Time

VENTURA prompts you to enter a file name and directory location for the new publication file. The following steps define the process for saving a new document for the first time:

1. Select Save **A**s from the **F**ile menu to open the Save Publication As dialog box as shown in figure 3.5.

2. Change to the drive and directory where you want to save the publication file and enter a file name in the File **N**ame box. You do not have to enter the file name extension .PUB; VENTURA does that automatically.

3. Click on OK. The publication file name appears in the title bar, and the chapter file name appears in the status line.

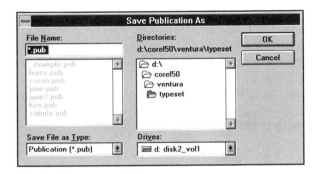

Figure 3.5
The Save
Publication As
dialog box.

After you initially save the publication file, you can use the Save command to save any subsequent changes to the publication. Simply select **S**ave from the **F**ile menu or click on the Save button in the ribbon bar. You only need to use the Save **A**s command described in the previous steps if you want to change the file name or directory location of your publication file.

Get into the habit of saving the publication file every 10 or 15 minutes to protect yourself from any power shortages or program errors.

Saving Style Sheets

As you prepare to build and design your publication, consider whether you plan to alter the style sheet information. For instance, do you anticipate changing the page margins or modifying the paragraph tags? Will you add headers and footers, or perhaps change the widow and orphans settings? Changes made to the style sheet affect all other documents using that style sheet. Therefore, you need to determine if you want to share any modifications you make to the style sheet with other documents. If not, save the style sheet with a new file name so that modifications only affect your new document.

It's a good idea to save all the publication, chapter, and style sheet files associated with a document in one directory, such as C:\VENTURA\DOCS. This makes the files for each publication easier to locate and manage.

II

Building a VENTURA Document

Sharing Style Sheets

The ability to share style sheets is ideal for maintaining consistency in larger documents such as a series of training manuals or a book with multiple chapters. As displayed in figure 3.6, using the same style sheet for all the chapters in a book makes it easier to achieve consistent formatting throughout the publication. For example, if you are beginning chapter two of a book and want it to look just like chapter one, you simply select the style sheet used to format chapter one.

Sharing style sheets also means that changes made in one chapter file affect all other chapter files using that style sheet. Suppose chapter one and chapter two of a publication use the same style sheet. If you change the layout in chapter two from a three-column to a two-column layout, chapter one will be modified to a two-column layout as well.

Saving Style Sheets with a New Name

There might be times when a particular style sheet meets most of your needs, but requires a little tweaking to be exactly what you want. If you want to modify a style sheet without affecting other documents using that style sheet, you need to rename the style sheet. Saving the style sheet with a new file name creates a new style sheet that is an independent copy of the original style sheet. You can then modify this new style sheet without affecting other documents.

For example, suppose that you built a style sheet called broch1.sty for your first brochure and selected this style sheet again to build a second brochure. In the second brochure, however, you want to change to a three column layout and use another font in the paragraph tags. To prevent these changes from affecting the first brochure, you would save the style sheet with a new name, possibly broch2.sty. Saving the style sheet with a new name creates a new style sheet with the same formatting information as the first. However, because they are now two separate style sheet files, any changes made to the second brochure do not affect the first brochure.

The Save Style Sheet As command is used to save a style sheet with a new name. The following exercise illustrates creating a new document with the brochure.sty style sheet, and then saving this style sheet with the new name salesbro.sty:

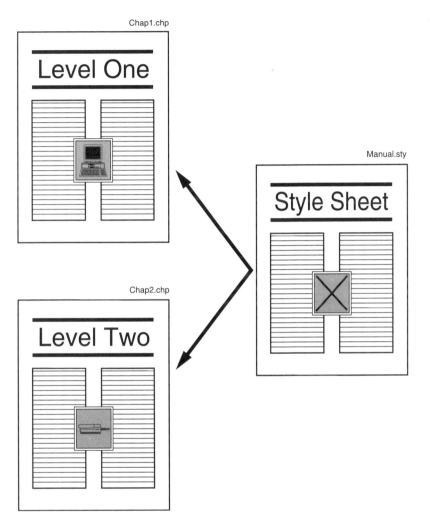

Figure 3.6
Sharing style sheets helps you achieve consistency in design.

1. Select **N**ew from the **F**ile menu or click on the New button. In the New Publication dialog box, click on the Load **S**tyle button.

2. In the VENTURA\VPSTYLE directory, select brochure.sty and click on OK. A new document is displayed. If you have the column guides feature turned on, three columns appear on the page, as shown in figure 3.7.

Figure 3.7
The brochure style sheet uses a three-column layout.

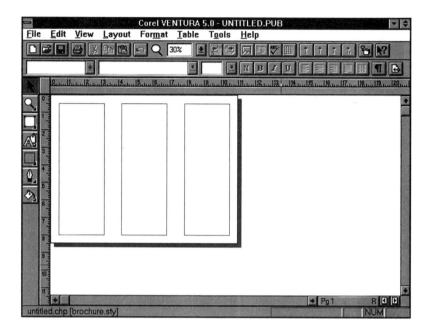

3. To save the brochure style sheet with a new name, select Save Style S**h**eet As from the **L**ayout menu. The Save Style Sheet As dialog box shown in figure 3.8 appears.

Figure 3.8
The Save Style Sheet As dialog box.

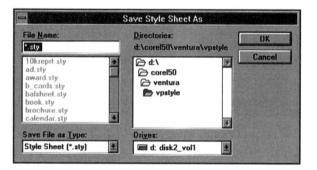

4. Change to the drive and directory where you want to save the style sheet file. Enter **salesbro** for the new style sheet name in the File **N**ame box and click on OK. You do not have to enter the file name extension .STY;

VENTURA does that automatically. The new style sheet file name salesbro.sty appears in the status line in the lower left corner of the screen.

You can change the name of the style sheet before or after saving the publication file. However, if you do change the style sheet name after saving the publication file, you will need to save the publication again to accept the change.

Saving Chapter Files

All VENTURA publications are composed of at least one chapter file. When you add other chapters, you must specify a separate file name for each chapter. The following exercise shows you how to save a chapter file:

1. Select Save Chapter As from the **L**ayout menu. The Save Chapter dialog box appears as displayed in figure 3.9.

2. Change to the drive and directory where you want the chapter file to be saved. Enter a file name in the File **N**ame box and click on OK. The new chapter file name appears in the status line in the lower left corner of the screen.

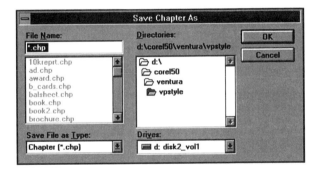

Figure 3.9
The Save Chapter As dialog box.

Understanding Additional Options for Saving Publications

VENTURA provides several options for backing up your work and modifying how the files in a publication are saved. The following options are found in the Preferences dialog box. You can set these features for the way you prefer to work. Once set, these features will remain in effect until modified again.

Creating Backup Files

To protect your work, VENTURA provides an option for creating backup copies of a publication file and its associated chapter, style sheet, and text files. Backups are made when you save a publication. These are copies of the .PUB, .CHP, and .STY files at the time they were last saved. These files will have the same name as the original files except that the first character of the file extension will be changed to a $. For example, a backup of the publication file autosale.pub would be named autosale.$ub. If you need to open these backup copies in VENTURA, you will have to rename them with the proper extension. For example, autosale.$ub, must be renamed as autosale.pub in order to open it in VENTURA.

 You can use the Windows File Manager to rename backup files. Refer to your Windows documentation for more information on file management techniques.

To activate the backup feature, choose Pre**f**erences from the T**o**ols menu. The Preferences dialog box as displayed in figure 3.10 appears. Click on the Make **B**ackup on Save option to place an *X* in the check box and click on OK. Be aware that enabling Make Backup on Save essentially creates a duplicate copy of each file you create. Thus, with this feature enabled, you could be consuming hard disk space with duplicate files.

Using Verbose Save

Normally, when you save a new publication, you are only prompted to enter a file name for the publication file. The name you specify for the publication is automatically applied to the first chapter file. If you want the chapter to have another file name, you must rename the chapter file with the Save Cha**p**ter As command. In addition, if the default style sheet was used to build the chapter, you also need to save the style sheet with the Save Style S**h**eet As command. The **V**erbose Save option can help to reduce some of these additional saving steps. When the **V**erbose Save option is enabled, VENTURA prompts you to enter file names for the publication, chapter, and style sheet files.

To enable **V**erbose Save, choose Pre**f**erences from the T**o**ols menu. Click on the **V**erbose Save option to place an *X* in the check box and click on OK. If the chapter and style sheet files already have file names, you are not prompted to save them, even when **V**erbose Save is enabled. For example, if one of the pre-designed style sheets is used to format the chapter, you are not prompted to save the style sheet.

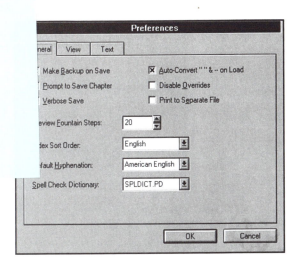

Figure 3.10
The Preferences dialog box.

Setting Up a Document

This section focuses on altering the page layout to set up your new document. These changes will affect the style sheet, so if you do not want the changes to affect other documents, make sure you rename the style sheet. In this section, you will learn how to change the page size and orientation and set up the document for single- or double-sided printing. The steps for selecting a page layout, setting the page margins, and establishing the number of columns are also covered. Remember, you only have to change these elements if the settings supplied by the style sheet are not what you need.

Setting the Page Size and Orientation

VENTURA provides several page size options, such as letter, legal, tabloid, and fanfold. The page sizes can be set to display in portrait or landscape orientation. As shown in figure 3.11, portrait displays the pages vertically, and landscape displays pages horizontally.

The following exercise illustrates setting up a chapter file using the tabloid page size and landscape orientation. You can substitute your own page size and orientation to fit your needs.

1. Select **C**hapter Settings from the **L**ayout menu. The Chapter Settings dialog box appears, as shown in figure 3.12.

2. By default, the Layout tab is selected. Under Page Size, click on the down arrow by the list box to reveal the available page sizes, and select Tabloid. A sample of the page appears in the preview box.

Figure 3.11
Portrait pages
print vertically;
landscape pages
print horizontally.

Figure 3.12
The Chapter
Settings dia-
log box.

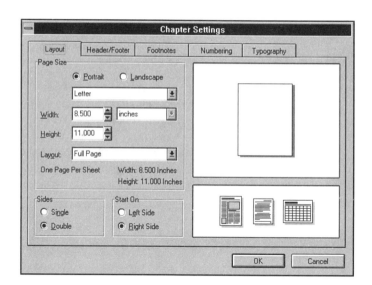

3. Click on the **L**andscape option to change the page orientation. The **W**idth and **H**eight boxes reflect the new page size—17×11 inches high.

4. Click on OK. The page is displayed with the new size and orientation. Notice the rulers indicate the page is 17 inches across.

Every page in the chapter file must use the same page size and orientation. If you want to change the page size and orientation within the same publication, you will have to add a new chapter file and select another style sheet for that chapter. You can then change the page size and orientation for that chapter file.

Specifying Single- or Double-Sided Printing

If your document will be printed on only one side of the paper, you are using single-sided printing. Because you no longer have facing pages, all of the pages in a single-sided chapter become right pages. If the document will print on both sides of the paper, as with this book, you are using double-sided printing. The format you choose determines how margins, headers, and footers are set up. For instance, in a double-sided chapter you can set a one-inch margin for all left pages and a two-inch margin for all right pages. Or set up a header that appears on only the right pages of the document. In a single-sided chapter, you can only set margins and headers for right pages.

 The Facing Pages Preview command is not available when a chapter is set up for single-sided printing.

Most of the predesigned style sheets are set up for double-sided printing. The following exercise illustrates selecting the single-sided printing option:

1. Select **C**hapter Settings from the **L**ayout menu. The Chapter Settings dialog box appears, as shown in figure 3.12.

2. In the lower left corner, select Si**n**gle in the Sides section of the dialog box and click on OK. All pages in the chapter are now right pages; there are no left pages.

Though single-sided documents are generally printed on the right side, you can specify the printing to begin on the left side. In this case, the pages in the chapter would all be "left" pages. A double-sided document can also be instructed to begin printing on the left side. To instruct a chapter file to begin printing on the left side, click on L**e**ft Side in the Start On section of the Chapter Settings dialog box.

Selecting a Page Layout

VENTURA offers a variety of "page layouts" designed specifically for greeting cards, invitations, and pamphlets—any type of document where the paper is folded. Think of the layouts as folding a piece of paper in different ways to create different page arrangements. You can select a page layout that folds into a booklet, or one that folds across the top or side. For instance, a side-fold folds the page in half vertically to create a front page, two inside pages, and a back page. Figure 3.13 illustrates the available page layouts.

Figure 3.13
VENTURA's
available page
layouts.

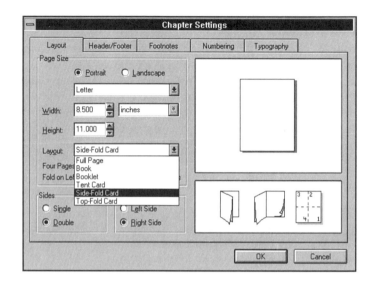

The following exercise illustrates setting up a landscape, letter-sized document with a booklet page layout. You might use a booklet when producing a small in-house training manual.

1. Select **C**hapter Settings from the **L**ayout menu. When the Chapter Settings dialog box appears, select a letter-size page with landscape orientation.

2. Click on the down arrow by Lay**o**ut. Select Booklet from the list of available page layouts. You can see a preview of the booklet in the lower right corner of the dialog box.

3. Click on OK. The first page of the booklet is displayed.

The booklet layout simulates folding a piece of paper in half to create two pages. Each page of the booklet is 5 1/2 inches wide, which is half the size of a landscape letter-size page. VENTURA's page layouts are a convenient way to quickly produce birthday cards, menus, table tents, and name cards.

Setting Margins and Columns

The page margins and column layout are part of the page frame settings. The page frame, which is the size of a full page, is automatically placed on each page of a document. You will have to select the page frame before changing the margin and column settings. The first tool in the toolbox, the Pick tool, is used to select frames. Click on the Pick tool—the tool darkens indicating it is active. Now

move inside the page area and click to select the page frame. As displayed in figure 3.14, eight gray selection handles appear around the outside edges of the frame.

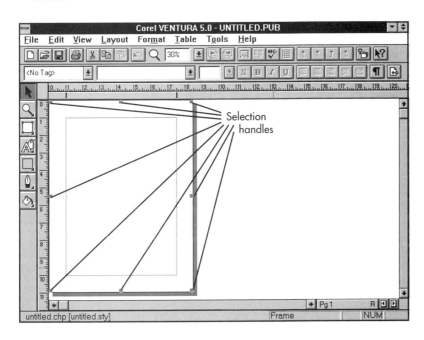

Figure 3.14
Selection handles indicate the page frame is selected.

Before setting the margins and columns, it is a good idea to display the column guides. The guides enable you to see the width of the margins and columns as you build the page layout. The option for displaying column guides is in the Preferences dialog box in the Tools menu. Refer to Chapter 2 for more information on showing column guides.

Setting Margins

Page margins are the white space around the edge of the page where text and graphics typically do not appear. The margin settings are stored with the style sheet information. With VENTURA, you can set margins for the top, bottom, left, and right side of the page.

When the base page is selected, small black lines called *margin boundary markers* appear in the ruler. Dragging these along the ruler is another way to adjust the page margins.

The margins for double-sided documents can be identical across the left and right pages. For instance, you might want a one-inch margin around the entire page for both the left and right pages.

The margins for double-sided documents can also be totally different for the left and right pages. For example, all left pages could use a one-inch top margin, with all right pages using a two-inch top margin.

You can even have the margin settings "mirror" across the left and right pages. In the book displayed in figure 3.15, the left page margins are mirrored, or flipped, on the right page. Notice the inside margin on the left page is wider, and the inside margin on the right page is wider. Mirroring the margins to allow for wider inside margins is ideal when your publication will be bound.

Figure 3.15
To allow for binding, add extra space to the inside margins in double-sided documents.

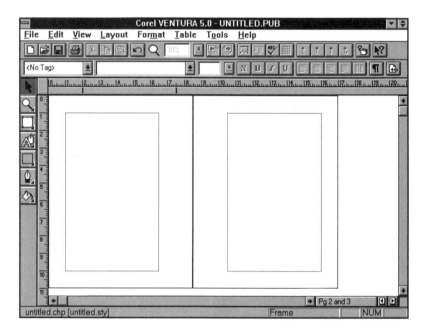

The following exercise illustrates setting page margins for a double-sided document. The margins will be set for the left pages and then mirrored to the right pages.

1. Select the base frame and choose **F**rame from the For**m**at menu. The Frame Settings dialog box appears.

2. Click on the Margins tab to display the options for controlling margins (see fig. 3.16). Under Inside Margins, click on the Left option by **P**ages to set margins for all left pages in the chapter.

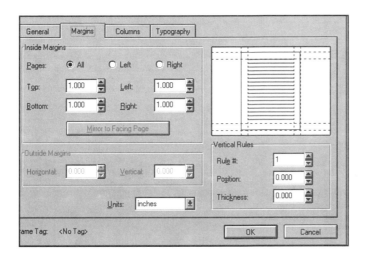

Figure 3.16
The Frame Settings dialog box with the Margins tab selected.

3. Enter **1.0** inch for the top, bottom, and left margins. Enter **1.5** inches for the right margin. Click on the **M**irror to Facing Pages button.

4. To preview the right page margins, click on the Right option by Pages. The left margin displays 1.5 inches, indicating the margins were mirrored. Click on OK to apply the margins.

If the column guides option is enabled, the margin boundaries are displayed on the page area. To see the margins mirrored on left and right pages, you will need to insert additional pages. The steps for inserting pages are covered later in this chapter. It's important to note that headers and footers are placed in the top and bottom margins. If you plan on using headers and footers, you might want to increase the size of your top and bottom margins to allow room for them.

Setting Columns

Multi-column layouts enhance the appearance and readability of your documents. Many of the predesigned style sheets for newsletters, magazines, brochures and catalogs use two- and three-column layouts. The maximum number of columns is eight. With VENTURA, you specify the exact width of the columns, as well as the space between the columns, called *gutters*.

As displayed in figure 3.17, the columns in your documents can be equal width or, for more variety, you can design columns in varying widths. The second image in figure 3.17 includes inter-column rules—thin, decorative lines that are placed between the columns. These rule lines can be turned on and off and adjusted for thickness. Several of the predesigned style sheets use the inter-column rules.

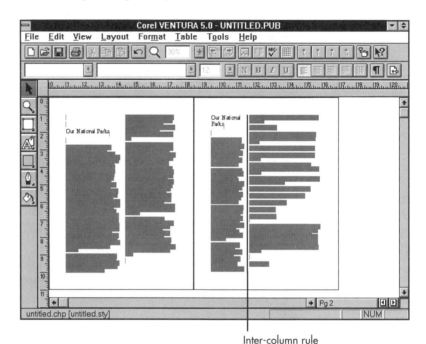

Figure 3.17
You can create equal or variable column widths in VENTURA.

Inter-column rule

If you are producing a double-sided document, the columns can be identical on both the left and right pages. In a report, for instance, you might use two equal columns on both the left and right pages. The columns can also be different on the left and right pages. For example, the left page could use a three-column layout, while the right page uses a two-column layout.

Setting Equal Columns

The following steps illustrate creating a three-column layout with equal column widths. The column layout will be identical on both the left and right pages.

1. Select the base frame and choose **F**rame from the For**ma**t menu. The Frame Settings dialog box appears. Click on the Columns tab to display the options for creating columns, as shown in figure 3.18.

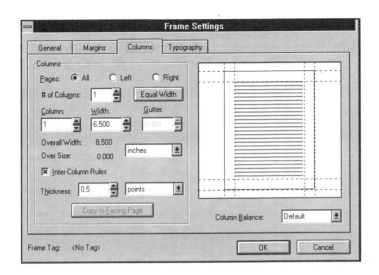

Figure 3.18
The Frame Settings dialog box with the Columns tab selected.

2. Under Columns, click on the All option to set columns for both the left and right pages. Enter **3** in the # of Colu**m**ns list box. The sample box displays three columns.

3. Enter **.25** in the **G**utter list box to add space between the columns. Click on the Equal Width button to make the columns and gutters the same width.

4. Click in the **I**nter-Column Rules option to turn the rule lines on and off. If an *X* appears by the option, a line will be placed between the two columns. You can see the line in the sample box. Use the T**h**ickness list box to control the thickness or *weight* of the rule line. If no *X* appears, the option is turned off.

5. When you are finished, click on OK. The base page is now set up for a three-column layout. If you add additional pages, they will also use the three-column layout.

Setting Up Variable Width Columns

When setting variable width columns, you must consider how wide the columns can be when elements such as the page size and margins are taken into account. All of these factors contribute to the overall page width. In figure 3.19, the page size is 8.5 inches wide. The left and right page margins are set at one inch. This leaves 6.5 inches for columns and gutters. The first column is set at 2 inches, and the gutter at .25 inches. This leaves 4.25 inches for the second column.

Figure 3.19
You must consider
the overall page
width when
creating uneven
columns.

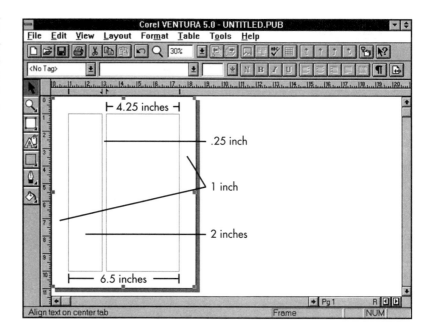

Figure 3.19
You must consider the overall page width when creating uneven columns.

VENTURA displays the overall page width as you enter the column widths. Use the Overall Width setting displayed below the column width to guide how wide your columns and gutters can be. For example, a portrait letter size page is 8.5 inches wide; you could adjust the column and gutter widths until the overall page width displays 8.5. The next steps illustrate creating a two-column layout with varying column widths on a portrait letter size page with one-inch margins.

1. Use the **C**hapter Settings command in the **L**ayout menu to set up a letter size page with portrait orientation. Select the base frame and choose **F**rame from the For**m**at menu. Click on the Margins tab and set a **1**-inch top, bottom, left, and right margin.

2. Click on the Columns tab in the Frame Settings dialog box. Under Columns, click on the All option to set columns for both the left and right pages.

3. In the # if Columns box, enter **2**. The **C**olumn box displays 1, indicating you are working with the first column. Enter **2** in the **W**idth box to make the first column two inches wide. Enter **.25** in the **G**utter list box. To set the width for the second column, return to the **C**olumn box and enter **2**. Enter **4.25** for the **W**idth box.

4. Directly below the **W**idth option, the Overall Width is displayed. In this case, the overall width is 8.5—the width of the letter size page. Click on OK. The varied column layout is displayed.

On the Columns tab of the Frame Settings dialog box, VENTURA provides an option for balancing the bottom of columns. On the left page in figure 3.20, the balance columns option has been turned on. This setting distributes the text so that both columns are the same height. The page on the right in figure 3.20 has Balance Columns turned off. In this case, the first column is filled, and any remaining text appears in the second column. To turn on the balance columns option, click on the down arrow by Column Balance and select On.

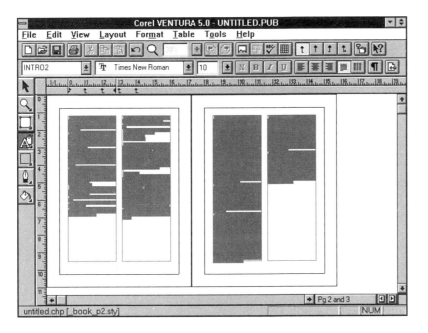

Figure 3.20
The Column Balance feature distributes the text evenly in the columns so they are vertically aligned.

II

Building a VENTURA Document

Adding Chapter Files

With VENTURA you can add additional chapters—for a total of 128 chapter files per publication. The obvious reason to add chapters is to divide the subject matter. For example, the chapters in this book separate the information for operating VENTURA into focused categories. When producing books and manuals, it is common to add chapters when a new topic is introduced. But even when there is not a change in subject matter, you might want to add chapter files to divide the information into smaller, more manageable sections. For example, a 200-page catalog would be much easier to work with when divided into four

50-page chapter files. The smaller chapters also enable you speed up your work by making it quicker to open, save, and print each of the chapter files.

Another important reason for adding chapters is the capability to apply a different style sheet to control the appearance of each chapter in the publication. For instance, as displayed in figure 3.21, you could build in a single publication file a sales presentation that included the speaker's script, a set of overheads, and audience handouts. This publication would include three chapter files all linked to different style sheets designed to format that particular section.

Figure 3.21
Linking chapter files to different style sheets enables you to create publication files that include several types of documents.

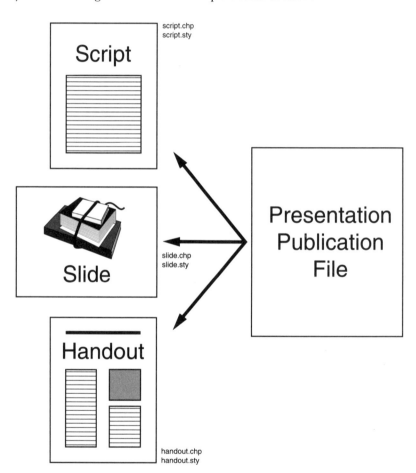

There are two options for adding chapter files to your publications. First, you can add blank chapters. Adding a blank chapter creates one page—a starting point upon which you can build and design the rest of the chapter. Second, you can add chapters from other publications to your current publication. A chapter

initially created for a stockholders report, for example, could be added to a company magazine, saving you the trouble of re-creating the chapter for the magazine.

New chapters are always added to the end of the publication. For example, if you add a chapter file to a publication with three chapter files, the new chapter becomes the fourth chapter file. To change the order of the chapters, use the Publication Manager in the **F**ile menu. Refer to Chapter 16 for more information on rearranging chapter files.

Adding Blank Chapters

In VENTURA, every chapter file is linked to a style sheet file. When you add a blank chapter file, the blank chapter automatically links to the style sheet file used in the current chapter file. For instance, if the chapter you are currently working in uses the techdoc.sty style sheet, a new blank chapter will also use the techdoc.sty style sheet. Use the following steps to add blank chapter files:

1. Select Add Ne**w** Chapter from the **L**ayout menu. If you have not saved changes to the current chapter, a message box appears asking you to save the current chapter file. Click on Yes to save any changes, or click on No to ignore the changes.

2. The first (and only) page of the new chapter is displayed. The new chapter does not yet have a file name, so Untitled.chp appears in the status line. The style sheet file name is also displayed.

When you add a blank chapter, a file name is not applied to the new chapter file. Use the Save Chapter As command discussed in the previous section to apply a file name. Because blank chapter files include only one page, you might need to use the I**n**sert Pages command covered later in this chapter to add additional pages.

Adding Chapters from Other Publications

Adding a chapter file from another publication is a quick way to copy information from one publication into another. The style sheet and all text and graphics files linked with the chapter file are placed in the new publication. When you add a chapter file from another publication, its links to the original publication remain intact.

In effect, as displayed in figure 3.22, it is the same chapter file linked to two publications. Any changes you make to the chapter file in the new publication also affect the chapter file in the old publication. For instance, if you change the page margins or delete some text, those changes occur in the chapter files in both publications.

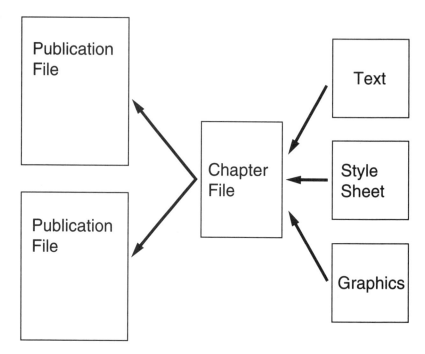

The following steps illustrate adding the Ventdemo.chp file to a new publication. Substitute the chapter file you want to add.

1. Select Add E**x**isting Chapter from the **L**ayout menu. If you have not saved changes to the current chapter, a message box appears asking you to save the current chapter file. Click on Yes to save any changes, or click on No to ignore the changes.

2. The Open Chapter dialog box appears as displayed in figure 3.23. Change to the drive and directory where the chapter file is located. The ventdemo.chp is located in the VENTURA\TYPESET directory.

3. Select the chapter from the list of file names and click on OK. The chapter is added to the end of the publication. Notice the status line displays the chapter and style file name.

With multiple chapter files in your publication, it frequently becomes necessary to move from one chapter to another as you build your publication. The steps for moving between chapters were introduced in Chapter 2, "Exploring a VENTURA

Document." Use the G**o** To Chapter command in the **V**iew menu and select the
chapter file you want to display. You can also use the keyboard shortcuts
Alt+PageDown to move to the next chapter and Alt+PageUp to move to the
previous chapter.

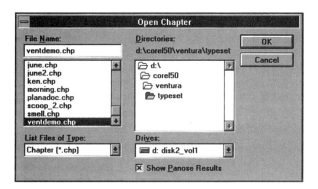

Figure 3.23
The Open Chapter
dialog box.

The fact that chapter files are linked can be somewhat limiting. For instance, if
you added a chapter file from a stockholders report to the company magazine,
you would probably want to alter the chapter information to fit with the magazine
design. At the same time, you would likely want the original information in the
stockholders report to remain unaffected by any modifications. To sever the
chapter files link to the other document, you must rename the chapter and style
sheet files. Use the Save Style Sheet As and Save Chapter As commands discussed
in previous sections to rename the style sheet and chapter files.

Loading Different Style Sheets

Each new chapter is automatically linked to a style sheet file. As discussed in the
previous section, if you add a blank chapter, the new chapter links to the style
sheet file being used when the new chapter was created. For instance, if the
current chapter file uses the thesis.sty style sheet, it also uses the thesis.sty style
sheet when you add a new chapter. If you add a chapter file from another publication, it uses the style sheet to which it was originally linked. In either case, you
should select another style sheet file for the new chapter. Use the following steps
to select another style sheet for a chapter file:

1. Select L**o**ad Style Sheet from the **L**ayout menu. The Open Style Sheet
   dialog box appears as displayed in figure 3.24.

II

Building a VENTURA Document

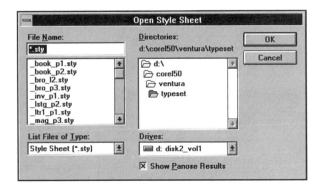

Figure 3.24
The Open Style
Sheet box.

2. Change to the drive and directory where the style sheet you want to load is located. Remember the predesigned style sheets are saved in the TYPE-SET and VPSTYLE directories.

3. Select the style sheet file name and click on OK. The chapter file is formatted according to the new style sheet specifications. The name of the style sheet appears in the status line.

Any time you select a style sheet rather than creating one from scratch, it is important to remember that you will be sharing it with any other documents that use the same style sheet. If you do not want to share the style sheet, you need to rename the style sheet file with the Save Style Sheet As command found in the Layout menu.

Inserting Pages

With VENTURA, you can insert pages at any time during the creation of your document. Each chapter can have a maximum of 9,999 pages. When you insert pages, you have the option to insert them before or after the current page.

Newly inserted pages use the margin and column settings from the style sheet. However, you can change the margin and columns for the inserted page. The capability to create different layouts on the inserted pages gives you a lot of design flexibility. For instance, you can create a newsletter with three-column layout on page one and a two-column layout on page two.

It's important to note that if you have a long text file that continues to flow across several pages, new pages will be added to the chapter using the margin and column layout specified on the page where the text file begins. For example, suppose page one uses a one-column layout and page two uses a two-column

layout. If your text file flows from page one to page two, a new page two is added that uses a one-column layout.

The following steps illustrate inserting ten pages after the first page in a chapter:

1. Display the first page of the chapter and select I<u>n</u>sert Pages from the <u>L</u>ayout menu. The Insert Pages dialog box appears, as shown in figure 3.25.

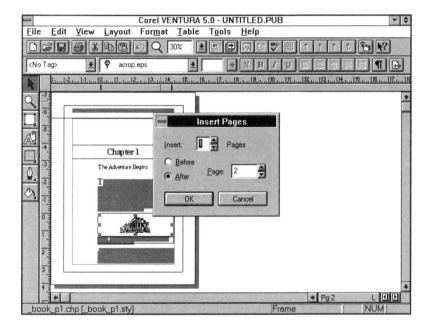

Figure 3.25
The Insert Pages dialog box.

2. Enter **10** in the Insert box—you can insert up to 99 pages at one time. By default, the pages will be inserted after the current page. Click on OK.

The new pages are inserted. The steps for moving between pages were covered in Chapter 2. You can click on the arrows in the Page Counter to move between the pages or use the keyboard shortcuts PgUp and PgDn.

Deleting Pages

If you add too many pages, or later need to reduce the size of a document, you can delete unwanted pages. For example, to add a new section to a publication, assume that you need three more pages. After adding those pages and inserting text and graphics, you discover that you need only two pages. To delete pages from your publication, follow these steps:

1. From the **L**ayout menu, choose Delete Page**s**. The Delete Page dialog box appears, as shown in figure 3.26.

Figure 3.26
The Delete Pages
dialog box.

2. In the **D**elete Page text box, enter the page number you want to delete. To delete a range of pages, click in the **T**hru Page text box and enter the last page number you want to delete.

3. Click on OK to delete the pages and return to the publication.

If a text file is flowed across several base pages, you cannot delete a page within that text flow. For instance, if text is placed on the base page, flowing from pages one to five, page three cannot be deleted. If deleted pages contain any free frames with imported text or graphic files, those files are deleted from the page, but remain in the Files list. If a deleted page contains graphics created with VENTURA's drawing tools, those graphics are lost.

Chapter Snapshot

Frames are the building blocks in VENTURA. You load your text and graphics into frames to construct your document. By using the various types of frames, you can create professional desktop publishing. In this chapter, you learn to do the following:

This chapter teaches you to draw and edit free frames to build your page layout design. This chapter teaches you the first steps to building a quality document.

CHAPTER

Working with Frames

In VENTURA, frames play an integral role in page design. Page layouts are built by adding frames to the page, into which you load text and graphics. Imagine a page from a magazine with lots of design elements such as text, photographs, and illustrations. If the page were designed in VENTURA, each element on the page would be placed in a frame. The frames determine where the text and graphics appear on the page.

Designing with frames makes it easy to build your page layout. When you want a graphic to appear at the top of the page, simply draw the frame at the top and load the graphic. Designing with frames also makes it easy to change your mind. If you want a previously placed graphic switched to the bottom of a page, just drag the frame to the bottom. The flexibility of working with frames makes it easy to experiment with different page layouts until you find just the right look.

This chapter focuses on using frames to design your page layout. First, the chapter explores the different types of frames, such as base page and free frames, that are used to build VENTURA documents. The latter portion of this chapter deals specifically with working with free frames. You will learn how to draw, size, and move free frames. The chapter ends with a look at some advanced frame options, such as rotating, locking, and repeating. For more advanced coverage on frames, refer to Chapter 10, "Advanced Free Frame Options."

Exploring VENTURA's Frames

VENTURA uses several types of frames to hold the text and graphics that appear on a page. Some frame types, such as footnote frames, are designed to hold text. Other frame types, such as free frames, are intended to contain text or graphics. Remember that text might be loaded from a file generated in a word processor or typed directly into the frame. Graphic files are the illustrations, charts, and logos created in drawing applications such as CorelDRAW. Each frame can hold only one file, either text or graphics. As displayed in figure 4.1, there are five types of frames.

Figure 4.1
VENTURA uses five types of frames for building your publications.

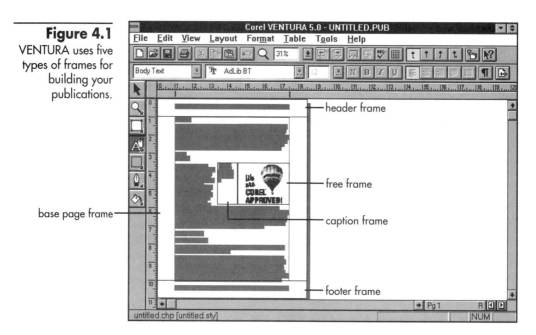

Understanding Base Page Frames

The *base page frame* is a frame that covers the entire page area. A base page frame is automatically placed on each page of a document. Because the base page frame is attached to the page area, it cannot be moved or sized. You can adjust the size of the page area, which in turn adjusts the size of the base page frame. To adjust the size of the page area, use the steps for changing the page size and orientation covered in Chapter 3. You will also find the steps for changing the margins and columns on the base page in Chapter 3.

Any changes made to the base page frame are saved with the style sheet. Remember, any changes made to the style sheet affect all documents using that style sheet. Refer to Chapter 3 for more information on saving style sheets.

The base page frame is generally used to hold the main text of the document. If you were producing a book, for instance, you could load a text file into the base page. When a lengthy text file is placed on the base page frame, VENTURA creates the number of pages needed to hold all of the text. VENTURA then automatically flows the text from base page to base page.

Understanding Free Frames

Very few documents are so uncomplicated that you can load text into the base page and be done with it. What if you want to add photos, illustrations, and charts to embellish the text? What if you want to place smaller text blocks, such as side-bars and pull-quotes within the main text? When your page layouts require a little more complexity, you will need to add *free frames*. As displayed in figure 4.2, two graphics appear in free frames which are drawn on top of the base page frame. The text on the base page flows around the free frame.

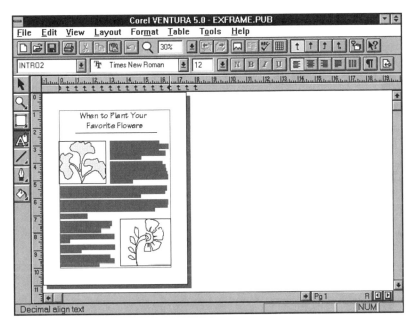

Figure 4.2
Text loaded into the base page flows around any free frames.

Building a VENTURA Document

Each free frame can have its own margin and column settings. The ability to modify each frame individually makes it easy to design pages with different column layouts on one page. For instance, one free frame can be set up with a two-column layout, and another free frame on the same page can be set up with a three-column layout. You can also control the background color and borders for each free frame. Free frames can be used in conjunction with the base page frame or to build the entire layout.

Generally, if a document has one main text file, such as a book, the text is loaded on the base page and all graphics are placed in free frames. However, as displayed in figure 4.3, if a document has several text files, such as a newsletter, all the text and graphics are loaded into free frames. Because all the page elements are in free frames, you can move, manipulate, and modify each frame to accommodate your design.

Figure 4.3
Building the entire layout from free frames makes it easy to experiment with different page layouts.

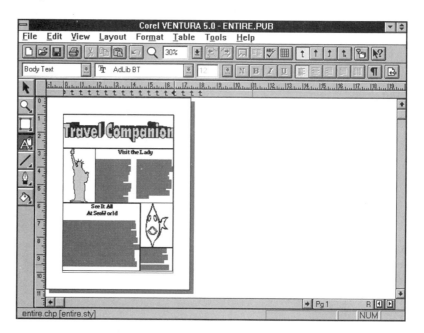

Understanding Caption, Header and Footer, and Footnote Frames

Caption frames are automatically created when you add a caption to a free frame. The caption frame is actually joined to the free frame, so when you move the free

aption frame is also moved. You can specify whether the caption
rs above, below, or to the left or right of the free frame. Refer to
or more information on adding captions.

nuals and books often use headers and footers to help guide readers
material. As displayed in figure 4.4, headers are placed in a *header*
ppears in the top page margin. Footers are placed in a *footer frame*
the bottom page margin. The bigger the margins, the bigger the
footer frames. Because their size is tied to the margins, you cannot
header or footer frames. Refer to Chapter 14, "Advanced Options
for Chapter Formatting," for more information on adding headers and footers.

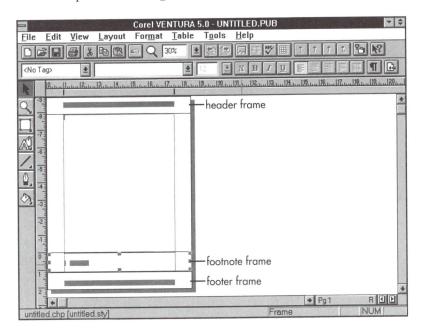

Figure 4.4
Header, footer,
and footnote
frames cannot be
moved or sized.

When footnotes are placed on a page, they appear in *footnote frames.* Similar to
header and footer frames, footnote frames cannot be moved and sized. As
displayed in figure 4.4, footnote frames are placed at the bottom of the page
directly above the footer frame. Refer to Chapter 13 for more information on
adding footnotes.

Creating Free Frames

Before adding free frames, take a moment to consider your page layout. For instance, are you loading text onto the base page? Or are you building the entire layout with free frames? In either case, determining how you want to build your layout makes it easier to begin adding frames. To get the creative juices flowing, some designers even sketch a rough draft of the layout on paper.

 As you learn about drawing and editing frames, you can practice on your own new publication files, or open one of the sample publication files included with VENTURA. Try opening the &book-p1.pub or &news-p2.pub publication files, which are stored in the VENTURA\TYPESET directory.

Drawing Frames

The Frame tool, the third tool in the toolbox, is used to draw free frames on the page. To select the tool, simply click on it with your mouse. The tool darkens, indicating it is selected. Drawing frames is similar to drawing rectangles in drawing applications such as CorelDRAW. Selection handles appear in the frame after it is drawn. Do the following exercise to draw a free frame:

1. Select the Frame tool. Move the mouse cursor into the page area. Notice that the mouse cursor changes shape.

2. Position the mouse where you want the top left corner of the frame to start. Hold the mouse button and drag diagonally. An outline of the frame appears as you drag.

3. When the outline of the frame is the desired size and shape, release the mouse button. The frame is created. As displayed in figure 4.5, selection handles appear inside the frame. Repeat these steps to draw additional free frames.

 If you want to draw several frames at one time, hold the Shift key as you draw the frames. This keeps the Frame tool selected so you can draw additional frames without having to select the Frame tool each time.

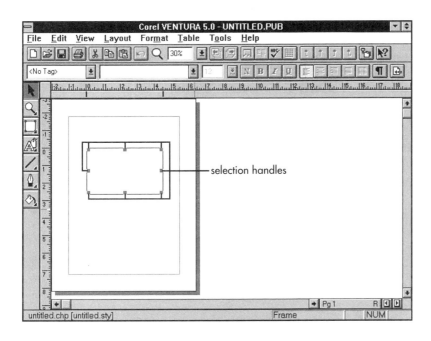

selection handles

II

Building a VENTURA Document

Figure 4.5
Selection handles appear inside a frame after it is drawn.

Selecting Free Frames

Before you can modify a frame in any way, it must be selected. As displayed in figure 4.5, selection handles appear in a frame when it is selected. The following exercise shows you how to select free frames:

1. If necessary, start a new document or open an existing publication file. Select the Pick tool, which is the first tool in the toolbox.

2. Position the mouse cursor inside the frame and click. Selection handles appear around the frame indicating that it is selected.

By default, only one frame is selected at a time. If you want to select several frames, hold the Shift key while clicking on other frames. If you want to move two frames at the same time, for example, select the first frame, then select the second while pressing Shift. Selection handles appear around both frames, indicating that both are selected. You can then move both frames together.

Deleting Frames

After drawing frames on your page, you might decide you added a few too many. To delete a frame, simply select it and choose Delete from the Edit menu. You can also press the Delete key to remove a frame. If a frame is accidentally deleted, use the Undo command in the Edit menu to retrieve the frame.

Free frames are the only frame type that can be deleted. When you delete a free frame, any caption frame linked to the free frame is also deleted. Base page frames, and footnote, header, and footer frames cannot be deleted.

If you delete a frame that is already loaded with a text or graphic file, the text or graphics are also deleted from the page. Deleted text or graphic files are deleted from the page only, *not* the chapter file. For more information about removing files from the chapter file, refer to Chapter 5, "Loading Text Into Frames."

Moving, Sizing, and Rotating Frames

To give you full control over the page design, you can move free frames anywhere on the page. Moving frames with the mouse is the quickest way to reposition a frame, although you can also enter exact coordinates for placing the frame in the Placement Roll-up.

You can also adjust the size of free frames. As with moving frames, the mouse provides the quickest way to resize a frame, though you can also enter exact dimensions in the Placement Roll-up for sizing a frame. The Placement Roll-up also includes an option for rotating frames. The Frame Settings dialog box provides another way to enter measurements for moving, sizing, and rotating frames. The Placement Roll-up, however, is much quicker and easier to use.

Roll-ups are unique to Corel applications. Double-click on the Control menu (the white bar) in the top left corner of the dialog box to close the roll-up. To hide the roll-up window, keeping just the roll-up's title bar on screen, click on the up arrow in the top right corner. Click on the down arrow to redisplay the roll-up window.

Moving Frames with the Mouse

Free frames can be moved anywhere on the page, even in the margin areas. If you have several frames selected, they will move together as a group. The following exercise demonstrates this feature:

1. Select the frame. Selection handles appear when a frame is selected.

2. Position the mouse cursor inside the frame. Hold the mouse button and drag the frame to a new place on the page.

3. An outline of the frame appears as you move the frame. Notice that the mouse cursor shape changes to a four-sided arrow. When the frame outline is in the desired location, release the mouse button.

Any text or graphics loaded into the frames are also moved. You cannot move a frame from one page to another. To move a frame to another page, use the Cut or Copy commands as discussed later in this chapter.

Moving a Frame with the Placement Roll-Up

The Placement Roll-up enables you to enter measurements indicating precisely where a frame is to be placed. As displayed in figure 4.6, the horizontal measurement specifes how far the left edge of the frame appears from the left edge of the page. The vertical measurement specifies how far the top edge of the frame appears from the top edge of the page.

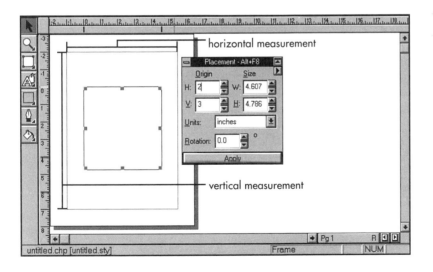

Figure 4.6

With the Placement Roll-up, you can enter exact coordinates for positioning frames.

II

Building a VENTURA Document

The following exercise illustrates positioning a frame exactly two inches from the left of the page and three inches from the top of the page:

1. Select **P**lacement Roll-Up from the T**o**ols menu. The roll-up appears as displayed in figure 4.7.

2. Select the frame you want to move. The Placement Roll-up shows the current horizontal and vertical position of the frame.

3. Under **O**rigin, enter **2** in the Horizontal box and **3** in the Vertical box. Click on the Apply button to move the frame. The selected frame is positioned accordingly. If desired, close the roll-up.

Figure 4.7
The Placement
Roll-up.

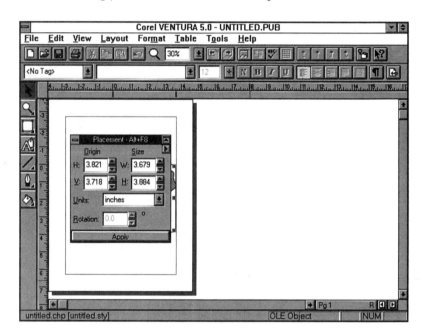

To use a measurement system other than inches for moving and sizing frames, click on the down arrow by **U**nits in the Placement Roll-up and select the desired measurement system.

Sizing a Frame with the Mouse

You can use selection handles to change the size of a free frame. As displayed in figure 4.8, use the corner selection handles when you want to adjust the width and height of the frame at the same time. Use the corner handles when you want to retain a frame's original shape as you reduce or enlarge it. Use the middle selection handles to size the frame in one direction only. For instance, sizing with the bottom middle button adjusts the height of the frame.

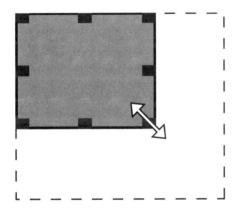

Dragging corner handles resizes objects proportionately.

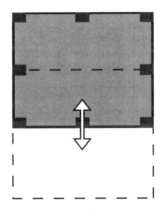

Dragging interior handles resizes objects in one direction.

Figure 4.8
The corner selection handles allow you to size a frame's height and width at the same time. The middle selection handles size the frame in one direction only.

The following exercise illustrates sizing a frame:

1. Select the frame and position the mouse cursor over one of the selection handles. The cursor changes to a double-sided arrow.

2. To enlarge the frame, drag away from the frame's center. To reduce the frame, drag toward the frame's center.

3. When the frame outline appears in the desired size, release the mouse button.

When a frame containing a graphic is sized, the graphic sizes along with the frame. For instance, if you reduce the frame size, the graphic in the frame is also reduced. (Graphics can also be sized independently of the frame—refer to Chapter 11, "Importing Graphics into Frames," for more information.) When a frame containing text is sized, the size of the text is not affected. For instance, when doubling the size of a text frame, the type size would not increase from 10 to 20 point. Instead, sizing a frame with text affects the amount of text that is displayed in the frame. If a frame is too small, the text will get cut off. Chapter 5 takes a closer look at working with frames that contain text.

Sizing a Frame with the Placement Roll-Up

With the Placement Roll-up you can enter exact measurements for the height and width of a free frame. If you've ever needed to place an object that is exactly 4.25 inches by 3.15 inches, you'll appreciate this feature. The following steps illustrate sizing a frame that is 3.25 inches wide and 2.5 inches tall:

1. If necessary, start a new publication file, or open an existing one. Draw a frame on the page. Select **P**lacement Roll-Up from the T**o**ols menu. The Placement Roll-up appears.

2. Select the frame you want to size. The Placement Roll-up shows the current height and width of the frame.

3. Under **S**ize, enter **3.25** in the Width box and **2.5** in the Height box. Click on the Apply button to size the frame. If desired, close the roll-up.

The Placement Roll-up includes options for applying the same frame size to a group of selected frames. The Same Size command enables you to instruct all selected frames to become the same size as the last frame selected. The Same Horizontal Size and Same Vertical Size commands enable you to instruct all selected frames to become the same horizontal or vertical size as the last frame selected.

The following exercise illustrates using the Same Size command:

1. If necessary, add several diferent size frames to your page. Select **P**lacement Roll-Up from the T**o**ols menu. The Placement Roll-up appears.

2. Select several frames. (Holding down the Shift key lets you select multiple frames.) The frame whose size you want to duplicate should be the last frame selected.

3. Click on the flyout menu arrow to reveal the menu (see fig. 4.9). Select Same Size. All of the selected frames are sized to match the size of the last selected frame.

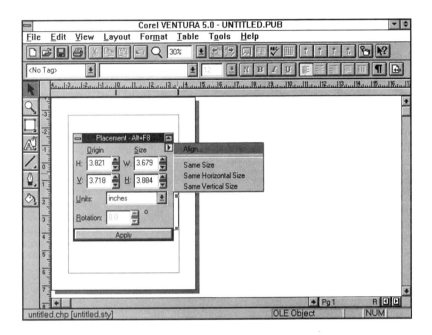

Figure 4.9
The Placement Roll-up with the flyout menu displayed.

Rotating Frames

To enhance your page design, you might want to rotate text or graphics to display at an angle (see fig. 4.10). Any free frame and its contents can be rotated. You can rotate only one frame at a time. All frames are rotated on the frame's center point and in a counterclockwise direction. The following exercise shows you how to rotate a free frame:

1. Select **P**lacement Roll-Up from the T**o**ols menu. The Placement Roll-up appears.

2. Select the frame you want to rotate. Enter the degree of rotation in the **R**otation box at the bottom of the roll-up. Click on OK.

Figure 4.10
Free frames and
their contents can
be rotated.

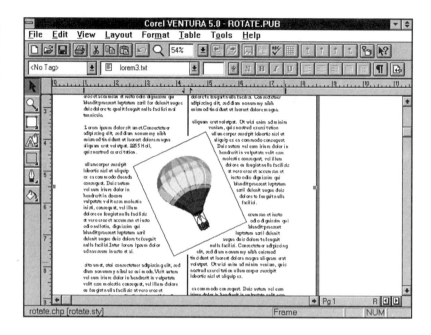

Before rotating a frame, consider how it will affect the text or graphic in the frame. For instance, rotating large amounts of text and graphics can detract from the document's readability. As a general rule, limit any rotation to short text blocks, such as titles and headings, and simple graphics, such as logos.

Aligning Frames

In some page designs, you might want the free frames to line up vertically or horizontally. For instance, in the catalog displayed in figure 4.11, the frames on the first page are vertically left-aligned. The frames on the second page are aligned horizontally across the top. With VENTURA, you can line up frames with your column guides or use the **A**lign command to line up a group of frames.

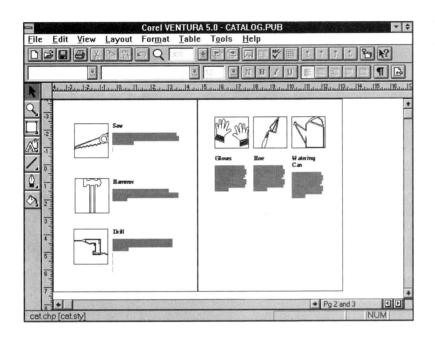

Figure 4.11
VENTURA makes it easy to align frames for a professional look.

Aligning Frames to Column Guides

The column guides on your page can have a magnetic pull that forces the sides of free frames to snap to the nearest column guide. In figure 4.12, the Snap to Columns feature was used to ensure that the frames are the same width as the column guides. To align frames with the column guides, select the Snap to Columns command in the **L**ayout menu. Now, when you move or size a frame close to a column guide, the frame *snaps to* or aligns itself with the guide. Click on the Snap to Col**u**mns command again to disable this feature.

The column guides do not have to be showing for the snap-to feature to work. However, displaying the column guides makes it easier to see what guides the frames are snapping to. Select the Column Guides option on the View tab of the Preferences dialog box under the Tools menu to display the column guides.

Figure 4.12
Enabling the Snap to Columns feature makes it easy to align frames with your column guides.

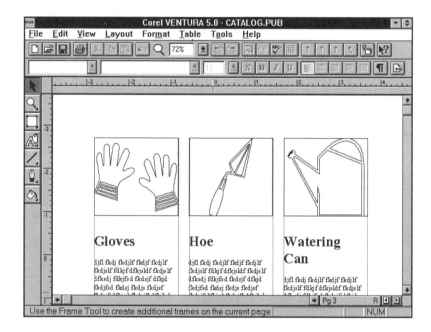

Arranging Frames with the Align Command

Rather than just eyeballing it when arranging frames vertically or horizontally, use the **A**lign command. Frames can be aligned with other frames or to the center of the page. The **A**lign command can also be used to align graphic objects drawn with VENTURA's drawing tools.

Aligning Frames with Other Frames

When aligning frames with each other, the last frame selected is used as the alignment guide—all other selected frames move to align with this frame. The following exercise illustrates horizontally aligning the three frames displayed on the first page in figure 4.13. The second page shows the frames after they are aligned, using the top frame as the alignment guide.

1. Select the three frames; make sure to select the frame to which you want the other two frames to align last.

2. Select **A**lign from the T**o**ols menu. The Align dialog box appears as displayed in figure 4.14.

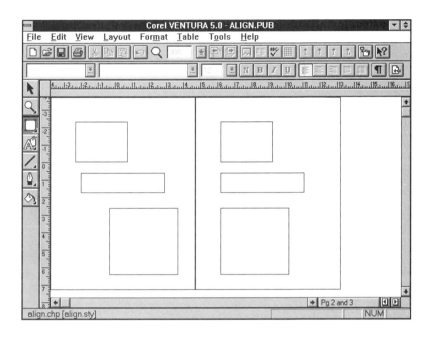

Figure 4.13
The Align
command gives
you a precise way
to line up your free
frames.

Figure 4.14
The Align dialog
box.

II

Building a VENTURA Document

3. Under Horizontally, click on the **L**eft option and click on OK. The frames are now lined up as displayed to the right in figure 4.13.

If you plan on using the Align command frequently, try the keyboard shortcut Ctrl+A to display the Align dialog box. You can also access the Align dialog box from the Placement Roll-up's flyout.

Aligning Frames to the Center of the Page

The Align dialog box provides an option for placing a frame in the exact center of the page. If several frames are selected, the frames will all be moved to the center of the page and overlap each other. By default, the Align to Center of **P**age option places the frame in the horizontal and vertical center of the page.

You can adjust this placement to fit your needs. In figure 4.15, for example, the frame is aligned to the horizontal center of the page, but not to the vertical center. The following exercise illustrates moving a frame to the horizontal center of the page.

Figure 4.15
Frames can be aligned to the vertical or horizontal center of the page.

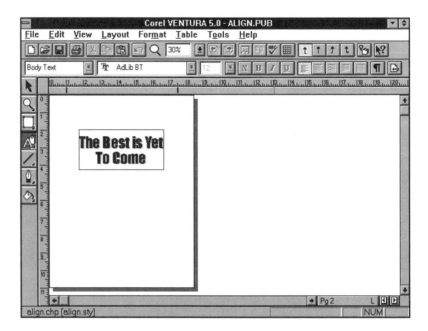

1. Select the frame you want to move.

2. Select **A**lign from the T**o**ols menu. In the Align dialog box, click on the Align to Center of **P**age option. Notice that the Horizontally and Vertically center options are selected.

3. Click on the Vertically C**e**nter option to turn off the vertical alignment. The *X* disappears when the option is disabled. Click on OK; the frame now appears in the horizontal center of the page.

Moving and Copying Frames to Other Pages

You can move or copy free frames to other pages. VENTURA uses the Windows Clipboard to store objects as they are moved or copied to other pages. As displayed in figure 4.16, the ribbon bar provides buttons for quickly moving and

copying frames. These same commands are also found under the **E**dit menu. If you are brand new to working with the Clipboard, refer to your Windows documentation.

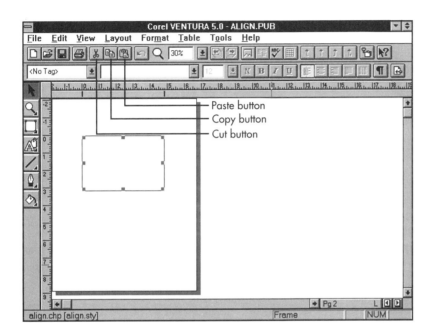

Figure 4.16
Cut, Copy, and Paste buttons are included on VENTURA's ribbon bar.

When you use the Clipboard to move or copy a frame, the contents of the frame are also moved or copied. This makes it easy to rearrange text and graphics as you build and design your document. For instance, you might decide that the frame containing a text file on page one would look better on page two. Or perhaps you want to place two copies of a frame containing a sales chart in your annual report.

Using the Cut Command To Move Frames

As with other Windows applications, VENTURA uses the Cut and Paste commands to move frames and their contents from one page to another. The following exercise illustrates how to move a frame to another page in a document:

1. Select the frame you want to move. Choose Cu**t** from the **E**dit menu, or click on the Cut button in the ribbon bar. The frame is removed from the page and stored in the Clipboard.

2. Move to the page where you want to place the frame. Select **P**aste from the **E**dit menu or click on the Paste button in the ribbon bar. The frame is pasted in the same position from which it was cut. You can move and size it as necessary.

You can move a frame from one publication to another. After cutting the frame, simply open the publication where you want the frame to appear and paste the frame on the desired page.

Copying Frames

When you want to place a copy of a frame on another page, use the Copy and Paste commands. The copied frame is not linked to the original frame, so you can modify either frame without affecting the other. The following steps illustrate placing a copy of a frame on another page:

1. Select the frame you want to copy. Choose **C**opy from the **E**dit menu or click on the Copy button in the ribbon bar. A copy of the frame is stored in the Clipboard.

2. Move to the page where you want to place the frame. Select **P**aste from the **E**dit menu or click on the Paste button in the ribbon bar. The copied frame is pasted in the same position as the original. You can move and size it as necessary.

You can copy a frame from one publication to another. After copying the frame, simply open the publication where you want the frame to appear and paste the frame on the desired page.

Locking Frames

After painstakingly sizing and aligning the frames on your page layout, you might want to lock the frames so they cannot be moved or sized. Because it is easy to accidentally move and size frames, locking them can prevent a lot of mistakes. By default, all free frames are unlocked. The following exercise shows you how to lock a frame:

1. Select the frame you want to lock.

2. Select **F**rame from the For**m**at menu. The Frame Settings dialog box appears as displayed in figure 4.17. The General tab is selected.

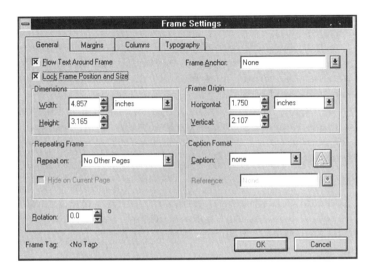

Figure 4.17
The Frame Settings
dialog box.

3. Click on the Loc**k** Frame Position and Size option at the top of the dialog box. An X appears, indicating the feature is enabled. Click on OK. The locked frame cannot be moved or sized.

Only one frame can be locked at a time. To unlock the frame, repeat the previous steps and disable the Loc**k** Frame Position and Size option. You do not need to unlock a frame before cutting or copying it to a new page. However, when pasted to its new location, the frame will also be locked and cannot be moved or sized until unlocked.

Creating Repeating Frames

Free frames can be repeated on every page of your document, or only on left or right pages. In an annual report, you might repeat a frame containing the company logo on every page. Repeating frames is much easier than copying and pasting the frame onto every page. Use the following steps to repeat a frame on all pages of your document:

1. Select the frame you want to repeat and choose **F**rame from the For**m**at menu. The Frame Settings dialog box appears with the General tab selected.

2. In the Repeating Frame section of the dialog box, go to the R**e**peat On list box and choose All Pages. Click on OK. The frame is repeated on every page of your chapter file.

By default, the frame is repeated on every page; however, you can hide the frame on certain pages if necessary. For instance, if you want the frame to appear on every page but the last, you could hide the frame on the last page. To hide a repeating frame on a particular page, select the frame. Then click on the Hide on Current Page option in the Repeating Frames section of the Frame Settings dialog box. An *X* indicates the option is enabled. Click on OK. The frame is hidden on the current page.

Remember, if you move or size any repeating frame, all copies of the repeating frame are affected. You cannot place a caption on a repeating frame. In addition, you must turn off the repeat frame feature before cutting, copying, or deleting the frame. Turn off the Repeating Frame option in the Frame Settings dialog box to disable the repeat frame feature.

Chapter Snapshot

As you construct documents, you often will take text generated by another person for inclusion in your VENTURA design template. If you are designing a newsletter, for example, you might get text that was created in several different word processing applications. In this chapter, you learn to do the following:

Managing files created in other software packages is easy when you use VENTURA's import features. This chapter provides hands-on exercises that show you how to take information created in over 25 popular file formats and use it within VENTURA.

5

CHAPTER

Loading Text into Frames

VENTURA excels at importing text from word processing applications, such as Word for Windows and WordPerfect. In companies that produce books and manuals, it is quite common to have one group of writers focusing on generating the text, another group focusing on creating graphics, and yet another group of designers specializing in building the page layout by merging the text and graphics. Writers generally enter text into word processing applications, and then hand the text files to the designers who bring it all together. The text files usually are generated with little or no formatting, because it is up to the designers to spruce up the text with attractive fonts and styles. VENTURA works well with this kind of assembly-line document production, by making it easy to import text from every popular word processing application.

This chapter examines the steps necessary to import text into VENTURA documents. First, the chapter discusses the text formats that VENTURA can import. The next section focuses on importing text into the base page frame or free frames. You will learn how to flow the text across the pages of your document. This chapter ends with a look at using the Files Roll-up to remove and rename the text files in your document.

Importing Text

Although VENTURA and your word processor might possess some similar tools, they each have very specific roles in document production. Your word processor is an excellent tool for generating the text that makes up your publications. VENTURA's extensive formatting capabilities provide all the tools you need to control the page layout, as well as the text and paragraph formatting of your document. You therefore should not need to spend much time formatting the text in the word processor because much of the formatting is ignored after it is imported into VENTURA.

Paragraph tags are used to format text in VENTURA documents. The tags specify the formatting attributes, such as fonts, line spacing, and alignment. You will learn more about paragraph tags in Chapter 7, "Formatting Tagged and Freeform Text." The formatting information in the paragraph tags overrides any formatting specified with the word processor. When text is imported, for example, the formatting assigned in the word processor—such as margins, fonts, indents, and tabs—is replaced by formatting specified in the paragraph tag. The exceptions are bold, italic, and underline type styles; these styles are retained when you import the text into a VENTURA document. After the text file is imported, the "Body Text" paragraph tag is automatically applied to all the paragraphs. As the name implies, the Body Text tag is designed for the main body text of a document.

After text is imported into a document, you can use VENTURA's text-editing tools to make any necessary changes. In fact, because VENTURA has many tools similar to a word processing application, some desktop publishers enter their text directly into VENTURA. The next chapter, "Entering and Editing Text," provides helpful information about editing your text after it is imported into VENTURA.

Importing Spreadsheet Data

VENTURA also can import spreadsheet data from popular spreadsheet programs such as 1-2-3 and Excel. VENTURA can directly import Excel 3.0 and 4.0 files saved in the XLS format, and Lotus 1-2-3 1A, 2.0, and 3.0 files saved in the WK* format. The spreadsheet data is imported into the document as a tabbed table. As displayed in figure 5.1, each cell of data is separated by a tab, and each row is a separate paragraph. (Click on the Show/Hide Returns button to view the tab and paragraph symbols.) See Chapter 8, "Managing Paragraph Tags," for more information on setting and aligning tabs.

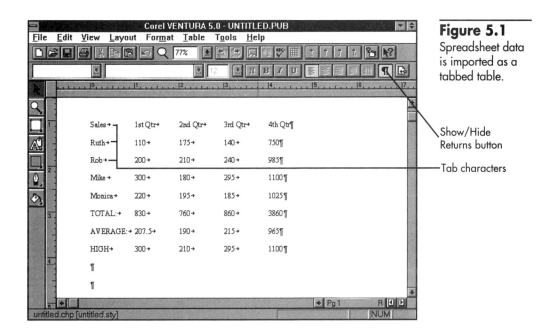

Figure 5.1
Spreadsheet data
is imported as a
tabbed table.

Show/Hide
Returns button

Tab characters

In addition to importing the spreadsheet data, you also can use the Windows
Clipboard to transfer data into VENTURA. Again, the spreadsheet data is placed
in the frame as a tabbed table. If you are unfamiliar with copying and pasting data
with the Windows Clipboard, refer to the section "Moving and Copying Text
From Within VENTURA" in the next chapter.

Use the Save As dialog box in Excel 5.0 to save workbook files (.XLS) as Excel
3.0 and 4.0 spreadsheet files. VENTURA currently does not support the Excel
5.0 file format.

If you want to retain the table format of an imported spreadsheet file, you can
import the spreadsheet as a Lotus or Excel print file. Figure 5.2 shows the data
that was imported in figure 5.1. As you can see, the imported data retained its
table format, with data placed in a cell structure rather than the tabbed structure
in figure 5.1. Most popular spreadsheet applications provide the capability to
print spreadsheet data to a print file. Refer to the documentation for your
spreadsheet application for more information on printing to a file. As you will see
in the next section about importing text into frames, you need to select the
Lotus/Excel Print Table (PRN) format to import a print file as a table.

Building a VENTURA Document

Figure 5.2
Importing a
spreadsheet print
file displays the
data in a table
format.

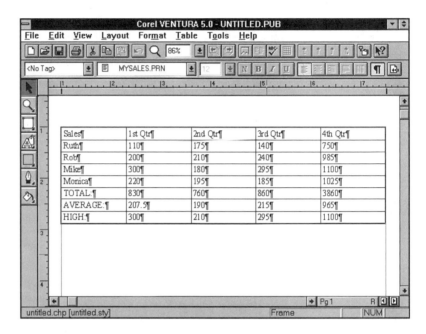

Looking at Text and Spreadsheet Formats Supported by VENTURA

VENTURA imports text files from most popular word processing and spreadsheet applications. Regardless of the word processing application you use, text files can be converted to the ASCII text format and then imported into VENTURA. Some spreadsheet and database applications also can export to ASCII format, which then can be imported into VENTURA. (See your software documentation for more information on exporting to ASCII.)

Table 5.1 lists the word processing and spreadsheet file formats supported by VENTURA.

Table 5.1
File Formats VENTURA Can Import

Application Format	File Extension
Ventura Generated	*.GEN
Ami Professional 2.0, 3.0	*.SAM
ANSI text	*.*

Application Format	File Extension
ASCII text	*.TXT
ASCII text (8-bit)	*.TXT
Excel for Windows 3.0, 4.0	*.XLS
Lotus 1-2-3 1A, 2.0	*.WK?
Lotus 1-2-3 for Windows 3.0	*.WK?
Lotus/Excel Print Table	*.PRN
Microsoft Word for Windows 1.*x*	*.*
Microsoft Word for Windows 2.*x*, 6.0	*.DOC
Microsoft Word 5.0, 5.5	*.*
Microsoft Word for Macintosh 4.0	*.*
Microsoft Word for Macintosh 5.0	*.*
Microsoft Rich Text Format	*.RTF
TagWrite—Style Match RTF	*.RTF
SGML/Custom Template	*.*
Style Match WP 5.*x*	*.*
Xywrite III, III Plus, IV	*.*
Xywrite for Windows 4.0	*.*
WordPerfect 4.2	*.*
WordPerfect 5.0	*.*
WordPerfect 5.1	*.*
WordPerfect 6.0	*.*
WordStar 3.3, 3.31, 3.45, 4.0, 5.0, 5.5, 6.0, 7.0	*.*
WordStar for Windows 1.*x*, 2.0	*.*

II

Building a VENTURA Document

Understanding How VENTURA Handles Imported Text

The text files you import into your VENTURA documents are not saved as a part of the chapter. Instead, they are saved separately from the chapter file as independent text files. As discussed in Chapter 2, when the chapter file is opened, pointers are sent out to retrieve the text files. One benefit of keeping the text files separate is that you can continue to edit text files in your word processor even after they have been imported into VENTURA.

Because the text file is linked to the VENTURA document, any changes you make to the file in your word processor are reflected the next time you open the document in VENTURA. Suppose that you open a text file in your word processor that already has been imported into VENTURA. Any editing changes made to the text also affect the text file in the VENTURA document. If you delete a paragraph, that paragraph also is deleted from the VENTURA document. Keep in mind that you do not have to return to the word processor to edit the text. As discussed in the next chapter, VENTURA provides many text-editing tools for modifying imported text.

If you do plan to edit the text in a word processor after it has been imported into VENTURA, don't be surprised if you see codes within the text. These codes identify VENTURA formatting information such as bold, italic, and paragraph tag names. Figure 5.3 displays a text file opened in Word for Windows after it has been imported into VENTURA. If a paragraph tag other than Body Text has been applied to a paragraph, the tag name appears in the text with an at sign (@) before it. Codes for formatting attributes such as styles and alignment are enclosed in <angle brackets>. The codes tell VENTURA how to format the text when it appears in the chapter file, so in most cases, you should not modify these codes.

VENTURA provides several options for altering the text in an imported file. First, the Preferences dialog box includes an option for converting inch marks (") to opening and closing quotation marks (""), and double hyphens (--) to a single em dash (—). Choose Pre**f**erences from the **T**ools menu to display the Preferences dialog box, as shown in figure 5.4. Click to place an *X* in the **A**uto-Convert ""&—on Load check box. Enabling this check box instructs VENTURA to convert the characters when a text file is imported. In addition, VENTURA converts multiple spaces into a single space plus a non-breaking space. See the following chapter for more information on non-breaking spaces.

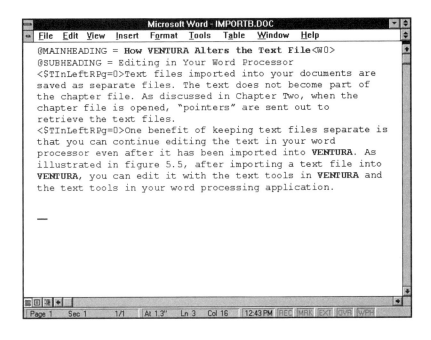

Figure 5.3
Codes that instruct VENTURA how to format the text are visible when you edit the text in a word processing application.

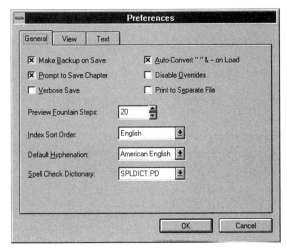

Figure 5.4
The Preferences dialog box.

Before importing text, take a minute to delete unnecessary spaces and extra carriage returns. Additional carriage returns create blank paragraphs in the text that are difficult to format. See the following chapter for more information on preparing your text for importing.

II

Building a VENTURA Document

VENTURA saves Microsoft Word for Windows 6.0 files as Word for Windows 2.0 files. When you try to open a file in Word for Windows 6.0 that was saved in Corel VENTURA, a prompt appears stating that the file was saved last in Word for Windows 2.0. After the file opens in Word, you can save it again as a 6.0 file.

After importing a text file, you might want to rename it, which creates a copy of the original file. You then can edit the copy without affecting the original text file. If you rename the text file, changes made to the original text file do not affect the VENTURA document. In addition, VENTURA's formatting codes do not appear in the original text. Renaming files is covered later in this chapter in "Using the Files Roll-Up."

Importing Text into the Base Page Frame

A base page frame is placed automatically on every page of the document. The base page frame fills the entire page area. The layout of the base page frame is determined by the style sheet. A style sheet for a magazine might specify a three-column layout on the base page frame, for example. The style sheet for a book might specify a one-column layout on the base page frame. It's not a bad idea to determine the page layout of the base page frame before importing text. If the base page frame uses a two-column layout and you want a one-column layout, you can change the layout before the text is placed in the document. To verify how the base page of your document is set up, see Chapter 3.

You can flow text across the page of one chapter file only. You cannot flow text across several chapter files.

Text files for documents, such as books and manuals, generally are imported onto the base page frame. VENTURA inserts as many pages as needed to display all the imported text. Text loaded into the base page frame flows continuously from page to page. As displayed in figure 5.5, each page uses the page layout specified in the first base page frame. Suppose that you import a text file of three pages into the first base page frame. VENTURA inserts the extra pages, with each page set up to use the same margins and column layout as the first base page frame.

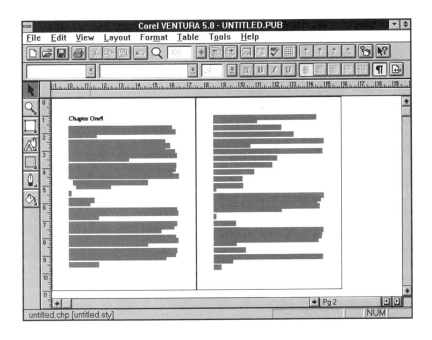

Figure 5.5

Text imported onto the base page flows continuously across the pages in your document.

In the following exercise, the file lorem3.txt is loaded onto the base page. The file is *greeked text*, meaning it is just random text, not real words and sentences. The file is located in the VENTURA\TYPESET directory. Substitute another file if desired. Perform the following to import text into a base page frame:

1. With the Pick tool, select the base page frame.

2. Choose Load **T**ext from the **F**ile menu.

   The Load Text dialog box appears (see fig. 5.6).

3. Change to the drive where VENTURA is located and move to the VENTURA\TYPESET directory.

4. Click on the down arrow beside List Files of **T**ype to display a list of text file formats. Select the format of the text you are importing. To import the lorem3.txt file, select ASCII Text (8-bit) (*.txt).

   The files in the specified format appear in the File **N**ame list box.

5. Select the desired file and click on OK. The text is flowed onto the base page and as many additional pages as needed.

Figure 5.6
The Load Text
dialog box.

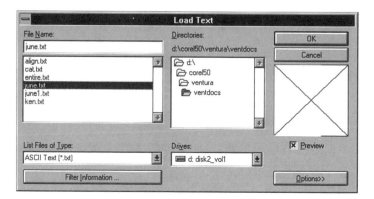

After importing, notice that the file name of the text appears in the Files list in the ribbon bar. The Files list includes the name of every text and graphics file placed in the chapter file. You will learn more about working with the Files list later in this chapter.

You can import another text file onto the base page frame of a newly inserted page. Suppose that you import text onto the base page frame that flows to page 10. You can insert a new page 11 and import another text file onto the base page frame of the new page. This text flows from page 11 onward.

It is important to note that inserting a page within a text flow interrupts the flow. Suppose that the text on the base page flows continuously from page 1 to page 10. If you insert a new page 5, the text flow skips the inserted page. The text flows across pages 1 through 4, and picks up again at page 6.

Importing Text into Free Frames

You add free frames with the Frame tool, and draw the frames on top of the base page frame. The steps for creating free frames are covered in Chapter 4. Free frames generally are used to build layouts for newsletters and brochures. As shown in figure 5.7, you can build your layout with multiple free frames. Each free frame can hold one text file. Importing text into free frames enables you to display several text files on one page.

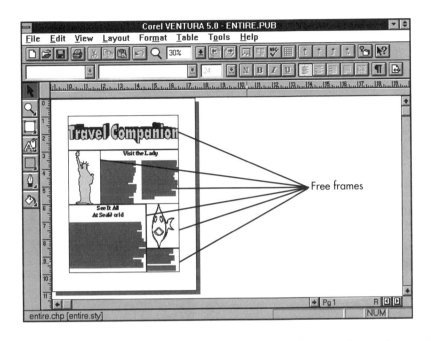

Figure 5.7
Importing text into free frames enables you to display several text files on one page.

Each free frame has individual frame settings for margins, columns, intercolumn rule lines, and borders. In figure 5.7, for example, the top frame containing text uses a two-column layout, and the bottom frames containing text use a one-column layout. The capability to establish separate settings for each frame makes designing with free frames very powerful. Before importing text into a free frame, you should establish the settings for the frame. After selecting the frame, choose **F**rame from the For**m**at menu. The Frame Settings dialog box provides several options for formatting frames. Chapter 4 provides detailed coverage on setting frame attributes. To import text into a Free Frame, do the following:

1. Select the free frame into which you want to import the text file.

2. Choose Load **T**ext from the **F**ile menu or use the keyboard shortcut F9.

   The Load Text dialog box appears.

3. Change to the drive and directory where the text file you want to import is located.

4. Click on the down arrow beside List Files of **T**ype to display a list of text file formats. Select the format of the text you are importing.

   The files in the specified format appear in the File **N**ame list box.

5. Select the file you want and click on OK.

The text flows into the free frame. The text file name appears in the Files list in the ribbon bar.

Keep in mind that the free frame might not be large enough to display all the text. Use the Zoom tool to view the bottom of the free frame up close. If the text is cut off, you might have to enlarge the frame size. Remember that you use the Pick tool to enlarge or reduce free frames.

If the Show/Hide Returns button on the ribbon bar is selected, VENTURA places an end-of-file marker (a small white box) at the end of the text file (see fig 5.8). Without the end-of-file marker, it can be difficult to determine the end of a text flow, especially if you were not the writer. If you see this marker, you know that all the text appears in the frame.

Figure 5.8
When flowing text into free frames, watch for the end-of-file marker to see whether all the text has been placed.

End-of-file marker

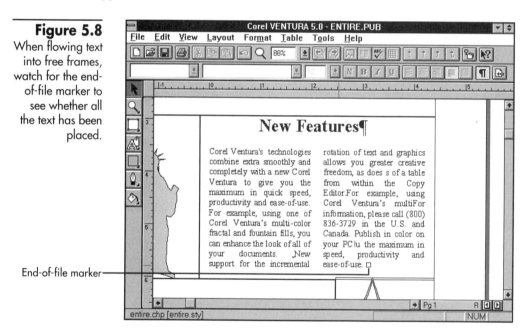

Flowing Text into Free Frames

Rather than displaying an entire text file in one free frame, you might decide to flow the text across several free frames. When designing a newsletter, for example, you might want to flow an article from a free frame on page one to a free frame on page three.

The following steps illustrate how to flow a text file across two pages. The file lorem3.txt, saved in the VENTURA\TYPESET directory, is used.

1. Begin a new document and insert one page for a total of two pages. Draw one free frame on both pages.

2. On page one, load the lorem3.txt file into the free frame.

   Remember that the entire text file is not visible in this frame.

3. Move to page two and select the free frame. The text will flow into this frame.

4. Click on the down arrow by the Files list in the ribbon bar. A list of files that appear in the chapter file are displayed.

5. Select the file lorem3.txt. The text is continued in the second frame.

Use this process to flow the text across as many free frames as needed. As mentioned earlier, watch for the end-of-file marker to see whether all the text is displayed in the final frame.

Changing the frame size affects the flow of the text. Suppose that you have a text file flowing in a free frame on page one to a frame on page two. Reducing the size of the first frame means that less text can be displayed in the frame. The text that no longer fits in the first frame is flowed into the second frame. Because more text is added to the second frame, watch for the end-of-file marker to determine if all the text fits into the second frame.

Using the Files List

The Files list displays the file names of all text and graphics files placed in the chapter file. To view the files in a chapter, select a frame and click on the down arrow by the Files list in the ribbon bar. The file loaded into the selected frame is highlighted in the list. In figure 5.9, the Files list indicates that there are five files loaded into the chapter. A small text icon appears next to text files, and a Corel balloon icon appears next to graphics files.

Clicking on a file name in the Files list loads that file into the selected frame. If you select a blank free frame and then select a text file from the Files list, for example, that text is imported into the selected frame. The file selected in the

Files list is loaded into the frame, even if the frame currently holds another file. Suppose that the selected frame holds the text file SALES.DOC. If you select the file LOSSES.DOC from the Files list, the LOSSES text replaces the SALES text in the frame. You can use the Files list to experiment with your page layout by placing different files in a frame.

Figure 5.9
The Files list displays the file names of all text and graphics files loaded into the chapter.

Corel balloon icon

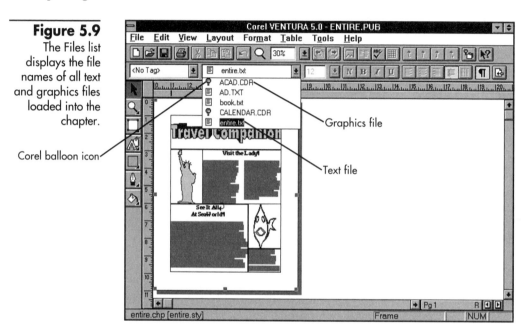

You can import files into the Files list without placing them into frames. Suppose that you have three text files to place in a brochure, but you aren't quite sure on which pages you want to place each file. You can load the three files into the Files list, where they reside until you decide to insert them into the document. The files now are easily available when you are ready to place them into frames. Use the following steps to load several files into the Files list.

1. Make sure that no frames are selected. If necessary, click on the Pick tool several times to deselect all frames.

2. Choose Load **T**ext from the **F**ile menu or use the keyboard shortcut F9.

   The Load Text dialog box appears.

3. Change to the drive and directory where the text file you want to import is located.

4. Click on the down arrow by List Files of **T**ype to display a list of text file formats. Select the format of the text you are importing.

   The files in the specified format appear in the File **N**ame list box.

5. To load a contiguous range of files, press Shift while clicking the first and last file in the list range. To load multiple files that do not appear in consecutive order, press Ctrl as you select the files.

   In figure 5.10, four contiguous files are selected.

6. After selecting the files, click on OK.

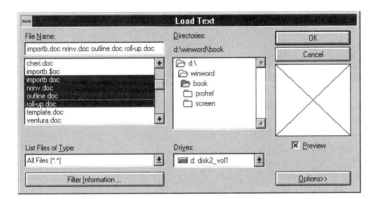

Figure 5.10
Press Shift while
clicking to select
multiple files.

The file names are listed in the Files list.

After the files are imported into the Files list, you can load them into frames. Simply select the frame where you want the text to appear, and select the file name you want to load from the Files list.

Importing Text at the Insertion Point

VENTURA provides an option for importing text at the insertion point that enables you to merge the contents of several text files into one frame. Generally, each text file is inserted into its own individual frame. But what if you want to add the contents of a second text file to the text already loaded into the frame? Suppose that one of the writers in your department writes an article on parenting styles, and you import this text file into the base page. Later, the writer hands you another text file containing a list of common questions meant to be inserted at the end of the parenting file. Importing the text at the insertion point, rather than into a frame, enables you to merge the contents of the second text file with the existing text. Import text at the insertion point by performing the following steps:

1. Select the Tagged Text or Freeform Text tool, which are discussed in Chapter 6. Click in the text to place the insertion point where you want to add the contents of another text file.

2. Choose Load **T**ext from the **F**ile menu or use the keyboard shortcut F9.

   The Load Text dialog box appears.

3. Click on the Insert at Cursor option, which appears at the bottom of the dialog box when you have the text tool selected while loading text.

4. Change to the drive and directory where the text file you want to import is located.

5. Select the text format from the List Files of **T**ype box.

6. Select the name of the file you want to import and click on OK.

The new text is imported at the specified location. Actually, you are not really placing two text files in one frame. VENTURA saves the inserted text as part of the first text file, rather than as a separate text file. In other words, the contents of the second file are merged with the existing text file.

Using the Files Roll-Up

The Files Roll-up makes it easy to manage all the text and graphics files loaded into your chapter files. You can use the Files Roll-up to load text and graphics files, to rename files, and even to remove a file from the chapter. Many of the commands available in the Files Roll-up also are available in the File menu. To display the roll-up, choose Files Roll-up from the T**o**ols menu. As shown in figure 5.11, each file in the current chapter is displayed in the list.

In addition to listing the files placed in the chapter, the Files Roll-up offers several options for managing your files. Click on the menu button to display a flyout of available commands. Use the first command, Place in Frame, to place a file from the roll-up into a frame. After selecting the frame, click on the name of the file you want to load into the frame. From the roll-up menu, choose Place in Frame to import the file into the selected frame.

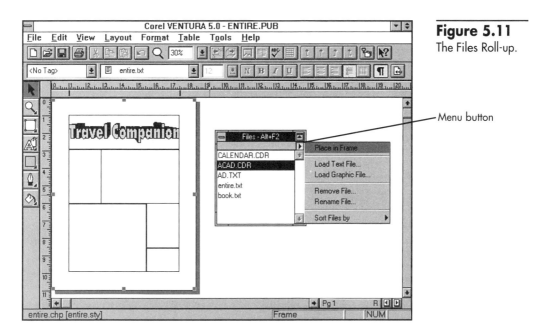

Figure 5.11
The Files Roll-up.

Menu button

The next two commands are an alternative way to load text and graphics into your document. The Load Text File command opens the Load Text dialog box. As previously discussed, you can use the Load Text dialog box to import a text file into a frame. The Load Graphic File command opens the Load Graphic dialog box. As you will learn in Chapter 10, "Advanced Free Frame Options," use this command to load graphics files into the frames of your document. The rest of the commands on the Files Roll-up are described in the following sections.

Removing Files

Use the Remove File command to remove a text file from the selected frame, or from the chapter entirely. Select the file you want to remove and click on the Remove File command. The Remove File dialog box appears, as shown in figure 5.12. Select the Remove from **F**rame option to remove a text file from a frame. You might use this command if you loaded the wrong file in a frame and now want to unload it.

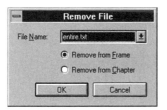

Figure 5.12
The Remove File
dialog box.

II

Building a VENTURA Document

Keep in mind that the Remove from **F**rame option does not remove the frame; it just removes the text file from the frame. Although the text is removed from the frame, it still is loaded in the chapter file. The file name still is listed in the Files Roll-up. The Remove from **F**rame option enables you to place the removed file into another frame in the chapter. When you want to remove the file from the chapter file entirely, select the Remove from **C**hapter option. This is handy when, after loading the file, you determine that you don't have room for it and want to eliminate it from the publication. After selecting the file you want to remove, click on OK.

Renaming Files

Use the Rename File command to assign a new file name to the selected text file. This command is useful particularly for those occasions when you want to modify a shared text file, but you don't want the modifications to occur in other documents where the file is being used. After you choose the Rename File option, the File Type/Rename dialog box appears (see fig. 5.13). This dialog box works much like the Save Publication As dialog box. Enter a file name and location for the renamed file. Use the List Files of **T**ype list box to select a file format for the newly renamed file. Click on OK to return to the document.

Figure 5.13
The File Type/
Rename dialog
box.

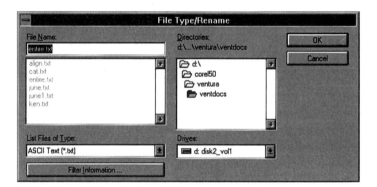

As a measure of caution, save the publication immediately after renaming the file, because the newly named file is not actually created until you save the document. The next time you open the document, VENTURA loads the renamed file, and the original file does not appear in the Files list.

Sorting Files

The Sort Files By option on the Files Roll-up enables you to control the order in which files appear in the Files list. Choose Sort Files By to reveal the flyout menu. The options are to sort files alphabetically by name or file extension. Sorting the files by extension is a great way to group together all files of a specific type, such as .TXT or .CDR.

II

Building a VENTURA Document

Chapter Snapshot

VENTURA combines the text-handling features of word processing with the page layout capabilities of desktop publishing packages. VENTURA's Copy Editor enables you to add or edit text. In this chapter, you learn to do the following:

This chapter covers the flexibility and ease with which you can enter text directly into VENTURA. With its capabilities, you easily can edit your documents.

CHAPTER

Entering and Editing Text

In the past, desktop publishing applications did not offer word processing features such as spell checking, thesauruses, and find-and-replace. Text was generally created in a word processor, such as WordPerfect or Microsoft Word, then imported into the desktop publishing application. Users who were forced to use two programs to get the job done began to express a need for text editing features directly in their desktop publishing applications.

Today, VENTURA combines the text-handling strengths of word processing with the page layout power of desktop publishing. If you elect to import text files from a word processing application, however, you have a broad range of options for placing the text in your VENTURA document. Regardless of how hard you work at perfecting the text before importing it into VENTURA, chances are good it will need to be modified somewhat after it is imported. Being familiar with the text editing tools in VENTURA make appending and editing imported text files much easier.

This chapter examines VENTURA's text-handling capabilities. Here, you will learn to enter a whole new block of text or append imported text. As you will see, text can be entered directly onto the page or into VENTURA's word processing facility, the Copy Editor. This chapter also examines controlling page and line breaks, and entering special characters. Of course, after the text is entered, you might need to make some changes, so the last section focuses on editing text.

Using VENTURA's Text Tools

VENTURA provides two tools for working with text. To see the tools, press and hold the fourth tool in the toolbox. A flyout toolbar appears, displaying the Freeform Text and Tagged Text tools (see fig 6.1). Simply click on the desired text tool to select it. You can also click on the Text tool to switch from one tool to the other. For instance, if the Tagged Text tool is currently visible, clicking on it will switch to the Freeform Text tool. After selecting a text tool, the shape of the mouse cursor changes to an I-beam when moved to the page area.

Figure 6.1
The Text flyout toolbar.

The main difference between the two text tools is the way each handles text formatting options, such as changing fonts and text alignment. You will learn how and when to use each tool for formatting text in the following chapter. For the purposes of entering and editing text covered in this chapter, the tools work identically. With either tool you can enter, delete, copy, and move text.

Entering Text

Considering VENTURA's extensive text-handling features, you might decide to enter and edit all of your text in VENTURA. Why use a separate word processing application when you can do it all in VENTURA? You won't have to worry about spelling blunders with the spell-check feature. The thesaurus can help you find just the right word for that snappy headline. With the new Type Assist feature, you can instruct VENTURA to correct mistakes automatically and create text shortcuts that simplify entering frequently used words and phrases. Everything you need to enter text in your document is here, in VENTURA.

However, don't completely rule out the need for importing text from a word processor. You may be in charge of laying out the document, for example, but not responsible for writing it. A contributing writer might prefer to use a word processor to create a story, then give it you to insert it in a publication. Whether you will be typing all your text or appending an imported text file, the steps for entering text in VENTURA are basically the same. You simply select the text tool, click where you want the text to appear, and begin typing.

 As you proceed with the exercises for entering text, you might want to start a new file or delete any entered text before beginning the next exercise.

Displaying the Insertion Point

Clicking with the Text tool in a blank frame or within an imported text block displays an *insertion point*. The insertion point is a blinking line that designates where newly added text will appear. If you are entering text into a new frame, the insertion point appears at the top of the frame. If there is already text in the frame, you can click anywhere in the text to position the insertion point. Before entering text, make sure you have positioned the insertion point exactly where you want the new text to appear.

Tips for Entering Text

Entering text in VENTURA is comparable to entering text in word processing applications. After ending a paragraph in a word processor, it is often customary to press the Enter key twice, creating two carriage returns between paragraphs. This is a practice to avoid with VENTURA because each carriage return is considered as an independent paragraph. Press Enter only once.

 As you will see in discussions on paragraph formatting, VENTURA offers control over the spacing between paragraphs by enabling you to assign specific spacing before or after each paragraph. If you have placed double carriage returns between paragraphs, the result will be additional unwanted space that is difficult to manage. Paragraph formatting is discussed fully in Chapter 7, "Formatting Tagged and Freeform Text."

Another text-entry habit that might be difficult to break is placing two spaces at the end of sentences. Though this practice may suffice for letters and memos, in the printing and publishing world, pressing the spacebar twice between sentences is strictly taboo. You can confirm this by glancing at any recently published book, magazine, or newspaper. It is extremely rare to find an instance where double spacing was used between sentences.

Unlike typewriters, computers can automatically tighten excess spacing between each character. Because the spacing is so well-controlled, you no longer need two spaces between sentences to delineate visually where sentences begin and end.

Entering New Text on the Base Page Frame

As discussed in Chapter 1, text in your document is not stored as part of the chapter file; text is stored in separate text files. The chapter files use pointers to locate the text and place it on the page. Place the insertion in the base page frame to begin entering text. Text entered into the base page runs continuously from page to page, making it ideal for working with long documents such as books and manuals.

If you attempt to enter text into another base page frame, you are asked to start a new text file. If you choose to start a new file, the New File dialog box appears for you to enter the new file name. The following exercise teaches you how to enter a new text block on the base page frame:

You can use any of the three views, Page Layout, Draft, or Copy Editor, to enter and edit text. Refer to Chapter 2, "Exploring a VENTURA Document," for more information.

1. Select either Text tool and click in the base page frame.

2. If you have previously entered text into a base page frame in the chapter file, the New File dialog box appears, as shown in figure 6.2. The List Files of **T**ype box indicates the text will be stored in ASCII format with file name extension .TXT. Change to the drive and directory where you want the text file to be stored. Enter a file name and click on OK.

3. The insertion point appears at the top of the base page frame. You can begin typing. Remember, a new page is inserted when you reach the bottom of the page. Text flowed across several pages is interrupted if you insert an additional page. For instance, suppose the text on the base page frame flows from page one through page three. If you insert a new page two, the text does not flow onto the new page. The text starts on page one, skips page two, and continues flowing on page three.

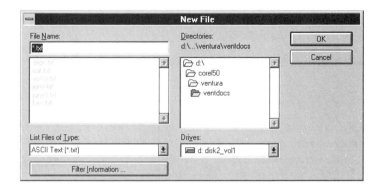

Figure 6.2
The New File
dialog box.

Entering Text into Free Frames

Shorter text files are generally placed into free frames. For instance, the articles in a newsletter are often placed in free frames. You can import text into free frames or enter text directly into the frame. Refer to Chapter 5, "Loading Text into Frames," for more information on importing text into free frames. The steps for adding text to an imported text file are the same whether you are working with the base page frame or a free frame. As described in the previous section, select either Text tool, click in the text to position the insertion point, and begin typing.

Text entered directly into a free frame is stored in a separate text file that uses the chapter file name with the extension .CAP. For instance, if you entered text in a free frame in a chapter named report.chp, a text file with the name report.cap is created. The .CAP text file stores all of the text entered into free frames for the whole chapter file. The text entered in a free frame on page one is stored in the same file as the text entered in a free frame on page two. Free frame text files cannot be used in other chapter files unless you rename the file using the Files Roll-up discussed in Chapter 5.

The following exercise shows you how to enter text into a free frame:

1. To draw a free frame, select the Frame tool and point to where you want the frame to begin.

2. Click and hold the mouse as you drag diagonally. Release the mouse button when the frame is the size and shape you want.

3. Select either Text tool and click inside the free frame in which you want to add text.

II

Building a VENTURA Document

4. The insertion point appears at the top of the free frame. You can begin typing. The text will wrap inside the frame.

It is possible to enter more text than the frame can display. If your text appears to be cut off, simply size the frame until it is large enough to display all of your text. VENTURA places an end-of-file marker at the end of every text flow. Without the end-of-file marker, it can be difficult to determine the end of a text flow, especially if you were not the writer. To ensure that all of a text flow is displayed in a frame, enlarge the frame until the end-of-file marker appears. To display end-of-file markers (small white squares) indicating exactly where a text block ends, click on the Show/Hide Returns button on the ribbon bar.

Entering Text into the Copy Editor

Desktop publishing applications have not been noted for speedy text handling. Waiting for the screen to catch up as you enter and edit text can be rather tedious, especially if the text is placed in columns and uses several fonts. To eliminate this problem, VENTURA provides the Copy Editor, a working environment more like a word processing application.

The Copy Editor enables you to enter, edit, and format text in the same way you might in any word processor. To speed up screen redraw, text in the Copy Editor appears without formatting. You can still format text in the Copy Editor, but it is not visible until you return to the Page Layout view. As shown in figure 6.3, text is displayed in one column using one font. The paragraph tags appear in the column on the left, and text appears on the right. Click on the Show/Hide Returns button on the ribbon bar to see paragraph symbols indicating the end of each paragraph.

In previous discussions, you learned to enter text directly into frames in the Page Layout View. Using the Copy Editor, you are still entering text in frames, only now you use the Copy Editor as a intermediary step by entering the text there first. When you exit the Copy Editor and return to Page Layout view, the newly entered text is placed in the frame with all text formatting visible.

This section examines entering a new text file using the Copy Editor. Editing with the Copy Editor is discussed later in the chapter. In the following exercise, you enter new text in a frame using the Copy Editor:

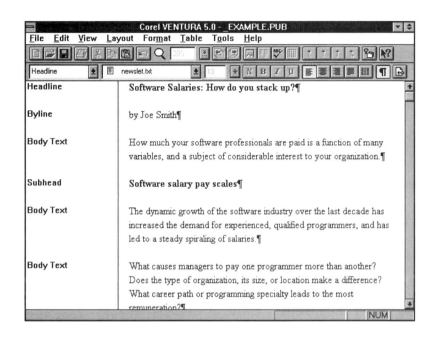

Figure 6.3
The Copy Editor is designed to expedite text entry and editing.

1. Select either Text tool and click inside the frame where you want to enter text. As described earlier, if you are entering text in the base page frame, you might need to assign a file name for the text.

2. The insertion point appears at the top of the frame. Select Copy **E**ditor from the **V**iew menu or press Alt+F10.

3. The screen changes to display the Copy Editor window. As displayed in figure 6.4, the insertion point appears, ready for you to begin typing.

4. When you are finished entering text, select **P**age Layout from the **V**iew menu or press Alt+F12. The text is placed in the selected frame.

There are a few important things to consider as you work in the Copy Editor. First, as you enter text in the Copy Editor, all new text uses the body text paragraph tag until assigned another tag. Each time you create a new paragraph by pressing Enter, another body text tag will appear in the left column. Second, many options such as printing, opening files, and zooming are not available in the Copy Editor View.

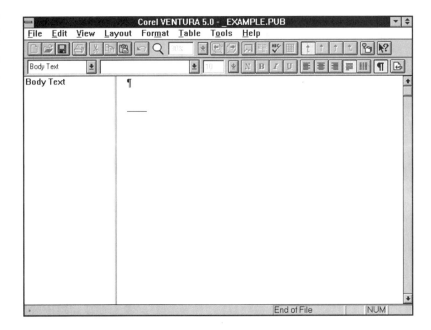

Figure 6.4
The Copy Editor window ready to receive text.

Entering Special Characters

VENTURA includes several features to give you added control as you enter text. For starters, VENTURA provides a wide selection of special characters such as trademark symbols, fractions, and accented letters that can be added to your text. VENTURA also provides an option to simplify entering the date and time on your documents. Finally, when you want to stack headlines or control how words break from line to line, you can use VENTURA's commands for creating line breaks and non-breaking spaces.

Many documents, such as marketing proposals and sales brochures, require the insertion of copyright marks and registered trademarks. Technical manuals might use fractions and other mathematical symbols to define concepts and theories. In addition, documents produced for international audiences might use a variety of currency symbols such as for yen and deutsche marks. VENTURA's special character roll-up lets you select from a wide array of special characters. The characters are available in almost every typeface.

In the following exercise, a trademark symbol is inserted after the word Corel:

1. Select either Text tool and click in the text to place the insertion point. Type the word **Corel**.

Select Character Roll-up from the Tools menu. The Character Set Roll-up appears, as displayed in figure 6.5.

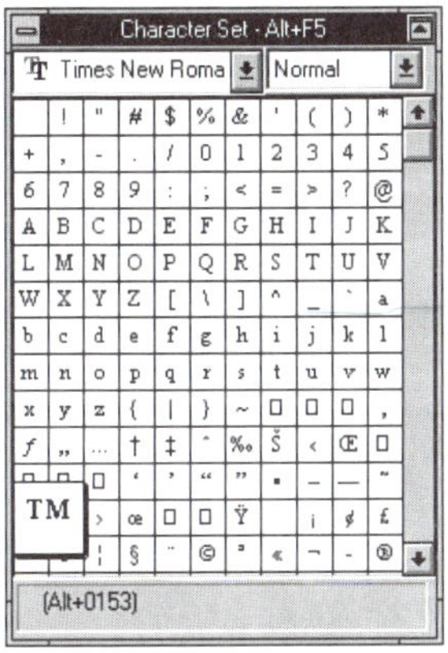

Figure 6.5
You can display the Character Set Roll-up by pressing Alt+F5.

3. Click on the down arrow by the Font List box and select the desired font; you might try Times New Roman. The special characters available in the desired font appear. You might need to scroll down to see all the available characters.

4. To see an enlarged view of a character, press and hold the character button. Double-click on the character button to insert the character into the text.

The special characters can be formatted as regular text characters. Chapter 7 discusses options for applying bold, italic, and underline to text. Use the delete and backspace keys to remove the special character.

As displayed in table 6.1, VENTURA provides several keyboard shortcuts for frequently used special characters. If you use one special character regularly, you could save time using the shortcuts instead of the Character Roll-up.

Table 6.1
Special Character Shortcuts

Press	To Create
Ctrl+Alt+M	Em dash —
Ctrl+Shift+M	Em space
Ctrl+Alt+N	En dash –

continues

II

Building a VENTURA Document

Table 6.1, Continued
Special Character Shortcuts

Press	To Create
Ctrl+Shift+N	En space
Ctrl+Shift+F	Figure space
Ctrl+Shift+T	Thin space
Ctrl+Shift+spacebar	Non-breaking space
Ctrl+-	Discretionary hyphen
Ctrl+Alt+Q	Open quote "
Ctrl+Alt+C	Closed quote "
Ctrl+Shift+R	Registered trademark ®
Ctrl+Shift+2	Trademark ™
Ctrl+Shift+C	Copyright Mark ©

Fixed-width spaces, such as em, en, thin, and figure spaces, are used for increased control of the spacing between characters. These fixed spaces do not increase or decrease in size when text is justified. For additional information on using fixed spaces, refer to your VENTURA documentation.

Inserting the Date and Time

VENTURA provides a feature that enables you to insert the current date and time into your document automatically. You have the option to insert the date as text, or as a code that automatically updates the current date each time you open a new document. For example, if you insert a date code into your document, when you open the document again next week, it will display that current date.

To insert a date into your document, first place your cursor at the location where you want the date inserted. Next, select Insert Special Ite**m** from the **E**dit menu. From the flyout menu, choose **D**ate and Time. The Date and Time dialog box appears as shown in figure 6.6.

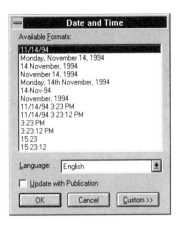

Figure 6.6
The Date and Time
dialog box.

Select the appropriate language from the **L**anguage list box, and the desired date format from the Available **F**ormats list. If you want the date to be inserted as a code that automatically revises to reflect the current date, place a check in the **U**pdate with Publication check box. Otherwise, the date is inserted as text only, and will thereafter display only the date that was originally entered. Click on OK to insert the date into the document.

If none of the available date formats suit your needs, you can create your own. Click on the Custom button to expand the Date and Time dialog box as shown in figure 6.7. To create your own custom date, use the syntax for the current date formats as a guide. For example, select any one of the available date formats and examine its structure in the Format St**r**ing text box. Using the structure of these date formats as a guide, you can easily create your own date format. After creating your custom date format, click on the **S**ave button to preserve the custom date format for further use. The **D**elete button removes a selected date format from the Available Formats list.

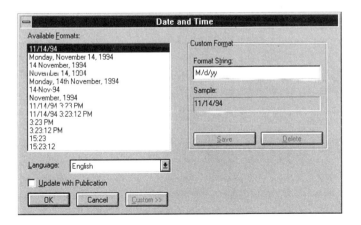

Figure 6.7
The Expanded
Date and Time
dialog box.

II

Building a VENTURA Document

Inserting Line Breaks

As you type, text automatically wraps to the next line when it reaches a margin or column guide. When you finish typing a paragraph, pressing Enter ends the current paragraph and begins another. If you want to end a line before it reaches the guide, without creating a new paragraph, you need to insert a line break. For instance, in figure 6.8, line breaks were used to stack the headline into three lines. If the Enter key had been pressed after every line, each line would be a different paragraph and thus require its own paragraph tag. By inserting line breaks, the headline could be stacked into three lines and still be considered one paragraph.

Figure 6.8
Line breaks help you stack lines of text.

To insert a line break, position the insertion point before the character you want wrapped to the next line. Press Ctrl+Enter or Shift+Enter to create the line break. If the Show/Hide Returns button is selected on the ribbon bar, a line break symbol appears indicating the presence of the line break.

Inserting Non-Breaking Spaces

Non-breaking spaces enable you to prevent a pair of words from splitting into separate lines. For instance, you might not want the lines of text to break between a person's first name and last name. Dates, titles, and phrases such as "United States of America," look best if they can appear together on one line.

To insert a non-breaking space instead of a regular space, press Ctrl+Shift+spacebar between the words you do not want separated. If the Show/ Hide Returns button is selected in the ribbon bar, a small symbol appears indicating the presence of the non-breaking space.

Editing Text

After entering or importing text, you can rearrange, revise, correct, and delete it with powerful text-editing tools built right into VENTURA. This section takes you through the steps for manipulating the text in your document. First, you learn how to select, cut, and copy text. Next, this section delves into VENTURA's powerful spell-check, thesaurus, and Type Assist utilities.

Moving Through Text

Although clicking the mouse to position the insertion point is quick, there are several keyboard shortcuts for moving the insertion point through the text. Table 6.2 examines these shortcuts.

Table 6.2
Shortcuts for Moving the Insertion Point

Press	To
Left arrow	Move one character to the left
Right arrow	Move one character to the right
Ctrl+left arrow	Move one word to the left
Ctrl+right arrow	Move one word to the right
Home	Move to the beginning of the line
End	Move to the end of the line
Up arrow	Move up one line
Down arrow	Move down one line
Ctrl+up arrow	Move up one sentence
Ctrl+down arrow	Move down one sentence

continues

II

Building a VENTURA Document

Table 6.2, Continued
Shortcuts for Moving the Insertion Point

Press	To
PgUp	Move up one window
PgDown	Move down one window
Ctrl+PgUp	Move to the top of current window
Ctrl+PgDown	Move to the bottom of current window
Ctrl+Home	Move to the beginning of the chapter
Ctrl+End	Move to the end of the chapter

Selecting Text

Before editing text, you must select the particular word, sentence, or paragraph that you want to edit. Selecting indicates to VENTURA which text on the page you want the editing command to modify. Before deleting a word, for example, you must select the word.

Either Text tool can be used to select text. After selecting a Text tool, position the I-beam directly before the first character you want selected. Now, press and hold the mouse button as you drag over the desired text. The selected text is highlighted in black. Release the mouse when the desired text is highlighted. If you did not get all of the text that you wanted to select, you need to start over again. To select multiple lines of text, drag down as you hold the mouse button. Table 6.3 illustrates shortcuts that can help you select the right amount of text.

Table 6.3
Shortcuts for Selecting Text

Action	To Select
Double-click on a word	A word
Hold the Control key	A sentence and click in a sentence
Hold the Control key	Multiple sentences and drag with the mouse

Action	To Select
Hold the Alt key	A paragraph and click in a paragraph
Shift+right or left arrow	Selects or deselects a character at a time
Ctrl+Shift+right or left arrow	Selects or deselects a word at a time, beginning at the insertion point
Ctrl+Shift+down arrow or up arrow	Selects or deselects a sentence at a time

Which View Is Best for Text Editing?

In VENTURA, you can edit text in the Page Layout or Copy Editor view. Use the View menu to switch between the two views. Editing text in Page Layout view enables you to see the editing changes, as well as any formatting changes that are taking place. For instance, when you delete several paragraphs, the remaining text moves up the page to fill in the space. In Page Layout view, you can see how deleting text affects your layout. If you join two paragraphs by deleting the paragraph mark between them, you can see how text formatting, such as bold and italic, is affected. Editing in Page Layout view lets you quickly determine how the editing changes affect the overall look of your page.

You can also edit text in Draft view. The page layout and text formatting are still visible, which makes the Draft view very similar to editing in the Page Layout view. However, all graphics are hidden in the Draft view. Refer to Chapter 2, "Exploring a VENTURA Document," for more information on VENTURA's page views.

One of the downsides of editing in Page Layout view is waiting for the text to redraw on the screen. This redraw time can slow you down—especially if you are editing text in a complex layout. As displayed in figure 6.9, the Copy Editor was designed to speed up editing by hiding the columns, fonts, and other text formatting. Working in Copy Editor view lets you focus on the text, making it readable and eliminating errors. After editing in the Copy Editor view, switch to Page Layout view to see the whole page design.

You might see *codes* enclosed in boxes scattered through the text in the Copy Editor. The codes indicate text attributes such as bold and italic, as well as special items such as index markers and footnotes. The codes do not print. You can hide the codes in the Copy Editor view by selecting Pre**f**erences from the T**o**ols menu. The Preferences dialog box appears as displayed in figure 6.10. Select the Text tab and click on the Show **C**odes option.

Figure 6.9
The Copy Editor.

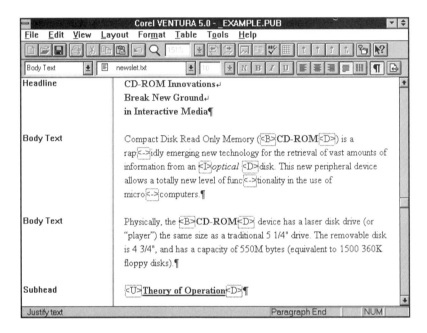

Figure 6.10
The Preferences dialog box with the Text tab selected.

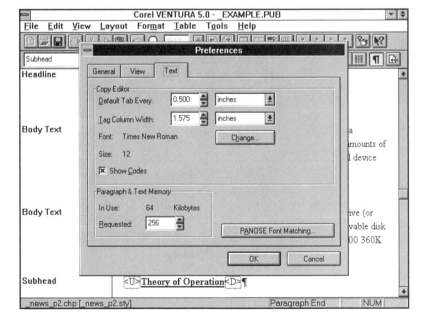

The Preferences dialog box also lets you specify which font is used to display the text in the Copy Editor. In the Copy Editor section of the dialog box, click on the C**h**ange button. Select a new font and click on OK. Click on OK again to return to the VENTURA screen. All text in the Copy Editor is now displayed in the selected font.

Moving and Copying Text

The Windows Clipboard provides an excellent way to move and place text in your VENTURA publications. The Clipboard is a temporary storage area where you can place text or graphics, then transfer them to a new location. The Clipboard offers two options for transferring text to new locations—moving and copying. With moving, you can cut text from its original location, then paste it in another. If you need to make a duplicate of the text to place in another location, you can place a copy of the text in the Clipboard leaving the original in its current location.

Moving and Copying Text from Within VENTURA

When working on a publication, you might find that you want to move a text block from one place to another. For example, for your company newsletter, you might decide that a story about a new employee would be better moved from page two to page three. The Clipboard provides a quick and efficient way to cut or copy text to a new location. The following exercise illustrates how to cut or copy text with the Clipboard:

1. Select the text you want to cut or copy. If you want to include any paragraph formatting with the selected text, be sure to select the paragraph symbol after the text. If you do not select the paragraph symbol, when you paste the text at its new location, it will assume the formatting of the paragraph where the text is pasted.

2. From the **E**dit menu, choose Cu**t** to remove the selected text from its original location, or **C**opy to place a duplicate of the selected text in the Clipboard.

3. With either Text tool, click to position the insertion point where you want to paste the text.

4. From the **E**dit menu, choose **P**aste, or click on the Paste button.

The text is placed on the page at the insertion point. The Clipboard holds the current selection so you can paste it in other locations. The contents of the Clipboard are replaced when you cut or copy another selection.

Copying and Pasting Text from Other Applications

Frequently, you might need to include text created in a word processor, such as Microsoft Word, in your VENTURA document. As discussed in Chapter 5, you can import text files from other applications into your VENTURA document. Another convenient way to move or copy text from your word processor into VENTURA is with the Windows Clipboard. The following exercise illustrates using the Clipboard to transfer text from a Windows word processor into the base page frame in VENTURA:

1. From VENTURA, switch to the application containing the text you want to place into your VENTURA document.

2. Select the text you want to transfer.

3. From the **E**dit menu, choose Cu**t** to remove the text from its original location or **C**opy to place a duplicate of the text in the Clipboard.

4. Switch back to your VENTURA document, select either Text tool and click in the base page where you want to place the text.

5. Click on the Paste button or choose **P**aste from the **E**dit menu.

You can paste text from the Clipboard into the base page frame, free frames, or the Copy Editor. In general, use the Clipboard to transfer shorter text blocks into VENTURA. The Clipboard is perfect for one or two paragraphs, or text blocks up to a page in length. Beyond that, importing is probably the most efficient way to transfer text from another application into VENTURA.

For more information on using the Windows Clipboard, refer to your Windows documentation, or *Inside Windows 3.11, Platinum Edition* by New Riders Publishing.

Using Spell Check

VENTURA provides a full-featured spell checking facility that identifies misspelled words and irregular capitalization. When you run the spell checker, VENTURA automatically scans your document to identify words not found in its dictionary. When VENTURA locates such a word, it provides a series of correction options, including suggested replacements for misspellings. Use the following steps to check your document's spelling:

1. Select **S**pell Check from the T**o**ols menu, or click on the Spell Check button on the ribbon bar. The Spell Check dialog box appears, as shown in figure 6.11.

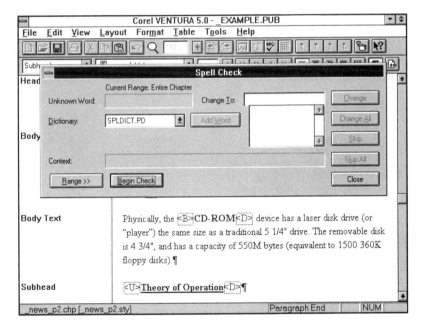

Figure 6.11
The Spell Check dialog box.

2. Specify the amount of text to be checked by clicking on the **R**ange button. By default, VENTURA will check the entire chapter. As shown in figure 6.12, the expanded Spell Check dialog box reveals other range options. For example, to check only specified text files, choose Selected F**i**les and select the files you want to check from the **F**iles list box. To spell check only a selected range of text, highlight the range to be checked with either text tool, then choose **S**pell Check from the T**o**ols menu. The option to check only the Selected Te**x**t will be active.

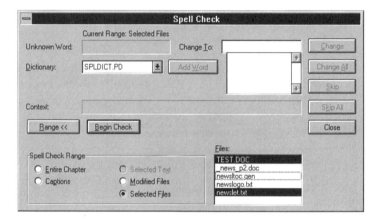

Figure 6.12
The expanded
Spell Check
dialog box.

3. Click on the **B**egin Check button to start the spell checker. When a word is found that VENTURA does not recognize, it is displayed in the Unknown Word text box. The Context text box displays the unrecognized word as it is used in a sentence.

4. The Change **T**o list box provides a list of suggested spellings for the unknown word. Select the correct spelling and click on the **C**hange button. If none of the suggested words are correct, you can type the correct spelling in the Change **T**o box and click on the **C**hange button. To change any additional occurrences of the same word, click on the Change **A**ll button. Click on the **S**kip button to ignore the unknown word, and S**k**ip All to ignore the word throughout the spell check range.

5. After the spell checker has finished checking your document, a confirmation dialog box appears telling you that the spell check is complete. Click on OK to return to your document. You can terminate the process at any time during the spell check by clicking on the Close button.

To avoid having to repeatedly check proprietary entries such as company names or other words not in VENTURA's dictionary, the spell checker enables you to add words to the dictionary. For example, if the name of your company is Cunningham Tools, you can add this name to the dictionary by clicking on the Add **W**ord button when the spell checker identifies it as an unknown word. Thereafter, the spell checker will no longer identify Cunningham Tools as an unknown word, unless it is misspelled.

VENTURA includes dictionaries in several different languages. You can also create your own custom dictionaries. For more information on these topics, refer to online Help, or your CorelVENTURA manual.

Using the Thesaurus

How many times have you known what you want to say, but just couldn't seem to find the right words to express your thoughts? For times like these, VENTURA's thesaurus is an indispensable writing tool. The thesaurus looks up any word and instantaneously provides a list of synonyms from which you can choose to replace the selected word. To use the thesaurus, select the word you want to look up, then choose **Th**esaurus from the **To**ols menu. The Thesaurus dialog box appears, as shown in figure 6.13.

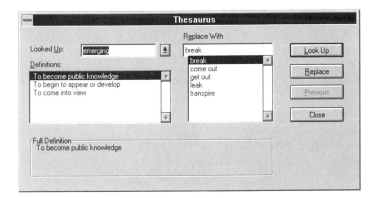

Figure 6.13
The Thesaurus dialog box.

If the word is in VENTURA's dictionary, the selected word appears in the Looked **U**p box. Beneath the word is a list of definitions for the selected word. Many words have multiple definitions. For example, the word "read" could be used as an active verb, as in "He will read to the class," or in the past tense, as in "She read to the children." If the entire definition is not visible in the **D**efinitions box, you can refer to the Full Definition entry below for a complete description. When you select a definition for a word, the R**e**lace With list box provides a list of potential replacement words.

If a replacement word is close, but not quite right, you can select it and search for its synonyms by clicking on the **L**ook Up button. The **P**revious button enables you to go back to the last word you looked up. The Looked **U**p list box provides you with a record of the words you have looked up, including the initially selected word. To go back to one of the words from the list, simply select it. When you find the perfect word to replace the word you looked up, click on the **R**eplace button. You are returned to your document with the new word in place. At any time you can return to your document without replacing a word by clicking on the Close button.

VENTURA includes thesauruses in several different languages. For more information, refer to online Help or your CorelVENTURA manual.

Using Type Assist

Type Assist enables VENTURA to correct your typing mistakes automatically. If you are like many people, you have one or two words you cannot type correctly to save your life. With Type Assist, you can instruct VENTURA to recognize those mistakes and fix them for you.

For example, if you frequently type "adn" instead of "and," or "teh" instead of "the," you can instruct VENTURA to recognize those mistakes and automatically correct them. Further, with Type Assist, you can "teach" VENTURA your own special brand of shorthand. For instance, you can instruct VENTURA to replace "govt." with "government," or your initials with your full name. After the misspelling or shortcut is entered, press the spacebar or type a punctuation mark. Type Assist then corrects the error or inserts the replacement text.

To enable the standard correction options, choose Type Assist from the Tools menu. The Type Assist dialog box appears, as shown in figure 6.14. Click on any of the options you want Type Assist to correct automatically. For example, if you often accidentally capitalize the first two letters of a sentence, check Correct Two Initial, Consecutive Capitals.

Figure 6.14
The Type Assist
dialog box.

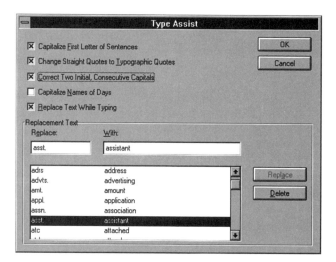

The Replacement Text section of the dialog box enables you to enter certain text shortcuts and have VENTURA replace them with a word or phrase. VENTURA includes a list of common replacement entries included with VENTURA, or you can define your own. To enable this replacement function, you must turn on the **R**eplace Text While Typing option.

Many replacement entries are included with the program. Before creating your own entry, check through the list to see what the entries already included. For example, included in the list is the shortcut "asst." which will be replaced by the word "assistant." If you want to eliminate a replacement entry, select it and click on the **D**elete button. To create your own replacement item, type the shortcut in the **R**eplace text box, then type the replacement word in the **W**ith box. For instance, you could type "univ" in the **R**eplace box, and "University" in the **W**ith box. Click on the **A**dd button to add the entry to the list, then click on OK to close the Type Assist dialog box. Now each time you type "univ," VENTURA will automatically replace it with "University."

Using Find and Replace

VENTURA provides a Find and Replace command similar to those found in most popular word processors. You can use Find and Replace to search for specific text in your publication, and, if necessary, replace it with other text.

 Searching and replacing paragraph tags is discussed in Chapter 8, "Managing Paragraph Tags."

The following steps illustrate using the Find and Replace command to search for a specific word to replace it with another:

1. From the **E**dit menu, choose Find and **R**eplace. The Find and Replace dialog box appears (see fig. 6.15).

2. Click on the Text radio button.

3. Type the text you want to find in the Fi**n**d What box. You can enter up to 60 characters.

4. Type the text you want to replace in the Replace **W**ith box. Again, you can enter up to 60 characters. If you only want to find a specific word without replacing it, leave the Replace **W**ith box blank.

Figure 6.15
The Find and
Replace dialog
box.

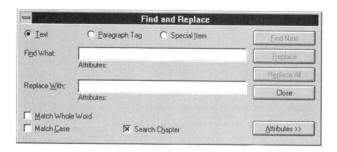

5. Place a check in the **M**atch Whole Word box to search for the entry as a complete word, not characters within a word. For example, check **M**atch Whole Word to find "cat" but not "scatter." Check Match **C**ase to confine the search to exact capitalization. To search through an entire chapter, check Search **Ch**apter. Otherwise the search occurs only from the insertion point to the end of the chapter.

6. Click on the **F**ind Next button to begin searching. The found text is highlighted. Click on the **R**eplace button to replace the highlighted text with the text in the Replace **W**ith box. Click on the Re**p**lace All button to replace all occurrences of the found text. Click on the **F**ind Next button to move the next occurrence of the specified text. Click on the Cancel button to halt the search and return to your document.

Find and Replace can also be used to locate certain character formatting to replace it with another formatting. For example, after completing a document, you decide that all bold formatting should be underlined. Rather than going through the document to change the items you want, you could use the Find and Replace command to perform the changes in a few seconds.

To search for specific character formatting, click on the **A**ttributes button to reveal the expanded Find and Replace dialog box shown in figure 6.16. In the Find Attri**b**utes section, choose the text formatting and font you want to find. In the Replace Attrib**u**tes section, choose the replacement text formatting and font. Choose Revert Text to clear the Replace Attrib**u**tes check boxes. If there are no replacement attributes chosen, the text found in the Find What box automatically reverts to the style attributes of the paragraph tag where the text is found.

You can use Find and Replace to search your document for special items such as footnotes or index entries. To search for special items, select the Special **I**tem radio button and choose the item you want to locate from the Fi**n**d What list box. Use the **F**ind Next button just as you would to locate text. When the special item

is located, click on the Close button to close the Find and Replace dialog box and perform any necessary changes. To resume the search, choose Find and **R**eplace from the **E**dit menu and continue as required.

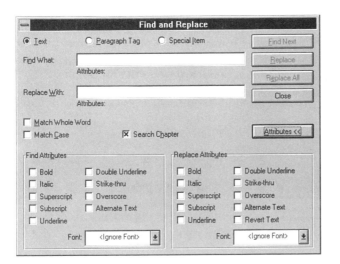

Figure 6.16
The expanded
Find and Replace
dialog box.

II

Building a VENTURA Document

 Footnotes and index entries are discussed in Chapters 14 and 17.

Chapter Snapshot

The wrong choice of fonts and text formatting can be disasterous. How your document looks is as important as what the words say. Learning to use text formatting options is an important part of designing with type. In this chapter, you learn to do the following:

This chapter covers all types of formatting concerns. You learn to apply formats across multiple paragraphs and use the Freeform Text tool to apply formatting to unique situations.

Formatting Tagged and Freeform Text

After importing, entering, and editing text, you're probably eager to begin formatting and designing with type. Searching for the perfect font and playing with type styles are perhaps some of the most creative and stimulating aspects of document design. Good text formatting catches the eye and draws the reader into the page. Inadequate text formatting can result in bland pages or overly done layouts that diminish the readability as well as the crediblity of your document.

This chapter focuses on formatting text in VENTURA documents. First, you learn about two text formatting techniques—paragraph tagging and freeform text formatting. Text formatting begins with the broad approach of tagging all the text in a document, then focuses on the specific formatting for each individual paragraph. This chapter takes a close look at working with paragraph tags. You learn how to apply tags, and how to modify them to fit your exact needs. Also covered here are selecting fonts, controlling alignment, and adjusting line spacing. This chapter ends with an examination of using freeform text where you will learn how to format individual paragraphs by overriding the paragraph tag formatting.

Formatting Text with VENTURA

VENTURA provides two methods for formatting and designing text. Paragraph tagging is the most powerful and comprehensive formatting method. *Paragraph tags*, which are collections of formatting attributes, are applied to text with the Tagged Text tool. Any formatting done with the Tagged Text tool automatically formats all paragraphs using the same tag. For instance, as displayed in figure 7.1, all headings use a tag designed to format headings. Applying paragraph tags to the text ensures consistency, an important element of text formatting. The tag controls the formatting, and every paragraph using a specific tag will be formatted identically.

Figure 7.1
Tagging establishes consistency in formatting within your documents.

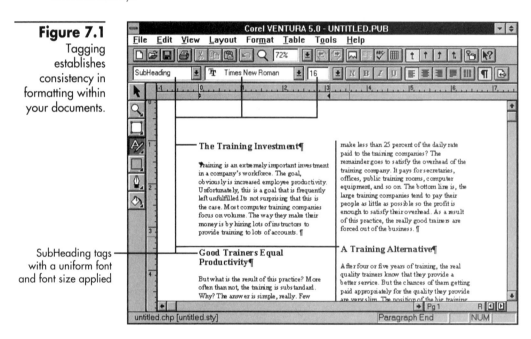

SubHeading tags with a uniform font and font size applied

Formatting text with the Freeform tool gives you the freedom to bend the rules. With freeform text you can change the attributes of one paragraph without affecting other paragraphs using the same tag. For instance, imagine you have one chapter title that you want to rotate. You can use the freeform method to rotate one title without affecting the other titles. Freeform text overrides the formatting attributes of paragraph tags.

Formatting in VENTURA works best if you start with the big picture and work your way in to the small stuff. Starting with the big picture means *tagging* all of the text in your document. A *paragraph tag* is a collection of formatting attributes, such as font, alignment, and color. For example, suppose you are compiling a technical manual. First, you would tag the chapter titles, headings, and

subheadings—all of the text in your document. Tagging establishes the format for each paragraph of text quickly. Tagging is a big step in text formatting. Consider that when all of the text has been tagged, you are probably close to 80 percent done with text formatting.

 The next chapter, "Managing Paragraph Tags," covers creating, deleting, and merging tags, as well as some specialized formatting options such as creating drop caps and bullets, and rotating text.

After tagging, you're ready to think about more specific details, focusing on the individual attributes of each paragraph. Freeform text enables you to break away from the rigid structure of paragraph tags. Rather than making a whole new tag for the one heading that requires a slightly different look, you can use freeform text to format that heading. For instance, suppose the paragraph tag for bulleted text specifies single line spacing, but there's one bulleted list you want double-spaced. With freeform text you can override the attributes in the paragraph tag to make one bulleted list double-spaced while the others stay single-spaced.

Keep in mind that many of the formatting commands for working with paragraph tags are the same as those for formatting with freeform text. With freeform text, however, you will only be formatting selected paragraphs, but with paragraph tags, the formatting affects all paragraphs assigned that particular tag.

Working with Paragraph Tags

VENTURA uses paragraph tags to format the text in your document. A tag is applied to each paragraph of text. Paragraphs are defined in VENTURA by carriage returns. Thus, a paragraph may contain several lines of text—or no text at all. Figure 7.2, shows some paragraphs with one-word headings and others containing several sentences. When a paragraph is tagged, the formatting attributes associated with that tag are applied to the paragraph.

Selecting the Right Style Sheet

Paragraph tags are stored as part of the style sheet file. As discussed in Chapter 2, style sheets also determine page layout information such as page size, orientation, and margins. Selecting the right style sheet is an important part of producing documents in VENTURA. When choosing a style sheet, consider the accompanying paragraph tags, as well as the page layout established by the style sheet. Of course, the text formatting in the style sheet can be altered, but the closer the formatting matches your needs, the less time you will spend modifying it.

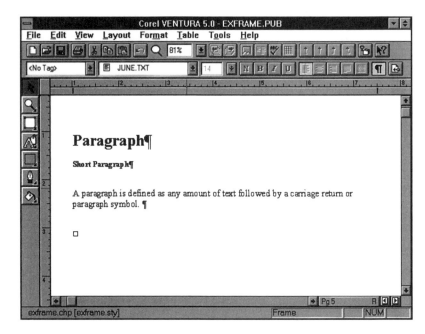

To select the right style sheet, browse through the Templates section of the Corel clip art book. The text displayed on the pre-designed style sheets is formatted using the tags available in that style sheet. When the text on the style sheet looks like what you had in mind for your document, you've found your style sheet. If you can't find a style sheet with text formatting that meets your exact needs, don't panic. This chapter also explains how to modify the text formatting. The next section discusses applying the tags that come with the selected style sheet.

Applying Tags

Tagging is a quick, one-step process that applies several formatting attributes at one time. By default, all text, whether imported from a word processor or entered directly in VENTURA, is automatically tagged with the *body text* tag. You only have to tag the titles, headings, lists, and other paragraphs requiring different formatting.

Clicking on the Tag list in the ribbon bar reveals the paragraph tags stored in the selected style sheet. If you selected the right style sheet, the tag names should be specific to the type of document you are creating. For instance, the calendar style sheet includes tags for month and day text, but the magazine style sheet provides tags for headlines and bylines. The magazine style sheet was used to format the text in figure 7.3. The first paragraph is tagged with the headline tag. The second paragraph is tagged as a deckhead.

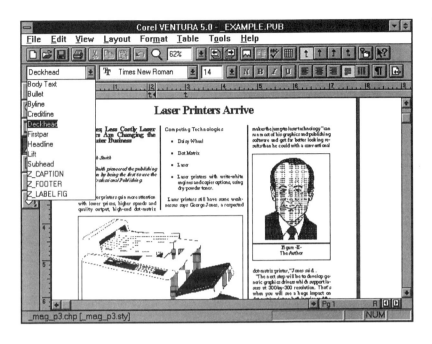

Figure 7.3
Paragraph tags are used to format text in VENTURA.

Either Text tool can be used to enter and edit text. However, when you begin tagging text, VENTURA requires that you select the Tagged Text tool. Press and hold on the text tool to reveal two tools. The Tagged Text tool displays a "tag," indicating it is used to work with tagged text. The following exercise shows you how to apply tags to the paragraphs in your document using the Tagged Text Tool:

1. Select the Tagged Text tool and click in the paragraph you want to tag. The insertion point appears in the paragraph.

2. Click on the down arrow by the tag list to reveal the paragraph tags. Select the desired tag.

3. The paragraph in which you had placed the insertion point is formatted to match the specifications of the selected tag.

The current tag name appears in the tag list. Repeat these steps to tag every paragraph in your document. Remember that the body text is already tagged. The next section discusses changing the formatting of paragraph tags.

Tagging Multiple Paragraphs

For long documents, tagging each and every paragraph in your document can become quite a task. You can simplify the tagging process by selecting several

II

Building a VENTURA Document

paragraphs and then tagging them all in one step. For instance, suppose you have five subheadings on a page. Rather than tagging each subheading separately, select all of the subheadings and tag them simultaneously.

You can select multiple paragraphs on different pages if you use the Go To Page command under the Edit menu. For example, you can hold the Alt key and click in a paragraph on page 1. Select the Go To Page command, enter 2 as the page number and click on OK. Now, on page 2, click in another paragraph while holding the Alt key. The paragraphs on both pages are selected, ready to be tagged. You cannot select multiple paragraphs across different pages if you use the arrows in the bottom right corner of the screen to move between the pages.

After selecting the Tagged Text tool, hold down the Alt key and click (*don't* click and drag) in every paragraph you want to tag. As displayed in figure 7.4, the shape of the mouse cursor changes to a "paragraph" and the selected paragraphs are highlighted. After the paragraphs are selected, choose a tag from the tag list. The formatting is applied to all of the selected paragraphs.

Figure 7.4
Applying paragraph tags to multiple paragraphs simplifies the tagging process.

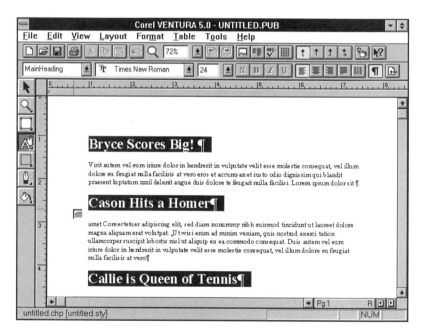

Using Hotkeys To Apply Tags

You can also speed up the tagging process by using keyboard shortcuts called *hotkeys*. Paragraph tags can be assigned a specific keyboard combination, such as Ctrl+9. To view the hotkey combinations assigned to each tag, select Ma**n**age Tag

List from the For**m**at menu. The Manage Tag List dialog box appears as displayed in figure 7.5. By default, the Paragraph Tags tab is displayed. The next chapter discusses using the **T**ag List to add, rename, and delete tags.

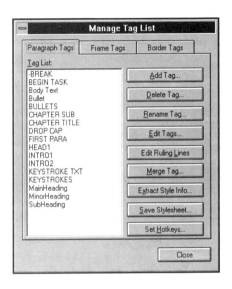

Figure 7.5
The Manage Tag List dialog box.

Click on the Set **H**otkeys button to reveal the Set Hotkeys dialog box as displayed in figure 7.6. The tag names appear in the first column, the point size of the type defined in the tag in the second column and the hotkey combination in the third. You can use the assigned hotkeys or define new ones. To set up a new hotkey combination, select the tag name, and click on the desired number button on the right. For instance, in figure 7.6, the BULLETS tag was selected and assigned the hotkey combination Ctrl+3. When you are finished, click on OK. Click on the Close button to close the Manage Tag List dialog box and return to the document.

To tag paragraphs using hotkeys, click with the Tagged Text tool to place the insertion point inside the paragraph, and press the hotkeys. Use the Alt key to select several paragraphs, then press the hotkeys to format the selected paragraphs in one step.

Modifying Paragraph Tags

Ideally, the paragraph tags supplied by the style sheet would work perfectly. However, almost every document requires adjusting the formatting set up in the paragraph tags. Maybe company standards dictate all headings use the Century

Schoolbook font, or perhaps the bullet paragraph tag uses a circle for the bullet character and your boss is fond of squares. Whatever the reason, VENTURA makes it easy to modify the attributes of a tag.

Figure 7.6
The Set Hotkeys
dialog box.

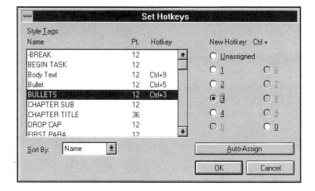

Any changes made to a tag affect all paragraphs using that tag. For instance, if you change the font of the heading tag to Century Schoolbook, all paragraphs using the heading tag are affected. You do not have to change each and every heading individually. As mentioned earlier, paragaph tagging is designed to save time and help you maintain consistency in text formatting throughout your document. With VENTURA, you can modify a tag knowing that the changes will be reflected in every occurrence of that tag.

You might want to begin by modifying the body text tag because it probably covers a majority of the text in your document. After the body text tag is formatted to meet your needs, move on to modifying the titles and other headings.

To modify a paragraph tag, you simply change the attributes of one paragraph using that tag. VENTURA automatically adjusts all other paragraphs that have been assigned the same tag. The following sections discuss modifying the font, type style, alignment, and spacing of paragraph tags. Refer to the next chapter for more advanced paragraph tagging formatting options.

Choosing Fonts and Type Styles

The type face you choose greatly influences the tone of your document. Type faces such as Times Roman are formal and business-oriented. Others, such as Hobo, are casual and instill a lighter, friendlier feeling. Type size is also a major consideration. Size helps determine the importance of the message. Notice in figure 7.7 that the size of the title establishes its importance over the other

smaller headings. Type styles, such as bold and italic, also lend emphasis to text. Headlines are often formatted to appear in bold to give them more prominence on the page. Selecting the right type face, size, and style for your text is essential to good page design.

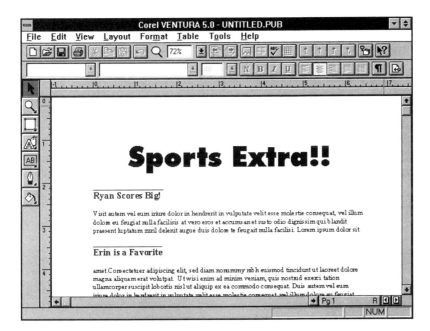

Figure 7.7
Type face, size, and style play an important role in page design.

The font and type style specified by the paragraph tag is applied to all of the text in the paragraph. Use the freeform text formatting method discussed later in this chapter if you want to change the font for just a word or sentence within the paragraph.

To modify the paragraph tag, it is essential that you select the Tagged Text tool. The Freeform tool is used when you want to modify only the selected paragraph. In addition, be careful that you *do not select* any text within the paragraph. Selecting instructs VENTURA to change just the attributes of the selected text, not the paragraph tag. The following steps illustrate changing the font and type style used in a paragraph tag:

1. Select the Tagged Text tool and click in a paragraph whose tag you want to modify. The insertion point appears in the paragraph.

2. Select Paragraph from the Format menu. The Override Paragraph Settings dialog box appears as displayed in figure 7.8. The Character tab

sheet is automatically displayed. The name of the tag you are modifying appears in the bottom left corner of the dialog box.

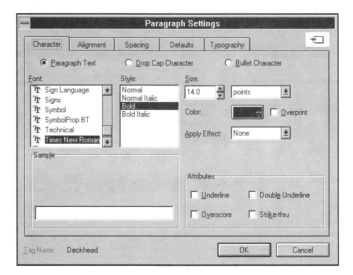

3. Select the desired type face from the **F**ont list box. You might have to scroll to view all of the fonts. A preview of the selected type face appears in the Sample box.

4. Select the desired type style from the St**y**le list box. Not all type faces offer bold and italic versions. The Technical type face, for instance, is only available in Normal and Normal Italic.

5. Enter the desired type size in the **S**ize box and click on OK. The formatting of all paragraphs using the modified tag has been changed.

Type size is generally measured in points. There are 72 points in an inch. To use another measurement system, such as inches, to measure your type, click on the down arrow by points in the Paragraph Settings dialog box and select the desired system.

The Character tab in the Paragraph Settings dialog box also offers options for changing the color of the type. Click on the Color button to display a palette of colors, and select the desired color. Also included in the dialog box are options for applying line attributes such as underlining, overscoring, and strike-thru. The sample box gives you a preview of the color and line attributes. As displayed in figure 7.9, the text color is white with the **U**nderline attribute turned on.

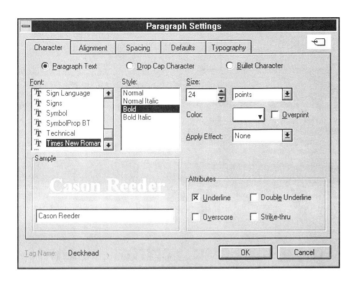

Figure 7.9
You can also apply text colors and line attributes with the Paragraph Settings dialog box.

The text in the Sample box defaults to "AaBbZz." As displayed in figure 7.9, however, you can enter the text characters you want to see previewed. Click in the white box below the sample text and begin typing. The preview in the sample box now displays the text you entered in the selected formatting.

Using the Ribbon Bar To Select Fonts

VENTURA's ribbon bar provides an alternate way to quickly select the type face and type size of your paragraph tags. When a Text tool is selected, the ribbon bar displays the Font and Font Size List boxes (see fig. 7.10).

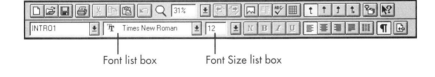

Font list box   Font Size list box

Figure 7.10
The ribbon bar provides another way to select fonts and font sizes.

Because this section focuses on modifying the paragraph tags, the Tagged Text tool is used. Remember any modifications made with the Tagged Text tool affect all paragraphs assigned a specific tag. Modifications made with the Freeform tool affect only the selected paragraph. The following exercise illustrates selecting a font and font size from the ribbon bar using the Tagged Text tool:

1. Select the Tagged Text tool and click in a paragraph whose tag you want to modify. The insertion point appears in the paragraph.

2. Click on the down arrow by the Font list box to reveal the available fonts. Select the desired font.

3. Click on the down arrow by the Font Size list box, and select the desired type size. If the size you want is not listed, you can type in the size in the box at the top of the Font list box. After entering the type size, press the Enter key. The formatting of all paragraphs using the modified tag has been changed.

The ribbon bar buttons for controlling type styles, such as bold, italic, and underline cannot be accessed when you are modifying a paragraph tag. You need to use the Paragraph dialog box as previously described to modify the type styles of a paragraph tag.

Controlling Horizontal and Vertical Alignment

VENTURA enables you to set the horizontal and vertical alignment for paragraphs. As illustrated in figure 7.11, horizontal alignment determines whether the text is left- or right-aligned, centered, or justified in the frame. Text entered into a free frame is aligned within the frame's boundaries. Text entered into a base page frame is aligned within the page boundaries. Generally, body text is left-aligned, while titles and other headings may be centered.

Figure 7.11
With Horizontal alignment you can align text with left, center, right, or full justification.

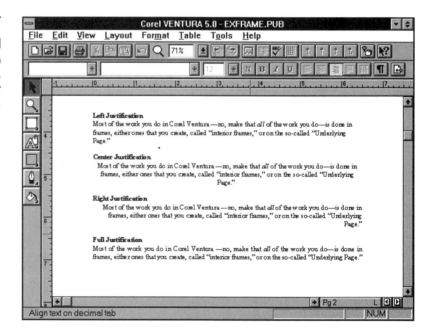

Vertical alignment controls whether the text sits at the top, middle, or bottom of the frame. Again, the text is vertically aligned within the boundaries of the free frame or base page frame. Almost all paragraph tags are set up for top vertical alignment. The text appears at the top of the frame and flows down. However, as displayed in figure 7.12, the chapter title was set up for bottom vertical alignment. In this case, every paragraph tagged as a chapter title begins at the bottom of the frame. Additional text begins flowing on the next page.

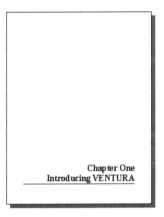

Figure 7.12

Vertical alignment allows you to create tags that position the text at the bottom of the frame.

The following exercise illustrates how to set up the horizontal and vertical aligment for a paragraph tag:

1. Select the Tagged Text tool and click in a paragraph whose tag you want to modify. The insertion point appears in the paragraph.

2. Select Paragraph from the Format menu. The Paragraph Settings dialog box appears. Click on the Alignment tab to display the dialog box in figure 7.13.

3. There are five buttons for setting **H**orizontal alignment: left, centered, right, justified, and decimal align. (Decimal align is examined later in this section.) Select the desired alignment button.

4. The three buttons for **V**ertical alignment are top, middle, and bottom. Select the desired button and click on OK. The alignment of all paragraphs using the modified tag is adjusted.

Figure 7.13
The Paragraph Settings dialog box with the Alignment tab displayed.

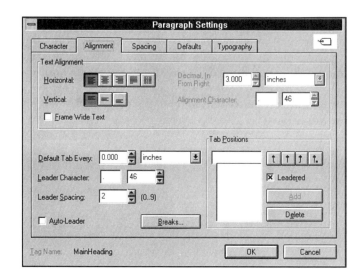

Specifying Frame Wide Alignment

Unless indicated otherwise, text is horizontally aligned within the column guides. For example, as displayed in figure 7.14, the subheadings are centered within the width of one column in a two-column layout. With VENTURA, you can also align text within the width of a frame. The main heading in figure 7.14 is aligned within the width of the whole frame, not the column guides.

Figure 7.14
Text can be aligned within column guides or the width of the frame.

Company Reaches Top Sales Again

Ruth Leads the Pack

Visit autem vel eum iriure dolor in hendrerit in vulputate velit esse molestie consequat, vel illum dolore eu feugiat nulla facilisis at vero eros et accumsan et iusto odio dignissim qui blandit praesent luptatum zzril delenit augue duis dolore te feugait nulla facilisi. Lorem ipsum dolor sit

Rob Voted Rookie of the Year

amet.Consectetuer adipiscing elit, sed diam nonummy nibh euismod tincidunt ut laoreet dolore magna aliquam erat volutpat. Ut wisi enim ad minim veniam, quis nostrud exerci

tation ullamcorper suscipit lobortis nisl ut aliquip ex ea commodo consequat. Duis autem vel eum iriure dolor in hendrerit in vulputate velit esse molestie consequat, vel illum dolore eu feugiat nulla

Manager Mike Tickled Pink

facilisis at vero eros et accumsan et iusto odio dignissim qui blandit praesent luptatum azril delenit augue duis dolore te feugait nulla facilisi. Lorem ipsum dolor sito amet, atoi consectetuer adipiscing elit, sed diam nonummy nibal as eui mode.Visit autem vel eum iriure

Centering headings across the width of the frame enables you to "stretch" the heading across several columns of text. To align the text within the frame width, click on the **F**rame Wide Text option located below the alignment buttons on the Alignment tab sheet in the Paragraph Settings dialog box (see fig. 7.13). Aligning text within the width of the frame works the same, regardless of whether the text is placed on the base page frame or in a free frame.

Using Decimal Align

VENTURA also provides an option for aligning numbers by their decimal points, as displayed in figure 7.15. Instead of using tabs, you can use the Decimal Align option to line up one column of numbers.

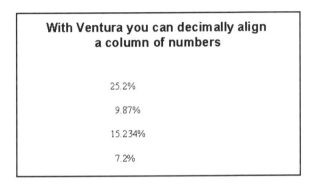

With Ventura you can decimally align a column of numbers

25.2%

9.87%

15.234%

7.2%

Figure 7.15
Decimal alignment enables you to align a column of numbers without using tabs.

Select the Decimal Align button (the fifth button for horizontal alignment) in the Alignment dialog box. Use the Decimal, **In** From Right box to specify the amount of space you want the decimals aligned. This option measures from the right column guide, so the greater the amount entered, the further the decimals align from the right edge of the frame. To select another character for alignment, click on the up and down arrows by Alignment **C**haracter. For instance, you might want the data to be aligned by slash marks (/), rather than decimal points.

Using the Ribbon Bar To Select Alignment

VENTURA's ribbon bar provides another way to quickly change the horizontal text alignment of your paragraph tags. When a Text tool is selected, the ribbon bar displays the alignment buttons as shown in figure 7.16.

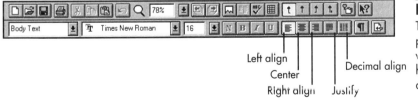

Left align
Center
Right align   Justify

Decimal align

Figure 7.16
The Ribbon Bar provides another way to change horizontal text alignment.

The following exercise illustrates changing the horizontal alignment using the ribbon bar. The changes affect the alignment of all paragraphs using the modified tag.

1. Select the Tagged Text tool and click in a paragraph whose tag you want to modify. The insertion point appears in the paragraph.

2. Click on the desired alignment button. The five buttons are left-align, right-align, center, justified, and decimal-align. The formatting of all paragraphs using the modified tag has been changed.

Adjusting Line and Paragraph Spacing

Adjusting the line and paragraph spacing in your text can improve the overall appearance and readability of your document. VENTURA enables you to control the spacing between lines of text within a paragraph. For instance, as displayed in figure 7.17, the spacing in the first paragraph is tighter, while more spacing is added between the lines of the second paragraph. You can also add spacing above and below specific paragraphs. In figure 7.17, spacing is placed above each heading to separate the sections of text. Line and paragraph spacing should be consistent throughout your document. Altering the spacing used in the paragraph tags changes every paragraph using that tag, thus ensuring consistency.

Figure 7.17
With VENTURA, you can control the line and paragraph spacing of your text.

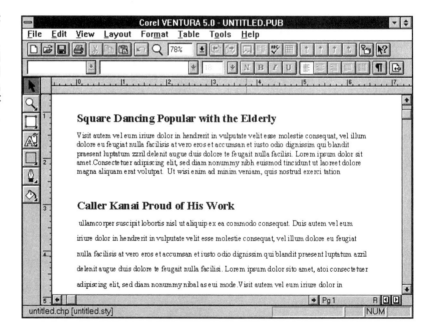

Inter-line spacing, often referred to as *leading*, is the distance between the baseline of one line of type to the baseline of another line of type. Above and below spacing is the amount of space placed above or below a paragraph of text.

With VENTURA, inter-line spacing can be measured in inches or as a percentage of the point size. It is recommended that you enter spacing as a percentage of the point size. Because type is measured in points, the spacing should be also. Measuring the line spacing as a percentage of the point size lets you enter a measurement relative to the size of the type. For instance, a measurement of 150 percent adds 50 percent of the point size to the inter-line spacing. For 12-point type, 50 percent would add 6 points of inter-line spacing. The 12-point type would rest on 18 points of inter-line spacing. For 72-point type, 50 percent would add 36 points. The 72-point type would rest on 108 points of inter-line spacing.

Line spacing should be proportionate to the length of the lines of text. Use minimal line spacing for short lines of type and increase the line spacing as the line length increases.

Spacing above and below paragraphs can also be measured in inches or as a percentage of the point size. Again, it is recommended that spacing be measured as a percentage of the point size. As an example, adding a measurement of 200 percent adds two times the point size above the paragraph.

The following exercise demonstrates how to adjust above, below, and inter-line spacing for a paragraph tag:

1. Select the Tagged Text tool and click in a paragraph whose tag you want to modify. The insertion point appears in the paragraph.

2. Select Pa**r**agraph from the For**m**at menu. The Paragraph Settings dialog box appears; click on the Spacing tab to display the dialog box in figure 7.18.

3. The Spacing section of the dialog box controls the paragraph and line spacing. Use the percent of Font Size to enter the desired amount in the **A**bove, **B**elow, and **I**nter-Line spacing check boxes. Click on OK. The spacing of all paragraphs using the modified tag is adjusted.

Using the Grow Inter-Line Space to Fit Option

The spacing option **G**row Inter-Line Space to Fit is designed to accommodate characters that may be larger than the normal paragraph font. For instance, as displayed in the first paragraph in figure 7.19, the line spacing was adjusted to

II

Building a VENTURA Document

accommodate the larger type size. The line spacing was not adjusted in the second paragraph.

Figure 7.18
The Paragraph Settings dialog box with the Spacing tab sheet displayed.

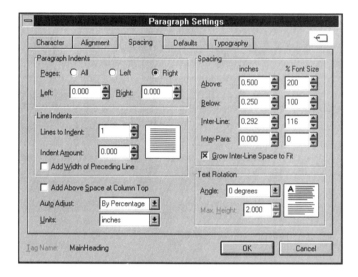

Figure 7.19
The Grow Inter-Line Space to Fit option adjusts the spacing if you add larger type sizes within a paragraph.

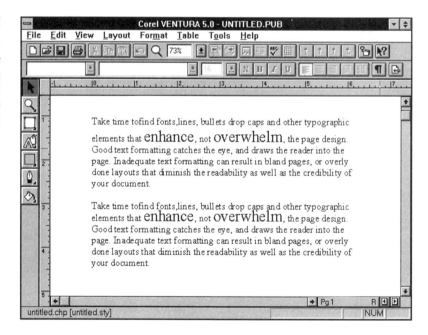

Adding Spacing at Column Top

By default, spacing added above paragraphs will not appear at the top of a page or column. For instance, the above spacing specified for the subheadings in figure 7.20 appears when the heading is preceded by text. However, the spacing is not added when the heading appears at the top of the first column.

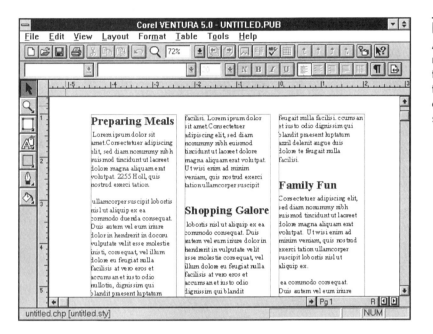

Figure 7.20
Above spacing is not added when text appears at the top of a page or column unless specified.

You can, however, override this behavior and instruct VENTURA to add the above spacing even when the text appears at the top of the page or column. To do this, turn on the Add Above Space at Column Top option in the Paragraph Settings dialog box.

Working with Freeform Text

Although paragraph tagging ensures consistency, it also is rather rigid. As described in the previous sections, any changes made to a paragraph tag affect all text using that tag. But what happens when you need to bend the rules a little? For instance, suppose there is one heading you want to display in the color red while the rest use black. Or perhaps you want to apply single-line spacing to one paragraph tagged as body text while the others retain double-line spacing. VENTURA supplies the Freeform Text tool when you need to break away from the rigid formatting set up by paragraph tagging.

Formatting with the Freeform Text tool lets you add a little flexibility to your text formatting by overriding the settings of the tag for a specific paragraph. The Freeform Text tool works similiarly to the Tagged Text tool except that changes made to the text affect only the selected paragraph, not all paragraphs using a particular tag. For instance, with the Freeform Text tool, you can change the font of a paragraph tagged as a subheading without changing the font of every other paragraph tagged as a subhead.

If you find yourself using the Freeform Text tool to make the same formatting changes to more than three paragraphs, consider making a new tag for the altered text paragraphs. A new tag cuts down on the number of steps and makes it easy to alter the text formatting later. Creating new tags is covered in the next chapter.

When the Show/Hide Returns button is selected in the ribbon bar, an "override diamond" is displayed at the beginning of paragraphs modified with the Freeform Text tool (see fig. 7.21). This diamond indicates which paragraphs have been altered from the original paragraph tag specifications. The diamond will not print. In addition, a "tag" appears by the tag name in the tag list when a paragraph is formatted with the Freeform Text tool.

Figure 7.21
When a paragraph is formatted with the Freeform Text tool, an override diamond is displayed over the first letter of the first word.

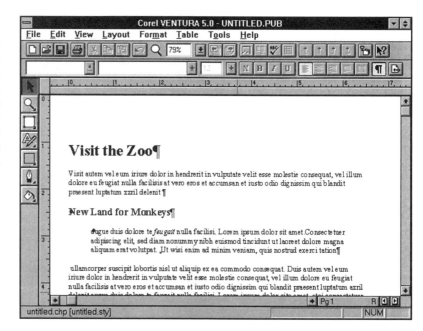

Freeform text provides even more flexiblity because you can change the attributes of the entire paragraph or just selected words and sentences. For instance, you might want to apply bold to all of the text in the paragraph, or just a word or two. VENTURA makes this simple. To affect the formatting of the whole paragraph, click anywhere in the paragraph. To affect only certain words and sentences, drag across those words to select them.

As described earlier, VENTURA provides the Freeform and Tagged Text tools for formatting text. Press and hold on the text tool to reveal both text tools. When you are working with paragraph tags, use the Tagged Text tool. When you want to modify a paragraph's formatting without affecting every other paragraph using the same tag, use the Freeform Text tool. Take the time to make sure you've selected the right tool for the task at hand.

The previous section, "Modifying Paragraph Tags," examined selecting fonts and type styles, changing alignment, and adjusting line and paragraph spacing. This section examines how the Freeform Text tool is used to modify these same formatting attributes. Because many of the steps are identical, the steps are abbreviated in this section. Refer to earlier sections for more information if needed.

II

Building a VENTURA Document

Selecting Fonts and Type Styles with the Freeform Tool

With Freeform text, you can choose another font for one paragraph without affecting other paragraphs using the same tag. For instance, as displayed in figure 7.22, you might want to set off a quote with italics or have the company name appear in a different font. Rather than creating a whole new tag for just one paragraph, use the Freeform Text tool.

Modifying the Entire Paragraph

To modify only a selected paragraph and not the paragraph tag, it is essential that you select the Freeform Text tool. Using the Tagged text tool changes the paragraph tag. To change the font or type style for the entire paragraph, just click anywhere inside the paragraph with the Freeform Text tool. The following exercise illustrates changing the font and type style for all of the text in a paragraph:

1. Select the Freeform Text tool and click inside the paragraph you want to modify. The insertion point appears in the paragraph.

Figure 7.22
With Freeform
Text you can use
different fonts and
type styles in
paragraphs
without affecting
the paragraph tag.

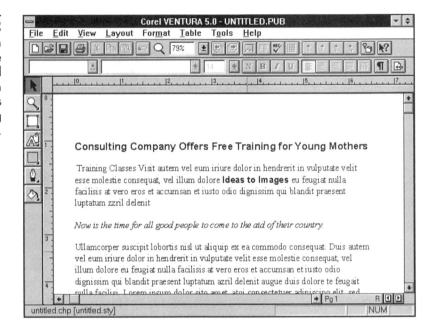

2. Select Paragraph from the Format menu. The Override Paragraph Settings dialog box appears with the Character tab automatically displayed.

3. Select the desired type face, type size, and type style. A preview of the selected type face appears in the Sample box. Not all type faces offer bold and italic versions.

4. Click on OK. The selected font and type style appears in the paragraph. Other paragraphs sharing the same tag are not affected.

As described in the previous section on selecting fonts, the Character tab offers options for changing the color of the type and applying line attributes such as underlining, overscoring, and strike-through. You can also enter text in the preview box to view how specific words look in the selected font and type style.

The ribbon bar provides an alternative to select fonts, font sizes, and type styles. After clicking in the paragraph with the Freeform Text tool, click on the down arrow by the Font list box and select a font. Click on the down arrow by the Font Size list box and select the desired type size.

Modifying Selected Text

You can use either Text tool to modify selected text. To apply the new font or type style to only specific words, drag across the words to select them. The following exercise illustrates changing the font and type style for selected text within a paragraph:

1. Select either Text tool. Select the text you want to modify by dragging across it. The text is highlighted.

2. Choose Selected Text the Format menu. The Selected Text Attributes dialog box appears as displayed in figure 7.23.

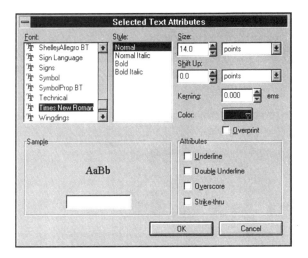

Figure 7.23
The Selected Text Attributes dialog box.

3. Select the desired type face from the **F**ont list. Select the desired type style from the St**y**le list. Not all type faces offer bold and italic versions. Enter the desired type size in the **S**ize box.

4. A preview of the selected type font appears in the Sample box. Click on OK. The highlighted words display in the selected font and type style.

The ribbon bar provides an alternate way to select fonts, font sizes, and type styles. After selecting the words with either Text tool, click on the down arrow by the Font list box and select a font. Click on the down arrow by the Font Size list box and select the desired type size. As displayed in figure 7.24, the ribbon bar also offers buttons for bold, italic, and underlining. After selecting the text, just click on the desired button to apply the type style. To remove the type style, select the text and click on the Normal (N) button.

Figure 7.24
The ribbon bar offers buttons for type styles when modifying selected text.

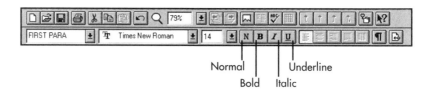

Normal

Bold Italic

Underline

Controlling Horizontal and Vertical Alignment with the Freeform Tool

With Freeform text, you can change the alignment of one paragraph without affecting other paragraphs using the same tag. For instance, in figure 7.25, the book passage is tagged as body text, but modified to be center aligned instead of left aligned. As discussed in the previous section on controlling alignment, VENTURA enables you to set the horizontal and vertical alignment for paragraphs.

Figure 7.25
With Freeform text, you can modify the alignment of one paragraph without changing other paragraphs using the same tag.

Shakespeare Festival Hit with College Students

Visit autem vel eum iriure dolor in hendrerit in vulputate velit esse molestie consequat, vel illum dolore eu feugiat nulla facilisis at vero eros et accumsan et iusto odio dignissim qui blandit praesent luptatum zzril delenit augue duis dolore te feugait nulla facilisi. Lorem ipsum dolor sit amet Consectetuer adipiscing elit, sed diam nonummy nibh euismod tincidunt ut laoreet dolore magna aliquam erat volutpat.

> I hold the world but as the world, Gratiano;
> A stage where every man must play a part,
> And mine a sad one.

Ut wisi enim ad minim veniam, quis nostrud exerci tation ullamcorper suscipit lobortis nisl ut aliquip ex ea commodo consequat. Duis autem vel eum iriure dolor in hendrerit in vulputate velit esse molestie consequat, vel illum dolore eu feugiat nulla facilisis at vero eros et accumsan et iusto odio dignissim qui blandit praesent luptatum zzril delenit augue duis dolore te feugait nulla facilisi. Lorem ipsum dolor sito amet, atoi consectetuer adipiscing elit, sed diam nonummy nibh al as eui mode. Visit autem vel eum iriure dolor in hendrerit in vulputate velit esse molestie consequat, vel illum dolore eu feugiat nulla facilisis at

Modifying the alignment affects the entire paragraph. Obviously, you cannot have one word of a paragraph centered while the rest remain left-aligned. The following steps illustrate changing the horizontal and vertical aligment for a paragraph:

1. Select the Freeform Text tool and click inside the paragraph you want to modify. The insertion point appears in the paragraph.

2. Select Pa<u>r</u>agraph from the For<u>m</u>at menu. The Override Paragraph Settings dialog box appears. Select the Alignment tab.

3. There are five buttons for setting <u>H</u>orizontal alignment: left-, centered, right-, justified, and decimal-align. Select the desired alignment button. (Decimal align is examined in the section "Modifying Paragraph Tags.")

4. The three buttons for <u>V</u>ertical alignment are top, middle, and bottom. Select the desired button and click on OK. The alignment of the selected paragraph is changed. Other paragraphs using the same tag are not affected.

Click on the <u>F</u>rame Wide Text option to align the text across the width of the frame not within the column guide. Refer to the previous section, "Specifying Frame Wide Alignment," for more information.

VENTURA's ribbon bar provides another way to quickly change the horizontal text alignment of your paragraph tags. After clicking in the paragraph with the Freeform Text tool, click on an alignment button in the ribbon bar. The five buttons represent left-align, right-align, center, justified, and decimal align.

Adjusting Line and Paragraph Spacing with the Freeform Text Tool

With Freeform text, you can adjust the line and paragraph spacing of one paragraph without affecting other paragraphs using the same tag. For instance, in figure 7.26, the address information is tagged as body text, but modified to be double-spaced instead of single-spaced. Rather than creating a whole new tag for the one paragraph, you can use the Freeform Text tool to modify the spacing of the address without affecting other body text tags.

As discussed in the earlier section, "Adjusting Line and Paragraph Spacing," inter-line spacing is the space between lines of text within a paragraph. Above and below spacing is the amount of space placed above or below a paragraph of text. Inter-line and above and below spacing can be measured in inches or as a percentage of the point size.

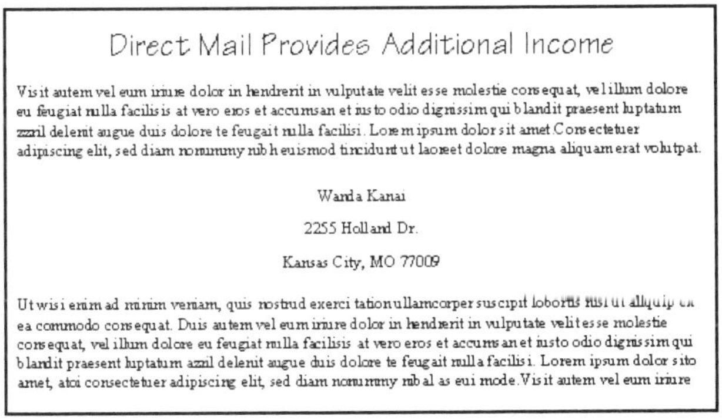

Figure 7.26
With Freeform Text, you can change the line and paragraph spacing of one paragraph without affecting other paragraphs using the same tag.

Changes made to the spacing affect the entire paragraph. The following exercise illustrates changing the inter-line, above, and below spacing for a paragraph:

1. Select the Freeform Text tool and click inside the paragraph you want to modify. The insertion point appears in the paragraph.

2. Select Paragraph from the Format menu. The Override Paragraph Settings dialog box appears; click on the Spacing tab.

3. The Spacing section of the dialog box controls the paragraph and line spacing. Enter an amount in the % of Font Size boxes for the desired amount of **A**bove, **B**elow, and **I**nter-Line spacing. Click on OK. The spacing of the selected paragraph is modified.

Click on the spacing option **G**row Inter-Line Space to Fit if some of the text within the paragraph will be formatted in a larger font. This option increases the line-spacing to accommodate the larger text. Click on the Add Above **S**pace at Column Top option to instruct VENTURA to add the above spacing even when the text appears at the top of the page or column.

Chapter Snapshot

The look and feel of every VENTURA document is governed by paragraph tags. Tags determine the font, the size, and other text attributes. In this chapter, you learn to do the following:

Managing the paragraph tags supplied with a style sheet is an essential part of producing a VENTURA document. Because each document you create will be unique, it's important to understand how to add tags and delete unnecessary ones.

CHAPTER 8

Managing Paragraph Tags

I t's no secret that paragraph tags are a major component of any document built in VENTURA. Paragraph tags govern the look of text in your document, ensuring consistency in formatting. The tags available when you begin a new document are determined by the style sheet selected to format the chapter file. For instance, the book style sheet offers tags for chapter titles, main headings, subheadings, and bulleted lists.

As discussed in the previous chapter, you can change the font, spacing, and alignment of tags to fit your exact needs. But what if you want to create a new tag, delete a tag, or perhaps change the tag name? As you will see, the tags supplied by the style sheet are only a starting point. VENTURA provides many options for managing the paragraph tags in your chapter file.

This chapter begins with the steps for creating new tags. Here, you will learn how to build and name a new tag. The next part of the chapter examines renaming and deleting tags to suit the requirements of your document. You will also discover how to copy or "merge" the tags from another style sheet into the current style sheet. In addition, this chapter provides a look at working with generated tags—tags that VENTURA applies automatically to text placed in captions, indexes, and tables of contents. The chapter ends with a look at printing the style sheet information and using the Find and Replace commands to help you quickly locate specific tags in a longer document.

Managing Paragraph Tags

VENTURA makes it easy to organize and manage the tags used to format your document. You can build new tags and modify existing ones to meet your exact needs. You can delete tags to shorten the Tag list and rename tags to apply tag names consistent with your documents. Managing your Tag list becomes especially important when you share style sheets among several chapter files or with other page designers. For example, if several people are involved in producing a book, an organized, succinct Tag list simplifies the tagging process, helping to prevent errors.

It is important to remember that any modifications made to the paragraph tags affect the style sheet, and any modifications to the style sheet affect every chapter file using that style sheet. For example, if you add a new tag, that new tag appears in every chapter file using the style sheet. If you do not want the changes to affect other documents, use the Save Style Sheet As command in the **L**ayout menu to rename the style sheet. Refer to Chapter 3, "Creating and Setting Up New Documents," for more information on working with style sheets.

Chapter 7, "Formatting Tagged and Freeform Text," discussed basic formatting options such as selecting fonts, changing alignment, and adjusting spacing. VENTURA also provides additional formatting options, such as drop caps, ruling lines, and indents. Refer to Chapter 9, "Advanced Text Formatting Options," for more information.

Creating New Paragraph Tags

The paragraph tags in the style sheets supplied by VENTURA are designed to meet *most* of your text formatting needs. Though the tags provided by the style sheet help to get you started, they are by no means guaranteed to solve all your formatting challenges. You will need to create new tags to meet all of the formatting requirements for your document.

For instance, suppose the style sheet provides heading1 and heading2 tags, but your document also requires a heading3 tag. Or perhaps the style sheet provides a tag for formatting bulleted lists, but you also need a tag for numbered lists. In cases like these, your best bet is to create new tags that address the required purpose.

You can include up to 128 tags in your style sheet chapter file.

When To Create a New Tag

As a general rule, build a new tag when you have several paragraphs requiring identical formatting and no tag to accommodate this formatting. For instance, suppose your manual includes numerous quotations from famous philosophers, and you want to emphasize the quotations by italicizing them. You could use the "body text" tag for the quotations and then apply the italics to each quotation individually. However, if there are several quotations, you will save time by making a "quote" tag. You could then quickly tag each quotation, instantly applying all the formatting attributes, including the italics. Making new tags also saves time if you plan on using the style sheet again.

If you just have one paragraph that requires specialized formatting, consider using the Freeform Text tool, rather than creating a whole new tag. Refer to Chapter 7 for more information on working with Freeform text.

Adding Paragraph Tags

New tags are built from the specifications of existing tags. When you create a new tag, you are asked to specify which existing tag will be used to build the new tag. The new tag starts out as a "copy" of an existing tag, which you then modify to meet specific formatting needs. Selecting a tag that closely matches the formatting needs of your new tag reduces the amount of work necessary to build the new tag. For instance, suppose you have a Main Heading tag formatted in 24-point Times Roman. You could use this tag to build a Sub Heading tag formatted in 18-point Times Roman. Only the point size would have to be changed for the new subheading tag.

Tag names are alphabetized in the Tag list. When entering tag names, use names that will place related tags together in the Tag list. For instance, the tag names Title 1 and Title 2 will appear together in the Tag list, whereas the names Chapter Title and Sub Title would not.

VENTURA does not require that you select a particular tool before creating tags. However, it's a good idea to select the Tagged Text tool because you will probably want to apply and modify the tag after creating it. The following exercise illustrates creating new paragraph tags:

1. Select Ma**n**age Tag List from the For**m**at menu. The Manage Tag List dialog box appears, as displayed in figure 8.1. The Paragraph Tags tab is selected. A listing of the current paragraph tags is displayed in the **T**ag List.

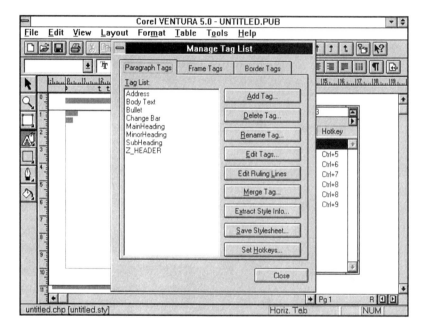

Figure 8.1

The Manage Tag List dialog box with the Paragraph Tags tab displayed.

2. Click on the **A**dd Tag button to display the Add Paragraph Tag dialog box shown in figure 8.2.

3. Enter a new tag name in the **T**ag Name box. You can use spaces in the tag name and enter up to 15 characters.

4. Click on the down arrow by **C**opy Attributes From and select the existing tag that will be used to build the new tag. The formatting options of this tag are automatically applied to the new tag.

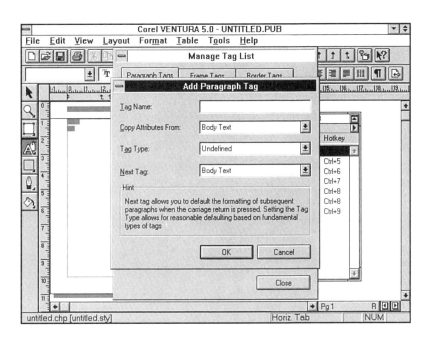

Figure 8.2
The Add
Paragraph Tag
dialog box.

5. Click on OK to return to the Manage Tag List dialog box. The new tag is added to the **T**ag List. The new tag is a copy of the existing tag until you reforma: it. Refer to the section "Editing Tags" in this chapter for information on formatting the new tag. Click on the Close button to return to your document.

The Add Paragraph Tag dialog box provides additional options for creating new tags. The T**a**g Type and **N**ext Tag commands are discussed in the following sections.

Selecting a Tag Type

The Add Paragraph Tag dialog box provides an option for selecting a tag type. The tag type classifies the new tag into a specific category such as body text, headings, lists, and tabbed text. When you select a tag type, VENTURA applies certain default attributes to the new tag. These attributes are consistent with the tag type. So Headings, for example, are formatted to be left-aligned with no hyphenation. Table 8.1 lists the default attributes applied to tags created by specifying a tag type.

Table 8.1
Defaults Applied to Tags Generated with Tag Type

Tag Type	Attributes Applied
Heading	Left Alignment, Top Vertical Alignment, No Left or Right Indent, Hyphenation Off, Allow No Breaks Within, No Tab Settings, No Special Effects, Line Break After, Space Above 20 points, Space Below 10 points, Keep with Next Paragraph On
Body Text	Justified Horizontal Alignment, Top Vertical Alignment, No Left or Right Indent, Hyphenation On, Allow Breaks Within, No Tab Settings, No Special Effects, Line Break After, Space Above 0, Space Below 0, Keep with Next Paragraph Off
List Item	Left Horizontal Alignment, Top Vertical Alignment, No Left or Right Indent, Hyphenation Off, Allow Breaks Within, No Tab Settings, Bullet Special Effects, Line Break After, Space Above 0, Space Below 0, Keep with Next Paragraph Off
Tabbed Text	Left Alignment, Top Vertical Alignment, No Left or Right Indent, Hyphenation Off, Allow Breaks Within, Six Tab Settings, No Special Effects, Line Break After, Space Above 0, Space Below 0, Keep with Next Paragraph Off
Table Text	Left Alignment, Middle Vertical Alignment, In from Left 3 points, In from Right 3 points, Hyphenation Off, Allow No Breaks Within, No Tab Settings, No Special effects, Line Break After, Space Above 2 points, Space Below 4 points Keep with Next Paragraph Off

These defaults can also be found in the CORELVP.INI file stored in the COREL50\CONFIG directory.

In the previous exercise for creating a new tag, the new tag was built by copying the attributes of an existing tag. Doing this in conjunction with selecting a tag type can produce unexpected results such as a conflict between the attributes from the tag type and the attributes of the copied tag. For instance, the attributes from the existing tag can specify right alignment, and the attributes for the tag type can specify left alignment. Because of the potential confusion resulting from this conflict, it is recommended that you use the Undefined tag type if you are building a new tag from an existing tag.

If all new tags are based on the body text tag, you might want to use the tag type as a way to separate the tags into categories. Sorting tags by type is covered later in this chapter in the section "Using the Tag Roll-Up."

Controlling the Next Tag

When you press Enter to end one paragraph and begin another, the new paragraph uses the same tag as the previous paragraph. The **N**ext Tag option in the Add Paragraph Tag dialog box enables you to build tags that are automatically followed by another type of tag.

Instead of following a heading tag with another heading tag, for instance, you could instruct the heading tag to be followed by a subheading tag. When you pressed Enter after a paragraph using the heading tag, the new paragraph would automatically be designated as a subheading tag. To specify that your new tag is followed by another paragraph tag, click on the down arrow by **N**ext Tag. Select the tag name from the list of tags and click on OK.

Editing Tags

New tags are created using the attributes of an existing tag. As described in the previous section, the new tag is an exact "copy" of the existing tag until you alter it. After creating a new tag, you need to edit the tag to meet your formatting requirements. There are two ways to do this. First, you can return to the document and apply the new tag to a paragraph. Then, use the Tagged Text tool to make all of the formatting changes to the new tag. The steps for formatting a tag are covered in the "Modifying Paragraph Tags" section of Chapter 7.

VENTURA provides a second way to format new tags. You can edit the tag while working in the Manage Tag List dialog box. The following exercise demonstrates how to edit a paragraph tag in the Manage Tag List dialog box. If you want, you can edit the paragraph tag built in the previous exercise.

1. After creating a new tag, select it in the **T**ag List in the Manage Tag List dialog box.

2. Click on the **E**dit Tags button to display the Paragraph Settings dialog box as displayed in figure 8.3. The Paragraph Settings dialog box is also used to format tags already applied to text.

Figure 8.3

The Paragraph Settings dialog box.

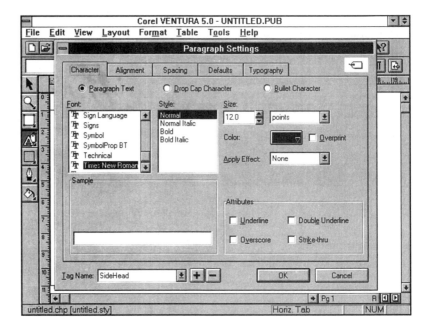

3. Use the various options in the dialog box to select font, style, control horizontal and vertical alignment, and adjust spacing.

4. Click on OK to return to the Manage Tag List dialog box. Click on the Close button to return to the document. The newly formatted tag is now ready to be applied to the text in your document.

Renaming Tags

VENTURA enables you to rename the tags in the Tag list. Renaming tags allows you to group them into alphabetical categories. You can change the tag names Main Heading and Sub Heading to Head1 and Head2. These two names would then appear together in the Tag List. Renaming tags also enables you to use names that are more in line with your type of work. For instance, a Chapter Title tag could be renamed as Course Topic to correspond with the needs of a training manual.

You can rename any tag except the Body Text paragraph tag. The following exercise shows you how to rename a paragraph tag:

1. Select Manage Tag List from the Format menu. The Manage Tag List dialog box appears. Select the tag you want to rename from the Tag List.

2. Click on the Rename Tag button to display the Rename Paragraph Tag dialog box shown in figure 8.4.

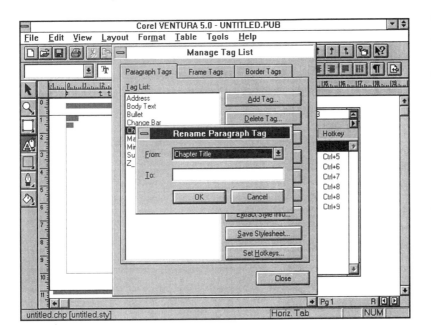

Figure 8.4

The Rename Paragraph Tag dialog box.

3. The tag to be renamed appears in the From box. You can click on the down arrow and select another tag if necessary. Click in the To box and enter the new tag name. Remember you can use spaces and up to 15 characters.

4. Click on OK to return to the Manage Tag List dialog box. The new tag name appears in the Tag List. Click on the Close button to return to your document. All paragraphs using the old tag name are automatically updated to use the new tag name.

Don't forget that renaming tags affects the style sheet. For instance, if you change the "main heading" tag to "section heading," this new name appears in all chapter files using the modified style sheet.

Deleting Tags

Scrolling through a long list of unused tags can make the whole tagging process cumbersome and frustrating. When you don't need all the paragraph tags supplied by the style sheet, just delete them. Deleting tags allows you to streamline the **T**ag List by removing unused tags. You can then focus on the tags specific to your document.

Changes made to the **T**ag List, such as creating new tags, renaming, and deleting tags are not saved as part of the style sheet until the publication or style sheet file is saved.

When deleting a tag, you are asked to specify which tag should be applied to any paragraphs using the deleted tag. For instance, if you remove a bullet tag, you can specify that the Number List tag is applied to all paragraphs using the deleted bullet tag. You cannot delete the Body Text tag. In the following exercise, you delete a paragraph tag:

1. Select Ma**n**age Tag List from the For**m**at menu. The Manage Tag List dialog box appears. Select the tag you want to delete from the **T**ag List.

2. Click on the **D**elete Tag button to display the Delete Paragraph Tag dialog box shown in figure 8.5.

3. The tag to be deleted appears in the **D**elete box. You can click on the down arrow and select another tag if necessary.

4. Click on the down arrow by the **R**eformat Text As box and select the tag you want applied to all paragraphs using the deleted tag.

5. Click on OK to return to the Manage Tag List dialog box. The deleted tag name is removed from the **T**ag List. Click on the Close button to return to your document. Paragraphs using the deleted tag name are automatically updated to use the tag selected to replace the deleted tag.

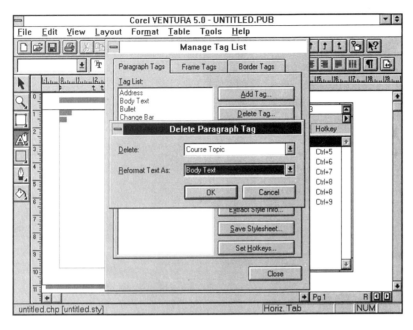

II

Building a VENTURA Document

Figure 8.5
The Delete
Paragraph Tag
dialog box.

Merging Tags

Paragraph tags can be copied or "merged" from one style sheet to another.
Merging tags allows you to "borrow" a tag from another style sheet, instead of re-
creating the tag in the new style sheet. For instance, suppose you produced a
report with a tag featuring a drop cap letter and want to use the drop cap tag in
your new magazine. Rather than spending time producing another tag with the
same formatting, you could copy the drop cap tag from the report style sheet into
the magazine style sheet.

The Body Text tag cannot be merged from one style sheet to another.

After you select the style sheet containing the tags you to copy, VENTURA
displays a listing of the tags. From there, you can choose the specific tags you
want merged into your document. If you merge a tag with the same name as a tag
already found in your document, the attributes of the merged tag overwrite the
existing tag.

For example, suppose the current style sheet includes a Heading tag formatted in 24-point Times Roman. If you merge a Heading tag from another style sheet that is formatted in 36-point Times Roman, the 24-point Heading tag is replaced by the 36-point Heading tag. If you do attempt to merge a tag with the same name as one found in the current style sheet, VENTURA displays the message box as shown in figure 8.6. Select Yes to overwrite the old tag, select No to cancel merging that particular tag.

Figure 8.6

You must confirm that the attributes of the new tag will overwrite the existing tag.

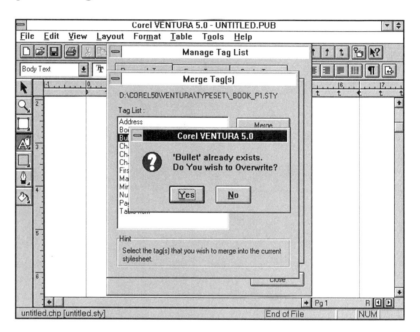

Use the following steps to merge tags from a specific style sheet into your current style sheet. If desired, you can merge the Headline paragraph tag from the mag.sty style sheet stored in the VENTURA\VPSTYLE directory.

1. Select Ma**n**age Tag List from the For**m**at menu. The Manage Tag List dialog box appears.

2. Click on the **M**erge Tag button to display the Open Style Sheet dialog box shown in figure 8.7.

3. Select the style sheet containing the tags you want to merge and click on OK. You might have to change the drive and directory. VENTURA's predesigned style sheets are stored in the VENTURA\TYPESET and VENTURA\VPSTYLE directories.

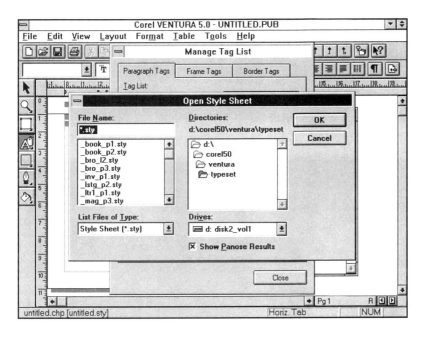

Figure 8.7
The Open Style Sheet dialog box.

4. The Merge Tag(s) dialog box appears as displayed in figure 8.8. The name of the selected style sheet appears at the top of the dialog box. The tags in the selected style sheet are listed in the Tag List.

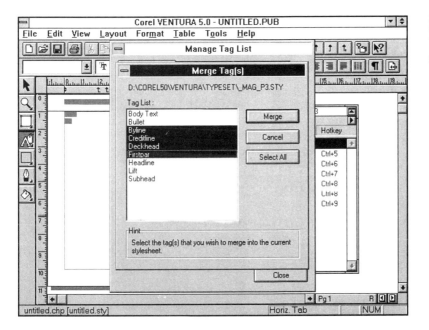

Figure 8.8
The Merge Tag(s) dialog box.

5. Select the tags you want to merge. You can select several tags simply by clicking on them with the mouse. In figure 8.8, four contiguous tags were selected.

6. Click on the Merge button. The new tags are added to the **T**ag List in the Manage Tag List dialog box. If any of the tags selected to be merged use the same name as a tag already in the document, a message appears asking you to overwrite the old tag.

7. Click on the Close button to return to your document. You can now apply the merged tags to paragraphs in your document.

There is no link between the merged tags in the current style sheet and the style sheet where the tags were originally copied. This means any changes made to the merged tags affect only the current style sheet.

Using the Tags Roll-Up To View and Manage Tags

The Tags Roll-up makes it easy to view and manage the tags used to format your document. The commands in the Tags Roll-up are also found in the Manage Tag List dialog box; however, you may prefer using the roll-up to access these commands. Using the Tags Roll-up you can add, rename, delete and edit tags. To display the roll-up, select **T**ags Roll-up from the T**o**ols menu. As shown in figure 8.9, each tag in the current chapter file is displayed.

In addition to listing the tags available in your document, the Tags Roll-up offers several options for managing your tags. Click on the menu button to display a fly-out of the following commands:

✔ Add Tag enables you to add new paragraph tags

✔ Delete Tag deletes paragraph tags

✔ Rename Tag enables you to rename tags

✔ Edit Tag lets you edit the text attributes of a tag

✔ Set Hotkeys displays a list of hotkeys to speed up paragraph tagging

The steps for adding, deleting, renaming, and editing tags were discussed in previous sections. Using hotkeys to apply tags is discussed in Chapter 7. The Sort Tags By and Show Generated Tags commands are discussed in the following sections.

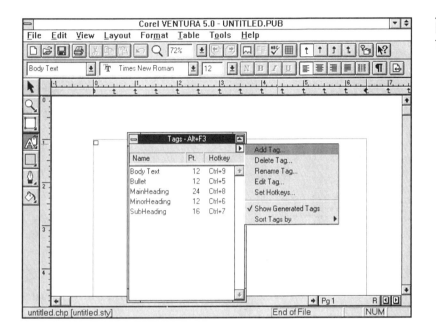

Figure 8.9
The Tags Roll-up.

II

Building a VENTURA Document

Sorting Tags

Sorting tags enables you to control the order the tags appear in the roll-up. Changing the sort order affects only how the tags are listed in the Tags Roll-up, not the order of the tags in the Tag list. Select the Sort Tags By option to reveal the flyout menu. As displayed in figure 8.10, you can sort the tags according to the tag name, point size, hotkeys, and tag type.

Both the point size and hotkeys sorting methods use ascending order. Tags using the larger point sizes appear at the bottom of the list. Sorting by tag type sorts tags into categories based on the tag type selected to make the tag. Refer to the previous section, "Selecting a Tag Type," for more information.

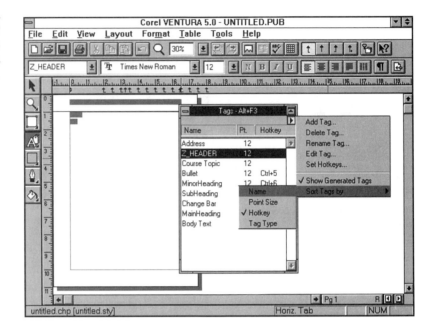

Figure 8.10
The Tags Roll-up
with the Sort Tags
By option selected.

Showing Generated Tags

The Show Generated Tags option displays paragraph tags used to format special text paragraphs, such as footnotes, and indexes. The generated tags will not be displayed in the Tags Roll-up unless the Show Generated Tags option is enabled. This command displays the generated tags in the Tags Roll-up only; it does not affect the display in the Tag list. The following section examines working with generated tags in more detail.

Working with Generated Tags

Generated tags are tags automatically created by VENTURA when you build certain types of text paragraphs, such as captions and headers and footers. For instance, when you create a header, VENTURA applies the generated tag Z_HEADER to the header text. Although you did not create the generated tag, you can modify the tag just as you would any other paragraph tag. Generated tag names, with the exception of the TABLE TEXT tag, are always preceded by the letter Z and an underscore (_).

By default, VENTURA does not display the generated tags in the Tag list. If you create a header and click in the header text with the text tool, the Tag list

appears blank. Actually, the Z_HEADER tag is used to format the header text, but the tag name is not visible in the Tag list. You must turn on the Generated Tags option to view the generated tag names.

Even though the generated tag names do not appear in the Tag list, you can still modify the attributes of the generated tag. Using the Tagged Text tool, click in the paragraph formatted with the generated tag and select Paragraph from the For**m**at menu.

To view the generated tags used in your document, select Pre**f**erences from the T**o**ols menu. In the Preferences dialog box, select the View tab to display the options, as shown in figure 8.11. Click to place an *X* in the G**e**nerated Tags option. Click on OK to return to the document. The generated tags used in the document appear in the Tags list. For instance, if you have created headers in your document, the Z_HEADER tag appears. However, if you have not created a caption, the Z_CAPTION tag does not appear.

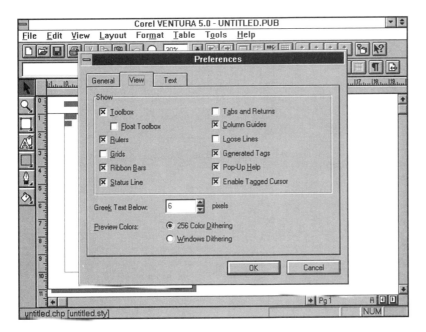

Figure 8.11
The Preferences dialog box with the View tab selected.

Other options in the View tab let you remove the toolbox, rulers, ribbon bar, and status line from the display. As discussed in Chapter 3, you can also turn on the column guides and show tab and return symbols in the dialog box.

Table 8.2 lists the generated tags applied by VENTURA.

Table 8.2
VENTURA's Generated Tag Names

Generated Tag	Applied to this Text Element
Z_HEADER	Header text
Z_FOOTER	Footer text
Z_SEC1 thru 10	Automatic section numbers
Z_TABLE TEXT	Text entered into table cells
Z_LABEL FIG	Automatic figure numbers
Z_LABEL TBL	Automatic table numbers
Z_CAPTION	Text entered into a caption frame
Z_LABEL_CAP	Additional Caption text
Z_TOC TITLE	Title for table of contents
Z_TOC LVL 1 thru 10	Levels for table of contents
Z_INDEX LTR	Index Letter
Z_INDEX MAIN	Main index entries
Z_INDEX SUB	Sub index entries
Z_INDEX TITLE	Title for Index
Z_FNOT #	Footnote numbers
Z_FNOT ENTRY	Footnote Text
Z_BOXTEXT	Text entered into Box text objects

You will learn more about formatting generated tags in later chapters focusing on footnotes, indexes, and tables of contents.

Printing Style Sheet Information

Printing the style sheet is an invaluable way to examine the page layout and paragraph tag information used in your document. Printing the style sheet gives you a "hands-on" copy of the formatting for each paragraph tag, enabling you to examine how the tags are set up.

Some paragraph tag formatting can get quite complex. For instance, headings often use the Keep With Next command, so the headings are always followed by text and don't appear alone at the bottom of the page. If you've ever tried to figure out the indents, spacing, or hyphenation of a tag, you'll appreciate the way printing the style sheet enables you to inspect the formatting of each tag. Figure 8.12 is an example of how tag information from the book_p1.sty style sheet looks when printed. As you can see, the attributes of the Major Heading tag are displayed in detail.

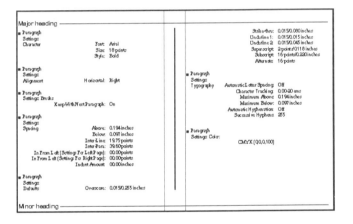

Figure 8.12
Example of printed style sheet information.

When instructed, VENTURA generates a text file of information about the style sheet currently in use. You can then start a new publication and import the generated text file into the chapter.VENTURA supplies the Stylog.sty style sheet to format the generated text file so that it can be easily read. After your style sheet information has been formatted, you can print.

II

Building a VENTURA Document

Tip

Printing the style sheet is a great way to facilitate the sharing of document formatting between a group of page designers all working on the same project.

For example, if the document you are currently working with uses the book.sty style sheet, VENTURA generates a file about the book.sty style sheet. Use the following exercise to print out a style sheet:

1. Select Ma**n**age Tag List from the For**m**at menu. The Manage Tag List dialog box appears.

2. Click on the E**x**tract Style Info button to display the File Save As dialog box shown in figure 8.13.

Figure 8.13
The File Save As
dialog box.

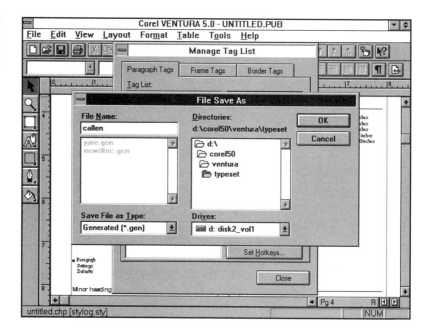

3. Change to the drive and directory where you want to save the generated text file. Notice the Save File As Type box displays "Generated (*.gen)."

4. Enter a file name in the File **N**ame box. It is not necessary to add a file extension; VENTURA automatically applies .GEN. Click on OK to return to the Manage Tag List dialog box. Click on the Close button to return to the document.

New Riders Publishing
INSIDE
SERIES

5. Begin a new publication, selecting the Stylog.sty style sheet. This style sheet is located in the VENTURA\TYPESET directory.

6. Select the base page frame with the Pick tool and choose Load **T**ext from the **F**ile menu. Change to the drive and directory where the generated text file was saved. Click on the down arrow by List File of Type and select VENTURA Generated File (*.gen).

7. Select the generated text file and click on OK. The text is loaded into the page.

8. Select **P**rint from the **F**ile menu and click on OK. The style sheet information is printed.

Printing issues and techniques are covered in depth in Chapter 19, "Printing in VENTURA."

Finding and Replacing Tags

VENTURA's Find and Replace feature enables you to search your document for a specific paragraph tag, then replace that tag with another. As an example, suppose after tagging your entire document you decide that the paragraphs using the "subhead" tag need more emphasis and should be tagged as "minor heading." Rather than visually stepping through the document to locate and change each "subhead," use Find and Replace to search the document for any occurrence of the "subhead" tag and replace it with the "minor heading" tag.

The following exercise illustrates the use of the Find and Replace command:

1. From the **E**dit menu, choose Find and **R**eplace. The Find and Replace dialog box appears; click on the **P**aragraph Tag radio button at the top of the dialog box. The Find and Replace dialog box is shown in figure 8.14.

2. Click on the down arrow by the Fi**n**d What list box and select the name of the tag you want to find.

3. Click on the down arrow by the Replace **W**ith list box and select the tag you want to use in place of the current tag.

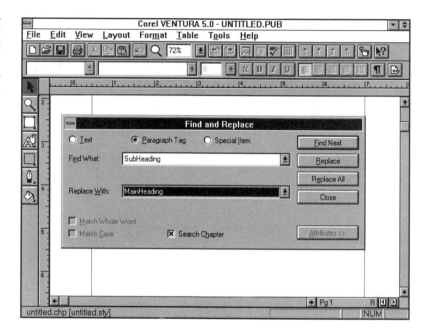

Figure 8.14
The Find and
Replace dialog
box with the
Paragraph Tag
radio button
selected.

4. Choose the Search **Ch**apter option to instruct VENTURA to search through the entire chapter. Otherwise, the search is conducted only from the insertion point to the end of the chapter.

5. Click on the **F**ind Next button to find the next occurrence of the tag in the document. Click on the **R**eplace button to change the tag. Click on the R**e**place All button to automatically change each occurrence of the tag. To terminate the search, click on the Close button.

It is important to note that character attributes applied with the Freeform Text tool will not be affected by changing the paragraph tag.

Part III

Advanced VENTURA Options and Techniques

Chapter Snapshot

The difference between an amateur and professional quality document often lies in the special type effects that the desktop designer uses. VENTURA enables the designer to really add visual impact to the printed word. In this chapter, you learn to do the following:

By using advanced text formatting options, you gain control over your page layouts. This chapter covers virtually every aspect of text manipulation.

9

CHAPTER

Advanced Text Formatting Options

There is much more to formatting text than simply selecting fonts and underlining important words. To produce good-looking documents, you must consider details, such as where text is positioned on the page and the spacing between words. Consider the use of tabs and indents to organize text into easy-to-read sections. While you're at it, it's a good idea to spruce up the page with some special effects by adding ruling lines and rotating text. VENTURA is noted for its many type design options, enabling you precise control of its flexible and powerful type features.

This chapter focuses on advanced text formatting options, beginning with an examination of the special effects available in VENTURA. Here, you will learn how to create big cap effects, rotate text, add bullets, and apply ruling lines to your text paragraphs. The next section discusses indenting text paragraphs and controlling the spacing and tracking between words. The chapter also discusses the options for setting line, column, and page breaks to control where text is placed on the page. The chapter ends with a look at setting tabs in VENTURA, exploring the types of tabs available, and using them to create tables of information.

Creating Good Page Designs

The essence of professional page design is the placement of page elements in a way that catches and holds the reader's eye. Explore the pages of magazines and newspapers to find ideas for special effects to enhance and decorate the pages of your document. The really well-done page layouts will pull you into the page and direct your eye around the layout in a way that unconsciously forces you to consume the information in a logical manner.

VENTURA provides options for creating dazzling page design effects. You can incorporate these effects into the formatting of your paragraph tags or to individual paragraphs. As discussed in Chapter 7, "Formatting Tagged and Freeform Text," use the Tagged Text tool to apply formatting to the paragraph tag. For instance, when adding bullets to text, you can add the bullets to the formatting specifications of a paragraph tag, enabling you to apply the bullets to multiple paragraphs. When the Freeform Text tool is used, the text formatting is applied to the selected paragraph only; the tag is not affected. You might, for example, want to rotate one paragraph of text without affecting other paragraphs using the same tag. Each of the effects covered in this section, with the exception of ruling lines, can be applied with the Tagged Text or Freeform Text tool.

Creating Drop Caps

The first letter in a paragraph can be enlarged to create a special effect known as a *big cap*, or *drop cap*. You can further enhance this effect by assigning a different font to the character. Big caps placed at the beginning of an article provide a visual transition between the headline and text. Big caps also help to cue the reader to the start of major sections in documents. As displayed in figure 9.1, big caps can be *dropped*, or set, into the paragraph they introduce. You can create a *raised* big cap effect where the letter sits on the first line of text, extending into the white space above the text they introduce.

VENTURA enables you to select the type face, type size, and color for the drop cap letter. By default, VENTURA will drop the letter into the first two lines of text. You can increase the number of lines for larger font sizes. For instance, a drop cap set in 60-point Avant Garde looks good when dropped into four lines of 12-point body text. VENTURA also provides options for nudging the letter up or down to achieve perfect placement. To create a raised big cap effect, change the number of lines to one. The letter then extends above the paragraph.

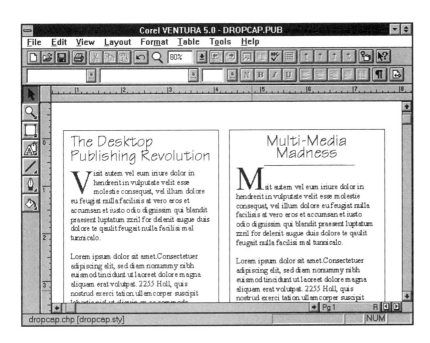

Figure 9.1
With VENTURA, you can create different effects with drop cap letters.

For the best effect, use a significantly larger type size for the big cap letter. For instance, in 12-point type, try a 30- or 36-point big cap letter. Big caps that are too small can distract from your page design.

When you want to incorporate the big cap effect to become part of the paragraph tag, use the Tagged Text tool. For example, you can create a tag called "first para" to add a big cap letter to the first paragraph of text following the heading. Use the Freeform Text tool when you want the big cap to be applied only to the selected paragraph.

The following steps illustrate creating a drop cap effect:

1. Select either the Tagged Text or Freeform Text tool and click inside the paragraph where you want to add the drop cap letter. The insertion point appears in the text.

2. Select Paragraph from the Format menu. If you are using the Tagged Text tool, the Paragraph Settings dialog box appears; if you are using the Freeform Text tool, the Override Paragraph Settings dialog box appears. Select the Character tab sheet and click on the **D**rop Cap Character option at the top to display the dialog box shown in figure 9.2.

III

Advanced VENTURA Options and Techniques

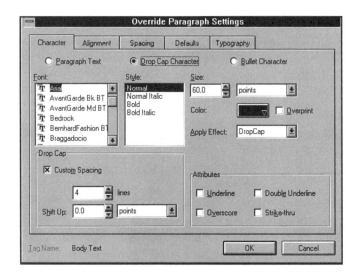

Figure 9.2
The Override
Paragraph
Settings dialog
box with the Drop
Cap Character
option selected.

3. Select the desired font, style, and size for the drop cap letter. Click on the Color drop-down list to choose another color for the drop cap.

4. The Custo**m** Spacing option is by default set to 2 lines, meaning the drop cap letter will drop two lines into the paragraph. To change the number of lines, click on the Custo**m** Spacing option and enter the desired line number.

5. Click on the **A**pply Effect drop down list and choose DropCap. (You will not get the effect if DropCap is not selected.)

6. Click on OK. The first letter of the selected paragraph is enlarged to your specifications. If you used the Tagged Text tool to add the drop cap, all paragraphs using the same tag are also affected.

You might have to experiment with the type size and line spacing to get the drop cap letter to look exactly as you want. Use the S**h**ift Up option found at the bottom of the dialog box to move the letter up or down in small increments until you get a precise fit.

Adding Bullets to Paragraphs

Placing bullets in front of items in a list is a great way to call attention to information, while adding visual diversity to the page. VENTURA provides a wide selection of symbols that can be used as bullet characters. Any character from any installed font can be used as a bullet. As displayed in figure 9.3, using the appropriate symbol can play a key role in communicating your message.

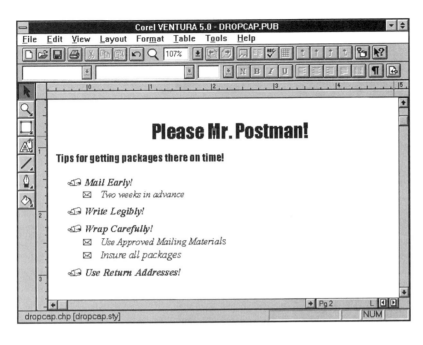

Figure 9.3
You can choose
from a variety of
symbols to build
bulleted lists.

When you add bullets, VENTURA automatically formats the paragraph with a hanging indent. In a *hanging indent*, the bullet character extends or hangs to the left of the rest of the text in the paragraph. You will learn more about setting indents later in this chapter.

 To preview all of the characters available for bullets, refer to the Character Sets in your VENTURA software documentation.

When you want the bullet to become part of the paragraph tag, use the Tagged Text tool. Use the Freeform Text tool when you want the bullet to be applied only to the selected paragraph. The following exercise illustrates adding a bullet to a paragraph:

1. Select either the Tagged Text or Freeform Text tool and click inside the paragraph where you want to add the bullet. The insertion point appears in the text.

2. Select Paragraph from the Format menu. The Paragraph Settings dialog box appears with the Character tab sheet selected. Click on the **B**ullet Character option at the top (see fig. 9.4).

III

Advanced VENTURA Options and Techniques

Figure 9.4
The Paragraph
Settings dialog
box with the Bullet
Character option
selected.

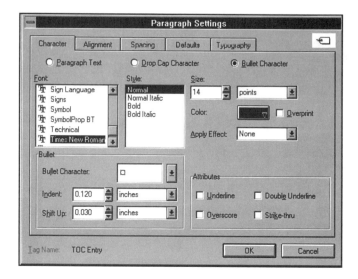

3. Select the desired font, style, and size for the bullet. For graphic symbols such as telephones, disks, and flags, select the symbol font called Wingdings. Click on the Color drop down list to choose another color for the bullet character.

4. Click on the down arrow by Bullet Character and select the desired bullet shape.

5. Click on the down arrow by **A**pply Effect and choose Bullet. (You will not get the effect if Bullet is not selected.)

6. Click on OK. The bullet character is added and the paragraph is indented. If you used the Tagged Text tool to add the bullet, all paragraphs using the same tag are also affected.

Use the **In**dent setting to adjust the spacing between the bullet and the text. For instance, entering 36 points indents the text 36 points from the left edge of the bullet character. Larger bullet shapes might require more spacing. Use the **Sh**ift Up option to move the bullet character up or down in small increments until you get a desirable position.

Another option for creating drop caps is to choose a letter for the bullet shape instead of a symbol. In this way, you can design "freestanding" drop caps that float in the left margin of the paragraph (see fig. 9.5). You may have to tinker with the **In**dent and **Sh**ift Up settings to get the character to position by the text correctly.

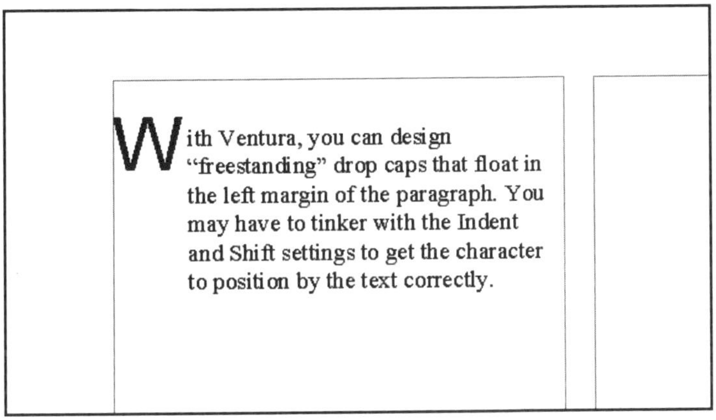

W ith Ventura, you can design "freestanding" drop caps that float in the left margin of the paragraph. You may have to tinker with the Indent and Shift settings to get the character to position by the text correctly.

Figure 9.5
You can create "freestanding" drop cap effects with the bullets option.

Rotating Text

Text can be rotated in 90-degree increments with VENTURA. Rotated text can be useful to create graphic tables and run credits along the side of a photograph, such as displayed in figure 9.6. The table in the figure was created with the box text graphic tool. Each name across the top is in a separate box. The text was then rotated in the box text.

The photo credit was placed in a free frame touching the photo frame. It is a good idea to draw the free frame larger than necessary and then size the frame after the text is rotated. Although you can rotate text on the base page, you will have better luck rotating text placed in a free frame, because you can move and size the frame to fit your needs.

With VENTURA, you can control how rotated text is placed in the frame. Use the Max **H**eight option to specify the maximum width a text line can occupy. If the text reaches the set limit, it wraps to a new line. By default, VENTURA sets rotated text to a maximum of three inches. In figure 9.6, the rotated text in the photo credit is set at two inches.

Rotating frames allows more flexibility in the amount of rotation. When you rotate a free frame, the text inside the free frame is also rotated. Refer to the next chapter, "Advanced Free Frame Options," for more information.

III

Advanced VENTURA Options and Techniques

Figure 9.6
Rotated text is great for annotating drawings and photo credits.

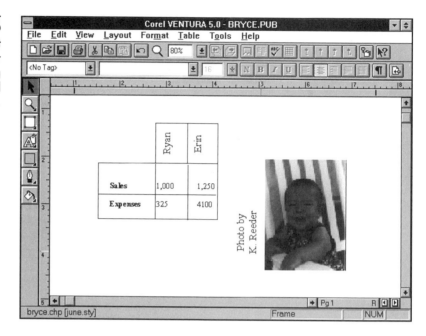

When you want the text rotation to be included in the paragraph tag, use the Tagged Text tool. Use the Freeform Text tool when you want to rotate text in only the selected paragraph. The following exercise illustrates rotating text 90 degrees:

1. Select either the Tagged Text or Freeform Text tool and click inside the paragraph you want to rotate. The insertion point appears in the text.

2. Select Paragraph from the Format menu. The Paragraph Settings dialog box appears. Click on the Spacing tab to display the dialog box shown in figure 9.7.

3. In the Text Rotation section of the dialog box, click on the down arrow by Angle and select 90 degrees. A preview of the rotation is displayed.

4. In the Max Height box, enter the amount of space you want to place between the text and the top of the frame.

5. Click on OK. The text is rotated 90 degrees. If you used the Tagged Text tool to rotate the text, all paragraphs using the same tag are also affected.

If you are not getting the rotated text to appear exactly where you want in the frame, try adjusting the horizontal and vertical alignment of the text. In addition,

try to complete all text editing before rotating text. When you attempt to edit rotated text, some of the text may simply disappear. If you must edit text after it has been rotated, use the Copy Editor to make viewing and editing the text easier.

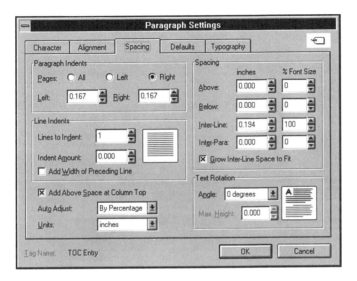

Figure 9.7
The Paragraph Settings dialog box with the Spacing tab selected.

Applying Ruling Lines

Ruling lines are often used to embellish titles and headings. As displayed in figure 9.8, the lines help organize text by joining headlines and body text or separating quotes from body text. With VENTURA, you can place up to three lines in varying thicknesses above, below, above and below, or around a paragraph of text.

Figure 9.8
Ruling lines lend organization to page layouts.

When setting up the ruling lines, you can select to have the line run the width of the text, the width of the column guides or frame, or from margin to margin. For instance, in figure 9.9, the line under the heading stretches across the entire frame area, while the lines above the subheadings stretch across the width of the text. You can also enter a custom width for the line. For example, you can specify that the ruling line be exactly three inches wide. VENTURA also enables you to adjust the spacing above and below the ruling lines.

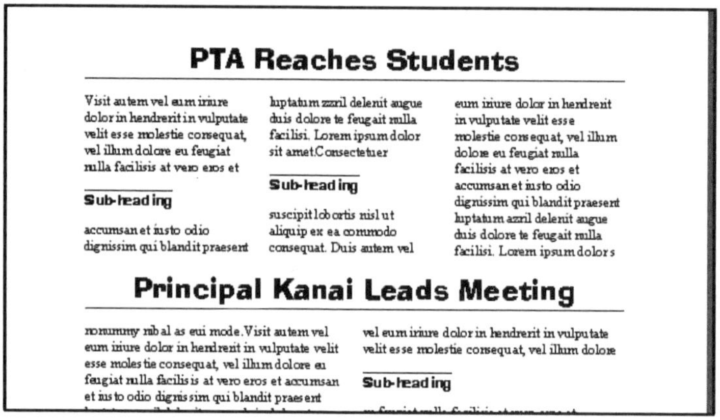

Figure 9.9
You can control the line width and spacing to accommodate your page design.

PTA Reaches Students

Visit autem vel eum iriure dolor in hendrerit in vulputate velit esse molestie consequat, vel illum dolore eu feugiat nulla facilisis at vero eros et

Sub-heading

accumsan et iusto odio dignissim qui blandit praesent

luptatum zzril delenit augue duis dolore te feugait nulla facilisi. Lorem ipsum dolor sit amet.Consectetuer

Sub-heading

suscipit lobortis nisl ut aliquip ex ea commodo consequat. Duis autem vel

eum iriure dolor in hendrerit in vulputate velit esse molestie consequat, vel illum dolore eu feugiat nulla facilisis at vero eros et accumsan et iusto odio dignissim qui blandit praesent luptatum zzril delenit augue duis dolore te feugait nulla facilisi. Lorem ipsum dolors

Principal Kanai Leads Meeting

nonummy nibh al as eui mode.Visit autem vel eum iriure dolor in hendrerit in vulputate velit esse molestie consequat, vel illum dolore eu feugiat nulla facilisis at vero eros et accumsan et iusto odio dignissim qui blandit praesent

vel eum iriure dolor in hendrerit in vulputate velit esse molestie consequat, vel illum dolore

Sub-heading

Ruling lines can only be created with the Tagged Text tool. The specified ruling line is then added to all paragraphs using the modified tag. The following exercise illustrates how to apply ruling lines to text:

1. Select the Tagged Text tool and click inside the paragraph where you want to apply ruling lines. The insertion point appears in the text.

2. Select Ruling **L**ines from the Fo**rm**at menu. The Ruling Lines dialog box appears as displayed in figure 9.10. There are three tabs—Above, Below, and Around.

3. The first box in the top-right specifies which tag will be affected by the ruling lines. Click on the down arrow by the **R**ule Style box and select where you want the ruling lines to appear: Above, Below, Above & Below, or Around. After you make a selection, VENTURA brings the appropriate tab sheet to the front.

4. Click on the down arrow by Border **W**idth and select the desired width the ruling line should span. The ruling line can run the width of the text, margin (line will run margin to margin), column, or frame, or can be

customized. If Custom is selected, enter the line width in the Custom Wi**d**th box. If you desire, enter an amount in the Custom **I**ndent box to indent the line from the left.

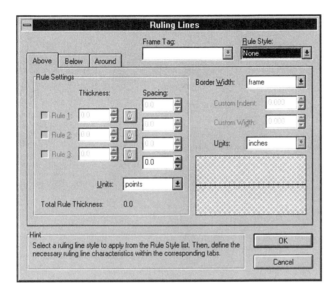

Figure 9.10
The Ruling Lines dialog box.

5. Under Rule Settings, click to place an *X* by the Rule 1 option. Enter the desired line thickness. For instance, if the Units option is set to Points, 1.0 creates a one-point ruling line.

6. Two spacing options are available. Enter the amount of space you want placed above the ruling line in the first box, and the amount of space you want placed below the ruling lines in the second box. The sample box provides a preview of your line width and spacing selections. In figure 9.11, the line width (thickness) is 4 points, the above spacing is 12, and the below spacing is 3.

7. Click on OK. The ruling line is added to the selected paragraph. All paragraphs using that same tag are also affected.

As previously mentioned, you can place up to three ruling lines above, below, or around a paragraph. To add a second or third line, click on the Rule 2 and Rule 3 boxes and enter the desired line thickness. The thickness of ruling lines is generally measured in points. There are 72 points in an inch. To use another measurement system (such as inches) to specify the line thickness, click on the down arrow by **U**nits in the Ruling Settings portion of the dialog box and select the desired system.

III

Advanced VENTURA Options and Techniques

Figure 9.11
The sample box
lets you preview
ruling line
selections.

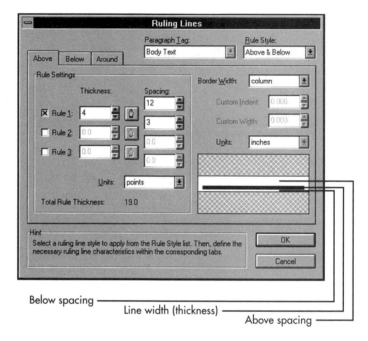

Figure 9.11
The sample box
lets you preview
ruling line
selections.

Below spacing ——————
Line width (thickness) ——————
Above spacing ——————

Additional Ruling Line Options

As displayed in figure 9.12, ruling lines can be embellished with arrowheads and dashed line styles. VENTURA provides a wide selection of arrows and dashed lines. The line thickness determines the size of the arrowheads and the spacing and thickness of the dashed line. In figure 9.12, the second line and arrowhead are larger than the first because the line thickness has been increased.

Figure 9.12
You can add
arrows and
dashed lines to
your ruling lines.

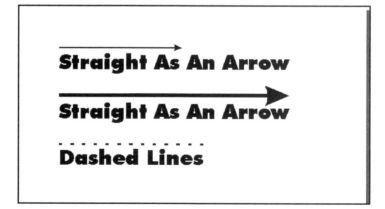

The following exercise illustrates adding color, arrows, and dashed lines to ruling lines:

1. In the Ruling Lines dialog box, an Outline button (with a pen nib on it) appears between the Thickness and Spacing options for each ruling line. Click on the Outline button to reveal the Outline Pen dialog box as displayed in figure 9.13.

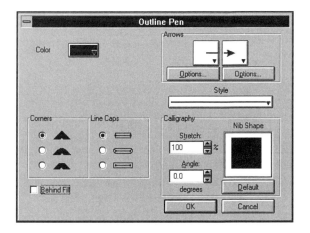

Figure 9.13
The Outline Pen dialog box.

2. To select another color for the ruling lines, click on the Color drop-down list. Select the desired color from the color palette.

3. The buttons in the Arrows section of the dialog box add arrowheads to your ruling line. Click on the first button to reveal a drop-down list of available arrowheads. Select the desired arrowhead for the beginning of the line. Click on the second button to select the desired arrowhead for the end of the line.

4. To add a dashed line style, click on the white button under Style and select the desired dashed line.

5. When you are finished making selections, click on OK. The line color and options are previewed in the sample box. Click on OK again to return to the document.

Controlling Paragraph Indents

Indenting paragraphs enables you to add space to the left or right sides of a paragraph. As displayed in figure 9.14, indenting is often used to call attention to quotes or to set off a series of numbered steps. In VENTURA, an indent is the amount of space from the column or margin guide to the beginning of the text. The steps in figure 9.14 have a $^1/_2$-inch left indent, and the quote has a one-inch left and right indent.

On the Homefront

Our resident handy person, Bryce Benjamin, offers these tips for decking the halls at your home.

1.   Get the right tools.

2.   Get a ladder.

3.   Check your electric capacity.

4.   Get a helper.

> *"The single most important safety precaution you can take is to get someone to help you do the job."*

With VENTURA, you can specify different indent amounts for the left and right pages of a document. For instance, you can format a "steps" tag to have a one-inch left indent on all right pages and a 1 $^1/_2$-inch left indent on all left pages. Setting separate indents for left and right pages can be especially important when you have uneven margins set up to accommodate the binding of the document. When you want the indents to be the same on both the left and right pages, choose the All option.

When you want the indenting to become part of the paragraph tag, use the Tagged Text tool. Use the Freeform Text tool when you want to indent the text in the selected paragraph only. The following exercise illustrates indenting text:

1. Select either the Tagged Text or Freeform Text tool and click inside the paragraph you want to indent. The insertion point appears in the text.

2. Select Paragraph from the Format menu. The Paragraph Settings dialog box appears. Click on the Spacing tab to display the dialog box shown in figure 9.15.

3. In the Paragraph Indents section of the dialog box, click on All, Left, or Right to select the pages that will reflect the new indent settings.

4. In the **L**eft box, enter the desired amount for the left indent. In the **R**ight box, enter the desired amount for the right indent.

5. Click on OK. The text is indented to your specifications. If you used the Tagged Text tool to indent the text, all paragraphs using the same tag are also affected.

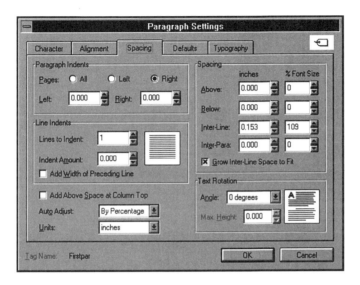

Figure 9.15
The Paragraph Settings dialog box with the Spacing tab selected.

The indent amounts are measured in whichever measurement system the Units option at the bottom of the dialog box is set to. For instance, if this option is set to inches, 1.5 creates a 1½-inch indent. In addition, remember when entering the amount for an indent that you are measuring from the margin or column guide, not from the edge of the page.

Adjusting Line Indents

You can set a separate indent amount for the first line of a paragraph. In figure 9.16, the entire first paragraph is indented ½ inch, with the first line indented another ½ inch. Entering a negative amount, such as –½, for the first line indent enables you to create *hanging indents* where the first line extends past the left side of the paragraph. The second paragraph in figure 9.16 shows a hanging indent. The paragraph has a left indent of one inch, with a first line indent of –½ inches.

Although it is more common to indent only the first line of a paragraph, VENTURA enables you to indent as many lines in a paragraph as desired, up to 99. For instance, you can indent the first two lines of a paragraph instead of just the first line.

III

Advanced VENTURA Options and Techniques

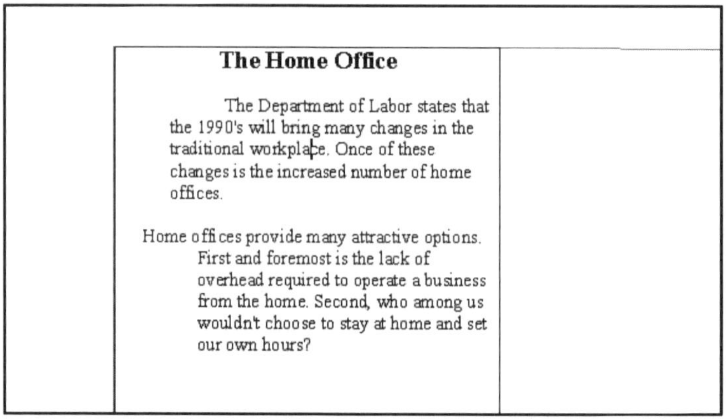

Figure 9.16

Setting a negative indent amount for the first line of a paragraph enables you to create hanging indents.

> ### The Home Office
>
> The Department of Labor states that the 1990's will bring many changes in the traditional workplace. Once of these changes is the increased number of home offices.
>
> Home offices provide many attractive options. First and foremost is the lack of overhead required to operate a business from the home. Second, who among us wouldn't choose to stay at home and set our own hours?

The following steps illustrate creating a hanging indent with a ¾-inch left indent and a –¼-inch first line indent. The All pages option is selected, so the hanging indent settings will be the same on all pages of the document.

1. Select either the Tagged Text or Freeform Text tool and click inside the paragraph you want to indent. The insertion point appears in the text.

2. Select Paragraph from the Format menu. The Paragraph Settings dialog box appears; click on the Spacing tab.

3. In the Paragraph Indents section of the dialog box, select the All option and enter **.75** in the Left box.

4. The Lines to Indent option indicates one line, the first line of the paragraph, will be indented. Enter **–.25** in the Indent Amount box.

5. Click on OK. The selected paragraph is formatted to create a hanging indent. If you used the Tagged Text tool to create the hanging indent, all paragraphs using the same tag are also affected.

To indent more than one line of a paragraph, enter the desired amount of lines to be indented in the Lines to Indent box. Click on the Add **W**idth of Preceding Line option to create first line indents that are equal to the last line of the previous paragraph (see fig. 9.17). This type of formatting is sometimes referred to as a *lead-in*.

Using the Ruler To Set Indents

The ruler provides another quick and easy way to set indents. When you click in a paragraph with either text tool, *indent markers* appear in the ruler, representing the first-line, left, and right indents of the selected paragraph (see fig. 9.18). You

can adjust the indents by dragging the indents markers along the measurements of the ruler.

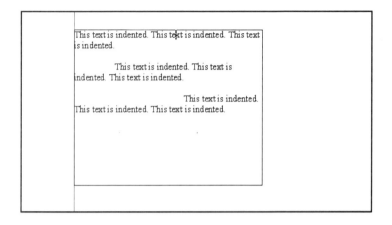

Figure 9.17
The Add Width of Preceding Line option creates first-line indents that are equal to the last line of the previous paragraph.

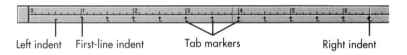

Left indent   First-line indent   Tab markers   Right indent

Figure 9.18
You can also set indents by dragging the indent markers along the ruler.

The following steps illustrate creating a one-inch left indent, a half-inch first-line indent, and a one-inch right indent using the rulers:

1. Select either the Tagged Text or Freeform Text tool and click inside the paragraph you want to indent. The insertion point appears in the text.

2. To set the left indent, position the mouse on the left indent marker and drag it to one inch on the ruler. The first-line indent marker will also be moved. The selected paragraph is indented one inch from the left.

3. To set the right indent, position the mouse on the right indent marker and drag it to the left (toward the center of the page) one inch. The selected paragraph is indented one inch from the right.

4. To set a first-line indent, drag the first line indent marker to one and a half inches on the ruler. The first line of the selected paragraph is indented.

When you drag indent markers along the ruler, notice that the markers jump from one ruler increment to another. For instance, you can line the markers up at ½ or ⅝ but not in-between. To place the indent markers between the ruler increments hold down the Control key as you drag.

Controlling Word Spacing

If you've ever had to fit three and one-half pages of text on three pages, you will appreciate VENTURA's word spacing feature. By decreasing the amount of space between words, you can tighten paragraphs of text, forcing the text to fit on fewer pages.

When you need to force text to fit on fewer pages, don't rely on word spacing alone. Try adjusting the line and paragraph spacing, or modifying the page margins and column widths.

With VENTURA, the amount of space between words can be increased or decreased. You adjust the spacing by altering the normal word spacing. The normal word spacing is set at 1.000. Entering 2.000 doubles the amount of space between words. Entering .500 cuts the word spacing in half. Actually, both of these values are extreme—you will most often use smaller settings such as .800 or .110 to decrease or increase the word spacing.

"Ems" are often used to control the amount of space between words. An *em* is a typographical measurement equal to the width of an uppercase M in a given paragraph font size. The em space between words in a 72-point headline is greater than the em space between words in a 12-point body text paragraph.

When you want the word spacing to become part of the paragraph tag, use the Tagged Text tool. Use the Freeform Text tool when you want to adjust the word spacing in the selected paragraph only. The following steps illustrate modifying the space between words:

1. Select either the Tagged Text or Freeform Text tool and click inside the paragraph whose spacing you want to adjust. The insertion point appears in the text.

2. Select Paragraph from the Format menu. If you used the Tagged Text tool to select the text, the Paragraph Settings dialog box appears. If you used the Freeform Text tool to select the text, the Override Paragraph Settings dialog box appears. Click on the Typography tab to display the dialog box shown in figure 9.19.

3. On the left side of the dialog box, you can see that Normal Word Spacing is set to 1.000. Enter the desired amount of spacing in the Proportion box.

4. Click on OK. The spacing of the selected paragraph is changed. If you used the Tagged Text tool to adjust the word spacing, all paragraphs using the same tag are also affected.

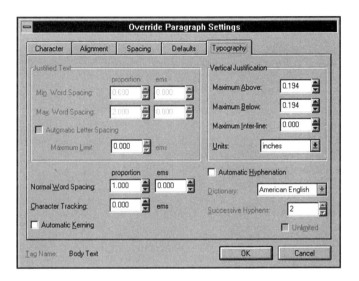

Figure 9.19
The Paragraph Settings dialog box with the Typography tab sheet selected.

If you are familiar with working with ems, you might want to adjust the word spacing by entering a measurement in the ems box. Otherwise, it is easier to set word spacing as a proportion of the normal word spacing as illustrated in the previous steps.

Controlling Word Spacing for Justified Text

The left and right margins of justified text paragraphs are flush or even. The spacing between words and letters is adjusted to spread out the text, creating even margins. As displayed in figure 9.20, additional word and letter spacing can add large amounts of white space that distort the readability of the text.

VENTURA provides special options for controlling the word spacing in justified text paragraphs. You can control the minimum and maximum amount of space placed between words. For instance, with the maximum setting, you can specify that no more than 1.5 ems are placed between words. As described in the previous section on word spacing, you can enter word spacing as a proportion of the normal spacing or in ems. Using the proportional method to adjust spacing is recommended.

Though with great difficulty I am got hither, yet now I do not repent me of all the trouble I have been at to arrive where I am. My sword, I give to him that shall succeed me in my pilgrimage, and my courage and skill to him that can get it. My marks and scars I carry with me, to be a witness for me, that I

You must select a paragraph with justified alignment before you can alter the word spacing for justified text. Use the following steps to control word spacing in a justified text paragraph.

1. Select either the Tagged Text or Freeform Text tool and click inside the justified paragraph whose spacing you want to adjust. The insertion point appears in the text.

2. Select Paragraph from the Format menu. The Paragraph Settings dialog box appears; click on the Typography tab.

3. The Justified Text section is in the top left corner of the dialog box. Enter the minimum amount of space you want placed between words in the Min Word Spacing box. Enter the maximum amount of space you want placed between words in the Max Word Spacing box.

4. Make sure the Automatic Letter Spacing option is turned on. This option tries to even out spacing in justified paragraphs by adding more space between the letters instead of the words in the paragraph.

5. To establish the maximum amount of spacing between letters, enter the desired amount in the Maximum Limit box.

6. Click on OK. The spacing of the selected justified paragraph is changed. If you used the Tagged Text tool to adjust the word spacing, all paragraphs using the same tag are also affected.

Adjusting Kerning

Kerning is the adjustment of space between selected pairs of letters. Sometimes, certain pairs of letters appear to be separated by too much space. The effect is especially apparent in larger titles and headings. For instance, in figure 9.21, the spacing between the letters in Hawaii looks better when kerned—the extra space has been removed. The spacing between the first two characters in Wave also looks better when kerned.

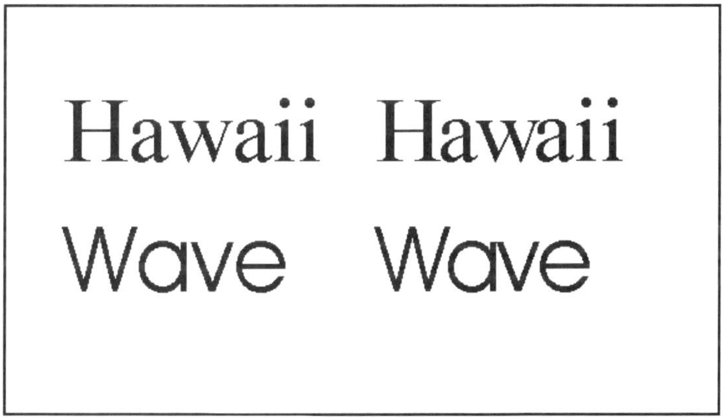

Figure 9.21
Kerning enables you to control the spacing between certain pairs of letters.

To have VENTURA automatically kern the letters in a paragraph, you can select the Automatic **K**erning option on the Typography tab sheet in the Paragraph Settings dialog box. However, the Automatic **K**erning option does not resolve all letter spacing problems. Certain letter pairs in words create spacing problems that can only be corrected by manually kerning the text.

Manual kerning requires that you select text; therefore, you can use either text tool. The kerning affects only the selected letters; the tag is not affected. Use the following steps to kern the spacing between two letters:

1. With either text tool, select the letters you want to kern by dragging across them. In figure 9.22, the second and third letters of Hawaii are selected.

2. Choose Sele**c**ted Text from the For**m**at menu. The Selected Text Attributes dialog box appears as displayed in figure 9.23.

3. In the Ke**r**ning box, enter a negative amount to move the selected letters closer together, and a positive amount to move the letters farther apart.

4. Click on OK. The spacing between the selected letters is adjusted to your specifications.

Figure 9.22
When manual kerning, select the letters whose spacing you want to adjust.

Figure 9.23
The Selected Text Attributes dialog box.

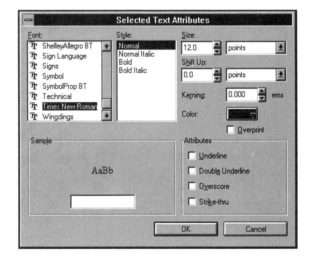

Use the following shortcuts to simplify kerning text. After selecting the letters you want to kern, press Ctrl+Alt+I to increase the kerning space. Press Ctrl+Alt+K to decrease the kerning space.

Working with Tracking

VENTURA's tracking feature enables you to add or subtract a specific amount of space between each letter in a paragraph. For instance, in figure 9.24, the same amount of space was added between each letter in the heading to "spread" the

text across the page. Unlike kerning, tracking adjusts the spacing between all of the letters, not just selected letters. As with word spacing, tracking is measured in ems.

Decreasing the tracking or subtracting space between each letter allows you to fit more words into the same amount of space. As displayed in figure 9.24, the text in the second column has less space between the letters in the paragraph. You will have better luck if you decrease the tracking in small amounts. If you decrease the tracking too much, the letters in the paragraph will "bunch up" on top of each other.

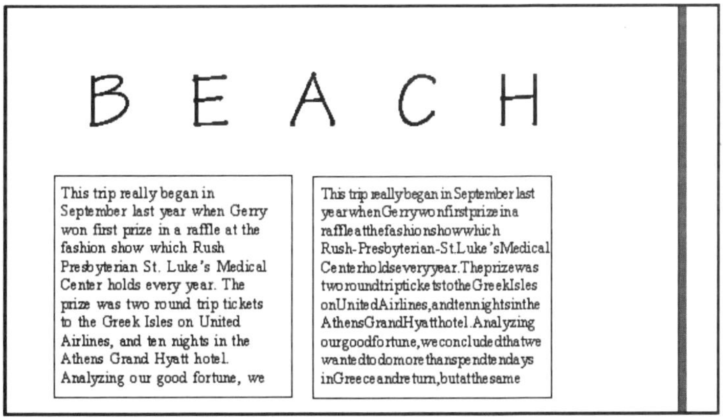

B E A C H

This trip really began in September last year when Gerry won first prize in a raffle at the fashion show which Rush Presbyterian St. Luke's Medical Center holds every year. The prize was two round trip tickets to the Greek Isles on United Airlines, and ten nights in the Athens Grand Hyatt hotel. Analyzing our good fortune, we

This trip really began in September last year when Gerry won first prize in a raffle at the fashion show which Rush-Presbyterian-St.Luke 'sMedical Center holds every year. The prize was two round trip tickets to the Greek Isles on United Airlines, and ten nights in the Athens Grand Hyatt hotel. Analyzing our good fortune, we concluded that we wanted to do more than spend ten days in Greece and return, but at the same

Figure 9.24
Expanding or condensing the tracking for a paragraph allows you to fit text in a given space.

When you want the tracking to become part of the paragraph tag, use the Tagged Text tool. Use the Freeform Text tool when you want to adjust the tracking for the selected paragraph only. The following steps illustrate adjusting the tracking:

1. Select either the Tagged Text or Freeform Text tool and click inside the paragraph where you want to adjust the tracking. The insertion point appears in the text.

2. Select Paragraph from the Format menu. In the Paragraph Settings dialog box, click on the Typography tab.

3. In the Character Tracking box, enter a positive number to increase the spacing between letters. Enter a negative number to decrease the spacing.

4. Click on OK. The tracking of the selected paragraph is adjusted. If you used the Tagged Text tool to adjust the tracking, all paragraphs using the same tag are also affected.

III

Advanced VENTURA Options and Techniques

Customizing Underlining, Superscript, and Subscript Attributes

With VENTURA, you can customize type attributes such as underlining and strike-through. If you work with a lot of underlined text, you might want to specify the thickness of the underline and shift the underline closer to or farther from the text (see fig. 9.25). You can also customize text attributes for superscript and subscript.

VENTURA enables you to shift the superscript and subscript letters up and down to fit your exact needs. Changes you make affect every occurrence of the line or text attribute within a paragraph tag or a selected paragraph. For instance, if you underline two words in a paragraph, both words use the same settings to format the underline.

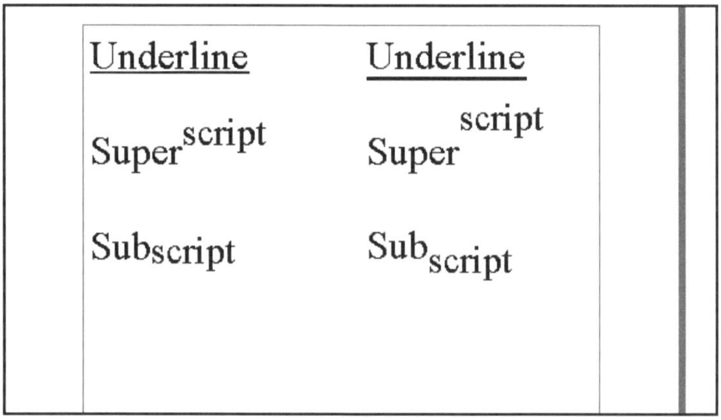

Figure 9.25
With VENTURA, you can control the formatting for underlining, as well as superscript and subscript specifications.

Underline   Underline

Super^script   Super ^script

Subscript   Sub_script

Modifying Line Attributes

Again, when you want the customized settings to become part of the paragraph tag, use the Tagged Text tool, and use the Freeform Text tool when you want to adjust the settings for the selected paragraph only. The following steps illustrate adjusting the line thickness and spacing of underlined text. You need to underline a word in the paragraph to see the changes that are made.

1. Select either the Tagged Text or Freeform Text tool and click inside the paragraph where you want to change the underline attributes. The insertion point appears in the text.

2. Select Paragraph from the Format menu. The Paragraph Settings dialog box appears. Click on the Defaults tab to display the dialog box shown in figure 9.26.

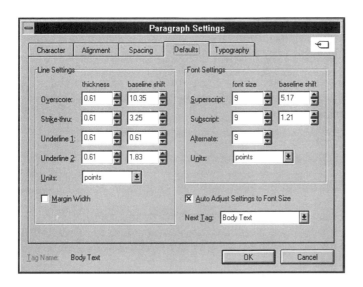

Figure 9.26
The Paragraph Settings dialog box with the Defaults tab sheet selected.

3. Turn off the **A**uto Adjust Settings to Font Size option by clicking to remove the *X*.

4. In the Line Settings section of the dialog box, enter the desired thickness for the underline in the Underline **1** thickness box.

5. To move the underline farther away from the text, increase the amount in the baseline shift box. To move the underline close to the text, decrease the amount in the baseline shift box. By default, the thickness and spacing are measured in points; click on the down arrow by **U**nits to select another measurement system.

6. Click on OK. Any underlined text in the selected paragraph is formatted to reflect the changes.

The Defaults tab sheet also offers options for controlling the thickness and placement of overscore and strike-through line attributes. Turn on the **M**argin Width option to run the underline, overscore, or strike-through line across the page from margin to margin

Modifying Text Attributes

As discussed in Chapter 7, you create superscript or subscript text by selecting the text you want to change, then clicking the right mouse button to display the pop-up menu where you can choose Superscript or Subscript.

With *subscript*, you "drop" letters with respect to the text, such as the 2 in H_2O. A letter is "raised" with *superscript*. For example, the 2 in 10^2. The following steps illustrate modifying the attributes of superscript and subscript text by shifting the text placement and adjusting the font size. To check how a superscript or subscript setting will look, apply it to a sample word in the paragraph.

1. Select either the Tagged Text or Freeform Text tool and click inside the paragraph where you want to change the text attributes. The insertion point appears in the text.

2. Select Paragraph from the Format menu. The Paragraph Settings dialog box appears; click on the Defaults tab.

3. The options appear gray until you turn off the **A**uto Adjust Settings to Font Size option.

4. In the Font Settings section of the dialog box, enter the desired font size for **S**uperscript or Su**b**script text in the font size boxes.

5. Use the baseline shift boxes to adjust the placement of superscript and subscript text. For superscript, enter a larger value to shift the text up, a smaller value to shift the text down. For subscript, enter a larger value to shift the text down, a smaller value to shift the text up.

6. Click on OK. Any superscript or subscript text in the selected paragraph is formatted to reflect the changes.

Setting Breaks in Paragraphs

Normally, each paragraph of text in your document is placed directly below the previous paragraph. When a page or column is filled, the following paragraph is placed at the top of the next page or column. As you design manuals and books, however, occasions will arise when you will need a title to appear at the top of a new page or a subheading to appear at the top of a column. *Breaks* are used to interrupt the normal flow of text and force a paragraph to begin at the top of the next page, creating a page break, or at the top of the next column, creating a column break.

Setting Page and Column Breaks

With VENTURA, you have several options for creating page breaks. First, you can place page breaks "before" the paragraph. A paragraph with a before-page break moves to the top of the next page. Because chapter titles generally appear on a new page, you might want to include a before-page break in the chapter title paragraph tag formatting. The break would force every paragraph tagged as a

chapter title to move to the next page. You can also place page breaks "after" a paragraph. Text following a paragraph with an after-page break is placed on the next page.

Some users force text to appear at the top of the next page or column by repeatedly pressing the Enter key to "push" the text forward. Setting page and column breaks provides more control and eliminates all of those blank paragraphs.

A paragraph with a before- and after- page break is placed on a new page, and any text after the paragraph is placed on the following page. Before- and after-page breaks enable you to place one paragraph on a page. For instance, in figure 9.27, the section title was formatted with a before- and after-page break, causing it to be the only text on the page.

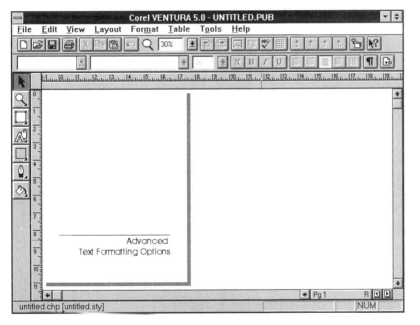

Figure 9.27

Before- and after-page breaks enable you to place one paragraph per page.

III

Advanced VENTURA Options and Techniques

The type of page breaks discussed thus far force text to appear at the top of the *next* page, regardless of whether it is a left or right page. You can also instruct the break to continue the text on either the next left or right page. Use the "before/until left"-page break to force the text to appear at the top of the next left page. Use the "before/until right"-page break to force the text to appear at the top of the next right page. You might use a before/until right-page break in a manual where you want all section headings to begin on a right page.

You can also apply page breaks with the Insert Breaks button on VENTURA's ribbon bar. Simply place the insertion point where you want to insert the break and click on the Insert Breaks button. Any text following the insertion point is pushed to the next page. This method does not affect the paragraph tag.

Many of the options for creating page breaks are also available when setting column breaks. You can choose a before-column break to force a paragraph to move to the top of the next column. For instance, you can format the headings in a flyer to include a before-column break so the headings automatically appear at the top of the columns.

Applying an after-column break pushes any text following a paragraph to the next column. A before- and after–column break breaks the text before and after the paragraph, enabling it to sit alone in a column (see fig. 9.28). Keep in mind that if you are working in a one-column layout and use a column break, the text moves to the next page, which is also the next column.

Figure 9.28
Before- and after-column breaks make it easy to place headings in a column all by themselves.

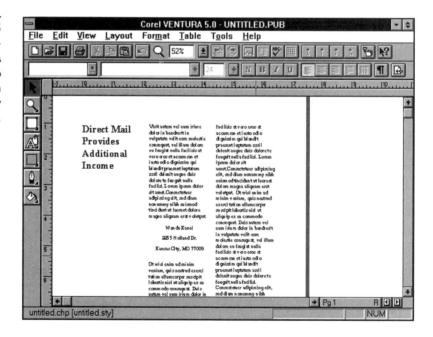

When you want the break to become part of the paragraph tag, use the Tagged Text tool. Use the Freeform Text tool when you want to apply the break to the selected paragraph only. The following steps illustrate adding page and column breaks.

1. Select either the Tagged Text or Freeform Text tool and click inside the paragraph where you want to apply the break. The insertion point appears in the text.

2. Select Br**e**aks from the For**m**at menu. The Breaks dialog box appears, as shown in figure 9.29.

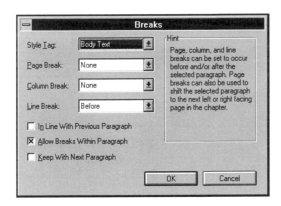

Figure 9.29
The Breaks dialog box.

3. If you are modifying a paragraph tag, the name of the tag that will be affected is displayed in the Style **T**ag list box.

4. To set a page break, click on the down arrow by **P**age Break, and select the desired style of break.

5. To set a column break, click on the down arrow by **C**olumn Break and select the desired style of break.

6. Click on OK. The break is applied to the selected paragraph. If you used the Tagged Text tool to apply the break, all paragraphs using the same tag are also affected.

It's important to make sure you've selected the correct text tool when applying breaks. Using the Tagged Text tool alters the paragraph tag, meaning if you add a break to a paragraph tag, all paragraphs with that tag move to a new column or page. This can be rather disconcerting if you did not plan it.

Setting Line Breaks

By altering the line breaks in a paragraph, you can create side-by-side paragraphs. Normally, a paragraph has an *after-line* break that forces the following paragraph to begin a new line that is vertically below the first paragraph (see fig. 9.30).

III

Advanced VENTURA Options and Techniques

Removing the after-line break enables the following paragraph to sit on the same vertical line as the first paragraph. Because the after-line break is gone, the paragraphs sit on top of each other. Subsequently, the text becomes tricky to read, and you must adjust the left and right indents to position the paragraphs side-by-side.

Figure 9.30
Altering line breaks in a paragraph allows you to create side-by-side paragraphs.

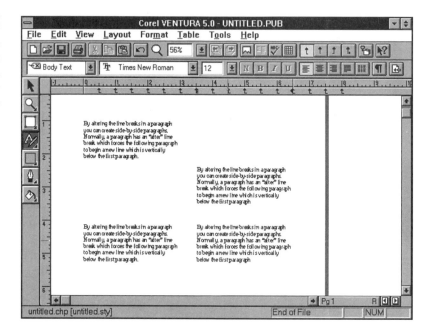

The following steps illustrate creating the side-by-side paragraphs shown in figure 9.30. In this example, the Freeform Text tool is used so only the selected paragraphs are affected.

1. With the Freeform Text tool, click in the paragraph you want placed on the left of the side-by-side paragraphs. Using the indent markers on the ruler, drag the right indent to 3 inches on the ruler. The lines of text in the selected paragraph all end at the new right indent.

2. Click in the paragraph you want placed on the right of the side-by-side paragraphs. Using the indent markers on the ruler, drag the left indent to 3 ½ inches on the ruler. The lines of text in the selected paragraph all begin at the new left indent.

3. Click in the first paragraph and select Breaks from the Format menu. In the Breaks dialog box, click on the down arrow by Line Break and select None. Click on OK. Because there is no line break to push the second paragraph down, the two paragraphs now line up side-by-side.

If you want to create paragraph tags to set up side-by-side columns, you will need two tags. The first tag is for the left paragraph with the right indent and no line break. The second tag is for right paragraph with the left indent.

Allowing Breaks within Paragraphs

When a multiple line paragraph is placed at the bottom of a page, VENTURA breaks the paragraph if there is not enough room for all of the text. Text that did not fit at the bottom of the page is continued on the next page.

Generally, it is acceptable to have breaks in longer paragraphs of body text. However, you might not want a break in a numbered step or bulleted item. In addition, you might not want to break a short paragraph consisting of three or four lines. Breaking a short paragraph leaves one or two lines at the bottom or top of a page, making the paragraph difficult to read.

VENTURA provides an option that enables you to control which paragraphs can break and which cannot. By default, the **A**llow Breaks Within Paragraph option is turned on for most paragraph tags, meaning these paragraphs can be divided across two pages. To prevent a paragraph from being divided, select Br**e**aks from the For**m**at menu. In the Breaks dialog box, turn off the **A**llow Breaks Within Paragraph option. An *X* indicates the option is on; no *X* indicates the option is off.

Keeping Paragraphs Together

Titles, headings, and subheadings are designed to direct the reader's eye into the body text. This transition is lost when a page ends immediately after a heading, causing the heading to appear alone at the bottom of the page. VENTURA provides the **K**eep With Next Paragraph option to ensure that certain paragraphs are kept on the same page as the following paragraph. For instance, rather than placing a heading at the bottom of the page, the heading would be moved to the next page with the paragraph that followed it.

Include the **K**eep With Next Paragraph option as part of your heading tag to keep the heading and the following subheading together. Use it again with the subheading tag to keep the subheading and the following body text together.

It's a good idea to include the **K**eep With Next Paragraph option in all of your heading tags. In fact, most of the heading tags supplied by VENTURA's style sheet already have this option enabled. To enable the **K**eep With Next Paragraph option, select Br**e**aks from the For**m**at menu. In the Breaks dialog box, turn on the **K**eep With Next Paragraph option.

Setting Tabs

Tab settings are fixed positions that run horizontally along your document. When you press the tab key, the insertion point moves to the next tab stop. With tabs you can create columns or tables of text. For example, in figure 9.31, tabs are set at one, three, and five inches on the horizontal ruler so that each column of information is perfectly left-aligned.

Figure 9.31
Use tabs to align text into columns or tables.

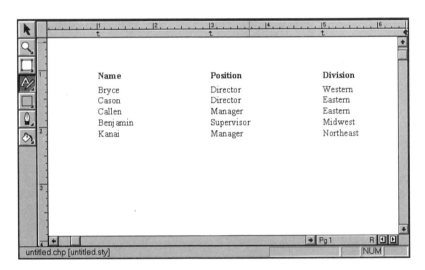

Tabs are measured from the left of the column or margin guide, not the left edge of the page. By default, VENTURA places tab stops at every half an inch for a total of up to 16 tabs per paragraph. As displayed in figure 9.31, when you click in a paragraph with either text tool, you can see the tab stops, represented by arrows, on the ruler. The ruler provides the quickest and easiest way to move, add, and delete tabs.

If the ruler is not displayed, choose Preferences from the Tools menu, then click on the View tab sheet and turn on the Rulers option.

VENTURA provides four different types of tabs: Left, Center, Right, and Decimal tabs. In figure 9.32, the four lines of text are all aligned to tab stops set at four inches. In the first tab, a left-aligned tab, the text is aligned to the left of the four-inch tab stop. The center tab is centered over the four-inch point. The right tab is aligned to the right of the tab stop, and the decimal tab is aligned so the decimal point sits precisely at the four-inch point on the ruler.

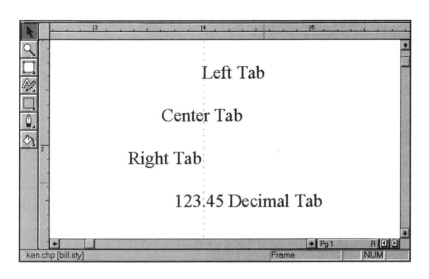

Figure 9.32
Four different tab types enable you to control how text is placed at the tab stop.

VENTURA's ribbon bar provides buttons for setting each type of tab (see fig. 9.33).

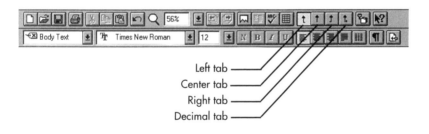

Left tab
Center tab
Right tab
Decimal tab

Figure 9.33
The ribbon bar provides buttons for selecting tab types.

Setting Tab Stops

If you want the tab settings to become part of the paragraph tag, use the Tagged Text tool. Use the Freeform Text tool when you want to set tabs for the selected paragraph only. The following steps illustrate setting tabs with the ruler:

1. Select either the Tagged Text or Freeform Text tool and click inside the paragraph where you want to set tabs. The insertion point appears in the text.

2. On the ribbon bar, click on the tab button that represents the type of tab you want to set.

3. To set a new tab, click in the gray bar below the ruler increments. A tab stop appears where you clicked. Because the maximum number of tabs per paragraph tag is 16, you might have to delete a tab before the new tab is accepted. Deleting tabs is covered in the next section.

Moving and Deleting Tabs

After setting a tab, you can adjust its placement by dragging the marker representing the tab stop to a new location on the ruler. For instance, suppose you set a tab at two inches and then wanted to move the tab stop to four inches. Using the ruler, you can drag the two-inch tab stop to four inches. By default, the movement is constrained to 1/8-inch increments. However, you can move the tabs more precisely by pressing the Control key as you drag the tab.

When you set a new tab, any existing tabs remain on the ruler until they are deleted. For instance, if you want the first tab stop to appear at three inches, you will have to delete any tab stops that precede the three-inch tab. Otherwise, when you press the Tab key, the insertion point moves to the first tab stop already on the ruler. To delete a tab, simply position the mouse on the arrow and drag it off the ruler and into the document area. When you release the mouse, the tab stop is deleted from the ruler.

Setting Tabs with the Paragraph Settings Dialog Box

In addition to using the ruler, you can set tabs in the Paragraph Settings dialog box where you can define the default tabs settings and create leader tabs. *Leader tabs* leave a trail of characters from the insertion point to the text at the tab setting. These character trails are used to assist eye movement. For example, the dotted leader in figure 9.34 helps associate each chapter with a page number.

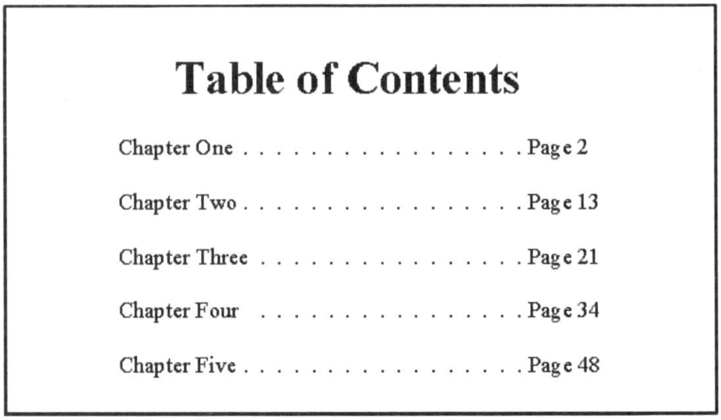

Figure 9.34
Leadered tabs
assist in eye
movement.

Table of Contents

Use the following steps to set tabs and create leadered tabs in the Paragraph Settings dialog box.

1. Select either the Tagged Text or Freeform Text tool and click inside the paragraph where you want to set tabs. The insertion point appears in the text.

2. Select Paragraph from the Format menu. The Paragraph Settings dialog box appears. Click on the Alignment tab to display the dialog box shown in figure 9.35.

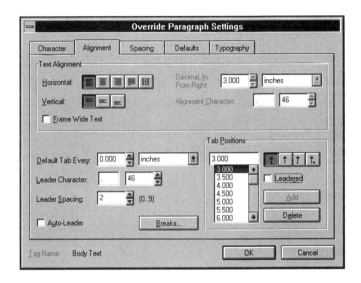

Figure 9.35

The Paragraph Settings dialog box with the Alignment tab sheet selected.

3. In the Tab Positions text box, enter the exact ruler position for the tab you want to set. Click on the Add button to add the setting to the tab list, then click on a tab button to select the desired tab type. Use this method to enter up to 16 tab stops.

4. To create a leadered tab, click on the Leadered check box before adding the tab. You can enter another character for the leader by typing the character you want in the Leader Character text box. For example, typing an asterisk displays a leader created with asterisks instead of dots. Use the Leader Spacing text box to adjust the spacing between leader characters.

5. Click on OK. The specified tab stops are displayed on the ruler.

As previously mentioned, VENTURA's default tab settings are set at every half an inch. You can adjust these settings in the Alignment tab of the Paragraph Settings dialog box. In the Default Tab Every text box, enter the desired measurement. For instance, enter **.75** to place a tab stop every ¾ of an inch. Notice that the tab list box displays the new tab settings in the specified interval. After making the desired changes, click on OK to return to the document.

III

Advanced VENTURA Options and Techniques

Chapter Snapshot

Building documents by using free frames opens up an almost endless amount of design possibilities. Free frames enable you to give your documents a multitude of looks. Each frame no longer has to look identical. In this chapter, you learn to do the following:

This chapter shows you how to set up documents with the use of free frames to modify the look of a column or a few pages.

10

CHAPTER

Advanced Free Frame Options

Frames are the building blocks of page layout in VENTURA. All text and graphics placed on the page are contained by frames. Each page of your document includes a base page frame that covers the entire page area. *Free frames* are drawn on top of the base page to hold graphics and smaller text blocks. In many complex layouts, such as newsletters and brochures, the base page is not used at all. Instead, the text and graphics are loaded into free frames. Free frames have a lot of flexibility because they can be moved, sized, and even rotated. You can flow text from one free frame to another. Free frames can also be formatted to have one or more columns; ruling lines and background colors or tints can be applied to them.

Chapter 4, "Working with Frames," examines drawing, sizing, and moving frames. The steps for locking, rotating, and repeating frames also are covered. This chapter delves deeper into designing and formatting documents with free frames. First, you will learn how to apply ruling lines to create borders for free frames. Next, the chapter discusses setting margins and columns for free frames. Advanced features such as adjusting widows and orphans, using vertical justification, and positioning text are discussed. The chapter ends with a look at adding captions to frames and working with frame tags.

Formatting Free Frames

Every free frame has individual formatting specifications, which makes it possible to design a multitude of page designs. Imagine the page designs you can create by formatting one frame in a two-column layout with borders, and another frame in a three-column layout with no borders. Take a moment to thumb through the style sheets and templates in the Corel clip-art book to analyze different page designs. Pretty soon, you will be looking through magazines and scrutinizing your junk mail for design ideas, contemplating how this or that effect can be accomplished with free frames.

Several chapters in this book discuss working with frames. Chapter 4, "Working with Frames," examines the basics of creating, selecting, and editing free frames; Chapter 5, "Loading Text into Frames," discusses importing text; and Chapter 11, "Importing Graphics into Frames," covers importing graphics. If necessary, refer to these chapters for more information.

Unlike base page frames, free frames are placed on the page with little formatting. By default, no lines, margins, or columns are applied in a new free frame. It is up to you to format the frame to meet your specifications. When you need several frames set up with the same formatting, apply the formatting and then use the Copy and Paste commands to make duplicates of the frame. The frame attributes are copied to the duplicated frames. As discussed later in this chapter, you also can use frame tags to build specific formatting guides for free frames.

Applying Ruling Lines to Frames

The boundaries of the frames you see on the page do not actually print. If you draw a free frame on a page, then print the page, the frame is not visible. Only the text and graphics loaded into the frames actually print. You can apply ruling lines to frames, however, to create a printable border for the frame. In the document in figure 10.1, ruling lines are placed around the frames containing text. As you can see, ruling lines are a good way to separate several text files on a page visually.

VENTURA provides several options for placing ruling lines. You can place ruling lines above the frame, below the frame, above and below the frame, or around the entire frame area. Up to three ruling lines can be placed on a frame, enabling you to create a variety of effects. Some of your options include placing two lines above a frame, one line around the entire frame, or three lines above and below a frame (see fig 10.2). To give you real design flexibility, VENTURA makes it easy to control the thickness and spacing of each of the lines.

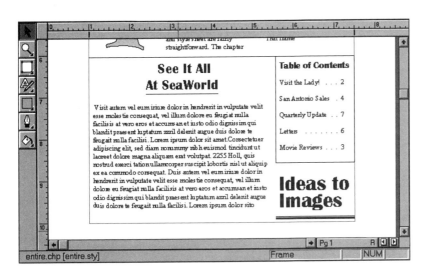

Figure 10.1
Applying ruling lines to frames is a good way to separate elements on a page.

Figure 10.2
You can place ruling lines above, around, and above and below free frames.

III

Advanced VENTURA Options and Techniques

You must select frames before you can apply ruling lines. You use the first tool in the toolbox, the Pick tool, to select frames. After selecting the Pick tool, move inside the frame and click. Eight gray selection handles appear around the outside edges of the frame, indicating that the frame is selected.

The following steps illustrate how to apply a two-point ruling line around a frame. You can use your own document or open the sample file academic.pub located in the VENTURA\VPSTYLE directory. In the academic.pub file, open the txtbook.chp file.

1. Select the frame to which you want to apply ruling lines. In txtbook.chp, select the frame containing text on the first page.

2. Choose Ruling **L**ines from the For**m**at menu.

   The Ruling Lines dialog box appears, as shown in figure 10.3. There are three tabs: Above, Below, and Around.

Figure 10.3
The Ruling Lines
dialog box.

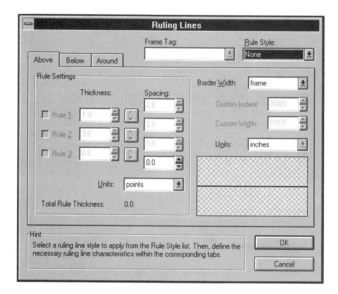

3. In the top right corner, click on the down arrow by the **R**ule Style box and select Around as the position for the ruling line. VENTURA displays the appropriate tab.

4. In the Rule Settings area, click to place an *X* in the Rule 1 check box. Click on the down arrow by Units to establish the system of measurement—in this example "points" is used. Enter **2** as the line thickness to create a two-point ruling line.

5. Two spacing options are available. Enter the amount of space you want placed between the edge of the frame and the first ruling line in the first box, and the amount of space you want placed between the first and second ruling lines in the second box.

   The sample box provides a preview of your line width and spacing selections.

6. To add a second and third ruling line, place an *X* in the Rule 2 and Rule 3 check boxes. Enter the line thickness you want. Use the Spacing boxes to add space between the lines.

7. Click on OK.

The specified ruling line(s) is added to the selected frame.

The thickness of ruling lines generally is measured in points. There are 72 points in an inch. To use another measurement system such as inches, click on the down arrow in the U**n**its field of the Ruling Lines dialog box and select the desired system.

You can apply ruling lines, margins, and columns to only one frame at a time. As explained later in this chapter, however, these elements can be stored as part of a frame tag and applied automatically.

Hiding the Frame Borders

Don't confuse the frame boundaries with the ruling lines. Remember, frame boundaries do not print. To get a better look at how the document will print, you can hide the frame boundaries. Choose Hide Frame **B**orders from the **V**iew menu. A check mark appears by the command, indicating that it is enabled. When the frame borders are hidden, only the ruling lines and any text or graphics loaded into the frames are visible. It also is a good idea to turn off the display of column guides from time to time so that you can see what actually will print. As discussed in Chapter 2, select Pre**f**erences from the T**o**ols menu to turn the display of column guides on and off. In figures 10.4A and 10.4B, the frame borders and column guides are visible in the first image and hidden in the second image.

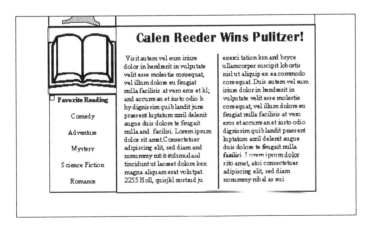

Figure 10.4A
The free frame with the frame borders visible...

III

Advanced VENTURA Options and Techniques

Figure 10.4B
...and hidden.

Obviously, when the frame boundaries are hidden, it is harder to select and work with the frames. To make the frame boundaries visible again, choose Hide Frame **B**orders from the **V**iew menu. The check mark is removed, indicating that the feature is off. If you find yourself hiding the frame borders frequently, take advantage of the keyboard shortcut Ctrl+K to turn the feature on and off.

Looking at Additional Ruling Line Options

You can embellish ruling lines around frames by using arrowheads and dashed line styles. VENTURA provides a wide selection of arrows and dashed lines. The line thickness determines the size of the arrowheads and the spacing and thickness of the dashed line. The same arrowhead is placed above both frames in figure 10.5, but the ruling line in the first frame is thicker, which creates a larger arrowhead.

Figure 10.5
Changing the ruling line thickness affects the size of the arrowheads.

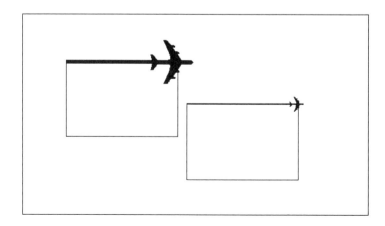

Adding Color, Arrows, and Dashed Lines to Ruling Lines

To add varying highlights to your ruling lines, use the following steps:

1. In the Ruling Lines dialog box (refer to fig. 10.3), an Outline button appears between the Thickness and Spacing options for each ruling line. Click on the Outline button to reveal the Outline Pen dialog box (see fig. 10.6).

2. To select another color for the ruling line, click on the Color button. You can select another line color from the color palette. Advanced line options are covered in Chapter 13.

3. To add arrows, click on the first button in the Arrows section and select the arrow for the beginning of the line. Click on the second button and select the arrow for the end of the line.

4. To add a dashed line style, click on the white button under Style and select the dashed line.

5. Click on OK.

   The line color and options are previewed in the sample box.

6. Click on OK again in the Ruling Lines dialog box to return to the document.

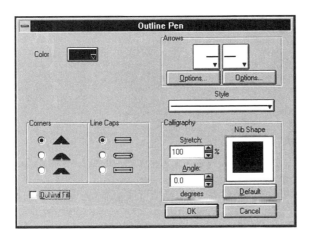

Figure 10.6
The Outline Pen dialog box.

Refer to Chapter 13, "Applying Fills and Outlines to Frames and Graphics," for more information on working with color palettes and selecting line widths, dashes, and arrowheads.

Avoid going overboard with lines and arrows. Too many of these elements distract from the readability of your document. The next section on adding margins to free frames becomes especially important when ruling lines are applied to frames.

Adding Margins to Free Frames

When text is loaded into a free frame, the text fills the entire frame area, touching the edges of the frame (see fig. 10.7). The same holds true for graphics; depending on the graphic's shape, parts of the graphic might bump against the edges of the frame. If two frames are placed side-by-side, the text from one frame can run right into the other. If a ruling line appears around the frame, the text becomes especially hard to read because it touches the edge of the frame. As you can see in figure 10.7, a margin is placed inside the frame on the right, adding a cushion of white space inside the frame so the text does not touch the frame edges.

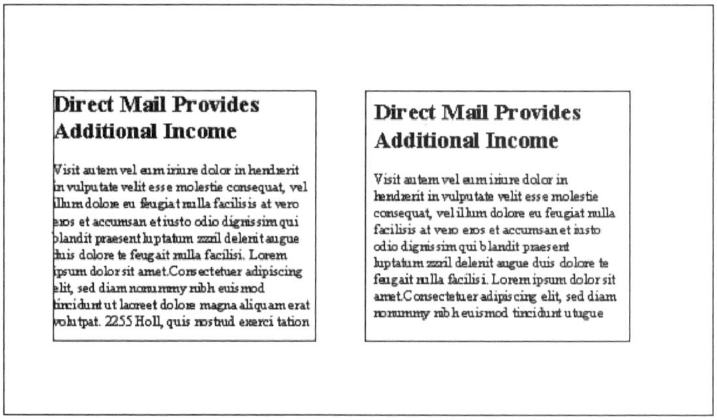

Figure 10.7
The frame on the right has an inside margin that prevents the text from touching the edges of the frames.

Direct Mail Provides Additional Income

Visit autem vel eum iriure dolor in hendrerit in vulputate velit esse molestie consequat, vel illum dolore eu feugiat nulla facilisis at vero eros et accumsan et iusto odio dignissim qui blandit praesent luptatum zzril delenit augue duis dolore te feugait nulla facilisi. Lorem ipsum dolor sit amet.Consectetuer adipiscing elit, sed diam nonummy nibh euismod tincidunt ut laoreet dolore magna aliquam erat volutpat. 2255 Holl, quis nostrud exerci tation

Direct Mail Provides Additional Income

Visit autem vel eum iriure dolor in hendrerit in vulputate velit esse molestie consequat, vel illum dolore eu feugiat nulla facilisis at vero eros et accumsan et iusto odio dignissim qui blandit praesent luptatum zzril delenit augue duis dolore te feugait nulla facilisi. Lorem ipsum dolor sit amet.Consectetuer adipiscing elit, sed diam nonummy nibh euismod tincidunt utugue

With VENTURA, you can set inside margins for the top, bottom, left, and right side of free frames. Generally, margins are added to all four sides of the frame. With graphics, however, you might not need to add all those margins. If a graphic is wide, for example, it might touch only the left and right edges of the frame, and you would need to add only left and right margins.

Note The steps for working with margins and columns are basically the same as those for the base page frame. Setting up the base page frame is covered in Chapter 3.

Adding Margins Inside a Free Frame

Use the following steps to add margins to a free frame:

1. Select the frame where you want to add margins and choose **F**rame from the For**m**at menu.

   The Frame Settings dialog box appears as displayed in figure 10.8. Click on the Margins tab.

2. By default, the margins are measured in inches. If desired, click on the down arrow by Units to select another measurement system. In the Inside Margins section, enter the desired spacing in the T**o**p, **B**ottom, **L**eft, and **R**ight boxes. For instance, enter .15 inches in all boxes to place a small margin around the inside of the frame.

   The preview box shows the margins you specify.

3. Click on OK.

III

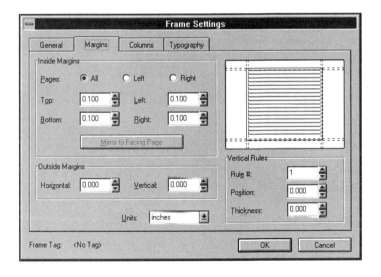

Figure 10.8
The Frame Settings dialog box with the Margins tab selected.

Margins are added to the selected frame. You do not see margin boundaries in the frame. The margins are apparent only after you load text or graphics into the frame.

Adding Outside Margins to Free Frames

Adding inside margins adds a cushion of white space inside the frame. You also might need a cushion of white space outside the frame at times. Suppose that text is loaded onto the base page, and a graphic is loaded into a free frame. As displayed in figure 10.9, the text on the base page might touch the outside edges of the frame. You can force the text away by adding an outside margin to the frame containing the graphic.

Figure 10.9
With no outside margins, text can run into the edges of a frame.

Computer Training
Increases Job Performance

Visit autem vel eum iriure dolor in hendrerit in vulputate velit esse molestie consequat, vel illum dolore eu feugiat nulla facilisis at vero eros et accumsan et iusto odio dignissim qui blandit praesent luptatum zzril delenit augue duis dolore te feugait nulla facilisi. Lorem ipsum dolor sit amet.Consectetuer adipiscing elit, sed diam nonummy nibh euismod tincidunt ut laoreet dolore magna aliquam erat volutpat.

2255 Holl, quis nostrud exerci tation ullamcorper suscipit lobortis nisl ut aliquip ex ea commodo consequat. Duis autem vel eum iriure dolor in hendrerit in vulputate velit esse molestie consequat, vel illum dolore eu feugiat nulla facilisis at vero eros eti blandit

praesent luptatum zzril delenit augue duis dolore te feugait nulla facilisi. Lorem ipsum dolor sito

Another way to control the spacing between a graphics frame and the text around it is to apply a text wrap path around the graphic. This option is discussed in the next chapter, "Importing Graphics into Frames."

You can apply vertical and horizontal outside margins to a free frame. Applying vertical margins adds spacing above and below the selected frame. Applying horizontal margins adds outside spacing to the left and right of the frame.

Adding Outside Margins to a Frame

The following four steps show how to highlight a frame with an outside margin:

1. Select the frame where you want to add margins and choose **F**rame from the For**m**at menu.

    The Frame Settings dialog box appears.

2. Click on the Margins tab.

3. In the Outside Margins section, enter the desired amount for the horizontal and vertical margins. You might enter .25 inches, for example, to place a small margin outside the frame.

   The preview box shows the margins you specify.

4. Click on OK.

Outside margins are added to the selected frame. Text that previously touched the edges of the frame now is pushed away. When you move the frame, the outside margins adjust to the new location. If you move a frame to the center of the page, for example, the outside margins still prevent text from touching the edges of the frame.

Adding Columns to Free Frames

Adding columns to free frames is another way that you can enhance the look of your page design. The columns control the flow of text in the frame. By default, each free frame is set up for a one-column layout. You can design individual column layouts for each free frame on the page, however, enabling you to design newsletters like the one in figure 10.10. One article is formatted in a two-column layout, and another article is formatted in a three-column layout.

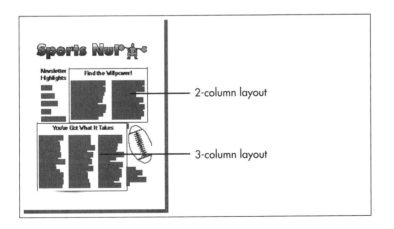

Figure 10.10
You can apply columns to free frames to control the flow of text.

III

Advanced VENTURA Options and Techniques

With VENTURA, you can add up to eight columns per free frame. Keep in mind that the more columns you specify, the narrower each column of text appears. Flowing text into extra narrow columns forces the reader's eye to jump from line to line. One rule of thumb is to use wider columns for larger text.

When adding columns, you control the exact width of the columns, as well as the space (or *gutter*) between the columns. As displayed in figure 10.11, the columns of text can be of equal width or, for more variety, in varying widths. In addition, you can include intercolumn rules to place thin, decorative lines between the columns. The second frame in figure 10.11 includes inter-column rules. These rule lines can be turned on and off and adjusted for thickness.

Figure 10.11

You can create equal or uneven column layouts in VENTURA.

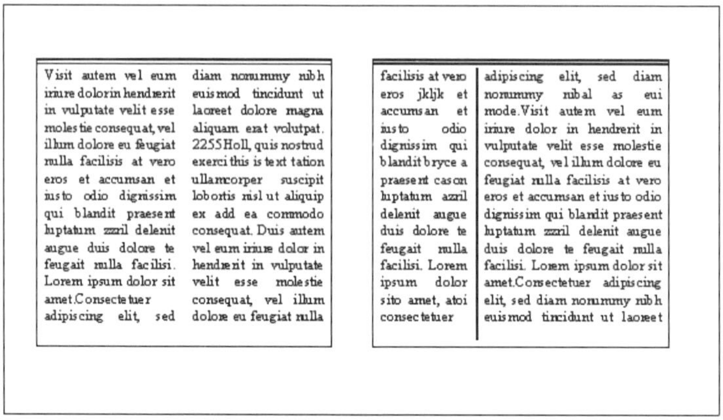

Creating Equal Columns

Perform the following to create equal columns:

1. Select the frame where you want to add columns and choose **F**rame from the For**m**at menu.

   The Frame Settings dialog box appears.

2. Click on the Columns tab to display the options for creating columns, as shown in figure 10.12.

3. In the Columns area, enter the desired number of columns in the # of Colu**m**ns list box.

   The sample box displays the specified number of columns.

4. Enter an amount in the **G**utter list box to add space between the columns. You might enter .20 inches as gutter spacing, for example. Keep in mind that with a two-column layout, there is one gutter; with a three-column layout, there are two gutters; and so on.

5. Click on the Equal Width button to make the columns and gutters the same width.

6. Click on the Inter-Column Rules check box to turn the rule lines on and off.

   If an X appears by the option, a line is placed between the two columns. You can see the line in the sample box. Use the Thickness list box to control the thickness or weight of the rule line. If an *X* does not appear, the option is turned off.

7. Click on OK.

The selected free frame now is set up for the specified number of frames. If inter-column rules are added to the column layout, the rule lines appear in the frame. If rules are not added, the frame appears blank, even after you have specified columns. The column layout becomes apparent when you load text into the frame. The Column Guides option in the Preferences dialog box displays column guides only on the base page frame—not in free frames.

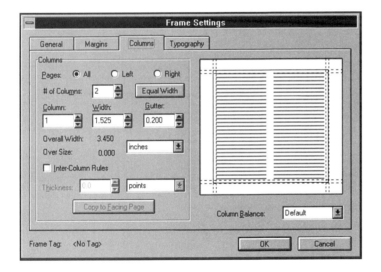

Figure 10.12
The Frame Settings dialog box with the Columns tab selected.

When creating columns of unequal widths, you must consider the overall width of the free frame. The total width of the columns cannot be wider than the frame itself. In figure 10.13, the free frame is 5 inches wide. The first column is set at 1 inch, and the gutter is set at .25 inch. This leaves 3.75 inches for the second column.

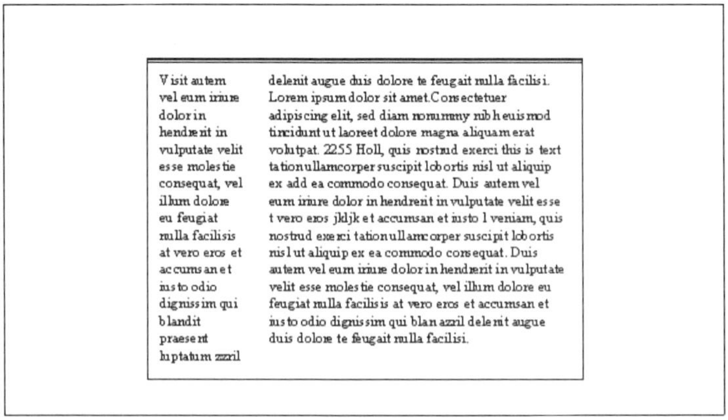

Figure 10.13
You must consider the overall frame width when creating uneven column layouts.

The overall frame width is displayed on the Columns tab of the Frame Settings dialog box (refer to fig. 10.12). Use the frame width setting to guide how wide your columns and gutters can be. If the frame width is 6 inches, for example, you should size the columns and gutters to meet the 6-inch width. If your specifications exceed the frame width, the Over Size indicator (under the Overall Width indicator) displays the amount of excess width. If your column and gutter specifications do not fill the frame width, however, this indicator changes to read Excess Space, which displays the amount of space that is left in the frame.

Setting Up Two Uneven Columns

Use the following steps to set up uneven columns:

1. Select the frame where you want to add columns and choose **F**rame from the For**m**at menu.

   The Frame Settings dialog box appears.

2. Click on the Columns tab.

3. Enter **2** in the # of Colu**m**ns list box to create a two-column layout.

   The sample box displays the specified number of columns.

4. The **C**olumn box displays 1, indicating that you are working with the first column. In the **W**idth box, enter the desired width for the first column. In the **G**utter box, enter the desired gutter width.

5. To set the width for the second column, return to the **C**olumn box and enter **2**. Enter the desired width for the second column in the **W**idth box.

Directly below the **W**idth option, the overall width is displayed. Remember that you cannot go wider than frame width.

6. Click on OK.

The uneven column layout is applied to the selected frame.

VENTURA also provides an option for balancing columns. As displayed in the first frame in figure 10.14, the Column **B**alance field in the Frame Settings dialog box distributes the text so both columns are the same height. The columns in the second frame are not balanced. When the columns are not balanced, the first column is filled, and any remaining text appears in the second column. To turn on the Column **B**alance option, return to the Columns tab of the Frame Settings dialog box and click on the down arrow by Column **B**alance and select On.

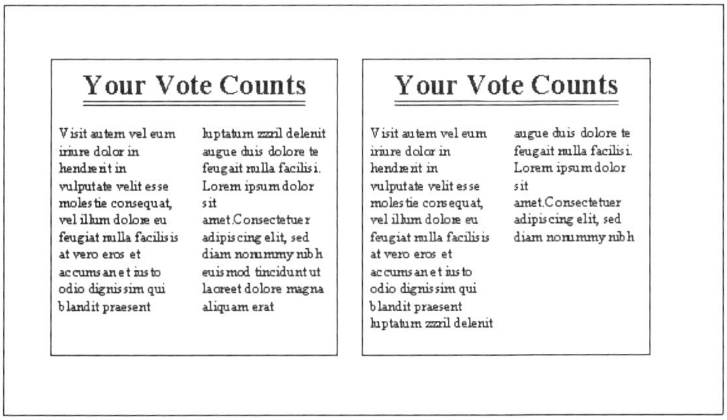

Your Vote Counts

Visit autem vel eum iriure dolor in hendrerit in vulputate velit esse molestie consequat, vel illum dolore eu feugiat nulla facilisis at vero eros et accumsan et iusto odio dignissim qui blandit praesent

luptatum zzril delenit augue duis dolore te feugait nulla facilisi. Lorem ipsum dolor sit amet.Consectetuer adipiscing elit, sed diam nonummy nibh euismod tincidunt ut laoreet dolore magna aliquam erat

Your Vote Counts

Visit autem vel eum iriure dolor in hendrerit in vulputate velit esse molestie consequat, vel illum dolore eu feugiat nulla facilisis at vero eros et accumsan et iusto odio dignissim qui blandit praesent luptatum zzril delenit

augue duis dolore te feugait nulla facilisi. Lorem ipsum dolor sit amet.Consectetuer adipiscing elit, sed diam nonummy nibh

Figure 10.14
The Column Balance feature distributes the text evenly in the columns in the left frame.

Adding Captions

Captions are used to add written support to the graphics on a page. A caption might explain the components of a new engine in a technical illustration, for example, or name the faces in a company party photo. With VENTURA, a caption is contained in a separate frame that is attached to the one containing the graphic (see fig. 10.15). The caption text is placed in this attached frame. The caption frame is linked to the free frame—if you move, cut, or copy a frame with a caption, the caption frame is moved, cut, or copied with it.

When adding captions, you have the option of adding a label and counter to the caption. The *label* consists of text, such as Figure or Table, and the *counter* consists of a number. Table 10.1 examines the available labels. The F represents the figure number, the T represents the table number, and the C represents the chapter number.

Figure 10.15
Captions are placed in frames that can be positioned above, below, or to the left or right of a free frame.

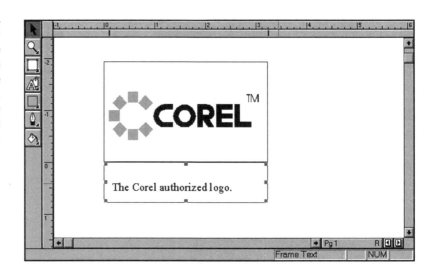

Table 10.1
Labels and Counters Available for Captions

Select this label	To create a caption with
Figure [F#]	Figure 1
Figure [C#]-[F#]	Figure 1-1
Table [T#]	Table 1
Table [C#]-[T#]	Table 1-1

Adding the label Figure [F#] to captions in your document enables you to number the figures in a chapter file automatically. The first caption would display Figure 1, the second Figure 2, and so on. The counters in the caption frames are renumbered if a frame is deleted or added. Figure 2 becomes Figure 1, for example, if the first frame is deleted.

After adding a caption frame and label, you can enter additional caption text. Simply place the insertion point after the paragraph marker, but before the end-of-file marker (the white square), and begin typing. You can enter as much text as necessary. Remember that you might need to enlarge the caption frame if you add much text. A generated paragraph tag is applied automatically to the label placed in a caption. Depending on the counter used, the tag name may be Z_LABEL_FIG, Z_LABEL_TBL, or Z_LABEL_CAP. Text entered after the label is formatted with the Z_CAPTION paragraph tag. Chapter 8 introduces the concept of generated tags.

Adding a Caption to a Frame

With VENTURA, you can place the caption frame above, below, or on either side of the frame containing the graphic. For design consistency, try to use the same positioning for all captions in a chapter file.

Use the following steps to add a caption to a frame:

1. Select the frame where you want to add a caption, and choose **F**rame from the For**m**at menu.

   The Frame Settings dialog box appears. The General tab is selected (see fig. 10.16).

2. In the bottom right corner of the dialog box, click on the down arrow in the **C**aption field. Select the desired caption positioning.

3. To add a label and counter, click on the down arrow in the Refere**n**ce field. Select the type of label you want to add to the caption.

4. Click on OK.

   A caption frame is attached to the free frame.

5. To enter additional caption text, select the Text tool and click after the paragraph symbol and before the end-of-file marker. Enter as much text as necessary.

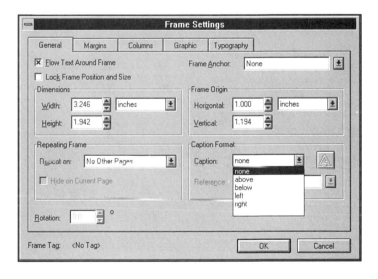

Figure 10.16
The Frame Settings dialog box with the General tab selected.

Keep in mind that sizing or moving the caption frame or the frame to which it is attached will affect both frames.

Adjusting Widows and Orphans in Free Frames

You can flow text across several free frames. Suppose that you load a text file into a free frame on page 1. If the free frame is not large enough to display all the text, you can continue to flow the rest of the text in another free frame. Flowing text across free frames often is done in newsletters, where an article might begin on page 1 and continue on page 3. Flowing text is covered in Chapter 5, "Loading Text into Frames."

When text flows across several frames, paragraphs of text often are split in two as the text continues to the next frame. In figure 10.17, for example, the paragraph at the end of the first frame is divided and continued at the top of the second frame. The paragraph at the bottom of the first frame is split at an unattractive place, leaving one isolated sentence at the top or bottom of a frame. As a page designer, you might be familiar with the terms widows and orphans. When you have one or two lines of text sitting alone at the bottom of a frame or page you have a *widow*. An *orphan* is one or two lines isolated at the top of a frame or page.

Figure 10.17
When text flows across several frames, the paragraphs can split leaving isolated lines at the bottom (widows) and top (orphans) of a frame.

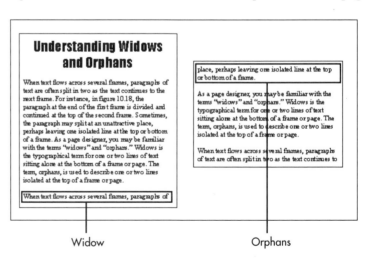

Sizing frames is one way to manage widows and orphans; you can enlarge or reduce the frame to control where a paragraph splits. Reducing the size of the first frame size forces more text to the next frame, and enlarging the first frame allows more text to be displayed. VENTURA provides a widows and orphans

feature, enabling you to control where a paragraph is split without sizing the frame. The widows and orphans feature enables you to specify the minimum amount of lines placed at the bottom of a frame (widows) and the minimum amount of lines placed at the top of a frame (orphans).

You can control the widows and orphans for text loaded into the base page frame by choosing the **C**hapter Settings command from the **L**ayout menu. See Chapter 14, "Advanced Options for Chapter Formatting," for a thorough look at adjusting the widows and orphans for a chapter file.

Specifying Widow and Orphan Control

In your page design, you might feel comfortable allowing two lines at the top or bottom of a frame, or perhaps you want a minimum of three lines. With VENTURA, you can specify from one to five lines. Selecting three lines for the widow setting, for example, means that no fewer than three lines must appear at the bottom of the frame. If there is not room for three lines, the text is forced to the next frame.

The following steps show how you can control widows and orphans:

1. Select the frame where you want to adjust the widows and orphans and choose **F**rame from the For**m**at menu.

    The Frame Settings dialog box appears.

2. Click on the Typography tab to display the Frame Settings dialog box shown in figure 10.18.

3. In the top left of the dialog box, click on the arrow to view the **W**idows drop-down list. Select the minimum amount of lines you want to appear at the bottom of a frame.

4. Open the Orp**h**ans drop-down list and select the minimum amount of lines you want to appear at the top of a frame.

5. Click on OK.

If possible, adjust the widows and orphans setting before loading text into the frames. If text already is loaded into the frames, the text might not reflow to meet the new Widow and Orphans settings. In this case, try manipulating the frame size to get the text to flow using the specified number of widow or orphan lines.

Advanced VENTURA Options and Techniques

Figure 10.18
The Frame
Settings dialog
box with the
Typography tab
selected.

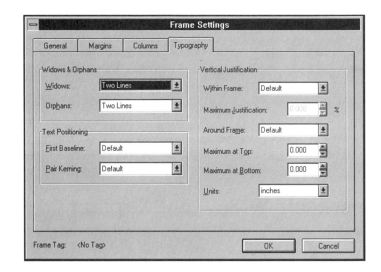

Figure 10.18
The Frame
Settings dialog
box with the
Typography tab
selected.

Controlling Vertical Justification

With VENTURA, you can turn on the vertical justification feature to ensure that text in a frame always reaches the bottom of the frame. Space is added between paragraphs and lines of text to spread out the text. Vertical justification was turned on for the first frame in figure 10.19, and turned off for the second frame. You can see how spacing is added to fill the frame.

Figure 10.19
Vertical
justification adds
space to ensure
that text reaches
the bottom of the
frame.

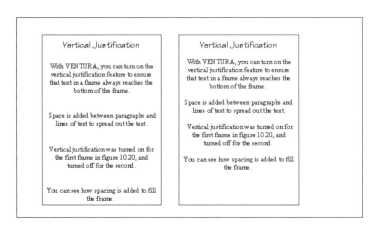

Some documents, such as advertisements and flyers, might look better when the frame is justified vertically so that the text completely fills the frame. This justification certainly is not required for all documents, however. When turning on vertical justification, keep in mind that added spacing plays havoc with text

spacing. The inter-line, as well as the before- and after- paragraph spacing, set up in the paragraph tags are no longer utilized, for example. If turning on vertical justification doesn't give you what you need, try spreading out the text manually by increasing the spacing between text paragraphs with the spacing options in the Paragraph Settings dialog box located under the Fo**rm**at menu. Refer to Chapter 7, "Formatting Tagged and Freeform Text," for more information.

You can control the vertical justification for text loaded into the base page frame by choosing the **C**hapter Settings command in the **L**ayout menu.

Setting Up Vertical Justification

You have two options for controlling the amount of space added to spread out the text. The Feathering option adds the exact amount of space required to make the text reach the bottom of the frame. The Carding option adds space using the inter-line spacing set up in the Body Text paragraph tag as a guide. As displayed in figure 10.20, the Carding option keeps the baselines of text even across several columns; the Feathering option does not. If you use the Carding option, text might not reach the bottom of the frame.

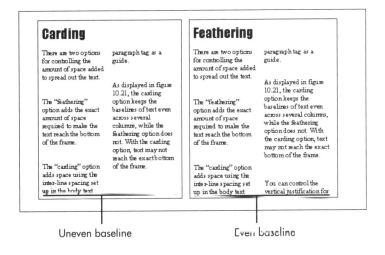

Figure 10.20
The Carding option keeps the baselines of text even across several columns. The Feathering option does not.

Uneven baseline   Even baseline

To set up vertical justification, follow these steps:

1. Select the frame where you want to apply vertical justification and choose **F**rame from the Fo**rm**at menu.

   The Frame Settings dialog box appears.

Advanced VENTURA Options and Techniques

2. Click on the Typography tab.

3. In the Vertical Justification section of the dialog box, click on the down arrow by Within Frame. Select Feathering or Carding.

4. Enter **100%** in the Maximum Justification box. A value of 0% turns off vertical justification.

5. Click on OK.

The text in the selected frame expands to fit the entire frame area.

If there is not enough text to fill the frame, the text does not reach the bottom of the frame. If you have three lines of text in a large frame, for example, VENTURA does not force it to fill the entire frame. The vertical justification feature is on, however, so if you add more text, the frame fills up.

Controlling Placement of the First Line of Text

VENTURA provides two options for specifying where the first line of text begins within a frame. As displayed in figure 10.21, the first line of text can begin at the very top of the frame, or it can be moved down slightly in an amount equal to the interline spacing.

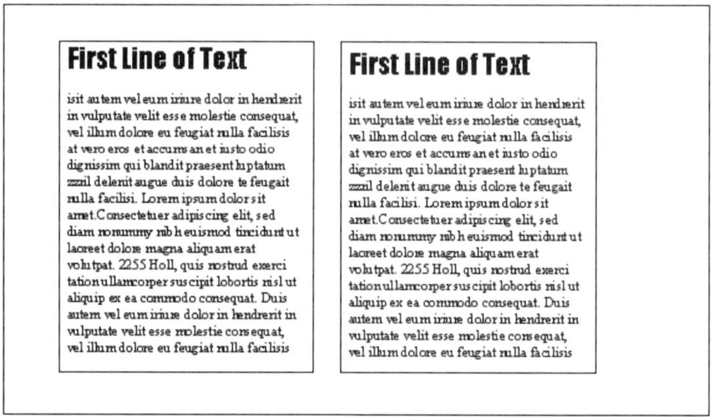

Figure 10.21
The first line of text can begin at the very top of the frame, or moved down slightly in an amount equal to the inter-line spacing.

First Line of Text

isit autem vel eum iriure dolor in hendrerit in vulputate velit esse molestie consequat, vel illum dolore eu feugiat nulla facilisis at vero eros et accumsan et iusto odio dignissim qui blandit praesent luptatum zzril delenit augue duis dolore te feugait nulla facilisi. Lorem ipsum dolor sit amet.Consectetuer adipiscing elit, sed diam nonummy nibh euismod tincidunt ut laoreet dolore magna aliquam erat volutpat. 2255 Holl, quis nostrud exerci tation ullamcorper suscipit lobortis nisl ut aliquip ex ea commodo consequat. Duis autem vel eum iriure dolor in hendrerit in vulputate velit esse molestie consequat, vel illum dolore eu feugiat nulla facilisis

First Line of Text

isit autem vel eum iriure dolor in hendrerit in vulputate velit esse molestie consequat, vel illum dolore eu feugiat nulla facilisis at vero eros et accumsan et iusto odio dignissim qui blandit praesent luptatum zzril delenit augue duis dolore te feugait nulla facilisi. Lorem ipsum dolor sit amet.Consectetuer adipiscing elit, sed diam nonummy nibh euismod tincidunt ut laoreet dolore magna aliquam erat volutpat. 2255 Holl, quis nostrud exerci tation ullamcorper suscipit lobortis nisl ut aliquip ex ea commodo consequat. Duis autem vel eum iriure dolor in hendrerit in vulputate velit esse molestie consequat, vel illum dolore eu feugiat nulla facilisis

Use the following steps to specify text placement:

1. Select the frame where you want to apply vertical justification and choose **F**rame from the For**m**at menu.

   The Frame Settings dialog box appears.

2. Click on the Typography tab.

3. In the Text Positioning section of the Frame Settings dialog box, click on the down arrow in the first Baseline field. Select Cap-Height to align the top of the tallest letter in the first line of text with the top of the frame. Select Inter-line to move the first line of text down by an amount equal to the interline spacing.

4. Click on OK.

The first line of text in the selected frame is positioned according to your specifications.

Working with Frame Tags

If your document requires that you create several identical frames, use frame tags. *Frame tags* store formatting attributes, such as size and ruling lines, much like paragraph tags store formatting information for text. Suppose that you are creating a 50-page document and every page needs a 3×5-inch frame formatted with ruling lines. Rather than creating 50 frames, carefully sizing them all and applying ruling lines to each of them, you can create a frame tag. The frame tag then is applied to frames, automatically sizing them and setting up the ruling lines.

Much like paragraph tags, any changes made to a frame with a frame tag affects all frames using the same tag. Suppose that you have five frames using a frame tag named Thick Lines. If you adjust the line thickness of any one of those five frames, all the other frames using that tag also are affected.

Unlike paragraph tags, frame tags are not stored as part of the style sheet file.

III

Advanced VENTURA Options and Techniques

Creating a Frame Tag

The size, margins, columns, ruling lines, and caption settings are saved as part of a frame tag. Generally, a frame tag is created from a frame that already is set up to match certain formatting requirements. The new tag stores the formatting, enabling you to quickly apply the same formatting to other frames.

Do the following steps to create a frame tag:

1. Create the frame on which you want to base the new frame.

   You might need to adjust the frame size, set up margins and columns, add captions, apply ruling lines, and add any other attributes you want saved in the frame tag.

2. Choose Manage Tag List from the Format menu.

3. Click on the Frame Tags tab to display the dialog box in figure 10.22.

4. Click on the **A**dd Tag button.

   The Add Frame Tag dialog box appears, as displayed in figure 10.23.

Figure 10.22
The Manage Tag List dialog box with the Frame Tags tab selected.

Figure 10.23
The Add Frame Tag dialog box.

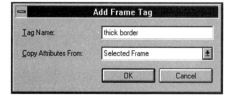

5. Enter a name for the new tag.

   You can use spaces in the tag name and enter up to 15 characters.

   The Copy Attributes From box displays `Selected Frame`, meaning that the formatting attributes of the selected frame are used to create the new frame tag.

6. Click on OK to return to the Manage Tag List.

   The new frame tag appears in the list.

7. Click on OK to return to the document.

Remember that if you change the formatting attributes of a frame that has been tagged, the changes affect every frame using the same tag name.

Applying Frame Tags

After creating the frame tag, you can apply this tag to other frames. All the formatting attributes stored in the frame tag are applied automatically. Perform the following to apply frame tags:

1. Draw a frame. The size is not important because the tag adjusts the frame size.

2. Make sure that the frame is selected, then click on the down arrow by the Tag list in the ribbon bar.

3. Select the desired tag from the list of tags.

The selected frame is formatted to meet the tag's specifications.

You can apply a frame tag to several frames at one time. Press Shift as you select the frames. When all the frames are selected, choose a tag from the tag list.

Other options in the Manage Tag List dialog box enable you to delete, rename, edit, and merge frame tags. These are the same options available when working with paragraph tags. Refer to Chapter 8 for a thorough look at these features.

III

Advanced VENTURA Options and Techniques

Chapter Snapshot

A publication gains instant visual impact with the use of graphics. VENTURA provides options for placing many types of graphical file formats within your documents. In this chapter, you learn the following:

Graphics are an integral part of communicating your message to the reader. This chapter teaches you how to import graphics and how to modify them.

CHAPTER

11

Importing Graphics into Frames

You've heard it a million times: *A picture is worth a thousand words.* Although words are the meat of your publications, the pictures certainly are the sizzle. VENTURA provides a wide range of options to add photos, illustrations, and other forms of graphics to your publications. You can import scanned photographs, graphics designed in illustration programs such as CorelDRAW, and charts and graphs created in presentation applications such as CorelCHART. You also can bring in clip art from VENTURA's extensive clip-art library.

This chapter shows you how to add graphics to your VENTURA documents. It begins with a discussion of the types of graphics that can be imported into VENTURA. You learn the ways in which VENTURA saves graphics files. You then examine the various ways in which to bring graphics into VENTURA, including importing and using the Windows Clipboard. The rest of the chapter focuses on manipulating graphics placed in a VENTURA document. You will learn how to size, pan, and crop graphics. This chapter concludes with a look at sprucing up your page design by creating customized text wraps around graphics objects.

This chapter focuses on transferring graphics into VENTURA by importing them and by using the Windows Clipboard. Another highly efficient way to transfer graphics into VENTURA is with CorelMOSAIC. For more information regarding using CorelMOSAIC, refer to your CorelVENTURA documentation or to the *The CorelDRAW 5 Professional Reference* by New Riders Publishing.

Working with Bitmapped and Vector Graphics

All graphics images fall into one of two basic categories: bitmapped or vector images. *Bitmapped graphics* are composed of dots that are arranged in a specific order to create an image. The seahorse in figure 11.1, for example, is a bitmapped drawing. The first image is full-size, and the dots that define the image are undetectable. When the figure is enlarged, however, as in the second image, the dots that comprise the seahorse can be seen clearly. Images created in CorelPHOTO-PAINT are bitmapped images. In addition, you are creating bitmapped images when you scan artwork or photographs. When you add bitmapped images to your VENTURA documents, remember that they can become distorted if you attempt to resize them. The bitmapped graphic format works well for photographs and images that you do not intend to scale or re-shape.

Figure 11.1

Bitmapped images are comprised of dots and can become distorted if you attempt to resize them.

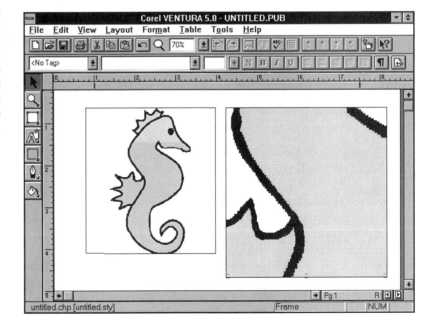

It is important to realize that bitmaps remain at the resolution at which they are scanned, and they cannot utilize the quality output of a higher resolution printer. Suppose that you scan the company logo at 300 dots per inch (dpi). When the art in placed in a newsletter that is printed on your desktop printer at 300 dpi, the scanned art is reproduced at its highest possible resolution. If you include the art in the company's annual report, however, which is reproduced at 2,540 dpi, the scanned logo still is reproduced at 300 dpi. The original scan of 300 dpi stays the same, regardless of the improved printing process.

Vector graphics are composed of lines and curves defined by complex mathematical calculations. CorelDRAW creates vector graphic images. When a vector graphic is resized, the lines and curves adjust, and the image remains smooth. The seahorse in figure 11.2 is a vector graphic. At full size, the vector seahorse might not appear much different from the bitmapped seahorse. Unlike its bitmapped counterpart, however, when the vector seahorse is magnified, its lines remain clean and smooth. Because you can adjust the size of vector graphics without deteriorating the image, they are the optimal option for illustrations that will be imported into VENTURA.

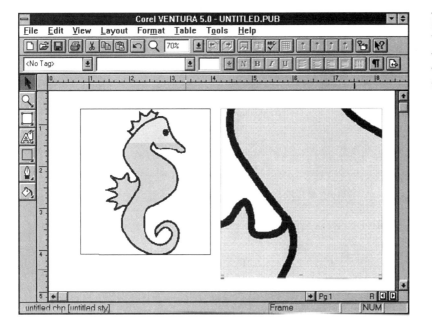

Figure 11.2

You can resize vector graphics without distorting the image.

III

Advanced VENTURA Options and Techniques

Table 11.1 lists the graphics file formats VENTURA can import.

Table 11.1
Graphics File Formats VENTURA Can Import

Graphics File Format	File Extension
Corel Presentation Exchange	*.CMX
CorelDRAW Graphic	*.CDR, *.PAT
CorelCHART	*.CCH
CorelTRACE	*.EPS
Windows Bitmap	*.BMP, *.DIB, *.RLE
CompuServe Bitmap	*.GIF
Computer Graphics Metafile	*.CGM
JPEG Bitmap	*.JPG, *.JFF, *.JTF, *.CMP
Paintbrush	*.PCX
Scitex CT Bitmap	*.CT, *.SCT
Targa Bitmap	*.ICB, *.TGA, *.VDA, *.VST
TIFF Bitmap	*.CPT, *.SEP, *.TIF
Windows Metafile	*.WMF
Adobe Illustrator	*.AI, *.EPS
AutoCAD DXF	*.DXF
GEM File	*.GEM
GEM Paint File	*.IMG
HPGL Plotter File	*.PLT
IBM PIF file	*.PIF
Lotus PIC	*.PIC
Macintosh PICT	*.PCT
Micrografx 2x, 3x,	*.DRW
EPS (Placeable)	*.AI, *.EPS, *.PS
WordPerfect Graphic	*.WPG

Understanding How VENTURA Saves Imported Graphics

Imported graphics are not included as part of the chapter file. Just as with imported text, imported graphics are stored as separate files. Chapter 1 examined the process VENTURA uses to save publication and chapter files. When a chapter file is opened, pointers are sent out to locate and retrieve the graphics files.

It is important to note that because imported graphics are separate files, any changes you make to the original graphic file will be reflected in the VENTURA imported graphic as well. Suppose that you import a CorelDRAW graphic into VENTURA. Thereafter, any changes you make to the original drawing in CorelDRAW also affect the image as it appears in VENTURA.

Graphic files placed in VENTURA are not saved as part of the document. You cannot delete the graphic file or move it to another location without also losing the graphic in your VENTURA document.

Understanding Graphics Display Options

After importing a graphic onto the page, you will notice that screen redraw is significantly slower. You can use two options to speed up screen redraw. You can display the graphics at a lower resolution, or you can hide graphics entirely. By default, imported graphics are displayed at low resolution. If you choose, you can display graphics at high resolution, although doing so increases the time it takes to redraw the screen. The resolution selected to display the graphics has no effect on printing. The graphics print at the resolution of the output device. To change the graphic display resolution, choose Graphics Resolution from the **V**iew menu. From the submenu, choose **L**ow or **H**igh Resolution.

Some vector images might not display at low resolution. The low resolution display image is actually a bitmapped image header. Not all graphics formats support the image header option.

Hiding graphics is the best way to speed up screen redraw. Hiding graphics also enables you to get a rough draft printout of the page layout without waiting for detailed graphics to print. You can hide all graphics in a chapter, or just selected graphics. To hide all graphics, choose **D**raft from the **V**iew menu. As shown in figure 11.3, in draft view, each graphic in the document displays as a box with a large *X.* Remember the graphic is still loaded into the frame. If you select the frame, the graphic file name appears in the File list in the ribbon bar at the top of the screen.

To print a rough draft with these representational boxes instead of the actual graphics, you must make sure that the Print **H**idden Graphics feature, found on the Options tab of the Print dialog box, is disabled. Otherwise, though the graphics appear as boxes, they will print as fully rendered images.

Figure 11.3

Choosing Draft view hides the graphics in your document and speeds up screen redraw.

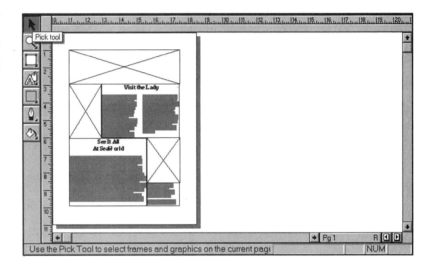

To hide selected graphics only, select the graphic and choose **G**raphic from the For**m**at menu. After the Frame Setting dialog box appears, click on the Graphic tab to display the dialog box shown in figure 11.4. Click to place an *X* in the Hide **G**raphics check box and click on OK.

Although hidden graphics cannot be viewed, you still can move and size them as you would a visible graphic. You learn how to move and size graphics later in this chapter.

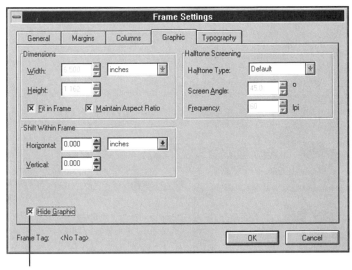

Figure 11.4
Turn on the Hide Graphic option in the Frame Settings dialog box to hide selected graphics.

Hide Graphic check box

Loading Graphics into Frames

As discussed in Chapter 5, "Loading Text into Frames," the base page frame can contain only a single file. Text generally is loaded into the base page frame and graphics are loaded into free frames. A free frame can hold one graphics file. If the frame currently holds text or a graphic, the item is replaced by the newly imported graphic. After a graphic is imported into a frame, it can be moved, sized, and cropped.

Chapter 10, "Advanced Free Frame Options," examines advanced frame formatting features, such as applying borders and captions, setting margins, and creating frame tags. After importing a graphic, you can refer to Chapter 10 for information on formatting the frame.

When importing graphics, it is important that you select the frame in which you want to load the graphic. If you do not select a frame, VENTURA automatically creates one as it imports the graphic. The frame for the newly imported graphic is the size at which the graphic was created. You can edit this frame just like any other free frame. If the imported graphic is larger than the page, VENTURA maintains the graphic's proportions but reduces it to fit the page. To import a graphic into VENTURA, use the following steps:

Advanced VENTURA Options and Techniques

1. With the Pick tool, select the frame in which you want to place the imported graphic.

   The selection handles appear when a frame is selected.

2. Choose Load **G**raphic from the **F**ile menu.

   The Load Graphic dialog box appears, as shown in figure 11.5.

Figure 11.5
The Load Graphic
dialog box.

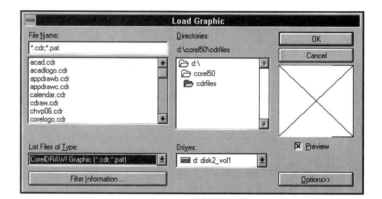

3. From the List Files of **T**ype list box, select the file format you want to import.

4. Navigate to the drive and directory where the file you want to import is stored. Select the file you want to import.

   If the **P**review option is enabled, a thumbnail of the graphic appears in the preview window.

The preview window in the Load Graphic dialog box displays thumbnails for bitmapped images and vector files that have bitmapped image headers, such as CDR, CCH, and EPS files.

5. Click on OK.

The graphic is loaded into the frame. Notice that the graphics file name appears in the Files list in the ribbon bar.

The Files list in the ribbon bar displays the file names of all text and graphics files placed in the chapter file. To view the files in a chapter, select a frame and click on the down arrow by the Files list in the ribbon bar. The file loaded into the

selected frame is highlighted in the list. In figure 11.6, the Files list indicates that there are five files loaded into the chapter. A small text icon appears next to text files, and a Corel balloon icon appears next to graphic files.

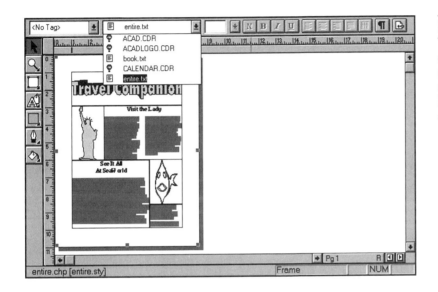

Figure 11.6
The Files list displays the file name of all text and graphics files loaded into the chapter.

Importing Multiple Graphics Files

You can import graphics files into the Files list without placing them into frames. Suppose that you have three graphics files to place in a report, but you aren't quite sure where you want to place each file. By loading the files into the Files list, you have them readily available when you are ready to place them into frames, as the following steps demonstrate:

1. Make sure that no frames are selected. If necessary, click on the Pick tool several times to deselect all frames.

2. Choose Load **G**raphic from the **F**ile menu or use the keyboard shortcut F10.

   The Load Graphic dialog box appears.

3. Navigate to the drive and directory where the text file you want to import is located.

4. Click on the down arrow by List Files of **T**ype to select the type of graphics file format you are importing.

5. To load a contiguous range of files, press Shift while clicking the first and last file in the list range. To load multiple files that do not appear in consecutive order, press Ctrl while you click to select the files.

6. Click on OK.

Click on the down arrow by the Files list to view the newly loaded files.

After the graphics files are imported into the Files list, you can load them into frames. Simply select the frame where you want the graphic to appear and select the file name you want from the Files list.

Copying and Pasting Graphics from Other Applications

The Windows Clipboard is a quick and easy way to transfer graphics into VENTURA from other Windows applications. You can copy a graphic from CorelDRAW, for example, and paste it into your VENTURA document. The Clipboard temporarily stores a graphic as it is copied from CorelDRAW and pasted into VENTURA. After an image is pasted into VENTURA, it can be manipulated just as an imported graphic (with the exception of panning and text wrapping, which are discussed later in this chapter).

For more information on using the Windows Clipboard, refer to your Windows documentation or to *Integrating Windows Applications*, by New Riders Publishing.

Unlike imported graphics, pasted graphics are stored as part of the chapter file. Pasted graphics are not stored as separate graphics files. The following steps show how to use the Clipboard to paste a graphic into VENTURA:

1. From VENTURA, switch to the application containing the graphic you want to import. Switch to CorelDRAW, for example.

2. Select the graphic you want to place in the VENTURA document. Choose Cut from the **E**dit menu to remove the text from its original location, or choose **C**opy from the **E**dit menu to place a duplicate of the graphic into the Clipboard.

3. Switch back to VENTURA and select the frame in which you want to paste the graphic.

4. Choose **P**aste from the **E**dit menu. Or click on the Paste button on the ribbon bar.

The graphic is placed in the selected frame.

In addition to being quicker, pasting graphics into VENTURA has another advantage over importing files. As discussed in the next section, *object linking and embedding* (OLE) provides a powerful way to work with graphics pasted into VENTURA.

Object Linking and Embedding (OLE)

As mentioned previously, imported graphics are stored as separate files that are retrieved when the chapter file is opened. To edit an imported graphic, you must open the application in which the graphic was created, make the changes, and save the file. The next time the VENTURA chapter file containing the graphics file is opened, the changes you made are evident. However, pasting a graphic into VENTURA creates a different type of connection between VENTURA and the graphic application. This connection is called object linking and embedding (OLE).

 Although OLE gives you a powerful way to edit graphics, embedded graphics can increase the size of your publication files significantly.

If the *source application* (the program where the graphic was created) supports OLE, the pasted graphic can be embedded in VENTURA. CorelDRAW supports OLE, for example, so when a CorelDRAW graphic is pasted into VENTURA, the graphic is embedded. Instead of having to return to the application in which the graphic was created to make changes, you can edit the graphic from within VENTURA.

Essentially, embedding enables you to open the source application while you are working in VENTURA. Suppose that you have paste embedded a graphic from CorelDRAW into VENTURA. To edit the graphic from VENTURA, simply double-click on the graphic. As shown in figure 11.7, this action causes CorelDRAW to open from within VENTURA. The embedded graphic appears on-screen, ready for any modification you want to make. After making the appropriate changes, choose E**x**it and Return from CorelDRAW's **F**ile menu. You are asked to update the latest changes to the document; click on Yes. CorelDRAW closes, and you are returned to the VENTURA document with the modified graphic in place.

III

Advanced VENTURA Options and Techniques

Figure 11.7
Double-clicking on an embedded CorelDRAW graphic launches the CorelDRAW application from within VENTURA.

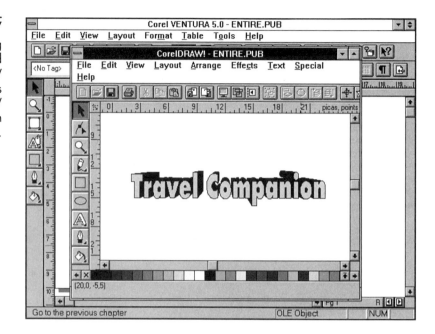

Modifying Graphics in VENTURA

After transferring graphics into VENTURA, you cannot manipulate the actual graphic. You cannot change the graphic's color or add or delete objects from the graphic, for example. You can, however, move and size graphics to suit the needs of your page design. As discussed later in this chapter, VENTURA also provides powerful features for scaling, cropping, and panning graphics to adjust which part of the imported graphic appears in the frame.

Adding Margins To Control Graphic Placement in the Frame

A graphic completely fills the frame and flows to the frame's edges. As a result, after importing a graphic, you might discover that it sits too close to other page elements. Text outside the frame, for example, might be placed too closely to the graphic. As you learned in Chapter 10, you can apply frame margins that add a cushion of white space inside and outside the frame to control the spacing. To adjust the frame margins, select the frame containing the graphic and then choose **F**rame from the For**m**at menu. Select the Margins tab and enter the desired margin settings. For more information on setting frame margins, see Chapter 10.

Moving Graphics

Moving a graphic means moving the frame containing the graphic. To move a graphic, you simply select the frame and drag it to a new location. As shown in figure 11.8, when a frame is selected, eight gray *selection handles* appear around the frame. Notice that the horizontal and vertical rulers adjust to create a *zero point* at the top left corner of the selected graphic. You can use the rulers to help you move a graphic a specific distance. Position the Pick tool along the top or left side of the image. When you drag the frame, tracking marks appear in the ruler, indicating how far the frame has been moved. Release the mouse button when the image is at the desired location.

Selection handles

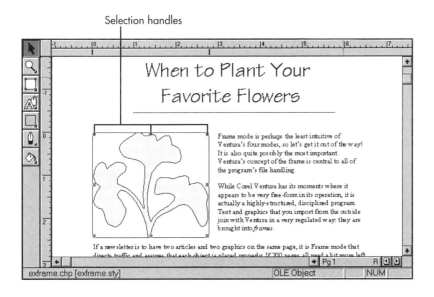

Figure 11.8
Selection handles appear around selected frames. The ruler also adjusts to display 0 at the top left corner of the frame.

Sizing Graphic Frames

When you bring a graphic into VENTURA, the size of the frame controls the size of the image. Even though the graphic might have been drawn originally at a different size, the graphic adjusts to the size of the frame when it is transferred into VENTURA. Frequently, any sizing you need to apply to a graphic can be accomplished by simply sizing the frame containing the graphic. When the frame is sized, the graphic enlarges or reduces to fit the adjusted frame size.

Tip

Bitmapped images cannot be sized without some compromise in image quality. If you must resize a bitmapped image, however, it is best to do so in halves and doubles. In other words, size the image to one-half (50 percent) or double (200 percent) its original size.

The easiest way to size a graphics frame is by using the mouse. Position the Pick tool on a selection handle and drag away from the frame to enlarge the frame; drag toward the center of the frame to reduce the frame size. Use the corner sizing handles to size the frame in both directions at once, and the interior handles to stretch the frame in only one direction at a time. When you size the graphics frame, VENTURA maintains the original proportions of the image, even when the frame is sized to an entirely different shape. The airplane frame in figure 11.9, for example, is wider than it is tall. Although the airplane frame might become bigger or smaller, you can see that the airplane maintains its basic proportions regardless of the frame size.

Figure 11.9
VENTURA maintains the original shape or aspect ratio of the graphic, even when the frame is stretched.

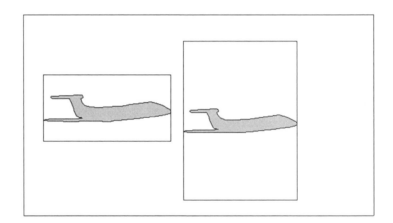

Sizing Graphics Independently of the Frame

For those times when you want more control over the size and shape of the graphic, VENTURA enables you to resize a graphic independently of the frame. With VENTURA, you can control the height, width, and proportions of a graphic. From the Format menu, select Frame, then click on the Graphic tab to display two options: Fit in Frame and Maintain Aspect Ratio (see fig. 11.10). These options give you the flexibility to enlarge, reduce, and stretch graphics to almost any dimensions.

When the Fit in Frame option is turned on, imported graphics assume the size of the frames. The size of the graphic appears in the Width and Height check boxes in the Dimensions area of the Frame Settings dialog box. Notice that the width and height are grayed out, and therefore cannot be altered. Turning off the Fit in Frame option displays the graphic at the size it was drawn originally. Suppose that your original graphic is five inches tall. If this graphic is loaded into a three-inch tall frame, the graphic is reduced to fit the frame. Turning off the Fit in Frame option displays the graphic at its original size, which, in this case, is larger than

the frame. In figure 11.11, the **F**it in Frame option is turned on for the first frame and off for the second. The graphic in the second frame is larger than the frame itself.

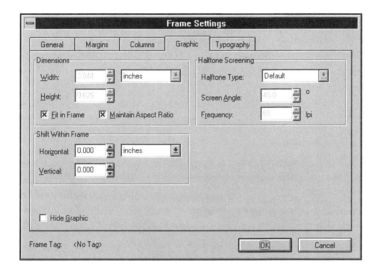

Figure 11.10
The Fit in Frame and Maintain Aspect Ratio options give you the flexibility to enlarge, reduce, and stretch graphics.

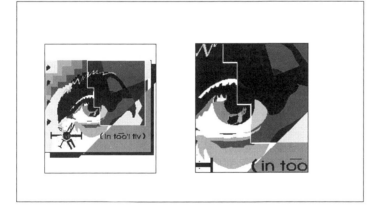

Figure 11.11
You can turn off the Fit in Frame option to adjust the size of the graphic without affecting the frame size.

When the **F**it in Frame option is turned off, the original size of the graphic is displayed in the **W**idth and **H**eight boxes. In addition to restoring the graphic to its original size, turning off the **F**it in Frame option enables you to change the size of the graphic. Notice that the **W**idth box no longer is grayed out. You can enter an amount to enlarge or reduce the width of the graphic. By turning off **F**it in Frame, you can adjust the size of the graphic while leaving the size of the frame intact.

The **F**it in Frame option generally is used to enlarge graphics that you want to crop. As discussed later in this section, cropping enables you to remove parts of the graphic from view.

The **M**aintain Aspect Ratio option ensures that the original shape of the graphic is maintained. As discussed, you can enter a new width for a graphic when **F**it in Frame is turned off. You cannot enter a new height, however, because the **M**aintain Aspect Ratio option is turned on. The **M**aintain Aspect Ratio option adjusts the height to match proportionally the amount entered in the **W**idth box. If you increase the width of a graphic, the height increases in an amount proportional to the graphic's shape.

Turning off **M**aintain Aspect Ratio makes the **H**eight option available. Now, you can stretch or distort the graphic's shape by entering dimensions in the **W**idth and **H**eight boxes. Suppose that your graphic was originally three inches tall and five inches wide. Turning off the **F**it in Frame and **M**aintain Aspect Ratio options enables you to change the shape to five inches tall and three inches wide. As displayed in figure 11.12, these options enable you to really reshape the proportions of your graphics. To resize graphics, use the following steps:

Figure 11.12
Turning off the
Maintain Aspect
Ratio option
enables you to
specify the width
and height of a
graphic.

1. Select the frame containing the graphic you want to adjust.

2. Choose **G**raphic from the For**m**at menu.

   The Frame Settings dialog box appears with the Graphic tab selected (refer to fig. 11.10).

3. To enlarge or reduce an image proportionately, disable the **F**it in Frame option but leave the **M**aintain Aspect Ratio option enabled. To stretch an image to new dimensions, disable the **M**aintain Aspect Ratio feature.

4. In the **W**idth and **H**eight boxes, enter the dimensions you want the graphic to assume.

5. Click on OK to make the changes and return to the document.

Cropping and Panning Graphics

After enlarging a graphic, you have complete control over the cropping of the image. *Cropping* determines what portion of the graphic appears in the frame. By default, when you size a graphic by disabling **F**it to Frame, the top left corner of the graphic is anchored at the top left corner of the frame. Although the rest of the image appears to be cut off by the frame, it is still accessible by moving the graphic *inside* the frame. Moving a graphic within a frame is called *panning*. The first frame in figure 11.13 displays the top left corner of an enlarged photograph. In the second frame, the image has been repositioned by panning, which is demonstrated in the following steps:

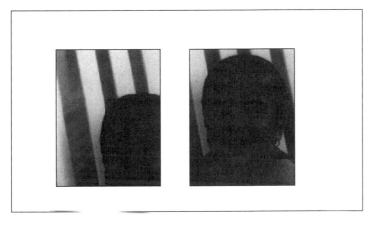

Figure 11.13
Panning enables you to control what portion of an image is visible in the frame.

III

Advanced VENTURA Options and Techniques

1. Select the frame containing the graphic you want to adjust.

2. While pressing Ctrl, drag with the mouse on the graphic.

The mouse shape changes to a hand. You might have to move slowly and wait for the repositioned image to redraw on-screen. When the area you want to appear in the frame is positioned, release the mouse.

You also can use the Shift Within Frame options in the Graphics tab of the Frame Settings dialog box to reposition a graphic within a frame. Enter the amount you want to shift the image in the Hori**z**ontal and **V**ertical boxes, then click on OK.

Wrapping Text Around Graphics

To add visual variety to your page layouts, VENTURA offers an option to depart from the traditional block structure of page design by creating text that conforms to the shape of your graphics. In figure 11.14, for example, the text wraps around the shape of the dinosaur for an interesting visual effect.

Figure 11.14
VENTURA's text wrap feature enables you to conform text to the shape of your graphics.

> ## Dinosaurs are Tops
> ## With Children and Adults
>
> Visit autem vel eum iriure dolor in hendrerit in vulputate velit esse molestie consequat, vel illum dolore eu feugiat nulla facilisis at vero eros et accumsan et iusto odio dignissim qui blandit praesent luptatum zzril delenit augue duis dolore te feugait nulla facilisi. Lorem ipsum dolor sit amet. Consectetuer adipiscing elit, sed diam nonummy
>
> Over 100,000 people visited the Dinosaur Exhibit at the City Town Mall in July.
>
> nibh euismod tincidunt ut laoreet dolore magna aliquam erat volutpat. 2255 Holl, quis nostrud exerci tation ullamcorper suscipit lobortis nisl ut aliquip ex ea commodo consequat. Duis autem vel eum iriure dolor in hendrerit in vulputate velit esse molestie consequat, vel illum dolore eu feugiat nulla facilisis at vero eros et accumsan et iusto odio dignissim qui blandit

To wrap text around a graphic, you must establish a path around the graphic to create a buffer between the text and the graphic. Otherwise, text might flow on top of the graphic, making it difficult to read. You can establish a path around a graphic in two basic ways. You can create a path that is the same shape as the graphic, or you can apply a preset path such as a diamond or heart shape for text to flow around. In figure 11.15, the text is wrapped around the graphic using the Oval Preset text wrap.

Text wrap can be applied only to imported graphics. You cannot apply text wrap to graphics pasted through the Clipboard. Use the following exercise to apply a text path to a graphic:

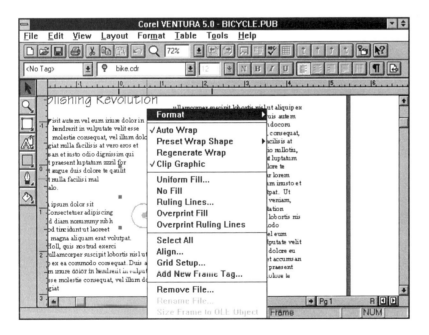

Figure 11.15
Wrapped text can conform to the shape of the graphic or follow a preset path shape.

1. Select the frame containing the graphic you want to wrap text around.

2. Click the right mouse button to reveal the pop-up menu shown in figure 11.16.

Figure 11.16
The pop-up menu with the available text wrap options.

Advanced VENTURA Options and Techniques

3. From the menu, choose Auto Wrap to insert a path the same shape as the graphic. Or, to pour the graphic into a preset shape, choose Preset Wrap Shape and choose a shape from the submenu list.

After selecting a text wrap path, a dotted path with a series of "nodes" appears around the graphic, and the cursor changes to the Node Edit tool. You can modify this path by moving and manipulating the nodes to change the path shape. You also can change the shape of the curve segments by clicking-and-dragging on the control points on either side of each node. This process is identical to the node editing performed in CorelDRAW. For even greater control, you can add new nodes and change the node type by double-clicking on the Shape tool to open the Node Edit Roll-up.

After reshaping the path, select Refresh **W**indow from the **V**iew menu or press Ctrl+W to redraw the screen with the new text wrap path. After the path is generated, you can move or resize the graphics frame, and text continues to wrap around the path. If you have distorted the original path to an unworkable level, you can restore the path to its original shape by clicking the right mouse button on the graphic and choosing Regenerate Wrap from the flyout. To remove the path from the graphic, select that path option again from the flyout. The graphic returns to its original status with no text wrap.

Working with Halftone Images

Halftoning is the process of printing photographs with a series of dots rather than the continuous tone images you see on your photographs. A black-and-white continuous tone photo might contain hundreds of shades of gray. Because printers are unable to reproduce this number of shades, the halftone process converts the shades to patterns of black dots. In the darker areas of your printed photos, the dots are larger and closer together, and in the lighter areas, the dots are smaller and farther apart, enabling the white of the paper to show through.

VENTURA provides controls for modifying the halftoning process. You can control the halftone screen type, the halftone screen angle, and the lines per inch. These options are set for you based on the printer you have chosen. In most cases, these defaults work very well. If you decide to modify the halftone options, they are available in the Graphics tab of the Frame Settings dialog box. These options are available only for grayscale bitmap images that are printed to a PostScript printer.

The halftone features are fairly advanced and should not be modified unless you are really sure of their properties and functions. For more information on working with these features, you should consult your documentation or speak with a representative from your printer or service bureau.

Chapter Snapshot

By including a drawing or other graphic in your document, you ensure that your page designs will attract and keep your reader's attention. In this chapter, you learn to do the following:

VENTURA's drawing tools enable you to embellish your pages with simple shapes. This chapter shows you how to use the tools and makes it easy for you to add visual impact to your text.

CHAPTER

Drawing and Editing Graphics in VENTURA

Graphics are a key element of good page design. The photos, technical drawings, charts, and illustrations included in your documents are atten tion-grabbers. They are designed to explain technical concepts, empha-size sales growth, and provide visual support to your text. Many of the graphics placed in your VENTURA documents are created by drawing applications such as CorelDRAW and CorelPHOTO-PAINT. These applications provide the kind of high-power tools needed to design professional, eye-catching graphics. You don't always have to use a separate drawing program to create graphics, however. To enhance a page with simple graphics, such as lines, circles, and squares, you can put the drawing tools provided by VENTURA to work.

This chapter examines drawing and editing with the drawing tools included in VENTURA. First, the chapter discusses attaching graphics to frames. You also will learn the steps for adding a grid to aid in sizing and positioning graphic shapes. You then will learn the ways in which you can use the drawing tools to create shapes. You will learn how to draw circles, squares, lines, and box text. The chapter then discusses editing these shapes. Finally, you will learn the steps for repeating, stacking, and adjusting the fill and line attributes of graphics.

Drawing Graphics with VENTURA

VENTURA provides a set of drawing tools that enable you to create simple illustrations, graphs, maps, and logos. The line graph in figure 12.1 is a sample of what you can create with basic shapes. After you draw an object, you can manipulate it by using a variety of methods. You can move a graphic, size it, or duplicate it, for example. You also can choose from a wide range of fill colors and line thicknesses to create even more enticing designs.

Figure 12.1

You can create a wide variety of designs with the drawing tools provided by VENTURA.

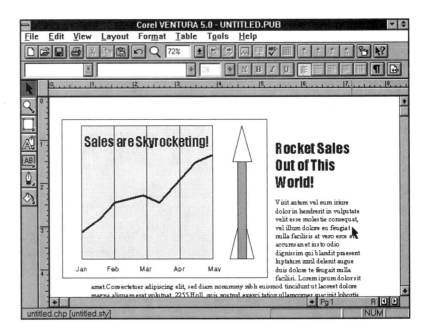

As explained in the following section, it is important to understand the ways in which graphics are attached to frames before you begin drawing and designing with graphics.

Attaching Graphics to Frames

VENTURA attaches shapes you create with the drawing tools to the base page frame or to a free frame. When a shape is attached to a free frame, the shape moves with the frame when it is moved, cut, or copied. Suppose that you attach a circle to a free frame. If you delete the free frame, the circle also is deleted. If you move the frame to page 10, the circle also moves to page 10. You can attach several graphics to a frame. In figure 12.2, one frame was selected when the circle

and square were drawn, meaning that both shapes are attached to the same frame. If you move the frame, the circle and square also move.

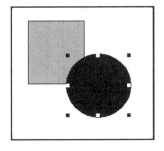

Figure 12.2
You can attach several graphics to a single frame.

Attaching several graphics to a free frame creates a connection between the graphics. If you are accustomed to drawing programs such as CorelDRAW, think of attaching several graphics to a free frame as being similar to creating a group of objects. Suppose that you create a logo with the drawing tools, attaching all the shapes that comprise the logo to a free frame. If you decide to reposition the logo on the page, you simply drag the frame to the desired location; all the graphics in the logo move with the frame. If you decide to copy the logo to another page or chapter, you simply copy the frame, and all the components of the logo are copied as well.

To attach a graphics shape to a free frame, you must select the frame before you draw the shape. If you are attaching several shapes to a frame, you must select the frame before you draw each shape. Remember that to select a frame, you can click in the frame with the Pick tool, and the selection handles appear around the frame. When you select a frame and then select a drawing tool, the selection handles turn light gray. In figure 12.3, the light gray handles around the frame indicate that it was selected when the rectangle shape was drawn.

Keep in mind that graphics attached to frames do not have to be placed in the frame. The frame can be at the top of the page, for example, and the attached graphic can be at the bottom of the page. As long as that frame is selected when the graphic is drawn, the shape is attached to the frame. This feature can be frustrating if you are not careful. You might not even realize graphics are attached to a frame until you delete the frame, and suddenly your graphics are gone. (If this happens, you can select <u>U</u>ndo from the <u>E</u>dit menu to return the frame and the attached graphics.)

The free frames to which you attach graphics can be set up to display a grid. The following section describes preparing your work area for drawing graphics by displaying a grid.

III

Advanced VENTURA Options and Techniques

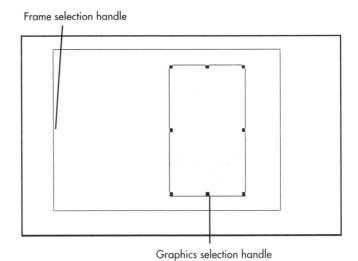

Figure 12.3
You must select a
frame before you
can add graphics
to it.

Frame selection handle

Graphics selection handle

Working with a Drawing Grid

When drawing graphics, you can set up a grid to aid in controlling the size and placement of the objects. A *grid* consists of horizontal and vertical lines that cover the entire page. *Grid markers* provide visual references for the grid. Figure 12.4 shows a grid used to align a group of objects and gauge their sizes. With VENTURA, you specify the amount of space placed between the gridlines. You can set up a grid in quarter-inch segments by placing four horizontal and vertical lines per inch on the page, for example.

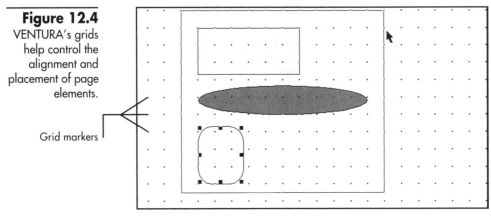

Figure 12.4
VENTURA's grids
help control the
alignment and
placement of page
elements.

Grid markers

New Riders Publishing
INSIDE
SERIES

Displaying Grid Markers

The grid markers represent the intersection of the horizontal and vertical gridlines. As figure 12.4 shows, the markers appear as black dots. To see the grid markers, choose Pre<u>f</u>erences from the T<u>o</u>ols menu. Click on the View tab, and enable the <u>G</u>rids option. An *X* indicates that the feature is turned on. Click on OK to display the grid markers on the page area. The <u>G</u>rids option remains selected until you return to the Preferences dialog box and disable the feature. The grid markers still are visible if you exit VENTURA and then restart the program.

Setting Up a Grid

You can define individual grid settings for each frame on a page. You can set up one frame with a grid in $^1/_2$-inch segments, and another frame with a grid in $^1/_4$-inch segments, for example. Any graphics attached to a frame adhere to that frames specific grid settings.

In VENTURA, the grid spacing or frequency is controlled by specifying the number of gridlines that appear per inch (or some other unit of measurement). To create a 1-inch grid, for example, you can enter 1 gridline per 1 inch. A $^1/_8$-inch grid is 8 gridlines per 1 inch. You can enter varying amounts for the horizontal and vertical gridlines.

Before creating a grid, turn on the display of the grid markers, as described in the preceding section. Otherwise, you will not be able to see your new grid setup. The following steps illustrate setting up a grid:

1. Select the free frame where you want to set up the grid.

2. Choose <u>G</u>rid Setup from the T<u>o</u>ols menu. You also can access this command by clicking the right mouse button in the frame and choosing Grid Setup from the pop-up menu.

   The Grid Setup dialog box appears (see fig. 12.5).

3. In the H<u>o</u>rizontal box, enter the number of horizontal gridlines you want to display per inch. In the V<u>e</u>rtical box, enter the number of vertical gridlines you want to display per inch.

4. Click on OK.

Grid markers appear on the page representing the new grid. Repeat these steps to set up a grid for another frame.

III

Advanced VENTURA Options and Techniques

Figure 12.5
The Grid Setup
dialog box.

You might have to zoom in if you do not see all the specified grid markers. If you set up a grid with 10 lines per inch, for example, not all the grid markers appear until you zoom in closer to the frame. In figure 12.6, a close-up of the frame displays 10 grid markers per inch.

Figure 12.6
You might have to
zoom in on the
page to see all
the specified
grid markers.

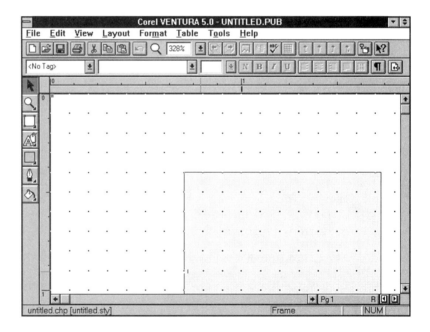

To use another measurement system for establishing the grid, click on the down arrow in the "per" field of the Grid Setup dialog box. Select a measurement system and enter a grid frequency. You can build a grid in picas by entering 1 line per pica, for example.

Using Snap To

The S**n**ap To Grid option in the Grid Setup dialog box applies a "magnetic-pull effect" to the gridlines. If the S**n**ap To Grid option is enabled when you move an object, the edges of the object are pulled to the grid markers. In figure 12.7, the S**n**ap To Grid option was used to align the bottoms of the rectangles to the same horizontal gridline. When you are drawing objects, the S**n**ap To Grid option forces the size of the new object to meet the grid markers. In figure 12.7, the S**n**ap To Grid feature made it easy to create rectangles that are 1-inch wide and a $^1/_2$-inch tall.

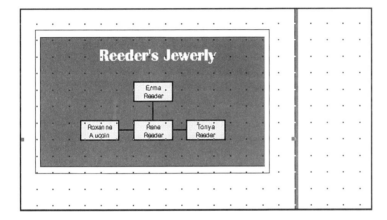

Figure 12.7
Turn on the Snap To Grid option to force objects to align with the grid markers.

To activate the S**n**ap To Grid feature, place an *X* in the S**n**ap To Grid check box in the Grid Setup dialog box when setting up your grid. Objects do not snap to the grid, however, until the Snap to **G**rid command in the **L**ayout menu also is enabled. A marker appears next to the Snap to **G**rid command when it is turned on. Both the S**n**ap To Grid option in the dialog box and the Snap to **G**rid command in the **L**ayout menu must be turned on in order for the Snap To feature to work.

Create a grid on the base page frame to align the free frames used to build the page layout.

After the S**n**ap To Grid option in the Grid Setup dialog box is enabled, you can quickly turn the Snap To feature on and off by pressing the keyboard shortcut Ctrl+Y. This shortcut enables you to access the power of Snap To **G**rid when desired, and quickly disable it when you do not want objects to pull to the gridlines.

Drawing Graphics

VENTURA provides a set of drawing tools for enhancing your page with basic graphics. The drawing tools are stored in a flyout toolbar (see fig. 12.8). To see the drawing tools, press and hold on the Rectangle tool, which is directly below the Text tool. When you select a drawing tool, it becomes active and remains displayed until you change to another drawing tool.

Figure 12.8
VENTURA's
drawing tools.

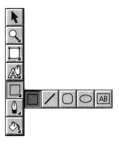

Table 12.1 examines the function of each drawing tool.

Table 12.1
VENTURA's Drawing Tools

Icon	Tool	Function
□	Rectangle	Draws rectangles and squares
/	Straight Line	Draws straight lines
○	Rounded Rectangle	Draws squares and rectangles with rounded corners
○	Ellipse	Draws ellipses and circles
AB	Box Text	Draws rectangles and squares in which text can be added

When you begin drawing shapes, each shape is formatted with preset attributes. These default settings determine the thickness of the lines and the color used to fill the shapes. After you draw a square, for example, the square might be filled with gray or some other color. The steps for changing the fill and outline attributes are covered later in this chapter. Advanced options, such as fountain fills, arrowheads, and dashed lines are covered in Chapter 13, "Applying Fills and Outlines to Frames and Graphics."

Selecting a Drawing Tool

You must select the appropriate tool before drawing a shape. To select a drawing tool, press and hold the Rectangle button to reveal the flyout toolbar. Click on the tool you want. As you move into the page area, notice that the shape of the mouse cursor changes to a crosshair.

Drawing Lines

You use the Straight Line tool to draw diagonal, horizontal, and vertical straight lines. As shown in figure 12.9, you can combine these lines to draw other objects, such as stars and triangles.

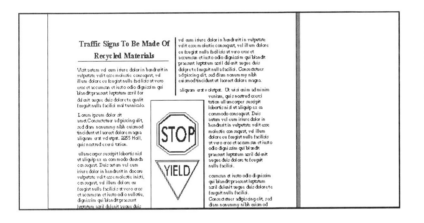

Figure 12.9
Use the Straight Line tool to draw diagonal, horizontal, and vertical lines.

1. If you want to attach a line to a free frame, select the frame now.

2. Select the Straight Line tool and place the crosshair where you want to begin the line.

3. Press and hold the left mouse button, drag to where you want to end the line, and release the mouse.

Press Ctrl while drawing to create lines that snap to 15-degree increments. Be sure to release the mouse button before you release Ctrl.

Drawing Rectangles and Squares

VENTURA provides two tools for drawing rectangles and squares. As shown in figure 12.10, the Rectangle tool draws the rectangle and square shapes with straight corners. The Rounded Rectangle tool draws rectangles and squares with rounded corners. Rounded rectangles often are used to add borders to fliers and brochures.

Advanced VENTURA Options and Techniques

Figure 12.10
VENTURA provides drawing tools that enable you to draw rectangles and squares with straight or rounded corners.

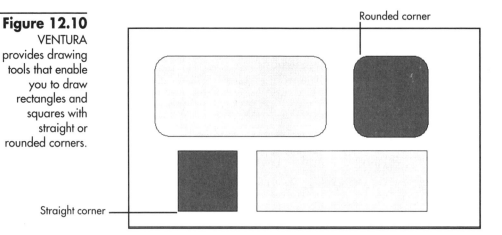

The process for drawing rectangles and squares with straight or rounded corners is the same, except for the drawing tool used.

1. If you want to attach the rectangle or square to a free frame, select the frame now.

2. To draw rectangles and squares with straight corners, select the Rectangle tool. To draw rectangles and squares with rounded corners, select the Rounded Rectangle tool.

3. Place the crosshair where you want the top left corner of the shape to appear.

4. Press and hold the left mouse button and drag down to the right (see fig. 12.11). You see an outline of the shape as you draw. Release the mouse button when the outline is the shape you want.

Figure 12.11
Drag down to the right to draw rectangles and squares. An outline of the shape appears as you draw.

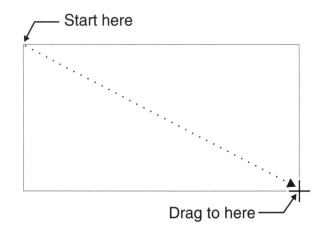

Press Ctrl while drawing to create perfect squares. Be sure to release the mouse button before you release Ctrl.

Drawing Ellipses and Circles

You can use circles and ellipses to create a variety of logos (see fig. 12.12). The following process for drawing ellipses and circles is very similar to the process for drawing rectangles and squares.

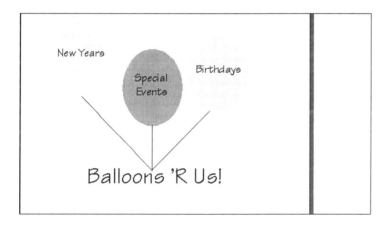

Figure 12.12
Use the Ellipse tool to add ellipses and circles to your page design.

1. If you want to attach the ellipse or circle to a free frame, select the frame now.

2. Select the Ellipse tool and place the crosshair where you want the top left corner of the circular shape to appear.

3. Press and hold the left mouse button and drag down to the right. An outline of the shape appears. Release the mouse button when the outline is the shape you want.

Press Ctrl while drawing to create perfect circles. Be sure to release the mouse button before you release Ctrl.

Drawing with the Box Text Tool

You can use the Box Text tool when you need to place text in your graphics. By using the Box Text tool, you can draw a rectangle or square, and then enter text into the shape. The box text object has an outline and fill color. If you remove the outline and fill, only the text is visible. You can remove the outline and fill to create a block of text and place it over a circle or other graphic.

Advanced VENTURA Options and Techniques

1. If you want to attach the box text object to a free frame, select the frame now.

2. Select the Box Text tool and place the crosshair where you want the top left corner of the box shape to appear.

3. Press and hold the left mouse button and drag down to the right. An outline of the shape appears. Release the mouse button when the outline is the shape you want.

   Press Ctrl while drawing to create perfect squares. Be sure to release the mouse button before you release Ctrl.

4. An end-of-file marker (a white square) appears in the box text object. Select the Text tool and click before the end-of-file marker.

   The insertion point appears (often called an *I-beam* for its shape), and you can begin entering text.

VENTURA automatically applies the generated paragraph tag Z_BOXTEXT to text placed in a box text object. Use the Tagged Text or Freeform Text tool to modify the attributes of the text. See Chapter 7, "Formatting Tagged and Freeform Text," for more information.

Drawing Several Objects at One Time

After you draw a shape, VENTURA automatically selects the Pick tool. After the Ellipse tool is selected and a circle is drawn, for example, the Ellipse tool is deselected and the Pick tool is selected. If you want to draw another circle, you must reselect the drawing tool. If you press Shift as you draw a shape, however, the selected drawing tool stays activated, enabling you to draw multiple shapes. Pressing Shift while drawing a circle, for example, keeps the Ellipse tool selected so that you can draw several circles at one time.

You also can use the *Pasteboard area*—the white space to the right of the document area—as extra work space for drawing objects. Objects in the Pasteboard area do not print.

Selecting Objects

Before moving, sizing, or formatting graphics created with VENTURA's drawing tools, you must select the graphic to be edited. Selecting indicates to VENTURA which graphic on the page you want the editing command to modify. Before

deleting a circle, for example, you must select it. Before changing the fill color of a square, you must select it. As figure 12.13 and the following steps demonstrate, selection handles appear around a graphic shape when it is selected:

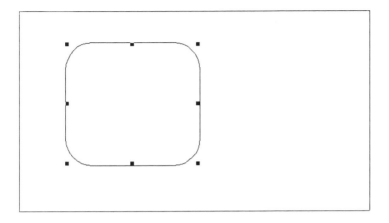

Figure 12.13
Selection handles appear around a graphic shape when it is selected.

1. Select the Pick tool (it is the first tool in the toolbox).

2. Position the mouse cursor on the shape and click. Selection handles appear around the object, indicating that it is selected.

In certain designs, you might want to stack or layer graphics on top of each other. This makes the bottom-most graphic rather hard to select. Press Alt while clicking to select graphics that are placed underneath other graphics.

 Working with the stacking order of graphics is discussed later in this chapter in the section "Layering Graphics."

By default, only one graphic can be selected at a time. If you want to select several graphics, press Shift while clicking on other graphics. To select two objects, for example, select the first object, press Shift, and click on the second object. Selecting several graphics at one time enables you to move or format several graphics at one time.

The pop-up menu provides another quick way to select multiple graphics. Place the mouse on the shape and click the right mouse button to reveal the pop-up menu. Choose Select All to select all other graphics attached to the same frame as the graphic on which you initially clicked the right mouse button.

Editing Graphics

Tinkering with the size and position of the graphics, adjusting line thickness, and selecting colors are all part of designing with graphics. This section focuses on editing, modifying, and formatting your newly drawn graphics.

Deleting Graphics

After drawing graphics on your page, you might decide that you added a few too many. To delete a graphic, simply select it and choose Delete from the **E**dit menu. You also can press Del to remove a graphic. If you accidentally delete a graphic, immediately choose **U**ndo from the **E**dit menu to retrieve it.

To delete several graphics at one time, press Shift to select multiple graphics before choosing the Delete command. Remember that you can delete all graphics attached to a free frame simply by deleting the frame.

Moving Graphics

You can move graphics anywhere on the page—even in the margin areas. The easiest way to move graphics is with the mouse; however, you also can enter exact coordinates for positioning a graphic by using the Placement Roll-up.

See Chapter 4 for more information about using the Placement Roll-up when sizing and moving frames.

To move several graphics as a group, press Shift and continue selecting all the graphics. Also, you simply can move a free frame to which graphics are attached.

1. Select the graphic. (Remember that you use the Pick tool to select frames.)

   Selection handles appear around the graphic when it is selected.

2. Place the mouse cursor on the graphic. Hold down the mouse button and drag the graphic to a new place on the page.

   An outline appears as you move the graphic. Also, the mouse cursor shape changes to a four-sided arrow.

3. When the graphic is in the desired location, release the mouse button.

You cannot move a graphic from one page to another by dragging. To move a frame to another page, use the Cut or Copy command, as discussed later in this chapter.

You can use the Placement Roll-up to enter coordinates for horizontal and vertical measurements, indicating precisely where a graphic is to be placed. The *horizontal* measurement specifies the distance from the left edge of the square to the left edge of the page. The *vertical* measurement specifies the distance from the top edge of the square to the top edge of the page (see fig. 12.14).

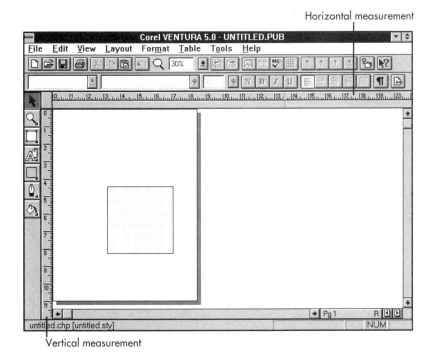

Horizontal measurement

Vertical measurement

Figure 12.14

You can use the Placement Roll-up to enter exact coordinates for positioning graphics.

The following steps illustrate positioning a rounded rectangle exactly two inches from the left of the page and three inches from the top of the page:

1. Draw a rounded rectangle anywhere on the page.

2. Choose **P**lacement Roll-Up from the T**o**ols menu.

   The Placement Roll-up appears, as displayed in figure 12.15.

3. Select the rounded rectangle. The Placement Roll-up shows the current horizontal and vertical position of the graphic.

Advanced VENTURA Options and Techniques

Figure 12.15
The Placement
Roll-up.

4. In the **O**rigin section, enter **2** in the Horizontal (H) box and **3** in the Vertical (**V**) box.

Click on the Apply button to move the graphic.

The rounded rectangle is positioned accordingly. Close the roll-up.

Sizing Graphics

It is rather tricky to get the perfect size for a graphic on the first try. VENTURA makes it easy to resize the ellipses, rectangles, and other graphics you have drawn on the page. As with moving frames, the mouse provides the quickest way to resize a frame, although you also can enter exact dimensions in the Placement Roll-up to size a frame.

When sizing with the mouse, you use the selection handles to size a graphic. If you press Ctrl as you size, the original shape of the graphic is maintained. For instance, if you hold Ctrl while sizing a perfect circle, the width and height of the circle are adjusted to maintain the circular shape. If you hold Ctrl while sizing an ellipse, the width and height of the ellipse are adjusted to maintain the original elliptical shape. You can distort the original shape of the graphic by not pressing Ctrl as you size the shape. Figure 12.16 illustrates how two copies of the same circle shape can be sized. The Ctrl key was held as the first circle was sized, maintaining the circle shape. The Ctrl key was not held when the second shape was sized, allowing the circle to be stretched into an ellipse.

1. Draw and select a circle.

2. Position the mouse cursor over one of the selection buttons.

   The cursor changes to a double-sided arrow.

3. To enlarge the frame, drag away from the graphic's center. To reduce the frame, drag toward the graphic's center. Press Ctrl while dragging to maintain the original circular shape as you reduce or enlarge the circle.

4. When the outline appears in the size you want, release the mouse button.

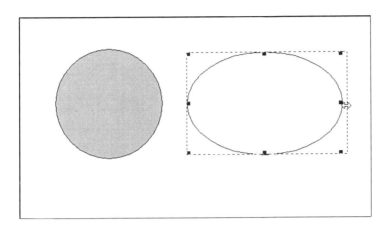

Figure 12.16
Hold the Ctrl key while sizing a graphic shape to maintain the original shape as you reduce or enlarge the graphic.

You can use the Placement Roll-up to enter exact measurements for the height and width of a graphic. As an example, the Placement Roll-up makes it easy to create a rectangle that measures exactly 4.25 × 3.15 inches. The following steps illustrate sizing a rectangle to be 4.25 × 3.15 inches tall.

1. Choose **P**lacement Roll-Up from the T**o**ols menu.

   The Placement Roll-up appears.

2. Select the rectangle you want to size.

   The Placement Roll-up shows the current height and width of the frame.

3. In the **S**ize section, enter **4.25** in the Width (W) box and **3.15** in the Height (**H**) box.

4. Click on the Apply button to size the frame. If desired, close the roll-up.

The Placement Roll-up includes options for applying the same size to a group of selected graphics. With the Same Size command, you can instruct all selected graphics to become the same size as the last graphic selected. The first set of squares in figure 12.17 shows three squares in various sizes. The second set shows the same three squares after their sizes have been adjusted to match the largest square. The following steps describe using the Same Size command:

1. Choose **P**lacement Roll-Up from the T**o**ols menu.

   The Placement Roll-up appears.

2. Select several graphics. Press Shift while clicking to select multiple graphics. The graphic of the size you want to duplicate should be the last graphic selected.

III

Advanced VENTURA Options and Techniques

Figure 12.17
The Same Size command forces all objects to assume the size of the last object selected.

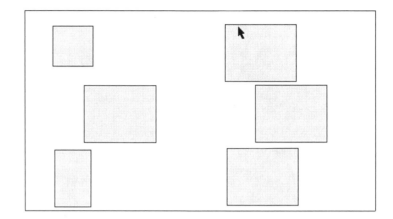

3. Click on the flyout menu arrow to reveal the flyout menu (see fig 12.18). Choose Same Size. All the selected graphics are sized to match the size of the last selected graphic.

Figure 12.18
The Placement Roll-up with the flyout menu displayed.

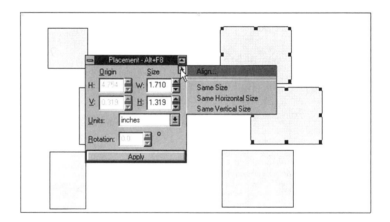

Layering Graphics

Graphics drawn with VENTURA's drawing tools are placed on the page in the order they were drawn or pasted on the page. The objects in figure 12.19 were drawn in this order: a circle first, then a rounded corner rectangle, and finally the square. Because the circle was drawn first, it is on the bottom, and because the square was drawn last, it is on top.

At times, you might want to change the stacking order of graphics by moving a graphic in front of or behind other graphics. For example, as in the stack of objects on the right in figure 12.19, you might want to place the circle on top of the square.

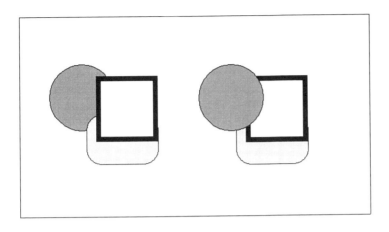

Figure 12.19
You can change
the stacking order
of graphics.

1. Select the image or images you want to reposition.

   Selection handles appear around selected objects.

2. Click the right mouse button to reveal the pop-up menu shown in figure 12.20.

3. Choose Send to Back or Bring to Front to reposition the selected objects.

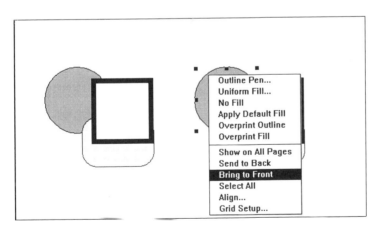

Figure 12.20
The pop-up menu
provides
commands to
change the
stacking order of
graphics.

You can change the stacking order of graphics only for graphics that are attached to the same frame. In other words, you cannot send a graphic attached to one frame behind a graphic attached to a previously drawn frame. Remember that graphics appear on the document in the order they were drawn. A graphic attached to one frame that appears beneath a graphic attached to another frame can be moved to the front by copying the first graphic to the Clipboard, and then pasting it back into its frame. Because the pasted graphic is the last element placed on the page, it will be on top of all other graphics.

Aligning Graphics

Rather than just "eyeballing it" when arranging graphics vertically or horizontally, use the Align command for precise alignment. You can align graphics with other graphics or to the center of the page. The Align command works only on those graphics that are in the same frame. You cannot align graphics in the base frame to graphics in a free frame, for example. In figure 12.21, the first set of shapes is vertically left aligned, and the second set of shapes is aligned horizontally across the top.

Figure 12.21
VENTURA makes it easy to align graphics for a professional look.

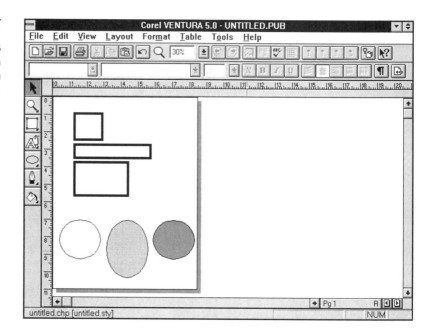

 You also can use the Align command when placing frames on the page. See Chapter 4 for more information.

When aligning graphics with each other, the last graphic selected is used as the alignment guide—all other selected graphics move to align with the last graphic you select, as demonstrated in the following exercise:

1. Select the graphics you want to align. Make sure that the graphic to be used as the alignment guide is selected last.

2. Choose **A**lign from the T**o**ols menu.

   The Align dialog box appears (see fig. 12.22).

3. Select the desired alignment. Select **L**eft in the Horizontally section to align the left sides of the graphics. Select **T**op in the Vertically section to align the top edges of the graphics.

4. Click on OK to perform the alignment.

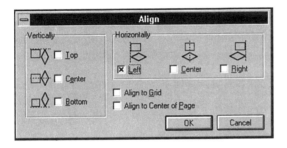

Figure 12.22
The Align
dialog box.

The Align command provides an option for placing graphics in the exact center of the page. If several graphics are selected, the graphics are moved to the center of the page and overlap each other.

1. Select the graphic(s) you want to move.

2. Choose **A**lign from the T**o**ols menu. In the Align dialog box, place an *X* in the Align to Center of **P**age check box. Notice that the Vertically C**e**nter and Horizontally **C**enter options are selected.

3. Click on OK.

The selected graphic(s) are moved to the center of the page.

By default, the Center to **P**age option places the graphic in the horizontal and vertical center of the page. You can adjust this placement to fit your needs. In figure 12.23, the graphic is aligned to the horizontal center of the page, but not to the vertical center. After selecting the Center to **P**age option, click on the Vertically C**e**nter or Horizontally **C**enter option to turn off that particular type of alignment. The *X* disappears when the option is disabled.

Advanced VENTURA Options and Techniques

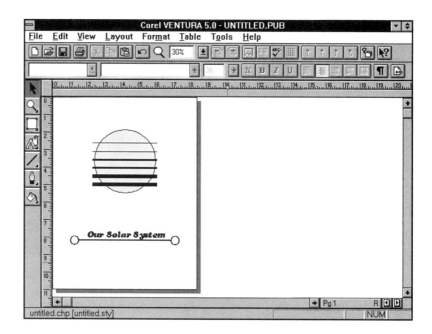

Figure 12.23
You can control an object's horizontal and vertical centering with the Center to Page command.

Cutting, Copying, and Pasting Graphics

On occasion, you might find it necessary to move a graphic drawn in VENTURA to another location, or to place a copy of a graphic in a new location. Suppose that you have created a graphic on page 6 with VENTURA's drawing tools, and then later decide that you want to move the graphic or use a copy of the graphic on page 9. The Windows Clipboard provides an efficient way to move or copy graphics to a new location.

1. Select the graphic you want to move or copy. Press Shift while clicking to select multiple objects.

   Selection handles appear around each object selected.

2. Choose Cut from the **E**dit menu. Or click on the Cut button on the ribbon bar to remove the selected object from its original location and place it in the Clipboard.

3. Choose **C**opy from the **E**dit menu. Or click on the Copy button on the ribbon bar to place a duplicate of the object in the Clipboard.

4. Go to the page where you want to place the graphic. Choose **P**aste from the **E**dit menu. Or click on the Paste button on the ribbon bar.

The graphic is pasted in the same position on the page as it originally appeared. After graphics are pasted, they can be moved, sized, and manipulated as any other graphics element drawn in VENTURA. It is important to note that if you cut or copy a free frame containing graphics, the graphics in the frame also are pasted at the new location.

Repeating Graphics

Suppose that you're working on a overhead presentation and want your company's logo to appear on every page. Rather than copying and pasting a copy of the logo on each page, you can use the Show On All Pages command to repeat the logo on every page of the chapter file, as the following steps show:

1. Select the graphic you want to repeat.

2. Place the mouse cursor over the graphic and click the right mouse button.

3. Choose Show on All Pages from the pop-up menu.

As discussed in Chapter 4, you also can repeat frames on every page of a chapter file.

Repeated graphics appear in the same spot on every page. It's important to note that if you move the graphic on one page, it also moves the graphics on every other page. In fact, any changes made to a repeating graphic are reflected on every page of the chapter file.

The graphic appears on every page. You cannot delete a repeated graphic on one page without deleting the graphics on all pages.

Select the repeating graphic and choose the Show on All Pages command again to disable the repeating feature.

Applying Line Widths and Fills to Graphics

Newly drawn graphics use a default line thickness, line color, and fill or interior color. You can change these attributes for any graphic drawn in VENTURA. This section discusses using preset line and fill options to change the appearance of graphics drawn in VENTURA. Chapter 13, explores the full range of options available for changing graphics attributes.

See Chapter 13 for the steps for changing the default attributes applied to new graphics.

Changing Line Attributes of Graphics

The Outline tool provides several preset options for modifying the appearance of lines created with VENTURA's drawing tools. These options apply to lines as well as to the outlines of objects such as ellipses and rectangles. Click on the Outline tool (the second to last tool in the toolbox) to display the flyout (see fig. 12.24).

Figure 12.24
Click on the
Outline tool to
reveal the flyout.

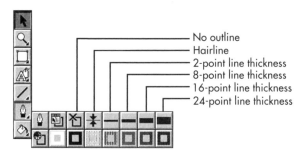

The last six buttons on the top of the flyout offer preset line thicknesses. The button marked with a square and a X removes the outline entirely. The next button enables you to apply a hairline thickness ($^2/_{10}$ of an inch). The final buttons apply 2-point, 8-point, 16-point, and 24-point line thicknesses. Use the buttons on the bottom row to display the line in white, black, or various percentages of black—including 10-percent black, 30-percent black, 50-percent black, 70-percent black, and 90-percent black. Figure 12.25 displays an 8-point line formatted as 30-percent black, and a circle with a 16-point solid black line.

1. Select the line or graphic to which you want to apply line changes.

2. Click on the Outline tool in the toolbar to reveal the flyout. Select the desired line thickness from the top row of buttons. Select the desired line color from the bottom row of buttons.

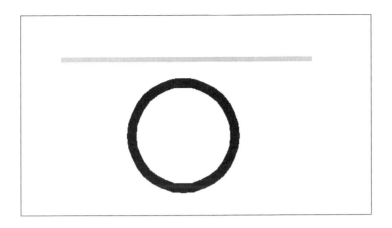

Figure 12.25
You have a wide range of line thicknesses to choose from when designing with graphics drawn in VENTURA.

When you position the mouse cursor on a button in the Outline tool, a pop-up note appears displaying the line thickness or fill color of that particular button. Creating custom line thicknesses, applying arrowheads and dashed line styles, and selecting line colors from a full-color palette are discussed in the next chapter.

Changing Fill Attributes of Graphics

The Fill tool (the last tool in the toolbox), provides options for changing the fill or interior color of graphics drawn in VENTURA. Click on the Fill tool to display the flyout toolbar (see fig. 12.26).

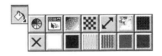

Figure 12.26
Click on the Fill tool to reveal the flyout.

The buttons on the bottom of the flyout offer a range of preset fills. The first button, which is marked with an X, removes the fill. Use the remaining buttons to fill graphics with white, black, and various shades of gray or percentages of black—including 10-percent black, 30-percent black, 50-percent black, 70-percent black, and 90-percent black.

1. Select the graphic to which you want to apply line changes.

2. Click on the Fill tool in the toolbar to reveal the flyout. Select the desired fill from the bottom row of buttons.

Selecting fills from a full-color palette and applying fill patterns such as fountain fills, texture, and patterned fills is covered in Chapter 13.

III

Advanced VENTURA Options and Techniques

Chapter Snapshot

VENTURA provides an incredible array of options for changing the appearance of frames and graphic objects. With these built-in features, you can create stunning graphical effects. In this chapter, you learn to do the following:

Take some time to experiment with the tools and features described in this chapter. The creative possibilities are endless.

Applying Fills and Outlines to Frames and Graphics

Imagine what page layout would be without color, texture, shapes, and shades to lead your eye around the page. It would all be, well…boring. Indeed, the printed page can be a fairly plain two-dimensional object, but with a little effort, you can give your pages depth, texture, and visual impact. VENTURA's outline and fill tools provide everything you need to bring your pages to life. Though color is an easy way to add spice to your work, there are many other tools available for creating eye-catching effects, without the expense of color.

This chapter examines the options for applying fills and outlines to frames and graphics drawn with VENTURA's drawing tools. In Chapter 12, "Drawing and Editing Graphics in VENTURA," you saw how to apply preset fills and outlines to objects. Here, you will learn about fill options for designing with color, gradated fills, textures, and patterns. Also included is a detailed look at line options, such as custom widths, color, line styles, and the various line end points such as arrows and drafting symbols.

Applying Fills

Fill and outline attributes can be applied to the base page frame and to free frames. Applying fill and outline attributes to frames enables you to create backgrounds for page elements, such as the masthead shown in figure 13.1.

Figure 13.1
Applying fills to frames can enhance a page layout.

Graphics drawn with VENTURA's drawing tools can also be enhanced with fill and outline attributes. You cannot modify the outline or fill of imported graphics or graphics transferred through the Clipboard; you can, however, change the outline and fill attributes of the frame holding the graphic.

Graphics or frames must be selected before you modify their fills or outlines. As discussed in Chapter 12, you can select multiple frames or graphics by holding Shift as you select. You cannot select multiple graphics if they are attached to different frames.

Use the Fill tool to apply fill colors and patterns to frames and graphics. Press and hold the mouse button on the Fill tool to display the flyout shown in figure 13.2.

As discussed in Chapter 12, the preset buttons on the flyout can be used to apply various shades of black to your objects. The white button applies a white fill to objects, and the X applies no fill to objects or creates an empty wireframe. The

top row of buttons on the flyout produces more elaborate fill styles. The color wheel, the first button on the top row, applies solid colors. The second button displays the Fill Roll-up. The third button is used to create gradient effects or "fountain fills." The fourth button, which looks like a checkerboard, applies two-color patterns. The fifth button, the arrow, applies full-color patterns, and the sixth button applies textured fills. The following sections examine the application of various types of fills.

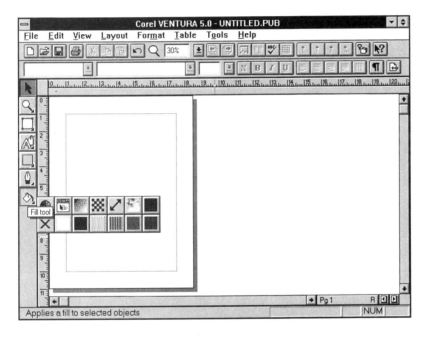

Figure 13.2
Press and hold the Fill tool to reveal the flyout toolbar.

The fills discussed in the section—patterned, fountain, and texture fills—increase a document's printing time. They also increase the size of files. It's best to limit using them as an entire background for a publication. Reserve them instead for filling smaller frames and graphics.

Applying Solid Fill Colors

Uniform, or solid, colors are applied with the Uniform Fill button. VENTURA uses the same color models, such as Pantone and Grayscale, found in CorelDRAW. The following steps illustrate applying uniform colors to graphics and frames:

Advanced VENTURA Options and Techniques

1. Select the object or frame to which you want to apply a color.

2. Click on the Fill tool and select the Uniform Fill button (the color wheel). The Uniform Fill dialog box appears, as shown in figure 13.3.

Figure 13.3
The Uniform Fill
dialog box.

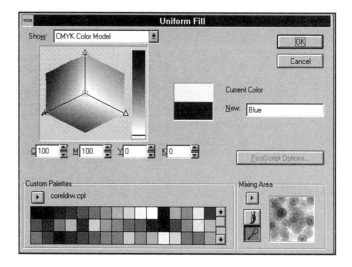

3. Click on the down arrow by Show and select the color model from which you want to choose colors. (Read the next section for more information on the color models.)

4. Select the desired color. The Current Color/**N**ew box displays the current color and the newly selected color.

5. Click on OK to apply the color to the graphic or frame and return to your document.

Understanding VENTURA's Color Models

The *CMYK* models refer to the four process ink colors used in full-color or "four-color" printing, cyan, magenta, yellow, and black. Essentially, a combination of these four inks are used to print the full-color images seen in books and magazines. Click your mouse somewhere on the color spectrum to choose a CMYK color. The color you select appears in the **N**ew box. You can adjust the numbers in the **C**yan, **M**agenta, **Y**ellow, and **B**lack list boxes to define a new color. For example, you could enter 100-percent cyan and 50-percent yellow to create a green.

The *RGB* color model uses percentages of red, green, and blue to create colors. Each color component has 255 levels of intensity, ranging from black to the component's full concentration. Thus, to produce pure green, for example, set Red to 0, Green to 255, and Blue to 0. Setting them all to 0 produces black. You can use the mouse to drag the red, green, and blue markers to new locations on the visual selector preview box. The Uniform Color model is also built from the RGB color percentages, but these colors are set at fixed percentages and cannot be altered. Notice that the **N**ew box displays the red, green, and blue percentages of each color selected.

HSB stands for hue, saturation, and brightness. This model builds colors based on their intensity and color purity. You can select a color by dragging the marker on the visual selector's color spectrum or define a new color by entering numbers in the Hue, Saturation, and Brightness list boxes. The Grayscale model displays controls for creating custom grayscales. You can set grayscales by entering a level between 0 (black) and 255 (white) in the Gray **L**evel box or by dragging the grayscale marker in the visual selector.

The *PANTONE Spot Color* model displays colors created using a standard color matching system. The colors are cataloged and exhibited in a guide similar to a paint swatch guide. Because your screen cannot give you an exact representation of any spot color, it is recommended that you refer to the Pantone spot color charts and enter the color number, and not attempt to match visually a specific color on the screen. With Pantone Spot Colors, you have the option of changing the tint or intensity of a color. For example, a 50-percent tint of red reduces the density by half and causes the color to reproduce as a light red.

If you are printing to a four-color printing press, you can choose from the predefined process colors provided in the PANTONE Process Color palette. Because printing presses cannot provide inks for each of the many colors in a full-color document, these process colors use the CMYK process inks to simulate the colors in the PANTONE Spot Color model. Because they simulate spot colors with the CMYK process inks, FOCOLTONE and TRUMATCH Colors are similar to the PANTONE Process Color model. Just as you would with the PANTONE Spot Color model, for all three process color models, refer to a color chart to help you find the exact color rather than gauging colors from your computer display.

When using PANTONE spot or process colors, TRUMATCH or FOCOLTONE color, click in the Sh**o**w Color Names check box to generate the listing of colors by name. Another handy tool is the Search box. After selecting a color from the color chart, simply enter the color number in the Search box. In this way you avoid scrolling through hundreds of color options to find a specific color and move directly to the color you want.

Creating Custom Colors

You can create and save your own custom colors. When using CMYK, RGB, HSB, and Grayscale color models, you can create colors by manipulating the various color levels. After you create a new color, you can save it for later use. For example, suppose after considerable tweaking, you've discovered using the HSB color model a color that is perfect for the company newsletter's masthead. For future reference, you can save that new color to the current color palette. The following steps illustrate how to save a custom color:

1. From the Uniform Fill dialog box, select the desired color model and create a new color.

2. Click in the **N**ew box and type a distinctive name up to 15 characters long.

3. Click on the Custom Palettes button. From the pop-up menu, select Add **C**olor.

The new color is added to the end of the current color palette.

Mixing New Colors in VENTURA

VENTURA provides a utility for mixing your own colors. Using the mixing tools, you can mix existing colors to create your own custom color variations. The following steps demonstrate how to create new colors with the mixing tools:

1. From the Uniform Fill dialog box, choose any of the color models.

2. Click on the Paintbrush button in the Mixing Area, then select a color from the visual selector.

3. Move to the Mixing area and drag with the Paintbrush tool to apply the chosen color in the Mixing area window.

4. Repeat the painting process with other colors from the visual selector.

5. Click on the Eyedropper button, then use the Eyedropper tool to click around in the Mixing Area window until you locate the color you want to pick up. The newly created color appears in the Current/New color box, on the visual selector, and in the color percentage boxes below the visual selector.

6. Click in the **N**ew text box and name your new color.

7. Click on OK to add the new color to the existing palette.

Adding Colors to the Color Palette

Occasionally you might want to add a color from another palette to the current color palette. For example, you have chosen a specific color from another color model that you intend to use throughout the document. To avoid having to locate that specific color every time you need it, you can make the color part of the current color palette. The following steps show how to add a color to the current palette:

1. Click on the Fill tool, then from the flyout, select the Uniform Fill tool.

2. From the Uniform Fill dialog box, select the color model and the color you want to add to the current palette.

3. Click on the Custom Palettes button (the black right-facing triangle at the bottom right of the dialog box). The pop-up menu shown in figure 13.4 appears.

4. From the pop-up menu, select Add **C**olor. The new color is added to the end of the current color palette.

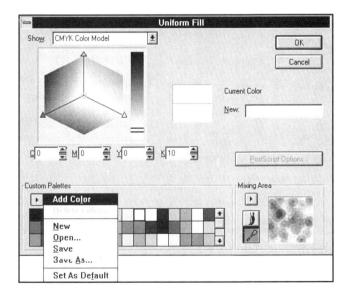

Figure 13.4
The Custom Palette
pop-up menu.

To remove a color from the color palette, select the color in the Custom Palettes section of the Uniform Fill dialog box, then choose **D**elete Color from the Custom Palettes pop-up menu.

Creating Custom Palettes

An alternative to adding colors to an existing palette is the creation of custom color palettes, which is a great way to access the exact colors you want quickly, without having to scroll though the many colors in other color palettes. The following steps illustrate how to create and save your own color palette:

1. From the Uniform Fill dialog box, click on the Custom Palettes button to reveal the submenu.

2. Select **N**ew to open the New Palette dialog box, as shown in figure 13.5.

Figure 13.5
The New Palette
dialog box.

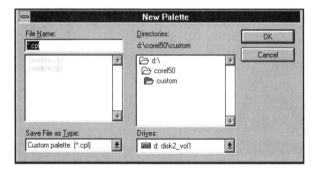

3. Navigate to the drive and directory where you want the new palette to be stored. It is recommended that you store all palettes in the default palette directory, Corel50\Custom, where VENTURA stores all other color palettes.

4. In the File **N**ame box, enter a name for the new palette. Click on OK to return to the Uniform Fill dialog box.

5. Select a color from any of the color models and click on the Custom Palettes button. Choose Add Co**l**or from the pop-up menu.

6. Repeat step 5 for each color you want to add to your custom palette.

7. Click on the Custom Palettes button, then choose **S**ave.

8. In the Uniform Fill dialog box, click on OK to return to the document with the new palette active.

To choose another color palette, click on the Custom Palette button in the Uniform Fill dialog box. From the pop-up menu, choose **O**pen. The Open Palette dialog box appears, as shown in figure 13.6. Navigate to the drive and directory where the palette is stored, then choose the desired palette and click on

OK. From the Uniform Fill dialog box, click on OK to return to your document with the new palette active.

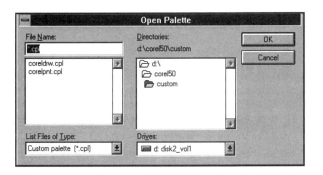

Figure 13.6
The Open Palette dialog box.

VENTURA's PostScript Printing Options

If you are printing spot colors to a PostScript printer, you can control the half-tone screens used to print the selected object's fill or outline. The PostScript printing features are discussed in Chapter 19, "Printing in VENTURA." If you are unfamiliar with the functions of screen frequency and angle, however, you might want to consult your service bureau or printer before manipulating these options.

Applying Pattern Fills

VENTURA provides two types of patterned fills: Two-color and Full-color. *Two-color* fills enable you to pick the foreground and background colors. They are comprised of simple patterns, such as polka dots and cross hatches. *Full-color* fills are more elaborate patterns, such as balloons and weaves, but the colors cannot be altered.

Applying Two-Color Fill Patterns

The following steps illustrate applying a Two-color fill pattern.

1. Select the frame or graphic to which you want to apply the pattern. Click on the Fill tool and select the Two-color fill button (the checkerboard). The Two-Color Pattern dialog box appears (see fig. 13.7).

2. Click on the large preview box to reveal additional pattern choices. You can scroll down to view more.

3. To select a pattern, double-click on it or click on the pattern and click on OK. The selected pattern appears in the preview box.

4. To change the background color of your pattern, click on the Back color button and select a color. To change the foreground color, click on the Front button and select a color.

5. To control the size of the pattern, click on the **S**mall, **M**edium, or **L**arge buttons. The preview box reflects your color and size choices.

6. Click on OK to apply the fill pattern to the selected frame(s) or graphic(s).

Figure 13.7
The Two-Color Pattern dialog box.

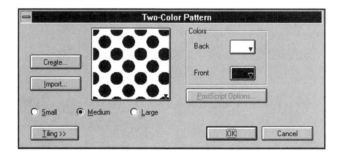

Applying Full-Color Fill Patterns

The steps for applying Full-color patterns are similar to the steps for using Two-color patterns.

1. Select the frame or graphic you want to fill. Click on the Fill tool and select the Full-color fill button (the diagonal line with the arrowheads). The Full-Color Pattern dialog box appears (see fig. 13.8).

2. Click on the preview box (the large X) to reveal additional Full-color pattern choices. Scroll down to view more patterns.

3. Double-click on the desired pattern, or select it and click on OK. Your selected pattern appears in the preview box.

4. Click on the **S**mall, **M**edium, or **L**arge buttons to control the size of the pattern. Click on OK to apply the fill pattern to your selected object(s).

Tiling Patterns

VENTURA provides several options for "tiling" Two-color and Full-color patterns. Click on the **T**iling button in the Two-Color Pattern dialog box to reveal the expanded Two-Color Pattern dialog box (see fig. 13.9). The following information also applies to tiling Full-color patterns.

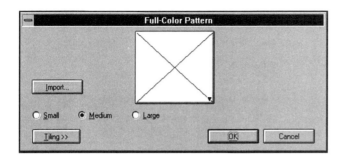

Figure 13.8
The Full-
Color Pattern
dialog box.

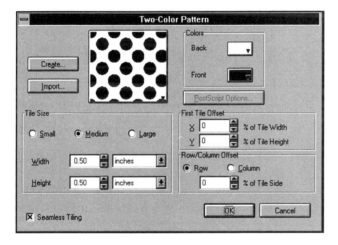

Figure 13.9
The expanded
Two-Color Pattern
dialog box.

III

Advanced VENTURA Options and Techniques

You can enter new values in the **W**idth and **H**eight boxes to adjust the pattern tile size up to 15×15 inches. The First Tile Offset option controls the placement of the first tile relative to the top left corner of the object's boundaries. Adjust the **X** values to shift the entire pattern horizontally within the object's boundaries and the **Y** values to shift vertically. Adjusting the Row/Column Offset values shifts the horizontal and vertical repetition of the pattern within the object. Change the **R**ow values to shift the pattern horizontally and **C**olumn to shift the pattern repetition vertically. Watch the preview of the pattern as you adjust the values for visual confirmation of your changes.

You can also create patterns from graphics created in other applications by clicking on the **I**mport button in both the Two-color and Full-color dialog boxes. Clicking on the Import button opens the Import dialog box. Navigate to the directory where the graphic is stored, select the graphic, and click on OK. The imported graphic appears as a pattern in the preview box. After the graphic is imported, you can manipulate it with the tiling features.

Creating Two-Color Patterns

To create your own two-color pattern, click on the Create button. The Two-Color Pattern Editor is displayed, as shown in figure 13.10.

Figure 13.10
VENTURA's Two-Color Pattern Editor.

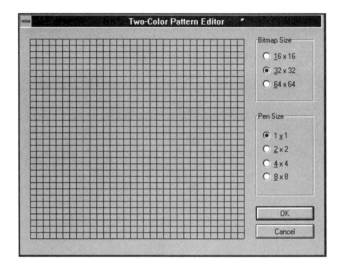

You can use the grid to design new patterns. Click with the left mouse button to fill in units of the grid. Use the right mouse button to erase. Press and hold the mouse buttons to quickly draw or erase broad areas of the grid. You can change the grid size by selecting from the three bitmap sizes, 16×16, 32×32, or 64×64. You can also change the size of the drawing pen from 1×1 to 8×8 grid units in size.

Applying Fountain Fills

Fountain fills, also known as *gradient* fills, blend one color into another. For example, a fountain fill might blend blue into green. Fountain fills are great for creating three-dimensional shading and highlighting effects.

Creating Linear, Radial, Conical, and Square Fills

VENTURA provides four different types of fountain fills: linear, radial, conical, and square (see fig. 13.11). *Linear* is the default fountain fill type, and it creates a fill using horizontal lines to blend directly from one color to another. *Radial* fills blend colors to the center with concentric circles. *Conical* fills blend between two

colors in a cone-line manner, and *square* fills blend colors to the center in concentric squares. The following steps illustrate the creation of a fountain fill.

Linear Fill   Radial Fill   Conical Fill   Square Fill

Figure 13.11
VENTURA provides four different types of fountain fills.

1. Select the frame or graphic you want to fill. Click on the Fill tool and select the Fountain fill button. The Fountain Fill dialog box appears (see fig. 13.12).

2. Click on the down arrow by **T**ype and select the desired fill type.

3. Click on the From and To button to select the blend colors. A preview of your fountain fill appears in the sample box.

4. Click OK to apply the fountain fill and return to the document.

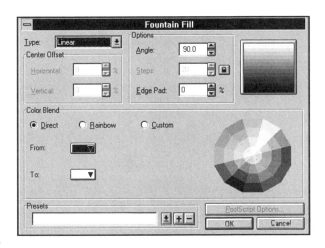

Figure 13.12
The Fountain Fill dialog box.

III

Advanced VENTURA Options and Techniques

There are two important options for controlling the appearance of fountain fills. First is the **S**teps command, which enables you to control the number of steps it takes to blend from one color into another. The higher the number, the smoother the blend. The default is 20 steps, but you can click on the Lock button and enter a new number. The Edge Pad command enables you to manipulate the blend rate. Increasing the value in the **E**dge Pad box controls how much of the

From and To colors appear at the edge of an object before the blending process begins.

Changing Direction of Fountain Fills

The Fountain Fill dialog box provides several options for modifying the direction of the fountain fill. With a linear fill, you can enter a value in the **A**ngle box under Options to change the angle of the fill. For instance, enter a value of 180 to create a vertical linear fill. You can also change the angle of the fill with the mouse. Place your mouse pointer in the preview box, then press and drag with the left mouse button. Position the representative line at the angle you want the fill to blend, and release the mouse.

For radial, conical, and square fills, you can change the location of the blend point with the Center Offset command. You can, for example, enter 25 percent horizontally and 25 percent vertically to shift the center of the blend up and to the right. You also can reposition the center point by dragging on the fill preview with the mouse.

Creating Rainbow Fills

Many fountain fills blend directly from one color to another. However, with a rainbow fill, the blend uses multiple colors on the color wheel as it blends from the selected From and To colors. The following steps illustrate how to create a rainbow fill:

1. Select the frame or graphic you want to fill. Click on the Fill tool and select the Fountain fill button. Click on the down arrow by Type to select the desired fountain fill type.

2. Click on the **R**ainbow radio button just above the From and To color buttons.

3. Use the From and To color buttons to select the beginning and ending colors.

4. Click on the circular arrow buttons next to the From and To buttons to move clockwise or counterclockwise around the color wheel. Notice the black line around the color wheel which shows which colors display, depending on the direction you "traveled" around the color wheel.

5. The preview box displays your fill. Click on OK to apply the Rainbow fill and return to your document.

Creating Custom Fills

Custom fills also blend multiple colors, but with custom fills, you determine which color blends into another. Instead of being stuck with the rainbow of colors around the color wheel, for example, you can control colors and position on the fountain fill blend. You can go from red to blue to yellow—the options are endless. You can select up to 99 colors for use in custom fills. The following steps illustrate how to create a custom fountain fill:

1. Select the object to which you want to apply a custom fill, then select the Fountain Fill tool from the Fill tool flyout.

2. Choose **C**ustom as the fill type. The custom fill preview box appears, as shown in figure 13.13.

3. Use the From and To color buttons to select the beginning and ending colors. Notice that the colors you selected appear in the preview of the blend.

4. To add more colors, double-click at the point on the color bar where you want to place another color. A small black triangle appears where you double-click.

5. Choose a color from the color palette. The selected color is blended into the preview at the position of the black marker. Continue adding colors by double-clicking along the color bar.

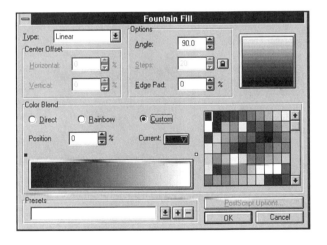

Figure 13.13
Use the Custom fill preview box to create your own blends.

When you add a new marker, it turns black, indicating it is the active marker and ready to be assigned a color. All other markers appear white. You can change the color at any marker by clicking on it to make it the active marker, and choosing a new color. You can reposition any marker by dragging it to a new location. You can add up to 99 markers in the fill. To delete a marker and its color, select the marker and press delete. The preview box displays your fill. You can change the type of fill if desired. Click on OK to apply the custom fill and return to the document.

Applying Texture Fills

VENTURA's texture fills are designed to simulate water colors, clouds, minerals, and much more. In addition, you can change the setting of each texture to create literally millions of variations. Depending on your computer's memory resources, texture fills can take a long time to display on the screen. They also take a long time to print and add considerably to the file size. As mentioned with other fill types, you should consider reserving them primarily for use with smaller graphic objects. The following steps illustrate how to apply texture fills to objects:

1. Select the object you want to fill and click on the Texture fill tool on the Fill tool flyout.

2. The Texture Fill dialog box appears, as shown in figure 13.14.

3. Choose a category of textures from the Texture **L**ibrary.

4. Scroll through the **T**exture List to see all the available textures. Select a texture to view it in the **P**review window.

5. Click on OK to apply the texture and return to your document.

Figure 13.14
The Texture Fill
dialog box.

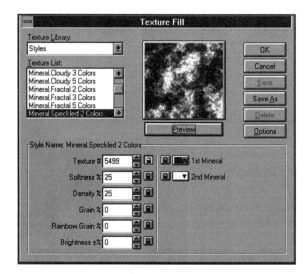

You can adjust the settings at the bottom of the dialog box to create new textures. This requires some experimentation. The settings are different for each texture you choose. After modifying the settings, click on the **P**review button to view the changes. To save the new settings, click on the Save **A**s button and enter a file name. The name is added to the list of textures, so you can use it again. Select a texture and click on the **D**elete button to remove it from the texture library.

New textures cannot be added to the Styles library. Though you can modify and save textures from the Styles library, they must be saved to a different library.

Using the Fill Roll-Up

The Fill Roll-up is another way to apply fills to objects. To display the roll-up, click on the second tool in the Fill tool flyout. The Fill Roll-up is displayed, as shown in figure 13.15.

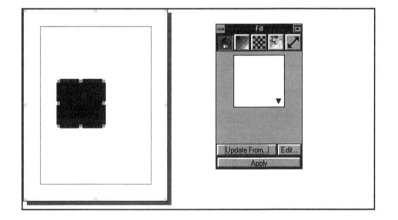

Figure 13.15
The Fill Roll-up.

The Fill Roll-up provides quick access to all the fill types and their relative options. Each fill type is represented by the buttons at the top of the roll-up. Click on the square in the center of the roll-up to reveal the fill options available for the type of fill you select. For example, if you select the Uniform fill button, clicking on the square reveals the colors available in the current palette.

Depending on which fill type you have selected, the options available in the Fill Roll-up change. For example, clicking on the Fountain fill button provides access to the From and To colors and the various types of fountain fills (linear, radial, and so on). When you click on a button to choose a fill type, you will find the options for modifying the fill are identical to the options available in various fill dialog boxes. The Edit button at the bottom of the Fill Roll-up opens the dialog box for whichever fill type you have selected. For instance, if you have the Two-Color fill button selected, clicking on the Edit button opens the Two-Color Pattern dialog box. After selecting the kind of fill you want, click on the Apply button.

You can use the Update From button to copy fill styles from one object to others—a handy way to repeat a fill on several objects. First, select the object or objects to which you want to copy fill attributes. Click on the Update From button to reveal a large black arrow labeled From?. Next, click on the object whose fill attributes you want to copy, then click on Apply and the fill attributes are copied to the selected object(s).

Using the Outline Tool

The Outline tool is used to control lines, curves, and the outline of graphics objects created with VENTURA's drawing tools. As discussed in Chapter 12, you can use the Outline tool to change the thickness of outlines. The Outline tool can, however, do much more; it can, for example, apply custom line thicknesses, set the line color, create dashed line effects, apply arrowheads, and create calligraphy effects.

Press and hold the mouse button on the Outline tool to display the flyout toolbar, as shown in figure 13.16.

Figure 13.16
The Outline
Pen flyout.

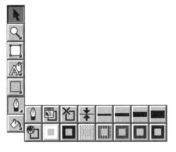

The first flyout button, the Outline attributes button, controls many line attributes covered in this section. The second button on the flyout is the Pen Roll-up. As discussed in Chapter 12, the remaining buttons on the top row are presets for changing an object's line thickness. Clicking on the button marked with an X removes the outline. The bottom row of buttons on the Outline tool flyout are presets for adjusting the outline color. The color wheel, the Outline Color tool, is used to apply colors to lines and outlines. Click on this button to open the Outline Color dialog box, which is identical to the Uniform Fill Color dialog box.

Creating Custom Line Thicknesses

In addition to the preset line widths available on the Outline tool flyout menu, you can create a custom line thickness. To apply a custom line thickness, select the object to be changed and click on the Outline attributes button in the Outline tool flyout. The Outline Pen dialog box appears, as shown in figure 13.17.

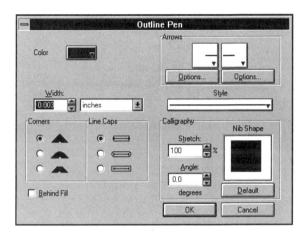

Figure 13.17
The Outline Pen dialog box.

The current thickness appears in the **W**idth box. Click on the down arrow by "inches" to reveal the other measurement systems you can use for sizing outlines. Points are a common way to measure line thickness in the printing and publishing industry. Enter the desired amount in the **W**idth box. You can also apply a new outline color by clicking on the color button and choosing from the pop-up color menu.

Applying Arrowheads and Symbols to Line Endpoints

VENTURA comes with a wide variety of arrowheads and symbols ideal for designing the lines and arrows in flowcharts and timelines. These symbols can be applied to the beginning and ending point of lines. The size of the symbol is determined by the line thickness, so for larger endpoint symbols, you might want to increase the outline width. The following steps illustrate how to add arrowheads and symbols to lines:

1. Select the line and click on the Outline attributes button in the Outline tool flyout.

2. On the right side of the dialog box are two buttons for placing arrowheads and symbols at the beginning and end of lines. To place an arrowhead or

III

Advanced VENTURA Options and Techniques

symbol at the beginning of the line, click on the first button to reveal the arrowhead submenu (see fig. 13.18).

3. Scroll through the choices and click on the desired arrowhead or symbol. To place a symbol at the ending of the line, click on the second button. Scroll down and click on your choice. The selected symbols are previewed on the arrowhead buttons.

4. Click on OK to apply the symbol endpoints to your selected object.

Figure 13.18
The arrowhead and symbol submenu.

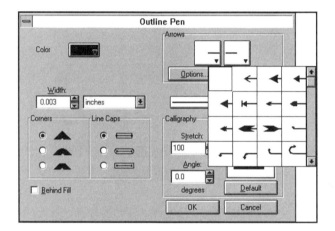

Applying Dashed Lines

Dashed lines are useful when creating maps, floor plans, and other graphics effects. VENTURA includes several types of dashed lines. As with arrowheads and symbols, the thickness of the dashes and the space in between them is determined by the line thickness. Unlike the symbols, dashed lines can be applied to graphics objects such as circles and squares, as well as to lines.

To apply dashed lines, select the object and click on the Outline attributes button in the Outline tool flyout. Click on the button under "Style" to reveal the dashed line choices shown in figure 13.19.

Scroll through the choices and click on the desired dashed line style. The selected style is previewed in the button. Click on OK to apply the dashed line style to your selected object.

The Corners options can be used to control the shape of corners on square and rectangular objects. The default is cusped, or mitred corners, but you can click on the accompanying radio buttons to change an object's corners to rounded or beveled. The Line Caps feature enables you to change the appearance of line

endpoints. The default squares the line off at each end. Click on the accompanying radio buttons to draw round caps extending beyond the ends of the line, or square caps extending beyond the ends of the line.

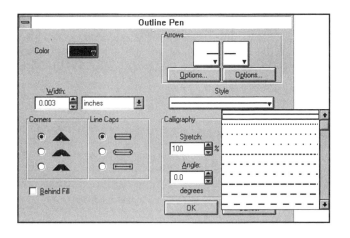

Figure 13.19
VENTURA provides a wide range of line styles.

Using the Calligraphy Tools

The Calligraphy options enable you to create curved lines that look like hand-drawn calligraphy. For example, figure 13.20 displays an ellipse with calligraphic effects applied. Notice how certain points of the curve are thick while others are thin.

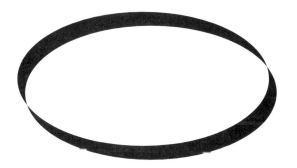

Figure 13.20
VENTURA's calligraphy tools enable you to vary the width of a line or outline.

These thick and thin lines are achieved by controlling the angle and the stretch values of the outline pen. Normally the outline pen is a perfect square shape of specified width. By angling the pen shape and narrowing its drawing width, you can force lines to become thinner at points on the curve drawn on the same slant as the pen angle. For example, because the angle of the pen is very thin and set at a 45-degree angle, the parts of the curves on the ellipse in figure 13.20 drawn at 45-degree angles are thinnest.

III

Advanced VENTURA Options and Techniques

To adjust the angle and the stretch of the pen—the *nib shape*—use the up and down arrows in the S̲tretch and A̲ngle boxes to enter the desired value. You can also adjust the nib shape with the mouse. When you place the mouse in the preview box, it changes to a cross-hair. Press the left mouse button and drag clockwise or counterclockwise to adjust the pen angle. Note the display in the A̲ngle box as you adjust the nib. To adjust the stretch of the pen, drag the crosshair toward the center of the preview to increase the pen width and away from the center to decrease it. Press the D̲efault button to return to the normal square-shaped pen.

Using the Pen Roll-Up

The second tool in the Outline tool flyout, the Pen Roll-up, is another way to access the controls for modifying outlines. Click on the Roll-up button in the Outline tool flyout to display the roll-up, as shown in figure 13.21.

Figure 13.21
The Pen Roll-up.

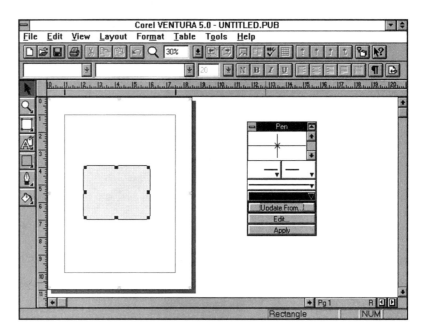

The top option is the Thickness Selector. Each click on the scroll arrows changes the thickness by .01 inches. Scroll down repeatedly to the big *X* to apply no outline. The Arrowhead Selectors are beneath the Thickness Selector and work identically to those in the Outline Pen dialog box. Click on the buttons and select the arrowheads you want. Click on the Line Style selector to choose a dashed line

effect. The last button is the Outline color button. To apply changes made in the roll-up, click on the Apply button. For more options, click on the Edit button to open the Outline Pen dialog box.

Though you cannot modify the outline or fill of imported graphics or graphics transferred through the Clipboard, you can change their frame outline and fill attributes.

Chapter Snapshot

If you are constructing a technical manual, you surely will need to know how to add footnotes, numbered figures, and headers and footers. In this chapter, you learn to do the following:

This chapter addresses the concerns of long and technical documents. With VENTURA's page numbering and footnotes features, it is easy to direct the reader to the right location.

Advanced Options for
Chapter Formatting

Browse through just about any technical manual and you'll see headers, footers, footnotes, and numbered figures. These *reader cues* are important tools for helping a reader understand and process information. Although the importance of cues is apparent, the time spent placing these elements in your document can be highly time-consuming. Imagine carefully numbering each of the 100 figures in your book, only to have to start all over because figure 5 is eliminated. (Does the phrase "busy work" mean anything to you?) VENTURA takes the drudergy out of creating reader cues, such as headers, footers, and footnotes, by simplifying the process and eliminating much of the busy work.

This chapter focuses on the generation of reader cues used in books, manuals, and other long documents. First, the chapter covers the steps for building and formatting headers and footers. You will learn how to insert page numbers, dates, and times into headers and footers. The following section explains VENTURA's powerful capability to generate footnotes. Numbering and formatting footnotes is covered. The chapter also examines the control of the numbering of the chapters, pages, figures, and tables in your document. The last section explores working with advanced typography attributes of the base page frame. There, you will discover how to adjust widow and orphan settings, utilize column balance, and enable vertical justification.

For the exercises in this chapter, you can work with one of your own chapter files or open the example.pub publication file and use the book_p1.chp or book_p1.chp chapter files. When working with sample files, note that some of the features discussed in this chapter might already be enabled.

Working with Headers and Footers

Headers and footers contain referential information to the body text and are located at the top or bottom of the page, respectively. The text in headers and footers typically consists of book or section titles, company names, and page numbers. This information serves as a road map to help the reader locate information quickly. In training manuals, the footer often includes a chapter number and title, making it easy for the reader to find specific information easily. In a sales proposal, the header might display a company name, keeping this information prominent in the reader's mind.

VENTURA places header and footer text in frames. The size of the header and footer frames is determined by the size of the margins on the base page frame. For instance, the top and bottom page margins in figure 14.1 are set at two inches. When headers and footers were added, the header and footer frames are set at two inches high. Select the base page frame and choose the Frame command from the Format menu to adjust the page margins.

Figure 14.1
The size of the header and footer frames is determined by the size of the base page margins.

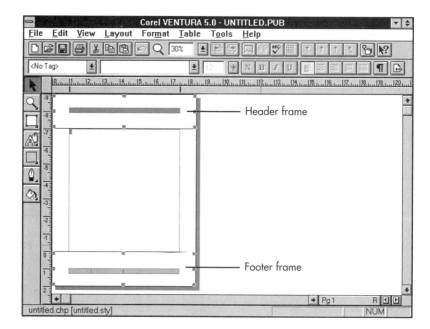

With VENTURA, you can have up to three separate entries for headers and footers. Text can be placed on the left, center, or right side of the header or footer frame (see fig. 14.2). For lengthy entries, the information can be stacked into two lines.

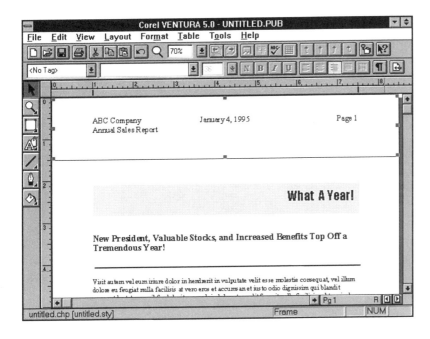

Figure 14.2
Text can be placed on the left, center, or right side of the header or footer frame.

Headers and footers for double-sided documents can be identical across the left and right pages. For instance, you might want the date to appear as header information on both the left and right pages. Headers and footers for double-sided documents can also be totally different for the left and right pages. The time, for example, could be displayed on all left page headers, and the date displayed on all right page headers. You can even have the headers and footers *mirror* across the left and right pages. Mirroring places the information to the outer edges of the pages where it is easily seen. Suppose, for example, you added a header where the chapter title appeared on the left side of all left pages. Mirroring the header would place this same information on the right side of all right pages.

VENTURA provides several buttons for automatically entering page numbers, dates, and other information commonly found in headers and footers. When you select one of these buttons, a code representing the selected information is inserted. For example, clicking on the Date button inserts the code "[D]" into the header or footer text. Although the code appears in the dialog box, the actual information appears in the header on the page. If the current date were October 7,

1995, for example, the dialog box would display the code [D], but the header displays "October 7, 1995." Table 14.1 examines the purpose of each button.

Table 14.1
Header and Footer Buttons

Button	Information Inserted	Code Entered
⊞	Inserts Chapter Number	[C#]
#	Inserts Page Number	[P#]
A	Applies Text Attributes	(see Formatting Headers & Footers)
🕐	Inserts Current Time	[H]
📅	Inserts Current Date	[D]
📄	Creates First Match Headers or Footers	(see next section)
📄	Creates Last Match Headers or Footers	(see next section)

Creating Headers and Footers

The following exercise examines the steps for adding headers and footers to a double-sided document. The left page header will be set up to display the text "Corel VENTURA" and the date. The left page footer will be set to display the chapter and page number separated by a dash (for example, the first page in Chapter 1 would display 1-1, the second page, 1-2). Both the header and footer information will be placed in the left side of the frame. The header and footer information will then be mirrored to the right pages.

1. Select **C**hapter Settings from the **L**ayout menu. Click on the Header/ Footer tab to display the dialog box in figure 14.3. Notice there are three boxes for entering text in the **L**eft, **C**enter, or **R**ight of the header or footer frame.

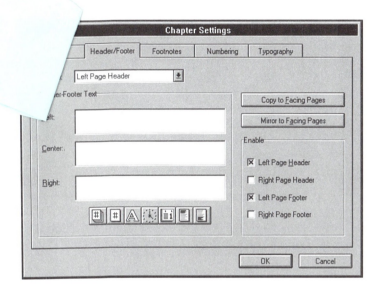

Figure 14.3
The Chapter Settings dialog box with the Header/Footer tab selected.

2. In the Enable section of the dialog box, click on the Left Page **H**eader and Left Page F**o**oter options.

3. To create the left page header, click on the down arrow by **D**efine and choose Left Page Header.

4. Click in the **L**eft text box to place the insertion point, and type **CorelVENTURA**. Press the Enter key to add a second line of information and click on the Date button.

5. Click on the Mirror to F**a**cing Pages button. The Ri**g**ht Page Header option under Enable is selected automatically. To see the right page header text, select Ri**g**ht Page Header from the **D**efine list box. The text is mirrored and displayed in the **R**ight text box.

6. To create the left page footer, click on the down arrow by **D**efine and choose Left Page Footer.

7. Click in the Left text box, then click on the Chapter Numbering button. Type in a dash and click on the Page Numbering button (see fig. 14.4).

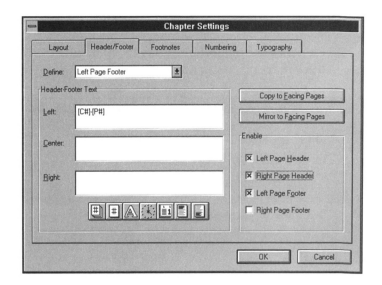

Figure 14.4
With VENTURA, you can use the Chapter Numbering and Page Numbering buttons to number the pages in your documents.

8. Click on the Mirror to Facing Pages button. Select Right Page Footer from the Define list box to verify the information was mirrored.

9. Click on OK. The header and footer information appears on the left side of all left pages and the right side of all right pages.

You must return to the Header/Footer dialog box to make editing changes to the header or footer text. You cannot type directly into the header or footer frame.

If desired, you can add ruling lines to header and footer frames to separate the information from other text on the page. Use the Ruling Lines command in the Format menu to add ruling lines to frames (refer to Chapter 10 for more information).

VENTURA does not automatically update the date and time placed in headers and footers except when you reopen the document. To update them while the document is open, select Refresh Window from the View menu.

Creating Running Headers and Footers

Headers and footers can also be used to summarize the content of each page, helping readers quickly locate information. Often called *running* headers and footers, the headers and footers vary across the pages displaying information about the current page. One example of running headers is the Yellow Pages. The header varies from page to page, displaying the types of businesses listed on the current page. Another example is the dictionary. The first word listed on the

left page is the left page header, the last word listed on the right page is the right page header. These running headers provide a quick reference to help the reader locate certain information.

VENTURA uses paragraph tags to create running headers and footers. Basically, you choose which tag is used to create the running header or footer. If a page contains a paragraph formatted with the tag you have chosen, the contents of that paragraph are displayed as the header or footer text. If the page does not contain a paragraph formatted with the tag, the text used in the most recent header is displayed again.

For example, imagine you are creating a how-to manual on photography. For consistency, the tag "Section Head" is applied to each of the section headings. To help the reader locate certain information, you decide to place the section heading in the header text. Because the headings are tagged as "Section Heads," this tag is used to create a running header. As shown in figure 14.5, the header in the manual changes to reflect the contents of the current page. On page 1, the header displays the first section heading. On page 2, the header displays the second section heading. There is no section heading on page 3, so the previous header text is used again. In this way, a section that continues across several pages uses the same headers. On page 4 the header changes again to display the current section heading.

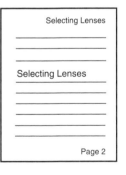

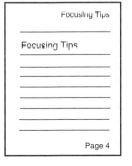

Figure 14.5
With VENTURA, you can create running headers and footers that summarize the contents of the current page.

III

Advanced VENTURA Options and Techniques

VENTURA provides the First Match and Last Match buttons (refer to Table 14.1) in the Header/Footer tab sheet of the Chapter Settings dialog box to select which tag is used to create the running header or footer. The First Match button displays the contents of the first paragraph on the page tagged with the selected tag. The Last Match button displays the contents of the last paragraph on the page tagged with the selected tag. For example, there are two section headings on the page in figure 14.6. When the First Match option is selected, the contents of the first section heading appear in the header. When the Last Match option is selected, the contents of the last section heading appear in the header.

Figure 14.6

Use the First Match or Last Match button to determine whether the first or last paragraph appears as the header or footer.

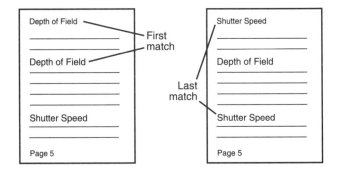

The following exercise examines the steps for creating a first match running header. A left page header will be created and mirrored to the right pages. The photography manual is used as an example, with the "Section Head" paragraph tag selected to create the running header. Use one of your own documents and substitute the desired tag name, or you can create a facsimile of the document in figure 14.6. Make sure you create a paragraph tag called "Section Head" and tag each of the section headings.

1. Select **C**hapter Settings from the **L**ayout menu or press F5. In the Chapter Settings dialog box, click on the Header/Footer tab sheet.

2. Under Enable, click on Left Page Header. Click on the down arrow by **D**efine and choose Left Page Header.

3. Click in the Left text box to place the insertion point. Click on the First Match button (second from the right) to display the Tags Roll-up as shown in figure 14.7.

4. Double-click on "Section Head" tag or on the tag name you want used to create the running header. The roll-up is removed, and the tag name appears in the Left box.

5. Click on the Mirror To F**a**cing Pages button to place the header on the right pages also. Click on OK. Running headers are created, and the contents of each section are displayed on the pages.

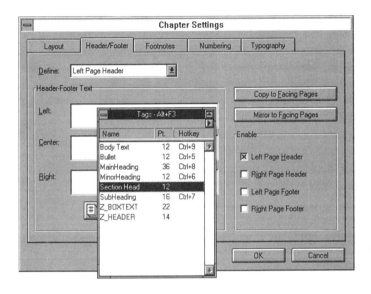

Figure 14.7
The Tags Roll-up appears when you click on the First Match button while creating a header or footer.

If you edit a paragraph tagged to display as a header or footer, the editing changes are not reflected in the header or footer until you select Refresh **W**indow from the **V**iew menu.

This section explains the concept of running headers and footers. However, for other advanced options, refer to the section "Adding Headers and Footers" in your VENTURA software documentation.

Formatting Header and Footer Text

VENTURA automatically tags header and footer text with the generated paragraph tags *Z_HEADER* or *Z_FOOTER*. For instance, when you create a header, VENTURA applies the generated tag Z_HEADER to the header text. Click in the header or footer text with either text tool to view the tag name in the Tag List. You cannot apply another tag to text in header or footer frames.

By default, generated tag names are not visible in the tag list. To view the generated tags used in your document, select Pre**f**erences from the T**o**ols menu. On the View tab sheet, turn on the G**e**nerated Tags option and click on OK to return to the document. Refer to Chapter 8 for more information about working with generated tags.

Advanced VENTURA Options and Techniques

Use the Tagged Text tool to modify the formatting of the Z_HEADER or Z_FOOTER paragraph tags. For instance, you can enlarge the font size or apply italics to the header or footer text. Recall that when a paragraph is formatted with the Tagged Text tool, all other paragraphs using the same tag are also affected. For instance, if you change the font of one paragraph tagged with the Z_HEADER tag, all other paragraphs using the Z_HEADER are changed. Formatting paragraph tags is discussed in Chapter 7. The Freeform Text tool cannot be used to format the Z_HEADER or Z_FOOTER paragraph tags. Although the Freeform text tool generally enables you to modify one paragraph without affecting other paragraphs using the same tag, this does not apply to header and footer text.

The Text Attributes button (see Table 14.1) in the Header/Footer tab sheet of the Chapter Settings dialog box provides another way to format header and footer text. With the Text Attributes button you can apply bold to selected parts of the header or footer text. For instance, in figure 14.8, the company name appears in bold, but the page number does not.

Figure 14.8
With the Text Attributes button, you can apply formatting to selected parts of the header or footer text.

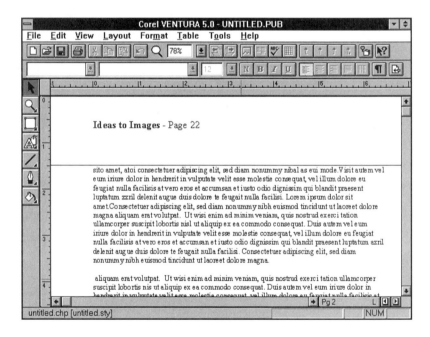

Applying formatting with the Text Attribute button places a code in the header or footer box. Codes are used to signal the beginning and ending of the new formatting. For instance, suppose the header text reads "<B>Acme Company<D>." The <B> turns on the bold formatting—all information following

the <B> is displayed in bold. The <D> code ends the bold formatting. Table 14.2 lists several codes used to create and format headers and footers.

Table 14.2
Header and Footer Codes

Code	Text Displayed
<I>Acme Company<D> <B>[H]<B>	*Acme Company* **12:40 p.m.**
<F"AvantGarde">[D]<D>	September 1, 1993
Chp. <B>[C#]<D> - Pg. <B>[P#]<D>	Chp. **1** - Pg. **1**

The following exercise shows the steps for creating a right page header and right page footer. The Text Attributes button is used to apply formatting. The date and page number are placed in the header, with the date formatted in bold. The time and company name appear in the footer, with the company name formatted in AvantGarde.

1. If desired, start a new document and insert several pages. Select **C**hapter Settings from the **L**ayout menu and click on the Header/Footer tab sheet.

2. Under Enable, click on **R**ight Page Header and **R**ight Page Footer. Click on the down arrow by **D**efine and select Right Page Header.

3. Click to place the insertion point in the **R**ight text box. To apply bold, click on the Text Attributes button (the letter A). The Selected Text Attributes dialog box appears as displayed in figure 14.9.

4. Select Times New Roman from the Font box, select Bold from the Style box and click on OK to return to the Header/Footer dialog box. The insertion point appears between the <B> and <D> codes. Click on the Date button. Press the End key, press the spacebar and click on the Page Numbering button. The completed code is <F"Times New Roman"B><B>[D]<D> [P#].

5. Click on the down arrow by **D**efine and choose Right Page Footer. Click in the Right Text box and click on the Time button. Press the spacebar and click on the Text Attributes button. Select AvantGarde from the **F**ont box and click on OK. Type in the company name, **Acme Company**. The completed code is [H] <F"AvantGarde">AcmeCompany<D>.

6. Click on OK to return to the document. The headers and footers appear on all right pages of the document.

III

Advanced VENTURA Options and Techniques

Figure 14.9
The Selected
Text Attributes
dialog box.

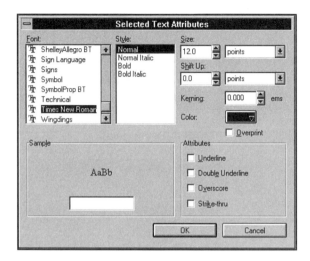

Hiding Headers and Footers

You can hide headers and footers on certain pages. For instance, it is a common practice to hide header and footer text from the first page of a report or manual. First, display the page containing the header or footer you want to hide. To hide the header, select Hide Page Header from the **L**ayout menu. To hide the footer, select Hide Pag**e** Footer from the **L**ayout menu. Checkmarks appear by the commands indicating the headers or footers are hidden. The headers and footers are hidden and will not print. Select the Hide Page Header and Hide Pag**e** Footer commands again to re-display the header and/or footer text.

Controlling Margins in Header and Footer Frames

Header and footer frames have margins that place a cushion of white space between the edges of the frame and the text. You can adjust these margins just as you would the margins on free frames. Select the header or footer frame with the Pick tool, and choose **F**rame from the For**m**at menu. As shown in figure 14.10, enter the desired margin spacing for the top, bottom, left, and right side of the header or footer frame on the Margins tab sheet.

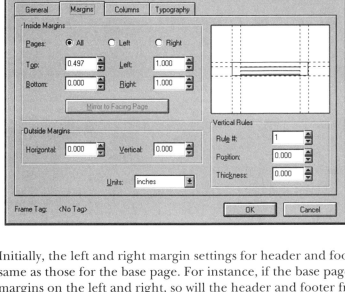

Figure 14.10
Use the Frame
Setting dialog box
to adjust margins
for header and
footer frames.

Initially, the left and right margin settings for header and footer frames are the same as those for the base page. For instance, if the base page uses one-inch margins on the left and right, so will the header and footer frames. If you change the base page margins after creating headers and footers, however, the margins in the header and footer frames do not conform to the changes. In figure 14.11, the left and right margins on the base page were set at a half inch when the footer was added. Then the left and right margins on the base page were changed to one inch. Because the margins in the footer frame did not adjust, the first image illustrates how the footer text is no longer aligned with text on the base page. In the second image, the Frame Settings dialog box was used to adjust the left and right margins in the footer frame to match those on the base page.

Figure 14.11

Figure 14.11
The margins in header and footer frames may have to be adjusted if the base page margins are altered after creating headers and footers.

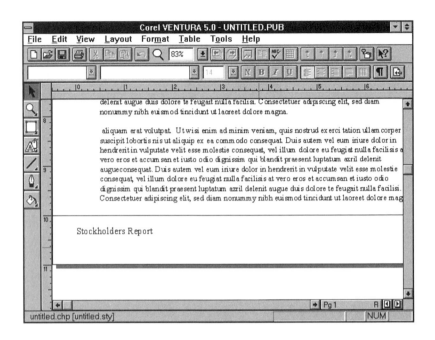

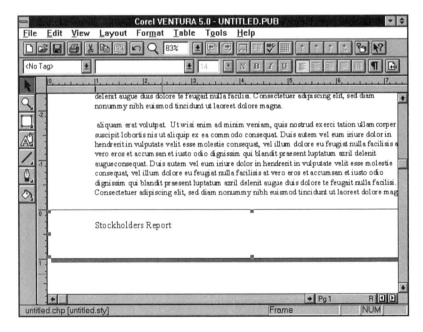

Working with Footnotes

In long documents, *footnotes* provide additional information about specific topics discussed on a page. When a passage from an article appears in the text, a footnote at the bottom of the page can be used to identify the author. When questionnaire results are cited in text, a footnote explains who conducted the survey (see fig 14.12).

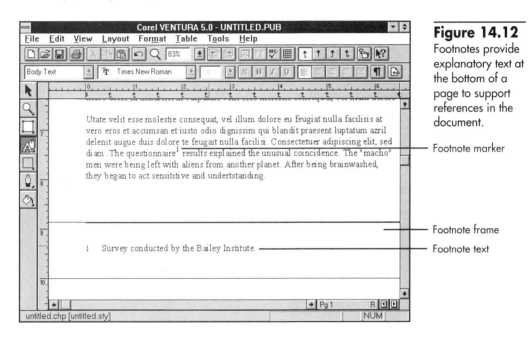

Figure 14.12

Footnotes provide explanatory text at the bottom of a page to support references in the document.

Footnote marker

Footnote frame

Footnote text

When a footnote is created, a *footnote marker,* either a number or some other symbol, is placed in the text. A *footnote frame* is placed at the bottom of the page in which you enter the footnote text. The size of the footnote frame automatically adjusts to get bigger as you enter footnotes and smaller when you delete them.

Footnotes can only be inserted in text placed on the base page.

Setting Up Footnotes

VENTURA provides several options for customizing footnotes. By default, a ruling line is added to separate the footnote text from text on the base page. You can remove this separator line or edit its length and thickness to meet your needs. In addition, you can edit the footnote marker to display in superscript, subscript, or normal (the marker sits on the baseline with the other text). In figure 14.13, the markers appear in superscript. You can also add parentheses, brackets, or dashes to the footnote reference in the footnote text. In the figure, parentheses appear around the footnote references in the footnote text.

Figure 14.13

You can control the placement of footnote markers and add parentheses to footnote references in the text.

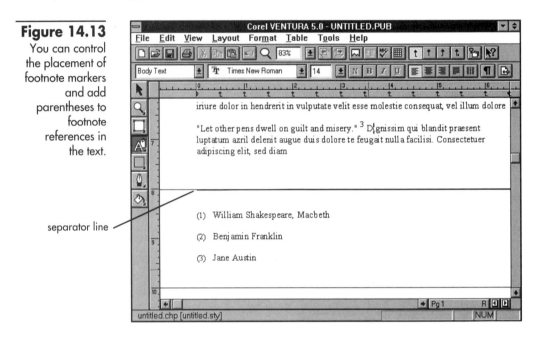

separator line

VENTURA also enables you to create custom numbering schemes for referencing footnotes. Although using numbers for footnote markers is pretty standard, you can use other characters instead. For instance, in figure 14.14, asterisks are used to identify footnotes. The first footnote displays one asterisk. The second footnote displays two, and so on. A custom numbering scheme continues up to four characters, then the scheme restarts with one character. If the fourth footnote marker is ****, for instance, the fifth footnote marker is * because the numbering scheme begins again.

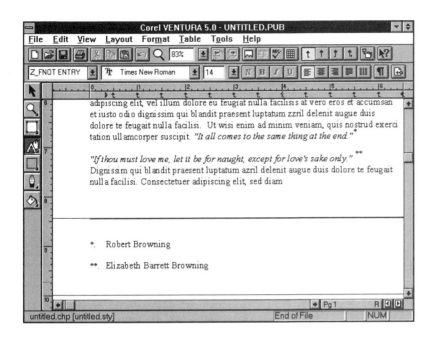

Figure 14.14
You can establish custom numbering schemes when you don't want to use numbers in the footnote markers.

The Footnotes tab in the Chapter Settings dialog box enables you to turn the footnotes on and off and control footnote settings. The following exercise illustrates the steps for turning on the footnote feature. The Numerical numbering scheme is used in the exercise. Footnote markers are formatted to appear in superscript, and brackets are added to the footnote references in the footnote text. The thickness of the separator line is also modified.

1. Select **C**hapter Settings from the **L**ayout menu and click on the Footnotes tab sheet to display the dialog box in figure 14.15.

2. Select the **N**umerical option at the top of the dialog box. (To create a customized numbering scheme, select the **C**ustom option and enter the character to be used in the scheme in the Reference box.)

3. To add parentheses to the footnote references in the footnote text, click on the down arrow by **T**emplate and select (#). To display footnote markers in superscript, click on the down arrow by **P**osition and choose Superscript.

4. The options in the Separator section of the dialog box control the ruling line placed above the footnote text. Enter the desired line thickness in the **T**hickness box. Click on the **A**dd Separator Line option to remove the line altogether.

5. Click on OK. You are now ready to begin inserting footnotes.

Figure 14.15

The Chapter Settings dialog box with the Footnotes tab selected.

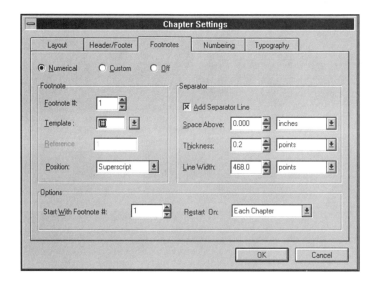

In addition to turning on the footnote feature in the Chapter Settings dialog box, you must select the En**a**ble Footnotes command from the **L**ayout menu. This command must be turned on for footnotes to appear on the page. If the En**a**ble Footnote command is not turned on, the footnote is still inserted, but it's invisible.

Inserting Footnotes

A footnote frame is created when you insert the first footnote. Subsequent footnotes added to the page also appear in this frame. It is important to note that footnote frames might appear on the next page if there is not room on the current page. In addition, lengthy footnotes might flow to a footnote frame on the next page. The following steps illustrate inserting footnotes:

1. With either text tool, click in the text to place the insertion point where you want the footnote marker to appear.

2. Select Insert Special Ite**m** from the **E**dit menu. From the submenu, choose **F**ootnote.

3. The footnote marker appears in the text. The marker is formatted to the specifications established when you set up the footnotes.

4. As shown in figure 14.16, a footnote frame appears at the bottom of the page. The footnote reference and the text "Text of Footnote" appear in the frame. Delete this text and enter your own footnote text. Footnotes are limited to one paragraph up to 8,000 characters long.

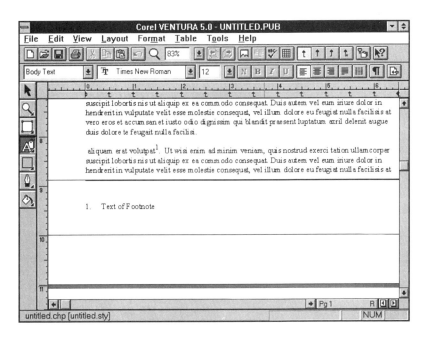

Figure 14.16

To enter footnote text, delete "Text of Footnote" and begin typing.

Footnote text can be edited as you would any other paragraph of text. Simply click in the footnote text and make the desired changes. VENTURA takes care of numbering the footnotes as you insert them. Each time you add or delete footnotes, the numbering is adjusted. For instance, if you add a new footnote between footnotes 2 and 3, the new footnote becomes 3, bumping the next one to 4.

Deleting Footnotes

Footnotes are deleted by removing the footnote marker from the text. To remove a footnote, place the insertion point immediately before the footnote marker. As displayed in figure 14.17, the status line displays the word "Footnote." If necessary, use the arrow keys to move the insertion point to the left or right until Footnote appears in the window's status line. Press Delete to remove the footnote marker. Although the footnote marker and footnote are deleted, you have to select Refresh Window from the View menu to clear the footnote text.

Figure 14.17

The status line
displays
"Footnote" when
the insertion point
is immediately
before the
footnote marker.

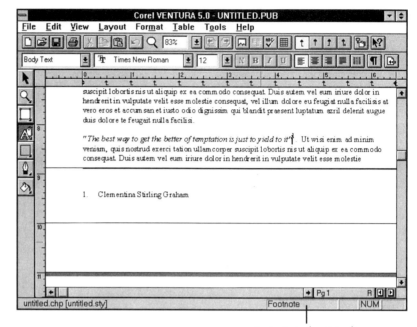

Footnote in the status line

Formatting Footnote Text

VENTURA automatically tags footnote text entered in the footnote frame with the generated paragraph tag "Z_FNOT ENTRY." The footnote marker is tagged as "Z_FNOT #." Click in the footnote text with either text tool to view the tag name in the Tag list. You cannot apply another tag to text in footnote frames.

The process for formatting footnote text and markers is similar to formatting header and footnote text. The Tagged Text tool is used to modify the formatting of the Z_FNOT ENTRY and Z_FNOT # paragraph tags. The Freeform Text tool cannot be used to override footnote paragraph tag formatting. Refer to Chapter 7 for information on formatting text.

Controlling Margins in Footnote Frames

Use the **F**rame command in the For**m**at menu to adjust the margins in footnote frames. When you first insert a footnote, the footnote frame uses the left and right margin settings set up on the base page. If the base page margins are changed after a footnote is inserted, the margins in the footnote frames do not conform to the changes. In figure 14.18, the left margin on the base page was set at one inch when the footnote was added, then the left margin on the base page

was changed to a half inch. The footnote text does not align with text on the base page because the margins in the footnote frame did not adjust. To remedy this problem, the left margin of the footnote frame was reset at a half inch using the <u>F</u>rame command in the For<u>m</u>at menu.

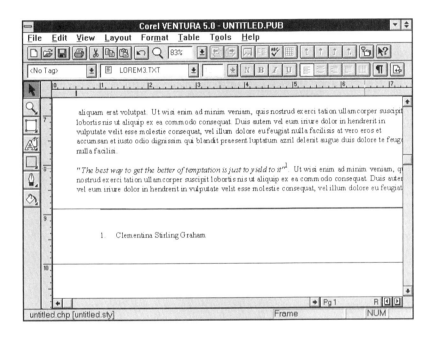

Figure 14.18
The margins in footnote frames might have to be adjusted if the base page margins are altered after creating footnotes.

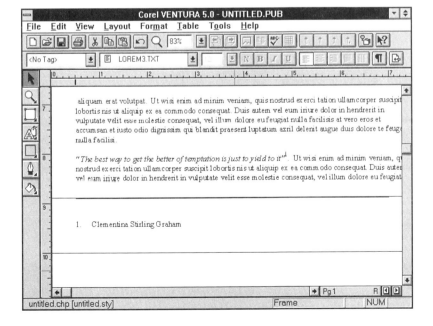

Working with Chapter, Page, Figure, and Table Numbering

Chapter, page, figure, and table numbering are important elements in helping readers locate information. What good would an index or table of contents be if the chapters and pages in a document weren't numbered? You have several options for modifying the numbering systems used to organize your document.

Chapter and page numbers are inserted when you add headers and footers to your page. Figure and table numbers are created when you add a figure or table reference to a caption frame. By default, each numbering system begins at 1, but you can specify another beginning number. You can, for instance, specify that page numbering begin at 10 instead of 1. VENTURA also enables you to number the elements sequentially throughout the publication. For example, you can specify that the page numbers run continuously across all the chapters in a book.

Creating headers and footers is discussed in the first part of this chapter. Refer to Chapter 10, "Advanced Free Frame Options," for more information about adding figure and table references to caption frames.

This section examines the creation of two numbering schemes prevalent in books and technical manuals. The two schemes have sequential numbering in common. For instance, chapter 2 appears after chapter 1. The two schemes differ in how the pages are numbered. In the first numbering scheme, sequential page numbering, the page numbers run continuously from chapter to chapter. The second numbering scheme, non-sequential page numbering, resets the page numbering to one for every chapter. Notice the page numbering in figure 14.19; sequential page numbering was used on the top two pages. The bottom two pages use non-sequential page numbering, forcing the page numbering to reset to one at the beginning of a chapter.

For the following exercise, use one of your own documents or create a sample publication file. To create your own, build a publication file with three chapters. Each chapter includes two pages with the chapter and page numbers set up in the header text. Numbered figures are also placed on the pages of the chapter files. If you plan to do both exercises, make a copy of the sample publication file for use with the second exercise.

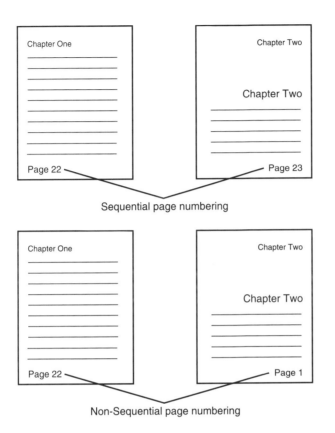

Figure 14.19
Page numbering
can run
sequentially
throughout your
document, or
begin anew with
each chapter file.

Working with Sequential Page Numbering Schemes

In the following exercise the chapter and page numbers are instructed to run sequentially throughout the three chapters. The command used to number the chapters and pages sequentially, however, also numbers the figures and tables sequentially throughout the document. The last three steps illustrate restarting the figure numbering to begin at one for each chapter.

1. If you created the sample publication, open it now. Otherwise, open your own publication file. Go to the first chapter in the publication. As the sample publication in figure 14.20 illustrates, the chapter, page and figure numbers all begin at one.

Advanced VENTURA Options and Techniques

Figure 14.20

In the first
chapter, the
chapter, page,
and figure
numbers all
begin at one.

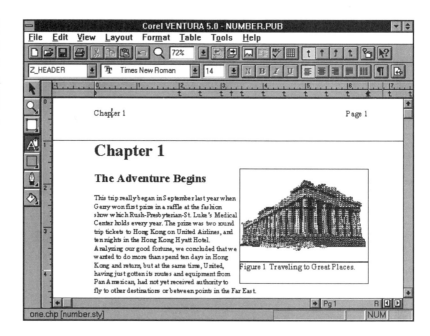

2. Select Renumber **P**ublication from the For**m**at menu. The message in
   figure 14.21 appears asking if you want to renumber the chapters, pages,
   tables, and figures in the publication file, click on Renumber.

Figure 14.21

A message
appears when
you select the
Renumber
Publication
command.

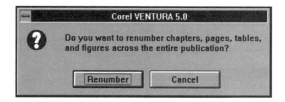

3. The status line displays the progress of the renumbering. When finished,
   select G**o** To Chapter from the **V**iew menu and select the second chapter.
   As the sample publication in figure 14.22 illustrates, the chapter, page,
   and figure numbering in the second chapter continues from the previous
   chapter. Use the G**o** To Chapter command to view the changes in the
   third chapter.

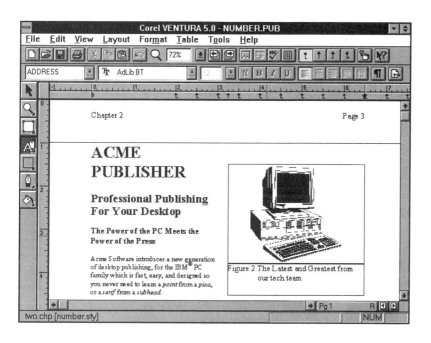

Figure 14.22
The Renumber command renumbers chapter, page, and figure numbers to run continuously through the publication file.

4. To adjust the figure numbering so it begins at one for each new chapter, display the second chapter and select **C**hapter Settings from the **L**ayout menu. Click on the Numbering tab to display the dialog box shown in figure 14.23.

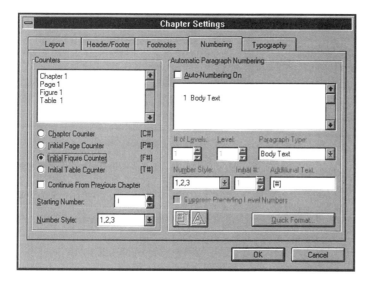

Figure 14.23
The Chapter Settings dialog box with the Numbering tab selected.

III

Advanced VENTURA Options and Techniques

5. Under Counters, click on the Initial **F**igure Counter box. Click to remove the *X* from the Continue from Pre**v**ious Chapter option. Enter **1** in the **S**tarting Number box and click on OK. The first figure in the second chapter is renumbered to begin at one.

6. Go to the third chapter and repeat steps 4 and 5. The figure numbering of each chapter begins at one.

Working with Non-Sequential Page Numbering Schemes

In this numbering scheme, only the chapters are numbered sequentially throughout the publication file. The page and figure numbers begin at 1 for each chapter. The steps here are condensed because they are similar to those in the previous exercise.

1. If you created the sample publication, open it now. Otherwise, open your own publication file. Go to the first chapter in the publication.

2. Select Renumber **P**ublication from the For**m**at menu. Click on the Renumber button to renumber the chapters, pages, tables, and figures in the publication file.

3. The status line displays the progress of the renumbering. When finished, check the second and third chapters to verify that the chapter, page, and figure numbers are adjusted to run continuously throughout the document.

4. To restart the page numbering at one for each chapter, return to the second chapter and select **C**hapter Settings from the **L**ayout menu. Click on the Numbering tab, and click on the **I**nitial Page Counter button to edit the page numbering system. Disable the Continue from Pre**v**ious Chapter option and enter **1** in the **S**tarting Number box (refer to fig. 14.23).

5. To restart the figure numbering at one, click on the Initial **F**igure Counter button. Again, disable the Continue from Pre**v**ious Chapter option and enter **1** in the **S**tarting Number box. Click on OK.

6. Go to the third chapter and repeat steps 4 and 5. The page and figure numbering of each chapter begins at one.

Selecting a Number Format

VENTURA provides several number format options when formatting the chapter, page, figure, and table numbers in your document. For instance, you can use roman numerals to identify the tables in your document. Table 14.3 lists the formats available in VENTURA.

Table 14.3
Numbering Formats

Number Style	Example
1,2,3	Figure 1
A,B,C	Table A
a,b,c	Table a
I,II,III,IV	Chapter III
i,ii,iii,iv	Figure iv
One, Two	Chapter One
ONE, TWO	Page ONE
one, two	Table two

The following exercise illustrates the steps for changing the number format for chapter and page numbering. The chapter numbers are formatted to display in words, and the page numbers in uppercase roman numerals. Use one of the sample documents supplied by VENTURA or your own publication file.

1. Open the chapter file in which you want to format the numbers. Select **C**hapter Settings from the **L**ayout menu and click on the Numbering tab.

2. Click on the C**h**apter Counter option. To select another number format, click on the down arrow by **N**umber Style. Select the option, One, Two.

3. Click on the **I**nitial Page Counter option. Click on the down arrow by **N**umber Style and select I,II,III,IV. Click on OK to return to the document. As displayed in figure 14.24, the format of the chapter and page numbering is altered.

Figure 14.24

You can apply different number formats to the chapter and page numbers.

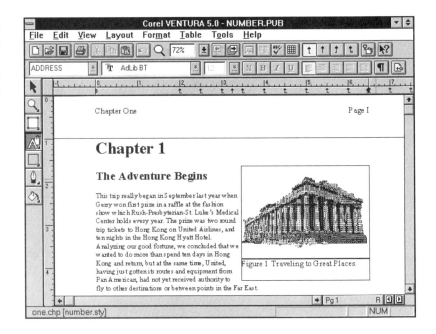

Working with Chapter Typography

VENTURA provides control over typographical settings, such as widows and orphans and vertical justification. This section examines the establishment of typography settings for an entire chapter. You can override these settings for any frame or page you have inserted manually. Refer to Chapter 10 for more information on controlling widows and orphans, vertical justification ,and placement of the first line of text for individual pages and frames.

Adjusting Widows and Orphans

When text flows across several pages or frames, paragraphs of text are often split in two as the text continues to the next page or frame. In figure 14.25, for example, the paragraph at the end of the first page is split, then continued at the top of the second page. Sometimes, the paragraph splits at an unattractive place, perhaps leaving one isolated line at the top or bottom of a frame. As a page designer, you might be familiar with the terms "widow" and "orphan." *Widow* is the typographical term for one or two lines of text sitting alone at the bottom of a page or frame. The term *orphan* describes one or two lines isolated at the top of a page or frame.

Orphan

Figure 14.25
You can control the number of lines isolated at the top or bottom of a page.

Widow

VENTURA provides a Widows and Orphans feature which enables you to control where a paragraph is split. The Widows and Orphans feature enables you to specify the minimum amount of lines placed at the bottom of a page or frame (widow) and the minimum amount of lines placed at the top of a page or frame (orphan).

In your page design, you might feel comfortable allowing two lines at the top or bottom of a page or frame, or perhaps you want a minimum of three lines. With VENTURA, you can specify from one to five lines. Selecting three lines for the widow setting, for instance, means that no fewer than three lines must appear at the bottom of the page or frame. If there is not room for three lines, the text is forced to the next page or frame:

The following steps illustrate controlling the widows and orphans for an entire chapter file:

1. Select **C**hapter Settings from the **L**ayout menu. Click on the Typography tab to display the Chapter Settings dialog box (see fig. 14.26).

2. The **W**idow and Orph**a**ns settings appear in the top left of the dialog box. Enter the desired number of widow and orphan lines in the appropriate boxes. For instance, entering 2 in the Orph**a**n box ensures that no fewer than two lines of text can appear alone at the top of a page or frame.

3. Click on OK. The widow and orphan settings have been established for the entire chapter file.

III

Advanced VENTURA Options and Techniques

Figure 14.26

The Chapter Settings dialog box with the Typography tab selected.

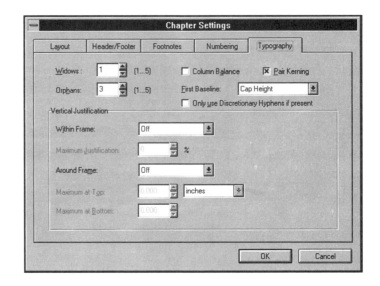

Balancing Columns

VENTURA provides an option for balancing columns. As displayed on the first page in figure 14.27, the columns are unbalanced because the first column is filled, and the remaining text is dropped into the second column. The columns are balanced on the second page where the text is distributed evenly in the columns.

Use the following steps to turn on column balance for an entire chapter file:

1. Select **C**hapter Settings from the **L**ayout menu and click on the Typography tab.

2. Click on the Column B**a**lance option and click on OK. Column Balance is enabled for the entire chapter.

Remember, Vertical Justification and Column Balance can also be applied to individual pages and frames. Refer to Chapter 10 for more information.

It is a good idea to turn on Column Balance when you have headings that extend across columns. The headings in figure 14.28 are set to display as frame-wide text. If Column Balance is not on, the headings can interrupt the flow of text between the columns.

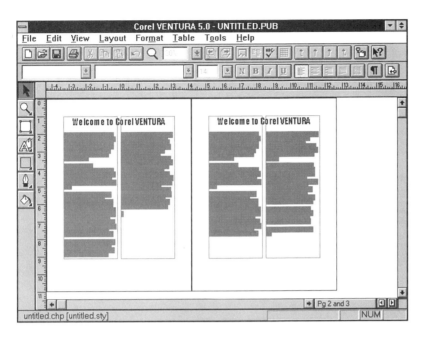

Figure 14.27
The Column Balance feature distributes text evenly in the columns.

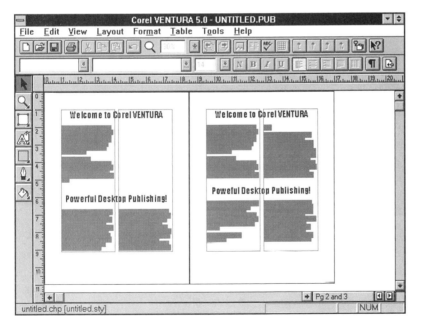

Figure 14.28
Turn on Column Balance when your document uses frame-wide text.

Advanced VENTURA Options and Techniques

Working with Pair Kerning

Kerning is the adjustment of space between selected pairs of letters. Certain pairs of letters appear to be separated by too much space. The effect is especially apparent in larger titles and headings. You can turn on the Pair Kerning option to have VENTURA automatically kern text in the chapter file.

Use the following steps to turn on pair kerning for an entire chapter file:

1. Select Chapter Settings from the Layout menu and click on the Typography tab.

2. Click on the Pair Kerning option and click on OK. Pair kerning is enabled for the entire chapter.

Turning on the Pair Kerning option does not resolve all letter spacing problems. Certain letter pairs in words create spacing problems that can only be corrected by manual kerning. Refer to Chapter 9 for a detailed discussion of manual kerning.

Controlling Vertical Justification

VENTURA enables you to turn on the vertical justification feature to ensure that text always reaches the bottom of the page or frame. Space is added between paragraphs and lines of text to distribute the text. Vertical justification was turned on for the first page in figure 14.29 and turned off for the second. You can see how spacing is added to fill the page.

You might want to turn on vertical justification when producing certain type of documents, such as advertisements and flyers, but it is certainly not required for all documents. Keep in mind that spacing inserted when you turn on vertical justification disregards text spacing. The spacing set up for inter-line and before- and after-paragraph spacing for each paragraph tags is no longer closely followed. More space might be added if needed. If turning on vertical justification doesn't give you what you need, try spreading the text manually by increasing the spacing between text paragraphs with the spacing options in the Paragraph Settings dialog box.

There are two options for controlling the amount of space added to distribute the text. The *feathering* option adds the exact amount of space required to make the text reach the bottom of the page or frame. The *carding* option adds space using the inter-line spacing set up in the body text paragraph tag as a guide. The carding option keeps the baselines of text even across several columns. With the carding option enabled, text might not reach the exact bottom of the frame.

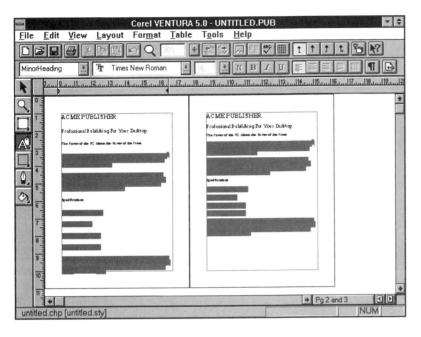

Figure 14.29

Vertical justification adds space to ensure text reaches the bottom of the page or frame.

When vertical justification is applied to a base page frame, spacing is added above and below any free frames on the page. VENTURA provides two options for determining how spacing is added to frames on the base page. With the first option, Fixed, spacing is only added below a frame so the frame stays in its original position. The Moveable option adds space above and below a frame. You can also specify the maximum amount of space that can be added between a frame and the text before and after it. This space is additional to the outside margins applied to the frame.

The following steps illustrate turning on vertical justification for an entire chapter file:

1. Select **C**hapter Settings from the **L**ayout menu and click on the Typography tab.

2. In the Vertical Justification section of the dialog box, click on the down arrow by W**i**thin Frame. Select Feathering or Carding.

3. Enter **100%** in the Maximum **J**ustification box. A value of 0% turns vertical justification off.

4. Click on the down arrow by Around Fra**me**. Select Fixed if you do not want any free frames on the base page to be moved. Select Moveable if the frames can be moved down to help vertically justify the page.

5. Enter values for the Maximum at T**o**p and Maximum at **B**ottom. For instance, entering .25 inches in the Maximum at T**o**p allows up to $1/4$-inch extra spacing to be added above a frame.

6. Click on OK. Vertical justification is turned on for the entire chapter file.

Controlling Placement of the First Line of Text

VENTURA provides two options for specifying where the first line of text begins on a page or frame. As displayed in figure 14.30, the first line of text can begin at the very top of the column guide, or it can be moved slightly down in an amount equal to the inter-line spacing.

The following steps illustrate setting the First Baseline feature for an entire chapter file:

1. Select **C**hapter Settings from the **L**ayout menu and click on the Typography tab.

2. Click on the down arrow by **F**irst Baseline. Select Cap-Height to align the top of the tallest letter in the first line of text with the top of the frame. Select Inter-line to move the first line of text down by an amount equal to the inter-line spacing.

3. Click on OK. The First Line feature is set for the entire chapter file.

Figure 14.30
The first line of text can begin at the very top of the frame or moved down slightly in an amount equal to the inter-line spacing.

…continues

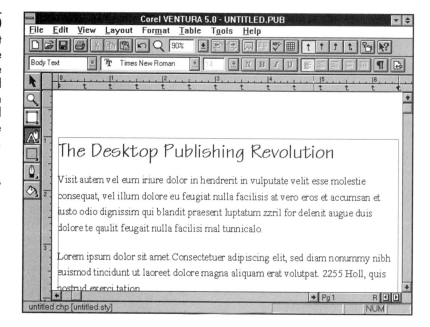

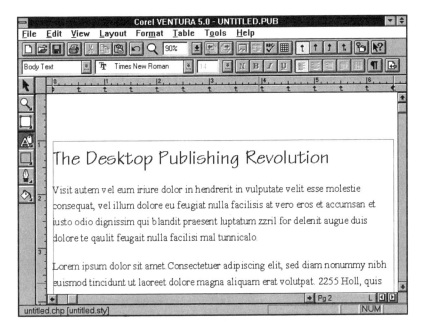

Figure 14.30

…continued

Chapter Snapshot

Almost any type of document occasionally includes the use of tables. Statistical information is almost always much easier to understand when presented in a tabular format. In this chapter, you learn to do the following:

Tables have a wide array of uses and this chapter helps you set up any type of table that you might want to use. You will learn not only how to set up a table, but how to format it and apply borders and shading.

CHAPTER

Working with Tables

CorelVENTURA has what many experts consider to be the most advanced and versatile table-creation feature of any desktop publishing package on the market.

A *table* consists of rows and columns of cells, all containing one paragraph. This paragraph can take on all the properties of any paragraph tag that has been created, as well as be changed with the Freeform Text tool. Because text in the cell wraps, text is not limited to one line. Text is limited to one paragraph, however.

After you begin to use tables, their uses become evident. Price lists, schedules, statistics, tables of figures, calendars, and even forms can be generated easily using the table feature.

This chapter discusses the ways in which you can enhance tables by using the many tools at your disposal. You can shade cells by using the fill qualities for frames found in VENTURA. You can add borders by using endless combinations of the rule lines. You can apply prebuilt border tags, or you can create and apply new tags.

You also will learn how to merge cells to give your tables a whole new look to better clarify your information.

This chapter discusses the ways in which you can input table text by using the Text tool or by importing it through CorelQUERY. (CorelQUERY is discussed in "Importing Data into Tables" later in this chapter.)

Creating a Table

Tables can be as small as one cell or as large as the memory on your computer allows. Tables can even span several pages. At first glance, tables are somewhat like a spreadsheet. You cannot directly insert a formula or calculation into a VENTURA table, however.

Inserting a Table

You begin your work by first choosing where you want to insert a table. To insert a table, follow these steps:

1. Select the Text tool and click in front of an empty paragraph symbol on the page.

   Tables can reside in the underlying base page frame or in a free frame. After you select the location of the table, you need to define the size of the table.

2. Click on the Table button in the button bar. Alternatively, choose Creat**e** Table from the **T**able menu (see fig. 15.1).

When the first table is created in the publication, a New Paragraph tag is added to the list. VENTURA automatically generates a Table Text tag that carries the same attributes as the current Body Text tag.

The Table Settings dialog box appears, with three tabs shown across the top of the box: General, Positioning, and Cell Borders (see fig. 15.2).

Setting Up the Table

After you have chosen the location of the table, you must define the makeup of the table. How many columns and rows of information will the table contain? Do you want to place a special border around the table? You specify this information in the General tab.

The General tab is divided into three sections: Rows & Columns, Column Widths, and Table Border. Define the size of the table by inserting the number of rows and columns in the appropriate boxes. Follow these steps to set up your table:

1. Enter **16** for the number of **R**ows.

2. Enter **7** for the number of **C**olumns.

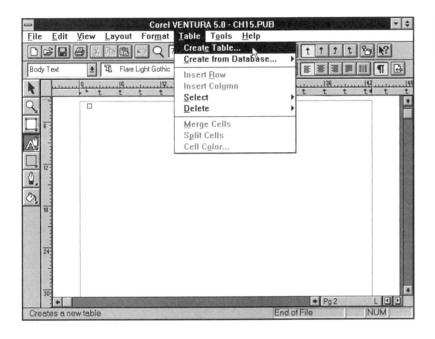

Figure 15.1
Inserting a table.

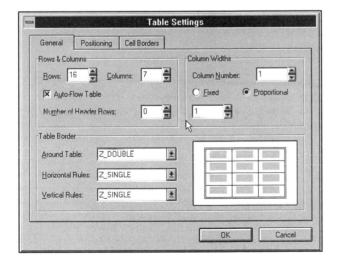

Figure 15.2
The General tab of the Table Settings dialog box.

3. Click on the Auto-Flow Table check box if the table is to occupy more than one frame. These frames can be the underlying page frame or multiple free frames on the same or different pages.

4. Enter the number of rows at the beginning of the table that will serve as the header rows in the Number of Header Rows box. Header rows will be repeated at the top of the table within each frame.

The table is not limited to the number of rows and columns set here. You can add, move, or delete rows and columns at any time. These procedures are discussed later in this chapter.

You can use the Column Widths section to customize column widths. If you do not make any changes in this section, all columns specified in the first section are spaced equally across the frame or column. If five columns are specified for a table that is being inserted into a five-inch wide column or frame, for example, each column will be one-inch wide until changes are made.

Before changing any column widths, it's a good idea to enter some or all of the text and then format the column widths for visual appeal and balance.

You use the Table Border section to apply border tags to the table. The default choices follow:

✔ **Z_DOUBLE.** Two 0.2-point rule lines separated by a white space of 0.7 points between them

✔ **Z_HIDDEN.** No rule lines applied

✔ **Z_SINGLE.** One 0.2-point rule line

✔ **Z_THICK.** One 2.2-point rule line

As you specify the rule lines in the drop-down lists, you can see how they will look on-screen in the sample box at the right of the dialog box.

VENTURA's default border settings are double rule lines around the entire table with single rule lines separating the rows and columns. Again, it is easier to work with the table if these lines are visible. Changing the rule lines is done more efficiently toward completion of the table. For this exercise, leave the rule lines at their default settings.

5. Select the second tab, Positioning, to display the four-sectioned dialog box shown in figure 15.3.

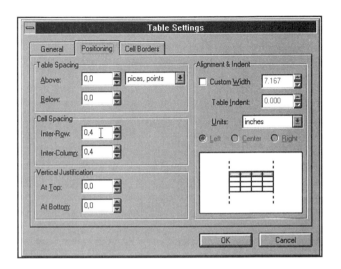

Figure 15.3
The Positioning tab of the Table Settings dialog box.

Table Spacing

In the Positioning tab, all table spacing is set. The spacing controls are on the left side of this dialog box. Following is a list of the spacing options and their purpose:

✔ **Table Spacing.** Specifies the amount of empty space left above or below the entire table. Entering a value of one pica above would move the table down one pica from the element immediately above it. A setting of one pica below would add one pica of space before placing the next element following the table.

✔ **Cell Spacing.** Places a buffer space inside the individual cells of the table to move text in from the cell borders.

✔ **Vertical Justification.** To limit the amount of space that VENTURA adds above and below a table when vertical justification is enabled for a column or frame of text and graphics, enter the maximum amount of space you will allow.

To set these measurements, use the following steps:

1. Select the unit of measure for space settings. In this example, choose "picas, points," which sets the measurements for all selections in the dialog box, except in the Alignment & Indent section.

2. Enter **1,0** in the <u>A</u>bove setting to begin the table 1 pica below the element or margin above it. For example, if the table is placed on the underlying page frame, your table will begin 1 pica below the top margin.

3. Enter **1,0** pica in the **B**elow box. Whatever follows the table will be moved 1 pica down.

4. Enter **0,4** in the Inter-R**o**w box to insert 4 points of spacing between the baseline of the text and the bottom of each cell. An equal amount of space is added above the text.

5. Enter **0,4** in the Inter-Colum**n** box to insert an in-from-left and in-from-right setting of 4 points within each cell.

6. Enter **2,0** in both boxes of the Vertical Justification setting. This will ensure that no more than 2 picas of space will be added At **T**op and At Botto**m** of the table should the frame or column be vertically justified.

Setting Up Table Alignment

The last setting in this dialog box defines the Alignment and Indent of the entire table. Just as paragraph text can be specified to span a column or the entire frame, so can a table. To specify a custom width for the table if it is not to be frame- or column-wide, place an *X* in the Custom **W**idth check box to enable that option. Enter a measurement for the width of the table. You can then enter an amount in the Table **I**ndent field to move the table to the right of the left margin.

For example, in figure 15.4, the total page margin is 43 picas. A 36-pica-wide table was created by checking the Custom **W**idth check box and entering **36,0** in the measurement box.

After the width is determined, a custom indent setting can be set in the Table **I**ndent box. Entering **7,0** picas in this box moves the table 7 picas to the right of the left margin (see fig. 15.5). Because 7 picas was the difference between the total margin width and the width of the table, the table was shifted to the right margin.

An easier way to right-align the table on your page is to leave the Table **I**ndent set to 0,0 and select the **R**ight button underneath the **U**nits box.

You can align a custom-wide table to the **L**eft, **C**enter, or **R**ight within the frame or column by selecting one of these option buttons. Selecting **L**eft aligns your table with the left margin. Tables can also be centered in the column or frame by choosing the **C**enter button.

Notice that the sample window in the dialog box illustrates your settings.

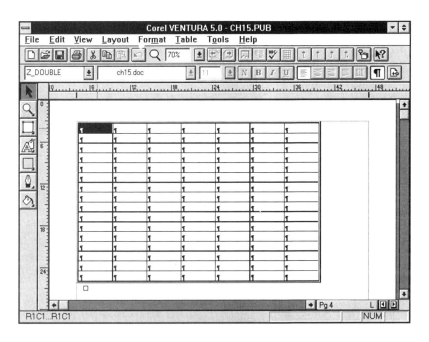

Figure 15.4
A custom width is applied to the table.

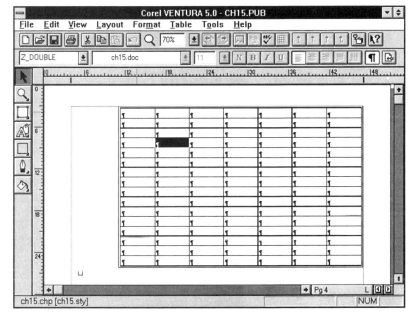

Figure 15.5
The same table has been indented seven picas from the left margin.

III

Advanced VENTURA Options and Techniques

The Table **I**ndent setting applies only if the table is left-aligned. The indent has no bearing if the table is right-aligned or centered.

Adding and Deleting Border Tags

Select the final tab in the Table Settings dialog box, Cell Borders, to make changes to the generated border tags or to create new border tags.

The Cell Borders settings do not change the currently highlighted cells border settings. This tab is only for specifying new border tags or deleting unwanted border tags.

You can specify up to three ruling lines with any spacing you want between them. Notice that the Pen button between the Thickness and Spacing settings enables you to customize each individual rule specified (see fig. 15.6). Clicking on this button opens the Outline Pen dialog box (see fig. 15.7), which controls the style and color of the rule lines. Because these setting are for each individual rule line, you can assign different colors and styles to each one.

Figure 15.6
The Cell Borders tab in the Table Settings dialog box.

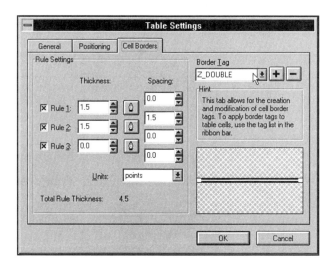

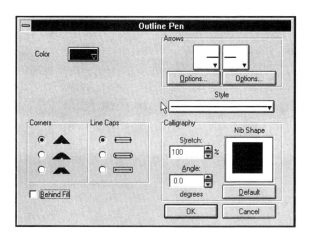

Figure 15.7
The Outline Pen
dialog box.

Creating a Border Tag

To create a new border tag, follow these steps:

1. To create a new border tag, click on the plus button to the right of the Border **T**ag list in the Cell Borders tab of the Table Settings dialog box. The Add Border Tag dialog box appears (see fig. 15.8).

Figure 15.8
The Add Border
Tag dialog box.

2. Enter the new **T**ag Name, such as "Triple rules," and click on OK. The new tag name appears in Border **T**ag pull-down list.

3. Because this border tag will have 3 rule lines, click on the check boxes in front of each rule line number to activate them.

4. Enter the thickness for each rule line. For this exercise, be sure that **U**nits is set to points. In the Thickness settings, enter **1** for Rule **1**, **2** for Rule **2**, and **4** for Rule **3**.

5. Enter **2** points of spacing between Rule 1 and 2, and between Rules 2 and 3 (see fig. 15.9).

III

Advanced VENTURA Options and Techniques

Figure 15.9

Setting thicknesses for the rules in the Cell Borders tab.

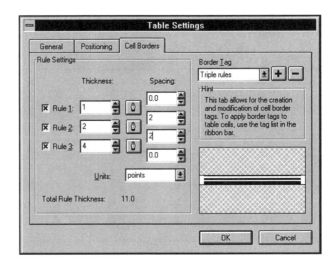

6. Customize the style of the ruling line by selecting the Outline Pen button between the Thickness and Spacing settings.

7. Click on OK when all rule styles are defined.

Deleting a Border Tag

If there are border tags that are not needed, they can be deleted. To remove a border tag, follow these steps:

1. Select the border tag name from the Border **T**ag list.

2. Click on the minus button to remove the tag and its settings.

Choosing Preset Format Options

Earlier in the book, you read that the Quick Format Roll-up offers preset formatting for paragraphs, ruling lines, columns, page layout, headers, footers, and tables. After you specify the initial settings for your table, you can use the Table option in the Quick Format Roll-up to specify quick formatting options. The Quick Format Roll-up applies cell shading, adds cell borders, or merges cells in the table. You can use these preset format options as the only formatting applied to the table, or you can use the options as a head start to your formatting. After you apply a Quick Format, you still can alter the table, but much of the formatting will have been done.

Quick Format does not alter the width of any of the table columns. You must change column width after the presets are applied.

To apply a Quick Format to your table, read the following steps:

1. Choose **Q**uick Format Roll-Up from the For**m**at menu (or press Ctrl+Q).

   The Quick Format Roll-up appears (see fig. 15.10).

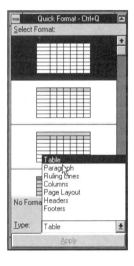

Figure 15.10
The Quick Format Roll-up.

2. Select the Pick tool.

3. Select the table by clicking inside one of the cells.

4. In the Quick Format Roll-up, choose the Table option from the **T**ype list.

5. Scroll through the different images of sample layouts and click on the one you want.

6. Click on **A**pply to format your table like the sample image.

Many of the Quick Formats include *merged cells*—cells combined to form one larger cell that spans the width or length of several cells. Applying a quick format to a table that already has some text entered might cause that text to be hidden. You can reveal the text again by splitting the cells. After you save and close the publication, however, all hidden text is lost. Merging cells is discussed later in this chapter.

III

Advanced VENTURA Options and Techniques

Entering Text into a Table

After you create a table, begin entering text into the cells by using the Text tool. You can maneuver around the table by using the arrow keys or by clicking the Text tool in the desired cell. Remember that each cell is limited to one paragraph, so pressing Enter does not produce a new paragraph within the cell. Line breaks (Ctrl+Enter), however, can be used to enter multi-line text in the cells.

It is a good idea to enter and format most of the table text before you change the appearance of the table—for example, adjusting column widths, merging cells, or adding shading and borders.

Selecting Cells, Rows, or Columns

When working with tables, you use the Pick tool to select cells. If no table is present, the Pick tool cursor appears as an arrow. When the cursor is positioned over a table, however, it changes to a white cross. This is the tool you need to highlight cells, rows, or columns.

Selecting a Single Cell

After the cursor changes to a white cross, simply click inside a cell to select it. The highlighted cell appears in reverse video (see fig. 15.11).

Figure 15.11
Selecting a cell.

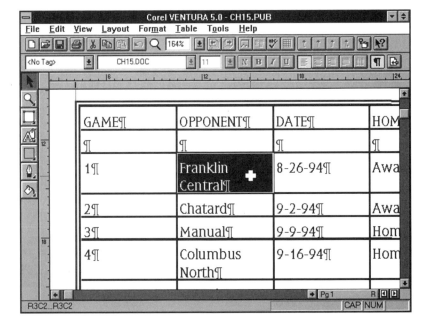

Selecting Multiple Cells, Including Rows and Columns

With the cursor, click-and-hold the left mouse button on the top, far left cell that you want to edit. Then drag the cursor to the bottom, far right cell. Release the mouse button to select the cells.

Alternatively, you can select the first cell by clicking inside it. Press Shift while clicking in the bottom, far right cell and then release Shift. All cells between are highlighted.

Adjusting Column Width

Remember that when you create a table, all column widths default to *proportional*. That is, all column widths are the same size, depending on how large the table is and how many columns there are. Because many tables contain text that varies in length, you should alter column widths to accommodate the text within them. Columns that contain numerical data, for example, might require less width than columns that contain words or phrases.

Changing Column Width by Dragging

Column width can be adjusted two ways: either dragging the right column border wider or smaller, or by entering a specific width in the General tab of the Table Settings dialog box which was used to create the table.

The following steps show how to adjust column widths by dragging:

1. Select the Pick tool.

2. Click in a cell in the column to be resized.

3. Using the reversed cell as a guideline for finding the right border of the column, move the cursor over the column border until it changes from a white cross to double vertical lines with arrows pointing to the left and right of the parallel lines (see fig. 15.12). Remember that columns must be sized using the right-hand border.

4. Press Ctrl while clicking and holding the left mouse button. Drag to the right or left to change the column width. Notice that if the rulers are enabled, you can adjust the column width using the top crosshair as a general guide.

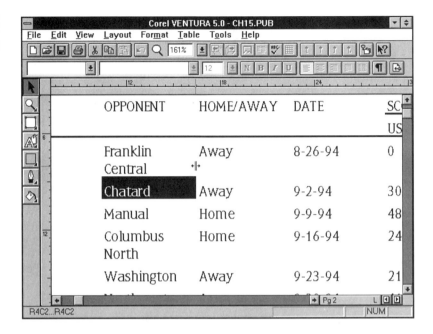

After you change the column width, all remaining columns designated as proportional resize equally to compensate for the new column.

Changing Column Width with a Dialog Box

You can change column width by following these steps:

1. Select the Pick tool.

2. Highlight a cell in the table.

   It is not important to select a cell in the column if the column width is changing. Any cell can be selected because you will designate the column number to edit in the dialog box.

3. Click the right mouse button to display the pop-up menu and select General.

   The Table Settings dialog box appears (see fig. 15.13).

4. In the Column Widths section, choose the Column **N**umber to be altered by cycling through the list with the arrow buttons, or by entering the column number in the box. Select column 2.

5. Choose whether the column is to be **F**ixed or **P**roportional. Selecting **F**ixed changes the measurement options below the radio buttons and enables you to enter a measurement and to specify the units of measurement.

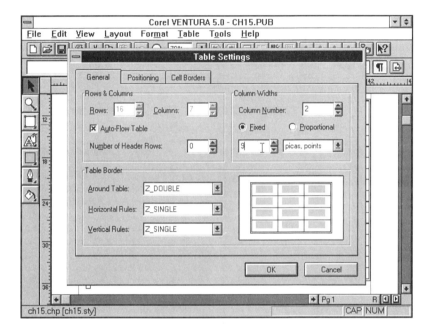

Figure 15.13

Specifying column widths.

For this example, select **F**ixed and change the units of measure to "picas, points." Entering **12** in the width box changes the column width to 12 picas. The remaining columns designated as **P**roportional share equally the remaining total table width as their column width.

Figure 15.14 shows all table columns proportionately spaced across the width of the table. After specifying a 12 pica width for column 2, all other columns share equally the remaining table width, as shown in figure 15.15.

If you choose **P**roportional, only one box appears below the radio buttons. Entering a number in this box assigns a proportionate amount of space to this column. For example, if you enter a 2, this column would be given twice as much width as the remaining columns; a 3 would make the column three times as wide as the remaining proportional columns that have a setting of 1.

After all column settings have been made, click on OK. The dialog box closes and the column widths change.

III

Advanced VENTURA Options and Techniques

Figure 15.14
Columns are equally spaced before column widths are changed.

GAME¶	OPPONENT¶	HOME/AWAY¶	DATE¶	SCORE¶		WON/LOST¶
¶	¶	¶	¶	US¶	THEM¶	¶
1¶	Franklin Central¶	Away¶	8-26-94¶	0¶	23¶	Lost¶
2¶	Chatard¶	Away¶	9-2-94¶	30¶	14¶	Won¶
3¶	Manual¶	Home¶	9-9-94¶	48¶	6¶	Won¶
4¶	Columbus North¶	Home¶	9-16-94¶	24¶	6¶	Won¶
5¶	Washington¶	Away¶	9-23-94¶	21¶	6¶	Won¶
6¶	Northwest¶	Away¶	9-30-94¶	41¶	14¶	Won¶
7¶	Scecina¶	Home¶	10-7-94¶	7¶	28¶	Lost¶
8¶	Broad Ripple¶	Home¶	10-14-94¶	51¶	7¶	Won¶
9¶	Brebuff¶	Home¶	10-21-94¶	57¶	7¶	Won¶
10¶	Chatard¶	Away¶	10-28-94¶	21¶	19¶	Won¶
11¶	Zionsville¶	Away¶	11-4-94¶	28¶	21¶	Won¶
12¶	Danville¶	Home¶	11-11-94¶	23¶	21¶	Won¶
13¶	Jasper¶	Away¶	11-19-94¶	10¶	6¶	Won¶
14¶	Tipton¶	Dome¶	11-25-94¶	35¶	14¶	Won¶

Figure 15.15
After the second column is expanded, the rest of the columns divide the remaining width of the table equally.

GAME¶	OPPONENT¶	HOME/AWAY¶	DATE¶	SCORE¶		WON/LOST¶
¶	¶	¶	¶	US¶	THEM¶	¶
1¶	Franklin Central¶	Away¶	8-26-94¶	0¶	23¶	Lost¶
2¶	Chatard¶	Away¶	9-2-94¶	30¶	14¶	Won¶
3¶	Manual¶	Home¶	9-9-94¶	48¶	6¶	Won¶
4¶	Columbus North¶	Home¶	9-16-94¶	24¶	6¶	Won¶
5¶	Washington¶	Away¶	9-23-94¶	21¶	6¶	Won¶
6¶	Northwest¶	Away¶	9-30-94¶	41¶	14¶	Won¶
7¶	Scecina¶	Home¶	10-7-94¶	7¶	28¶	Lost¶
8¶	Broad Ripple¶	Home¶	10-14-94¶	51¶	7¶	Won¶
9¶	Brebuff¶	Home¶	10-21-94¶	57¶	7¶	Won¶
10¶	Chatard¶	Away¶	10-28-94¶	21¶	19¶	Won¶
11¶	Zionsville¶	Away¶	11-4-94¶	28¶	21¶	Won¶
12¶	Danville¶	Home¶	11-11-94¶	23¶	21¶	Won¶
13¶	Jasper¶	Away¶	11-19-94¶	10¶	6¶	Won¶
14¶	Tipton¶	Dome¶	11-25-94¶	35¶	14¶	Won¶

Moving, Copying, and Pasting Tables

VENTURA enables you to copy or move a table easily—whether it has text before and after it, or whether it is all by itself. Before you can make these changes to a table, however, you must select it.

Selecting a Table

The following steps demonstrate how to select a table in your document:

1. Click-and-hold the left mouse button in the top left cell of the table and drag the cursor to the bottom right cell of the table.

2. Release the mouse button.

As an alternative to steps 1 and 2, you can click in any cell of the table and then choose **S**elect from the **T**able menu.

The entire table is highlighted.

Copying or Moving a Table

To copy or move a table, use the following steps:

1. Select the entire table.

2. Choose Cu**t** from the **E**dit menu (or press Ctrl+X), or choose **C**opy from the **E**dit menu (Ctrl+C).

   A dialog box appears, asking you to confirm that you want to cut or copy the entire table to the Clipboard.

3. Choose Entire Table.

4. Choose the Text tool and click in the new location of the table.

5. Choose **P**aste from the **E**dit menu (Ctrl+V).

The entire table is pasted from the Clipboard to its new location.

Deleting a Table

To totally remove a table from the document, follow these steps:

1. Select the entire table as described above.

2. Press the delete key on the keyboard or choose De**l**ete from the **E**dit menu.

If there is text above or below the table that you are copying or moving, and you want to move the text with the table, highlighting with the Text tool **will** include the table. Simply click-and-drag the Text tool over the text and table and proceed as normal. Choose Cu**t** from the **E**dit menu (or press Ctrl+X) or choose **C**opy from the **E**dit menu (Ctrl+C). Position the text cursor in the new location, then choose **P**aste from the **E**dit menu (Ctrl+V).

Copying, Deleting, and Moving Rows and Columns

At times, the information that appears in your table might not be in the order you want. You can manipulate rows and columns to present the information in the most effective way.

Manipulating Rows and Columns

The following exercise explains how to copy, move, and delete rows or columns:

1. Select the Pick tool to highlight the rows or columns to be manipulated. You can choose only rows or columns.

2. Highlight the row(s) or column(s) to be copied, moved, or deleted.

   Remember that you can click, hold, and drag to highlight, or you can select the first and last cell of the desired row or column if you press Shift while making your selections.

3 To delete the selection, choose De**l**ete from the **E**dit menu or press Del.

   To copy the selection, choose **C**opy from the **E**dit menu or press Ctrl+C.

   To place the selection in the Clipboard, choose Cu**t** from the **E**dit menu or press Ctrl+X.

After each operation, a dialog box appears asking you to confirm whether you want to delete, copy, or cut row(s) or column(s). Choose the appropriate selection (see fig. 15.16).

Figure 15.16
Confirming your
operation.

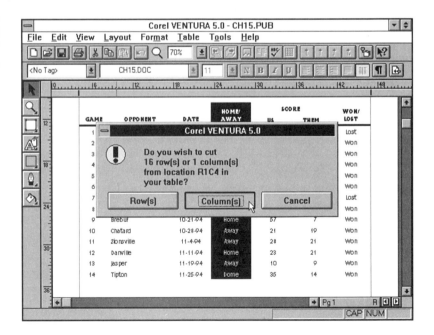

Individual cells cannot be cut, copied, pasted, or deleted by themselves. Therefore, it is not necessary to highlight an entire row or column to perform one of the operations above. Highlighting one cell in the row or column and then selecting the operation (cut, copy, paste, or delete) opens a dialog box to confirm the operation. In that dialog box, you are asked to confirm the operation for a row or column (you can cancel the operation, as well). When a row is selected, the selected cell's row is affected. If column is selected, the cell's entire column is affected. If multiple cells are selected, the operation is completed on all rows or columns that intersect the selected cells.

If your intent is to paste a cut or copied column or row into another table location, use the following steps:

Pasting Rows

These steps show how to paste a row into the table:

1. Highlight a cell in the row below the new location of the pasted row(s).

2. Choose **P**aste from the **E**dit menu (or press Ctrl+V).

3. Confirm that the cut or copied row(s) is to be pasted above the highlighted cells row.

Pasting Columns

These steps show how to paste a column into the table:

1. Highlight a cell in the column to the right of the new column location.

2. Choose **P**aste from the **E**dit menu (or press Ctrl+V).

3. Confirm that the cut or copied column(s) is to be pasted in front of the highlighted cells column (see fig. 15.17).

Inserting Blank Rows and Columns

As indicated earlier, tables are not limited to the initial settings made at the time the table is created. You can add rows and columns at any time during the editing process.

Figure 15.17
Confirming your
pasting operation.

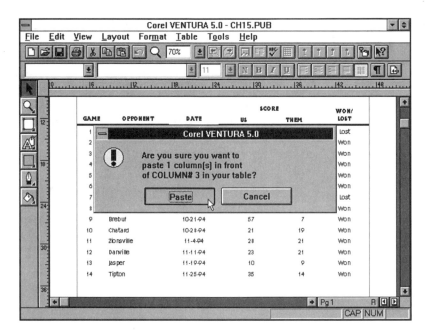

Inserting Blank Columns

The process of inserting a blank column is very similar to the process for pasting a cut or copied column. Use the following steps:

1. Select the Pick tool.

2. Click in a cell in the column that will follow the newly inserted blank column.

3. To insert the new column or columns, choose Insert Column from the Table menu. Or, you can click the right mouse button and choose Insert Column from the pop-up menu (see fig. 15.18).

   The Insert Column(s) dialog box appears (see fig. 15.19).

4. Enter the number of columns to be inserted in the dialog box and click on OK.

The designated number of columns will be inserted in front of the highlighted column. These new columns will default to a proportional width.

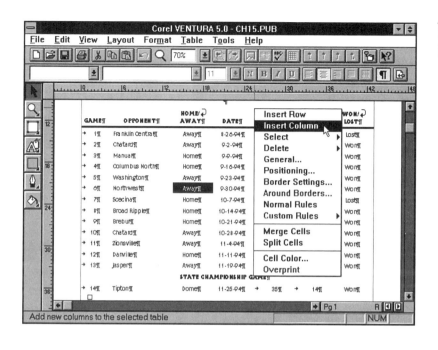

Figure 15.18
Inserting a column.

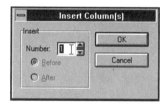

Figure 15.19
The Insert
Column(s) dialog
box.

Inserting Blank Rows

You can insert blank rows anywhere in the table either above or below the currently selected row. The following steps show how to insert blank rows into a table.

1. Select the Pick tool.

2. Click inside one cell of the row that will directly follow or precede the inserted row.

3. Choose Insert **R**ow from the **T**able menu or click the right mouse button and choose Insert Row from the pop-up menu.

   The Insert Row(s) dialog box appears (see fig. 15.20).

4. Enter the number of rows you want to insert. Choose whether to insert these rows above or below the currently selected row by selecting the **B**efore or **A**fter option.

5. Click on OK.

Figure 15.20
The Insert Row(s)
dialog box.

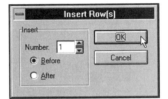

The designated number of rows is inserted in the selected location.

Merging and Splitting Cells

After all or most of the text is in your table, you can begin to customize the appearance of the table. One way to make a table more readable and attractive is by merging cells to create headings across columns, instead of including repetitive headings in each cell.

Merging Cells

When cells are merged, all text except the contents of the top, far left cell is hidden while editing. When you save the publication, however, hidden text is deleted.

Another thing to keep in mind is that merged cells are split when pasting and inserting rows or columns in the table. This happens only when they intersect with the merged cells. If splitting occurs, cells easily can be merged again.

Use the following steps to merge cells:

1. Select the Pick tool.

2. Highlight the cells to be merged by clicking-and-dragging the cursor or by pressing Shift while selecting the first and last cell to be merged. Figure 15.21 shows two cells being selected.

3. Choose **M**erge Cells from the **T**able menu. Or, click the right mouse button and choose Merge Cells from the pop-up menu (see fig. 15.22).

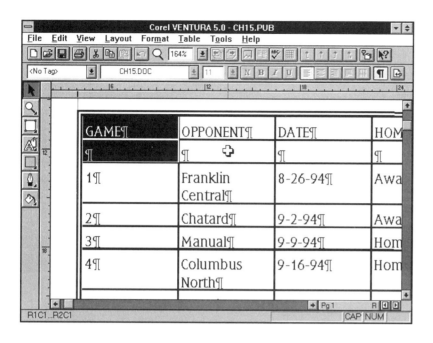

Figure 15.21
Selecting cells.

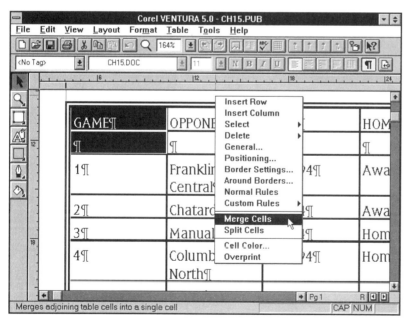

Figure 15.22
Choosing Merge Cells from the pop-up menu.

III

Advanced VENTURA Options and Techniques

You now see one cell with one paragraph spanning the width or height of the highlighted cells. Figure 15.18 shows the cells selected in figure 15.23 after they have been merged.

Figure 15.23
Merging cells.

Figure 15.23
Merging cells.

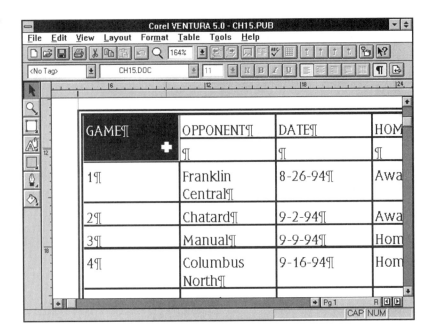

In the table shown in figure 15.24, notice that there are two header rows. Cells in rows 1 and 2 in columns 1, 2, 3, 4, and 7 have been merged. The paragraph tags for column headers are bottom-aligned.

Figure 15.24
A table with two header rows.

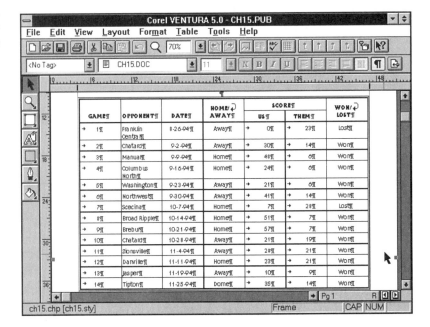

Looking at the headers in columns 5 and 6, notice that the two cells in the top row have been merged to span over the two header cells below. Rather than repeat "Score" over "Us" and "Them," the two cells were merged. In order for "Score" to appear above the two columns, two separate header rows were needed.

Similarly, in the example shown in figure 15.25, all cells in the highlighted row were merged so that the table subhead spans the entire width of the table.

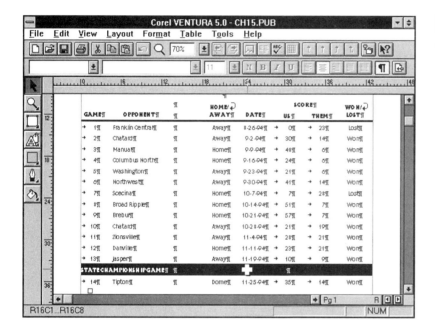

Figure 15.25

Merging cells.

Splitting Cells

You can split cells just as easily as you can merge cells. You can split them individually or as a group if merged cells are in succession.

Use the following steps to split cells:

1. Select the Pick tool and highlight the cells to be split.

2. Choose Split Cells from the Table menu or click the right mouse button and choose Split Cells from the pop-up menu.

Applying and Removing Borders

After entering and formatting the text and merging cells, you might want to apply a custom look to the table. If you used the Quick Format feature on the table, some of the work already might be done. You might need to make some other alterations to the table, however. You can apply borders to the table to clarify key columns and rows or to facilitate easier interpretation of the table information.

Recall that initially, VENTURA's default border settings were to place a double rule line around the table and single rule lines between rows and columns. To change these settings, you first must change the border settings in the General Table Settings dialog box.

Hiding Table Borders

Use the following exercise to hide table borders:

1. Select the Pick tool and click on one cell in the table.

2. Click the right mouse button and choose General from the pop-up menu.

   The General Table Settings dialog box appears.

3. Change all Table Border settings to Z_HIDDEN (see fig. 15.26). Even though no borders will be visible on the table, all columns and rows still are intact. (Remember, the border tag is called Hidden!)

4. Click on OK.

Adding Borders around Cells

Borders are not limited to entire columns or rows. Selected cells also accept borders. Follow the steps in the subsequent exercise to add borders to a group of cells.

1. Highlight all cells to be included within the border.

   You can apply borders to entire rows, columns, or any group of cells.

2. Click the right mouse button and choose Around Borders from the pop-up menu.

   The Cell Borders dialog box appears.

3. Select one of the predefined Border **T**ags available in the list or create a new border tag by clicking on the plus button and adding a border.

4. Click on OK.

The border is applied to the highlighted cells.

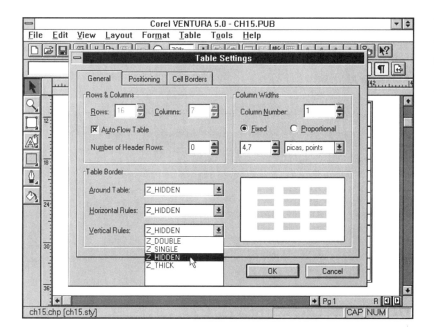

Figure 15.26
The table now should have no rule lines visible on the page.

Applying Borders to Individual Cells

It also is possible to apply ruled borders to the top, bottom, or on either side of a group of cells. Again, this option is not limited to entire rows or columns. You can apply a border to any group of highlighted cells. You can apply a rule line under a header row, for example, or you can place a rule line running along the right or left side of a column to divide it from the rest of the columns.

Use the following steps to apply a border to an individual cell:

1. Highlight the group of cells that is to receive the border by using the Pick tool.

2. Move the cursor over the border that is to receive the rule line setting. The cursor should change so that it looks like the letter H on its side (see fig. 15.27).

412 **Chapter 15:** *Working with Tables*

3. Click the left mouse button on the cell's border to select it. (You can click again on the same border to deselect it.)

4. Select a border tag from the tag list in the button bar. Alternatively, click the right mouse button to access the table pop-up menu and choose "Custom Rules." Select the rule from a list of VENTURA's predefined border settings.

Figure 15.27
Choosing the border to receive the rule line setting.

Cursor

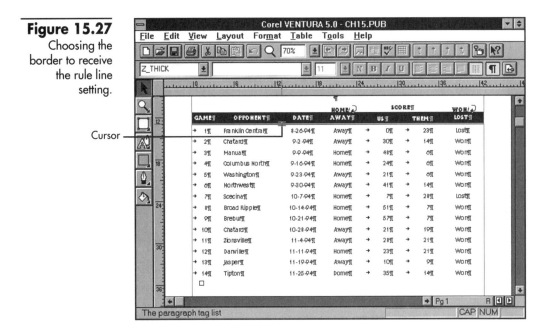

After choosing the border tag, it is applied to your selection.

Selecting an entire row with merged cells might be difficult using the click, hold, and drag method. Back in figure 15.22, a border was to be applied below the header rows. Because the column cells in rows 1 and 2 were merged in all columns except the Score column, the merged cells in row 2 could not be highlighted with the mouse. The only way to select this entire row is to click on a cell in the row that has not been merged. After the cell is highlighted, click the right mouse button to access the pop-up menu. Choose Select from the list to get the flyout choices. Select Row from the list. Your row will be highlighted and the border is now selectable to assign a border tag.

A second option to accomplish the same task would be to highlight the row underneath this row and select the top border to assign the border tag.

Applying Shading to Cells

You can apply shading or color to any cell or group of cells in the table to add emphasis or attractiveness. Cell color and shading is applied in the same manner as applying borders.

Adding Shading to Cells

Use the following steps to add shading to a group of cells:

1. Select the Pick tool.

2. Highlight the cells to be shaded.

3. Choose Cell C**o**lor from the **T**able menu. Alternatively, click the right mouse button and choose Cell Color.

   The Cell Color dialog box appears (see fig. 15.28).

4. In this dialog box, VENTURA provides many ways for you to select the right color for filling the cells.

5. Select the cell color.

6. Click on OK.

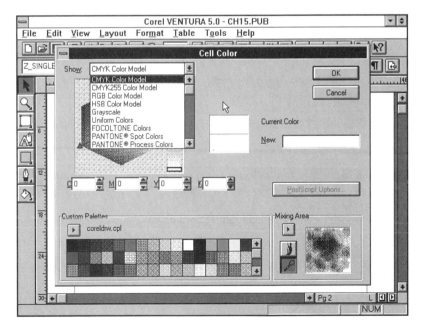

Figure 15.28
The Cell Color dialog box.

III

Advanced VENTURA Options and Techniques

The cell selection is filled with the chosen color.

Remember that because the cells are made up of individual paragraphs, the Freeform Text tool is available to change the color of any of the text. This feature is useful to keep in mind when, for example, you want a reverse type for a darkly shaded cell.

Importing Data into Tables

Often, information needed for a table in VENTURA is located in a database or spreadsheet elsewhere on the computer. Because most spreadsheet programs enable you to save data in a database format, importing information into VENTURA through CorelQUERY can be a simple process. Once imported, tables can be modified like any other table created within VENTURA.

CorelQUERY will seem easy to those who are familiar with database retrieval (SQL) techniques. QUERY is a front-end program that helps build search conditions to extract desired information from one or many spreadsheets or databases of information. QUERY accumulates the data, sorts it, and combines it into one table.

Because QUERY uses Microsoft's Open Database Connectivity (ODBC) facility, this must be installed before it can work.

Figure 15.29 shows a screen capture of a database in Lotus Approach. This database of computer supplies has 2,241 records and consists of five fields, three shown with two off-screen. For the purposes of this example, all other records were filtered out except the items coded as NPIJ. This code was created solely to group like items and enable those items to be exported together.

Creating a Table from an Existing Database

You can create a table with existing information using the following steps:

1. Select the Pick tool and click in front of an empty paragraph symbol on the page where the table is to be placed.

2. Choose **C**reate from Database from the **T**able menu, then choose **N**ew (see fig. 15.30).

   CorelQUERY is launched, and an ODBC (Open Database Connectivity) Data Source is requested.

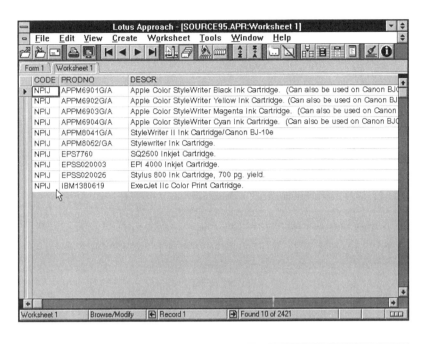

Figure 15.29

A database in Lotus Approach.

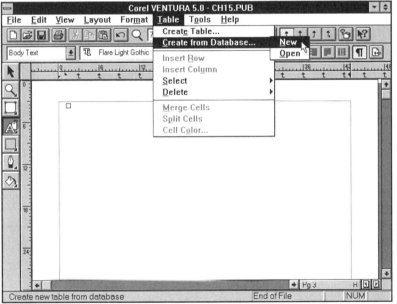

Figure 15.30

Choosing Create from Database from the Table menu.

III

Advanced VENTURA Options and Techniques

3. If a source for your database is listed, select its icon and click on Configure.

The ODBC Setup dialog box appears (see fig. 15.31).

Figure 15.31
The ODBC Setup
dialog box.

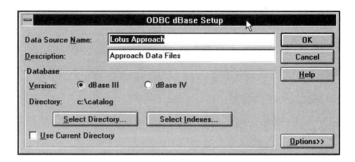

4. Enter the Data Source **N**ame and a **D**escription. The Data Source **N**ame is the program from which the information is coming. The **D**escription can define the file contents. Because this sample is from Lotus Approach, enter it in the Data Source **N**ame box. For the description, enter **Approach Data Files**.

   Because the Approach file is dBASE III compatible, check that radio button.

   Examine the Directory: setting. If this is not where your data is stored, click on **S**elect Directory and locate the data file.

   If an index has been created for this data file, locate it by choosing the Select **I**ndexes.

5. Click on **S**elect Directory and locate the database file.

6. If there are any indexes applicable to this database file, click on Select **I**ndexes and locate the drive and directory where they are located.

7. Click on OK.

   After the database is located, the Query Builder dialog box with four tab sheets appears (see fig. 15.32).

8. In the first tab, Select, double-click on the database file to be used.

   A list of all fields appears in the box to the right.

9. Double-click on each field to be imported into the table.

You can fill in the **H**eading box, but this text is not imported into the table. The text is used only as column headers in CorelQUERY after the data is extracted.

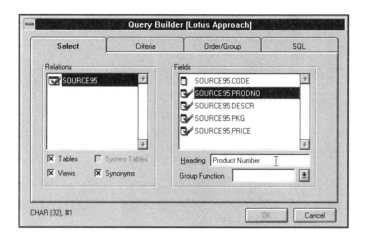

Figure 15.32
The Query Builder dialog box.

10. Select the Criteria tab (see fig. 15.33). This menu enables you to specify search specifications. Recall that this example was only to extract those items with the code of NPIJ.

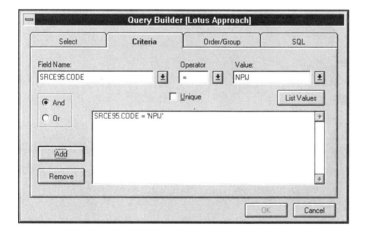

Figure 15.33
Making selections in the Criteria tab of the Query Builder dialog box.

11. Selecting the Field Name CODE, the Operator =, and a Value of NPIJ tells the query builder to find all records where NPIJ is listed in the CODE field.

Remember that this section is only an overview of using CorelQUERY to extract data from a database. You can specify other criteria to include or exclude other field data. Another criteria also can be built to exclude those items over a certain price. For now, a simple search illustrates how to import database information into a table.

12. After each criteria is built, click on the Add button to include it in the list. (The And and Or choices are for adding additional criteria and linking them together.)

13. To provide some order to the imported data, the third tab, Order/Group, enables you to sort on field contents or values (see fig. 15.34). In this example, the product numbers will be in **A**scending alphanumeric order.

Figure 15.34

Making selections in the Order/ Group tab of the Query Builder dialog box.

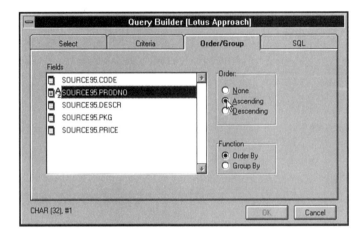

14. Select the SQL tab (see fig. 15.35). Here, the information entered into the three previous dialog boxes is combined to create a search of the database and extract all information requested.

Figure 15.35

Making selections in the SQL tab of the Query Builder dialog box.

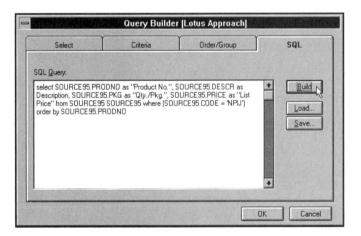

15. Click on **B**uild to build an SQL query. You have the option of saving the query to avoid having to rebuild it again. If a query already has been saved, you can load it at the outset by selecting this tab first. Changes can be made, if necessary, and the query built again.

16. Click on OK.

    After searching the database to extract the information requested, a table of the search results appears in CorelQUERY.

17. After the data is in CorelQUERY, select the columns or rows that you want to include in the VENTURA table. In this case, by clicking on the *X* in the upper left corner of the worksheet, all rows and columns are selected for inclusion (see fig. 15.36).

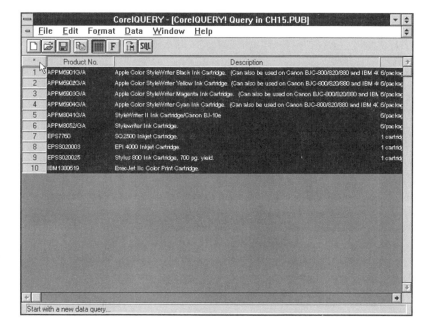

Figure 15.36
Selecting rows and columns for inclusion.

18. Select the **F**ile menu. Choose **Exit** and Return to *publication name,* which is the name of the active VENTURA publication that is to receive the found data.

    A confirmation box asks whether you want to save changes made in CorelQUERY to the publication (see fig. 15.37).

Advanced VENTURA Options and Techniques

Figure 15.37
The CorelQUERY
confirmation box,
asking whether
you want to save
your changes.

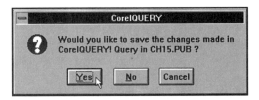

19. Click on **Y**es to transfer the highlighted rows and columns to the table location you originally specified.

The results appear somewhat like the table shown in figure 15.38, depending on your data. After the data is imported, you can format the table as described earlier in this chapter using borders, shading, and cell merging.

Figure 15.38
A table created
from an existing
database.

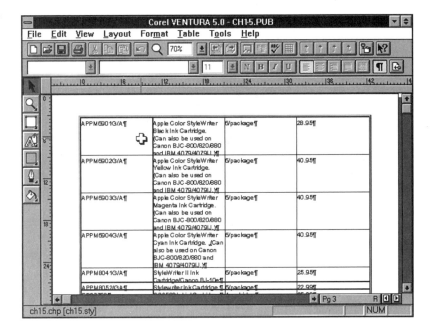

Chapter Snapshot

After you have completed all your individual files that will make up your complete document, you are ready to assemble your publication. Learning to use the Publication Manager is essential in managing your chapters. In this chapter, you learn to do the following:

Publication Manager enables you to safely move, copy, or delete chapter and publication files without fear of damage to VENTURA's pointer system.

Assembling Publications

Earlier chapters in this book described "structure" of a publication. CorelVENTURA publication files consist of one or more chapters, which are made up of text, a style sheet, and graphics. VENTURA's strength as a desktop publishing package is its pointer system which describes the location of any file that is included in the publication. VENTURA does not absorb these component files, so it does not create a monstrous publication file.

This chapter shows you how to manage VENTURA's publication and chapter files. Copying, moving, or deleting these files through Windows' File Manager or from the DOS prompt causes disastrous results. *Publication Manager*, a customized utility included in VENTURA, enables you to safely move, copy, or delete chapter and publication files without fearing damage to VENTURA's pointer system.

Chapter and publication files are files that instruct VENTURA which chapter, style sheet, text, and graphic files to load for that particular publication or chapter. You can open these in a word processor and see firsthand VENTURA's file management (see fig. 16.1). Among the code, you can see the familiar names of the very files that make up that chapter or publication. In the figure, the top line indicates the style sheet used. Each text and graphic file listed below it includes a drive and subdirectory which enables VENTURA to locate the needed file and load it.

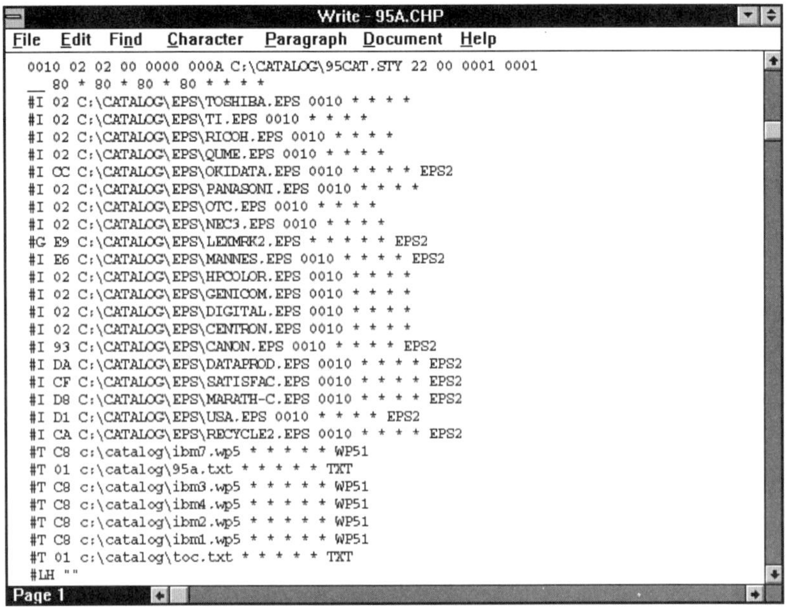

Figure 16.1
A CorelVENTURA
CHP file points to
component files.

```
                              Write - 95A.CHP
 File   Edit   Find   Character   Paragraph   Document   Help

  0010 02 02 00 0000 000A C:\CATALOG\95CAT.STY 22 00 0001 0001
 __  80 * 80 * 80 * 80 * * * *
 #I 02 C:\CATALOG\EPS\TOSHIBA.EPS 0010 * * * *
 #I 02 C:\CATALOG\EPS\TI.EPS 0010 * * * *
 #I 02 C:\CATALOG\EPS\RICOH.EPS 0010 * * * *
 #I 02 C:\CATALOG\EPS\QUME.EPS 0010 * * * *
 #I CC C:\CATALOG\EPS\OKIDATA.EPS 0010 * * * * EPS2
 #I 02 C:\CATALOG\EPS\PANASONI.EPS 0010 * * * *
 #I 02 C:\CATALOG\EPS\OTC.EPS 0010 * * * *
 #I 02 C:\CATALOG\EPS\NEC3.EPS 0010 * * * *
 #G E9 C:\CATALOG\EPS\LEXMRK2.EPS * * * * * EPS2
 #I E6 C:\CATALOG\EPS\MANNES.EPS 0010 * * * * EPS2
 #I 02 C:\CATALOG\EPS\HPCOLOR.EPS 0010 * * * *
 #I 02 C:\CATALOG\EPS\GENICOM.EPS 0010 * * * *
 #I 02 C:\CATALOG\EPS\DIGITAL.EPS 0010 * * * *
 #I 02 C:\CATALOG\EPS\CENTRON.EPS 0010 * * * *
 #I 93 C:\CATALOG\EPS\CANON.EPS 0010 * * * * EPS2
 #I DA C:\CATALOG\EPS\DATAPROD.EPS 0010 * * * * EPS2
 #I CF C:\CATALOG\EPS\SATISFAC.EPS 0010 * * * * EPS2
 #I D8 C:\CATALOG\EPS\MARATH-C.EPS 0010 * * * * EPS2
 #I D1 C:\CATALOG\EPS\USA.EPS 0010 * * * * EPS2
 #I CA C:\CATALOG\EPS\RECYCLE2.EPS 0010 * * * * EPS2
 #T C8 c:\catalog\ibm7.wp5 * * * * * WP51
 #T 01 c:\catalog\95a.txt * * * * * TXT
 #T C8 c:\catalog\ibm3.wp5 * * * * * WP51
 #T C8 c:\catalog\ibm4.wp5 * * * * * WP51
 #T C8 c:\catalog\ibm2.wp5 * * * * * WP51
 #T C8 c:\catalog\ibm1.wp5 * * * * * WP51
 #T 01 c:\catalog\toc.txt * * * * * TXT
 #LH ""
 Page 1
```

Do not attempt to edit this file unless you are experienced with CorelVENTURA code. Deleting or changing even one space or letter could cause the chapter or publication to become "trashed" and unusable again.

VENTURA's file pointer system can also cause headaches when copying, moving, or deleting publications and chapters. Files imported into VENTURA can reside in other drives or subdirectories. In addition, many supplementary files are created by VENTURA when a new publication is created. Keeping track of these files and their locations can be impossible and frustrating.

Understanding the Publication Manager

Publication Manager is the best tool for managing CorelVENTURA publications. Not only will this utility copy, move, and delete publication files, it also gives you more information concerning publications or chapters, including:

✔ Displaying all chapters or publications in a defined search

New Riders Publishing
INSIDE
SERIES

✔ Full copying of all files related to a publication or chapter, even to multiple floppy disks

✔ Deleting chapter and publication files, including those created by VENTURA

✔ Moving publications or chapters to a different destination, including to multiple floppy disks

✔ Listing all files associated with a chapter or publication, including the file size, date, and time

✔ Giving total file space necessary to copy or move an entire chapter or publication, including all component files

✔ Helping find files you might have on your system without using Windows File Manager

✔ Adding chapters to or removing chapters from a publication

✔ Reordering chapters in a publication

These functions can be carried out easily by selecting the **F**ile menu and choosing Pu**b**lication Manager.

When you first select Publication Manager, VENTURA scans the directories specified in the last directory scan. If no drives or directories have been specified, the current open publication will be listed.

When you select **F**ile, Pu**b**lication Manager, two menus appear: File Operations and Scan Directories. File Operations is used to move, copy, and delete chapters and publications, along with other unique tasks. You have to point the way to other publications unless the only chapter or publication you want to manipulate is the one that is currently open.

The Scan Directories menu can filter out unnecessary chapters or publications and thereby speed up the scanning operation. It can also be used to find publications or chapters that have been misplaced!

Scanning Directories

Scanning directories is a simple operation. On the left side of the Scan Directories tab is a list of the **A**vailable drives on your system. On the right side is where you build the list of which drives or specific subdirectories VENTURA will scan for any publication and chapter files (see fig. 16.2).

Figure 16.2
Subdirectories are
revealed by
double-clicking on
the Drive icon.

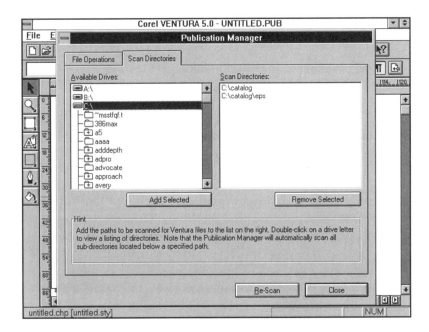

To access a list of the subdirectories for a certain drive, double-click with the left mouse button on the desired drive icon. VENTURA will search and list all subdirectories underneath the drive icon. Subdirectory icons (which look like a file folder) that have a + inside indicate that there are more subdirectories underneath. To reveal these, double-click on the file folder icon.

After all the desired directories and subdirectories are revealed, click once with the left mouse button to highlight a directory you want to scan. Select the A**d**d Selected button, and the drive or subdirectory will be added to the Scan Directories list on the right. You can only add one drive or subdirectory at a time. The A**d**d Selected button must be chosen for each.

Adding a drive to the Scan Directories list adds all subdirectories to the scan.

If a drive or subdirectory in the Scan Directories list needs to be removed, highlight that entry in the list and choose R**e**move Selected. If there are multiple selections to be made, use the Shift key to highlight the first and last choices to select all consecutive drives or subdirectories. When nonconsecutive selections need to be made, hold the Control key and click once on each drive or subdirectory to highlight individual entries. After these selections are made, choose R**e**move Selected to withdraw these from the listing.

The Control and Shift key techniques work for removing items from the Scan Directories list, but do not work when adding items to the scan list from **A**vailable Drives.

When the scan list is finished, select **R**e-Scan; VENTURA creates a new list of publications and chapters to be added to the File Operations tab menu.

If VENTURA gives an error or crashes while scanning the specified drives or directories, try removing several subdirectories and re-scan. It is possible that a corrupt chapter or publication has been encountered during the scan. Should this occur, quit VENTURA and restart it.

File Operations

The File Operations tab menu has multiple purposes for handling chapters, publications, and files. Switching between the Publication and File radio buttons reveals different functions. Generally, the File radio button is selected to copy, move, or delete chapters, publications, or files. The Publication radio button enables you to add or delete chapters to publications, as well as reveal information about the publication, chapter, or individual file. The final selection, **S**ave Info, sends the chapter- or publication-specific information that appears in the File **I**nformation: box to an ASCII text file for documenting the details of a chapter or publication.

Retrieving Detailed File Information

In the list of Publications, double-clicking on the publications name reveals all its chapters. Double-clicking on the chapter name lists all Component Files within that chapter. Clicking once on the file name gives the size, date, time, and attributes of that file. Every time you double-click on a publication, chapter, or file, the File Information box reveals detailed information about that selection.

To return to the previous list, double-click on the "..[*chapter name* or *publication name*]" at the top of the list or select Publication or Chapter from List Files of **T**ype.

Saving Information to File

At any time, the data in the File **I**nformation box can be saved to an ASCII text file. When **S**ave Info is selected, a dialog box prompts for the drive, directory, and file name of an ASCII file to save the information. The default extension given to the file is .TXT. Once saved, the file can be opened in any ASCII text editor, such as NotePad or Windows Write, and can be used to track a publication, insert notes about files, or file away for future reference.

Managing Publications

With the List Files of **T**ype set to Publication, the found publications are listed in the top box. When one of the publications is selected (see fig. 16.3), the File **I**nformation box lists detailed information pertaining to that publication: its location, whether a table of contents or index has been generated, the last date and time stamp on the publication file, and a list of all chapter files included in the publication.

Figure 16.3
File Information gives details on the currently selected chapter or publication.

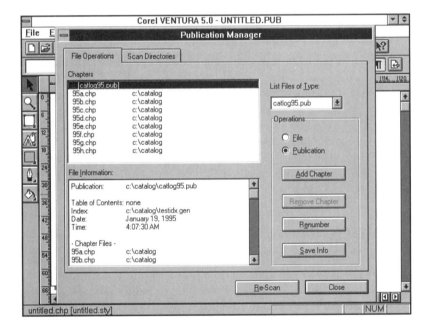

Adding a Chapter

Double-clicking on the publication file name in the Publication list filters out all other publications and lists the selected publication's chapters. Notice after double-clicking on the publication name that the box heading changes to Chapters and the List Files of **T**ype now includes the publication name.

Chapters may be added to this publication by choosing **A**dd Chapter in the Operations section. When **A**dd Chapter is selected, a chapter can be found using the Add Chapter dialog box (see fig. 16.4).

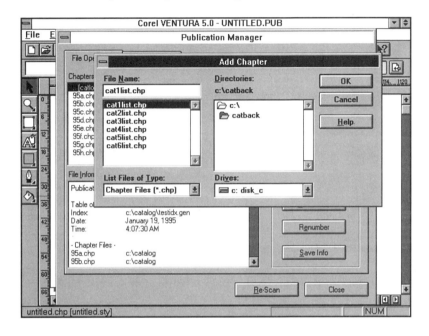

Figure 16.4
Adding a new chapter to the current publication.

Chapters may also be added if the publication name is highlighted in the list of all found publications. However, chapters cannot be removed unless the publication has been selected and its chapters listed.

Removing Chapters from a Publication

If a chapter is in the publication that is no longer needed, you can remove it in two-steps:

1. Choose the chapter name in the Chapters list

2. Select Re**m**ove Chapter from the Operations box (see fig. 16.5)

III

Advanced VENTURA Options and Techniques

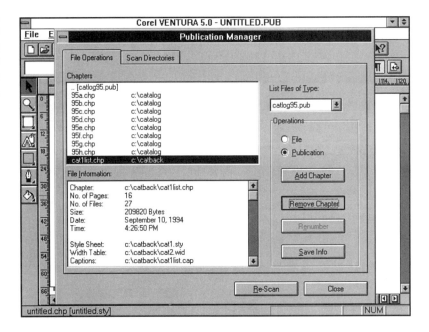

Removing a chapter does not delete it from your system. It only removes it from this publication.

Reordering Chapters in a Publication

When printing your publication, you are given the choice of printing the current chapter or entire publication. Chapters need to be in the proper order for the pages to print in order. The order listed in Publication Manager is the current chapter order.

If chapters need to be shuffled to change the order, simply select and drag, as follows:

1. Highlight the chapter name to move in the Chapter list.

2. Click and hold the left mouse button. The cursor changes to the moving icon with a pointer (see fig. 16.6).

3. Drag the chapter name to the desired location in the list using the pointer as a guide.

4. Release the mouse button. The chapter drops in place and all other chapters automatically flow below it.

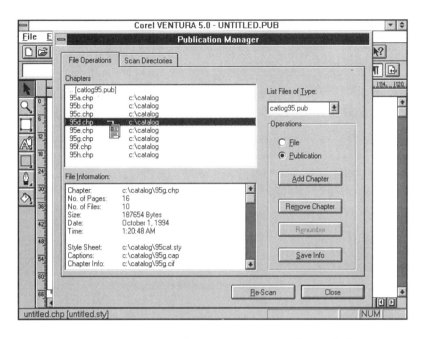

Figure 16.6

Make changes in the chapter order by using click and drag.

Renumbering Chapters and Publications

The auto-numbering system in VENTURA is one of the most extensive and sophisticated features of any desktop publishing program. This feature depends on accurate auto-numbering settings in each of the chapters as well as the order that chapters appear in the publication list. For further inforamtion on auto-numbering, see Chapter 14, "Advanced Options for Chapter Formatting."

If chapters are moved or deleted, the numbering sequence within and between chapters needs to be updated. Publication Manager allows renumbering multiple chapters and includes the numbering sequences within those chapters. By choosing the publication name in the file list and selecting Renumber, not only are chapter and page numbers updated, but any generated figure or table numbers are automatically updated. The following steps show how to do it:

1. Choose the publication name in the file list. (Notice that the Renumber selection is not available when working with chapter files.)

2. Select Renumber (see fig. 16.7).

3. All chapters within the publication will be scanned and their auto-numbering updated.

III

Advanced VENTURA Options and Techniques

Figure 16.7
Publication
Manager
renumbers all
chapters in a
publication.

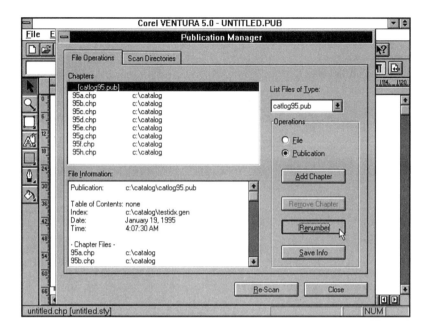

Finding Files

Have you ever needed a file that somehow strayed or was lost? VENTURA makes losing files a lot more difficult. Built within Publication Manager is a simple, versatile file search utility.

When Find Files in the Operations box is selected, a dialog box appears prompting for the file name (see fig. 16.8). The down arrow reveals a list of common file extensions created by or loadable into VENTURA.

File names are either chosen from the list or typed into the box. Wildcards are acceptable when searching for files. For example, entering **95*.chp** lists Component Files whose file names start with "95" and have a "CHP" extension. Multiple searches can be made by separating the file specifications with a semi-colon. For example, all EPS and CGM files can be found by entering ***.EPS;*.CGM** in the box.

Be sure to leave out spaces, especially after the semicolon. Anything following the space is ignored in the search.

VENTURA scans for these files only in the subdirectories specified in the **S**can Directories listing.

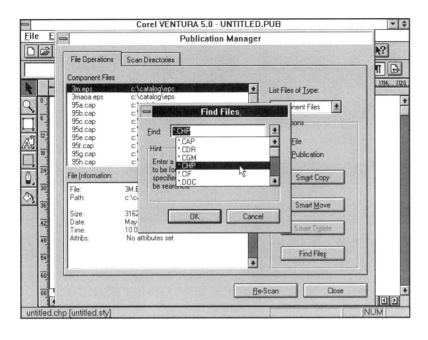

Figure 16.8
Choose the file type to find from those available in the drop-down list.

After clicking on OK, the results of the search appear in the Component Files box; file details are indicated in the File **I**nformation box. Notice that the Operations options have changed to Sm**a**rt Copy and Smart **M**ove.

Copying, Moving, and Deleting Files

VENTURA's "Smart" file operations for copying, moving, or deleting publications, chapters, or files are designed to protect the integrity of other chapters or publications that may share the same files. This section describes briefly each of these operations.

Smart Copy and Smart Move

Sm**a**rt Copy is a helpful VENTURA feature that allows chapters, publications, or individual files to be copied to a different drive or subdirectory in their entirety. All linked files will be found and copied to the destination directory specified. This ensures that any chapter or publication using the same file(s) can still load the file because these files stay in their original location.

Should an individual file be chosen to copy, VENTURA copies the file to the new destination and updates the file pointers in the chapter.

III

Advanced VENTURA Options and Techniques

Smart **M**ove moves chapters, publications, or individual files from their current location to a new destination. However, VENTURA checks all chapters and publications in the scanned search path(s) specified to see if a file is used in any other chapter or publication. If it is, selecting the option **C**opy if Shared copies instead of moves a file if it is found in any other documents in the active list. If this option is not checked, VENTURA moves the file and updates the pointers in the remaining publications in the scanned list so they can find the file in the new destination drive and directory.

If files are being moved to a floppy disk, VENTURA automatically copies a shared file. This ensures that all chapters and publications using the file are able to find it again should the disk not be available when opened.

Another option in the Smart Move dialog box, Reference if Read Only, copies files specified as Read Only when their chapter or publication is copied. For example, if a style sheet has been designated as Read Only so that no alterations may be made to it, the style sheet would have to be copied or the chapter or publication would be useless and not load.

If several users in a network environment altered a style sheet, their changes could cause problems with the final output of the document. The designer of the style sheet can apply a Read Only attribute to the file so that style sheet changes cannot be made.

Copying and Moving Individual Files

When copying or moving individual files, a Browse dialog box (see fig. 16.9) appears so that the new destination can be specified.

When a file is moved, all references to that file in other publications or chapters in the search list are updated to reflect the new drive and subdirectory. If the file is copied, there is no need for updating the pointers because the original is still in the pointer location.

Copying and Moving Chapters or Publications

After a publication or chapter has been tagged for copying or moving, select Sm**a**rt Copy or Smart **M**ove from the Operations box. A dialog box appears (see fig. 16.10). The Smart Copy dialog box is the same as Smart Move except for two items in the Smart Move dialog box, Copy if Shared and Reference if Read Only. These options were all discussed in the previous section, "Smart Copy and Smart Move."

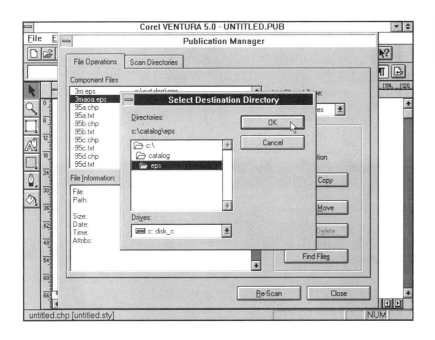

Figure 16.9

Selecting a new location for files.

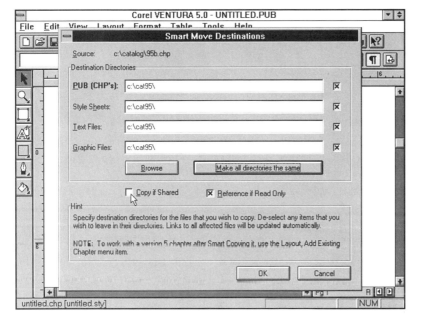

Figure 16.10

The Smart Move dialog box.

III

Advanced VENTURA Options and Techniques

File organization is a matter of preference among VENTURA users. Some store all the files for a publication in one subdirectory, keeping style sheets, graphics, text, and chapter and publication files in one subdirectory. Others organize similar files in separate subdirectories: text in one, graphics in another, style sheets in another, and chapter and publications in yet another. There is no one right way.

Publication Manager can satisfy either way of file organization when using Smart **M**ove or Sm**a**rt Copy. Destination Directories are separated in four categories: **P**UB (CHP's), Style S**h**eets, **T**ext Files, and **G**raphic Files. This system of selecting destinations for moved or copied files can satisfy many file organization preferences.

Each of these categories in the Smart Move or Smart Copy Destinations dialog box has a check box. When checked, the specified files are copied or moved to the drive and subdirectory typed in the box. If the check box is unchecked, the files remain in their current location, and the publication and chapter pointers are changed to reflect this.

Also, if no directory is entered for a specific category, the files remain in their current location. Publication and chapter files are updated to indicate their location.

Following are the categories and an explanation of the file types that fall under these headings.

- ✔ **PUB (CHP's).** All chapter and publication files, including the files created for the publication or chapter by VENTURA. This includes CAP, CIF, VGR, and FRM, if the chapter was from a previous version of VENTURA.

- ✔ **Style Sheets.** The associated style sheets will be moved or copied. If the chapter was created in an earlier version of VENTURA, this would include the width table.

- ✔ **Text Files.** Any files loaded as text. This does not include any text typed into a frame; that text is stored in the CAP file.

- ✔ **Graphic Files.** Any file loaded into the publication or chapter as a graphic.

By entering the drive and subdirectory into the four locations, the selected chapters or publications will be copied or moved into these new locations. If the check box to the right of the file type choices is not checked, those files will not be copied or moved. If a nonexistent directory is specified, VENTURA will create it.

To locate a specific drive and directory, select the **B**rowse button. The Select Destination Directory dialog box appears (refer to fig. 16.9). Select the desired drive and directory in this dialog box, and click on OK. The drive and directory chosen will be placed in the **P**UB (CHP's): box.

If the new destination is to be the same location for all files, type the drive and subdirectory into the first box and select the **M**ake all directories the same button. For example, if a publication is finished and you want to archive it on disk, enter the disk drive in the **P**UB (CHP's): box. Clicking on the **M**ake all directories the same will repeat the drive letter in all category boxes that was entered in the **P**UB (CHP's): box.

File Safeguards

VENTURA has several safeguards built into Publication Manager's file management functions.

✔ **Aborting.** Aborting a move or copy function could damage the file that was interrupted when Cancel was selected. VENTURA waits to abort the function until the file that is being processed is completely finished.

✔ **Space.** Storage space might be short on the destination drive. VENTURA figures the total size of all files in the publication or chapter, and compares this total with the amount of free space on the destination drive. If there is not enough free space to complete the operation successfully, VENTURA cancels the operation.

✔ **Multiple Floppy Disk copying.** Disk copying used to be extremely difficult in previous versions of VENTURA. Should a floppy drive be specified as the destination directory and the publication or chapter requires multiple disks to store, VENTURA prompts for additional floppies to be inserted until the entire document is stored. The first floppy disk will need to be reinserted at times to update the chapter file pointers.

Smart Delete

Copying or moving files used in publications is not as scary as deleting them. After all, you could copy them back to their original location. But deleting a file can be disastrous if it is used by another chapter or publication. Using Smart Delete gives VENTURA the opportunity to scan the file pointers of all the publications and chapters defined in your search list to see if it is needed elsewhere. If a file is used by another publication or chapter, VENTURA warns you and gives the choice to delete or not. To begin Smart Delete, do the following:

III

Advanced VENTURA Options and Techniques

1. Be sure that the List Files of **T**ype field is set to Publications or Chapters.

2. Choose the Chapter or Publication to be deleted from the list of chapters or publications.

3. Choose Smart D**e**lete. A dialog box asks to confirm that you want to continue with the requested deletion. VENTURA goes through the list of component files to prepare for deletion. Once assembled, another dialog box appears and offers the following choices (see fig. 16.11):

   a. Select Yes to confirm deletion of chapter files and style sheets individually.

   b. Select Yes to All for all publication, chapter, and component files to be deleted, including the style sheet.

   c. Select No to abort deletion of the current file shown in the dialog box and proceed to the next file.

   d. Select Cancel to abort the operation entirely.

Figure 16.11
Choices for
deletion of
VENTURA CHP
or PUB files.

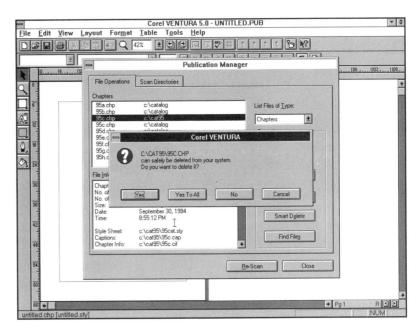

VENTURA only checks the chapters and publications in the defined search to see if the files to be deleted are used by any other chapter or publication. If files are used by any other chapter or publication that is not in the defined search, the files are deleted upon your OK. The file, however, will not be found by the chapter or publication that is not in the scan list the next time it is opened.

Individual files cannot be deleted through Publication Manager. The option to delete is only available when deleting entire publications or chapters.

Chapter Snapshot

Your publication won't be good to a reader unless the information is accessible. Providing a good table of contents and index is essential. In this chapter, you learn to do the following:

This chapter teaches how you set up and construct not only a table of contents, but also how you tag text that you want included in an index.

CHAPTER

Creating Tables of Contents and Indexes

T he table of contents (TOC) and the index are two important parts of a
document's structure, and they help the reader find information quickly.
Typically, the table of contents is placed at the front of a document and the
index at the back, although this is not always the case. Many Microsoft manuals
have the indexes for each section immediately following the section and not at
the back of the book.

You will also learn the importance of structuring your tables of contents and
indexes in a logical and helpful manner. By following the advice and examples
given in this chapter, you will be in the position to produce better tables of
contents and indexes that will do justice to the rest of your book.

Your readers will find it easier to locate the tables of contents and indexes if you place them where they expect to find them. For most countries, tables of contents are found in the front of the document, and indexes are found in the back.

Documents that are longer than a few pages usually have a table of contents and many will also have an index. VENTURA enables you to create both tables of contents and indexes for your documents quickly and easily. This chapter shows how you can use the consistent formatting applied to your document by tags to produce your table of contents. It also demonstrates how to use the Index Roll-up in VENTURA to produce an effective index.

Setting Up a Table of Contents

If you look near the front of this book, you will see that the Table of Contents provides a breakdown of each chapter and gives an indication of what is contained within each section of each chapter.

A good table of contents leads you by the hand through the structure of the document in a logical and well thought-out manner. It provides enough information for you to understand what is in each chapter of the book without swamping you with too much information. In short, a TOC should act as a signpost to set you on the right path to the information you want to read.

Identifying Tags To Be Used

If you examine this book's Table of Contents, you will see that each entry is a copy of one of the headings used throughout the book. In addition, the headings are hierarchical with different emphasis for each heading level. This hierarchical structure is common to all well-designed documents.

A TOC's hierarchical structure is easily reproduced using VENTURA's paragraph tags. By creating a paragraph tag for each heading level, the desired formatting can be applied to each heading level. The style sheet containing the paragraph tags can be used for each chapter in the publication to provide a consistent hierarchical appearance which, in turn, can be used for the table of contents. A complete discussion of how to implement this sort of hierarchy with tags is provided in Chapters 8 and 9.

At this point, all you need to understand is that the table of contents is produced directly from the hierarchical structure present in the documents you produce. It is easy to identify the tags that are needed for producing a table of contents. The structure of some documents is dictated by their purpose. Many of the examples that follow, for example, are taken from an Environmental Impact Assessment (EIA), following guidelines set by the Environmental Protection Agency. Figure 17.1 shows this document's Table of Contents.

TABLE OF CONTENTS

Figure 17.1
The Table of Contents from the Environmental Impact Assessment.

III

Advanced VENTURA Options and Techniques

The EIA has a hierarchical structure with four headings consisting of a chapter name and three subheading levels. VENTURA's autonumbering facility (see Chapter 14) was used to generate the section numbers automatically to give a 3.2, 3.2.1, and 3.2.1.1 numbering scheme. These automatically generated paragraph tags, as well as page numbers, are used in the table of contents.

The structure of the table of contents shown in figure 17.1 enables you to find sections of interest quickly and to see immediately if any of the recommended sections of an Environmental Impact Assessment have been omitted. This document's TOC also provides the page number of the section and the overall chapter title so that you can go directly to the desired section. In short, this EPA document meets all the requirements defined earlier for a table of contents.

Use the Publication Manager found under the **F**ile menu to examine each chapter in your publication to see which style sheets are used by the document (see fig. 17.2). Double-click on the publication to display a list of chapters, then double-click on each chapter to see the style sheet used. If you find that more than one style sheet is being used, check that the tags used in each style sheet have the same names for each type of heading you want included in your table of contents.

Figure 17.2
Examine each chapter using the Publication Manager to find the style sheets used in the document.

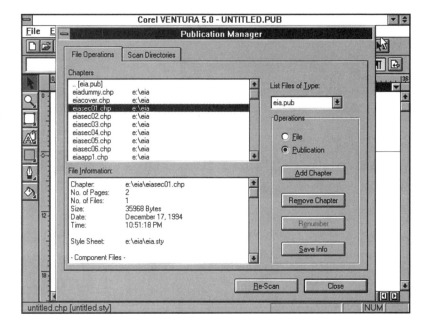

Searching through every chapter in a publication can be time consuming. A shortcut is to use the Smart Copy feature to copy all the files to a temporary directory and then to use File Manager to find STY files to see which style sheets are used in your publication.

When you know what style sheets are used and after you have checked the tags to ensure they are named consistently, it is easy to identify the tags to include in the table of contents. Simply load a chapter that contains the headings to be used as shown in figure 17.3, and examine the tags you set up for your headings. Make a note of the tags you want to include. If you're not sure which tags to include, read the tag chapters in Part II of this book to make sure you have selected the right tags.

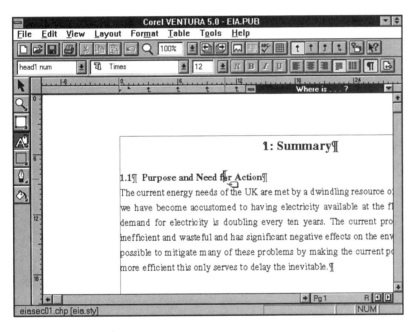

Figure 17.3

Open a chapter and examine the headings you want to include and make a note of the tag names.

It is useful to add reference information about the tags you are going to use for your table of contents to a dummy chapter at the start of the publication. This gives you one central place to look for information on tags. In addition, it can be used for other items you might need easy access to, such as variables and index entries. Using a dummy chapter in this way provides a wealth of easily accessible information. Add the chapter to the start of your publication using Publication Manager. Remember to exclude it from the numbering of your publication because it is only present for ease-of-reference and not as part of your final printed document.

Advanced VENTURA Options and Techniques

III

The dummy chapter for the following example has information about the following tags: Z_SEC2 for the 3.1 level numbers, and head1 num for the associated text "No Development Option"; Z_SEC3 for the 3.2.1 level numbers, and head2 num for the text "Tidal Power Units"; Z_SEC4 for the 3.2.1.1 level numbers, and head3 num for the text "Rotors."

Preparing the Table of Contents

Armed with a list of tags, you can begin the process of generating a table of contents. To start, you need to open the TOC & Index dialog box, set the number of levels required for the table of contents, then select what you want to include. To do this, follow these steps:

1. Open your publication and load the dummy chapter (see fig. 17.4).

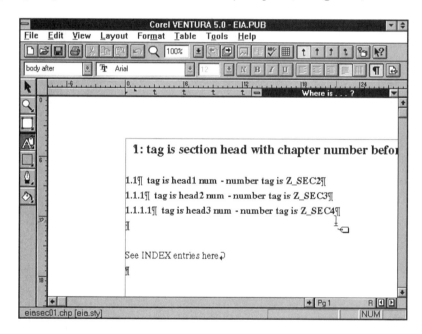

Figure 17.4
Loading the dummy chapter displays reference information about tags.

2. From the For**m**at menu, click on TOC & Inde**x** to get the dialog box (see fig. 17.5).

3. Leave the **T**itle as TABLE OF CONTENTS.

4. Set the # of Level**s** to **4** so that you can create a four-level table of contents and include all the tags you want from the dummy chapter in the table of contents.

5. In the Reference Tag list, select a tag. In this example, the section head tag has been selected (see fig. 17.6). VENTURA automatically adds this tag to the Table of Contents Text field for you.

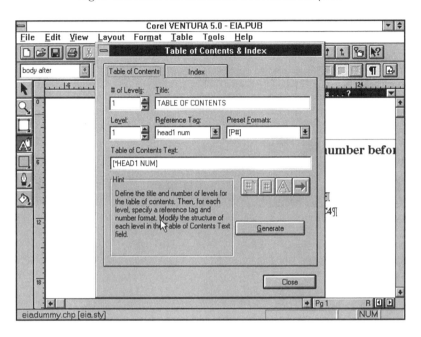

Figure 17.5
The TOC & Index dialog box with the Table of Contents tab selected.

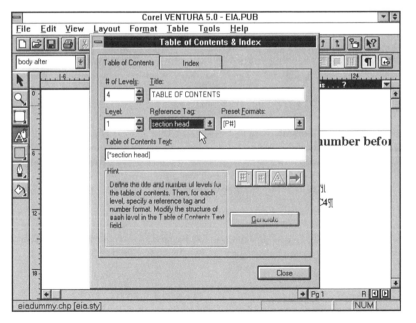

Figure 17.6
Select a tag from the tag list, and it is added to the Table of Contents Text field.

III

Advanced VENTURA Options and Techniques

Do not use blank paragraphs to create space in your document. These can be picked up by the table of contents process and will appear as blank lines in the TOC.

6. Move to the end of the Table of Contents Te**x**t field, click on the tab button (the farthest right button with the arrow on it), then the page number button (second from the left (see fig. 17.7) to add these to the formatting of the entry.

Figure 17.7
Adding a tab and page number to the entry for a section head.

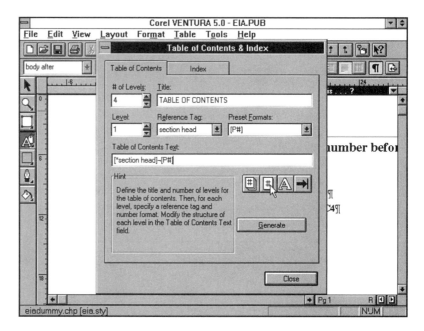

Now you need to enter the formatting for the next level. It is slightly different from the previous level because you want to include the section numbers applied using the autonumbering.

7. Increment the Le**v**el so that you are working with level two. Select the Z_SEC2 tag to include the first level of autonumbering from the **R**eference Tag list and input a tab (see fig. 17.8).

8. Type **[*head1 num]** to include the text for the first level of the TOC and follow it with a tab and page number using the buttons described above (see fig. 17.9).

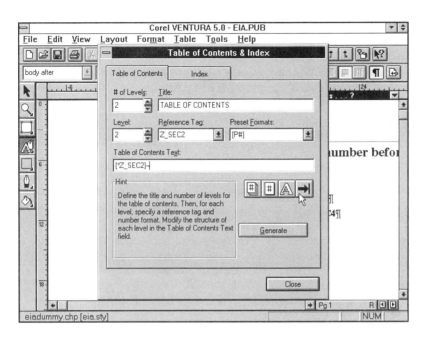

Figure 17.8
The Z_SEC2 tag is entered with a tab to offset it from the following text.

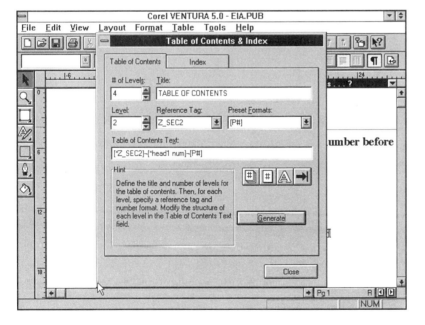

Figure 17.9
The complete TOC entry for level two.

III

Advanced VENTURA Options and Techniques

You can only use the R**e**ference Tag list for the first tag you want to enter. Using it again will replace the first tag selected. All subsequent tags must be entered by hand. Don't forget to use the correct syntax of [*tagname] for tags entered into the Table of Contents Te**x**t box; otherwise, your TOC will not work.

9. Repeat steps 6 to 8 for the remaining TOC entries required so that they look like figures 17.10 and 17.11.

Figure 17.10
Entry for third
level of the TOC.

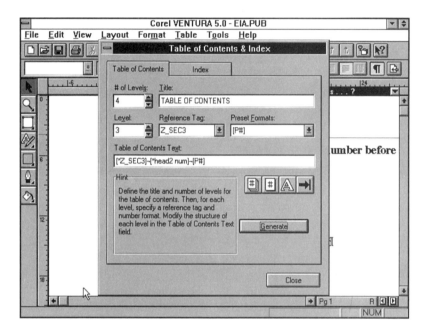

Generating a Table of Contents

After you have finished preparing the table of contents entries, you need to generate the TOC by clicking on the **G**enerate button in the bottom right of the dialog box. You are prompted for a file name for the entries that VENTURA generates for you. Type a suitable directory and file name (see fig. 17.12), but remember to keep the extension as .GEN for ease-of-identification. The .GEN extension is used to identify files *generated* by VENTURA from information you specify. The two most common GEN files produced are the table of contents GEN file and the index GEN file.

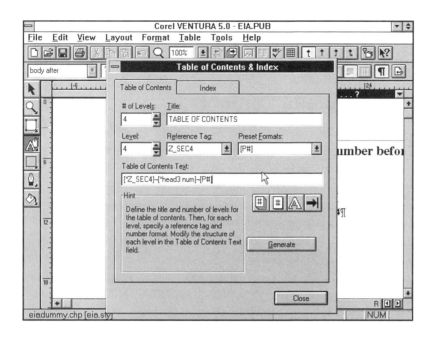

Figure 17.11
Entry for the fourth level of the TOC.

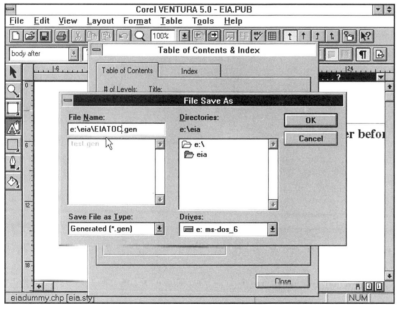

Figure 17.12
Selecting a file name for the generated TOC.

You are prompted to save your publication if there are any changes that have not been saved. VENTURA then generates a GEN file containing entries for every occurrence of all the tags you specified in every chapter of your publication. While VENTURA is generating the TOC, it provides a status report in the bottom left corner of the screen showing the chapter currently being processed.

Formatting a Table of Contents

You need to know how to format paragraphs and set tabs to format your table of contents correctly. You also need to know about Publication Manager to place the table of contents in your publication correctly. All these skills have been covered in detail in earlier chapters; you'll only cover the basics here. Use the following to format your TOC:

1. Add a new chapter to the publication using **L**ayout, Add Ne**w** Chapter.

2. Use **F**ile, Save **A**s to save the chapter with a suitable name.

3. Load the generated table of contents using **F**ile, Load **T**ext option (F9), and select the GEN filter under List Files of **T**ype (see fig. 17.13) to locate the file you created.

Figure 17.13

Loading the generated table of contents file.

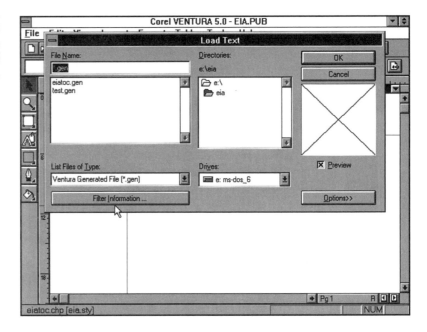

4. When the table of contents file is imported, the text will already be pre-tagged with generated tags. As discussed earlier in the book, these tags are based on the default body text settings for your document (see fig. 17.14) and need to be modified to format the TOC.

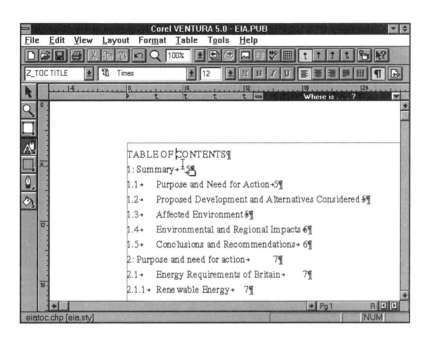

Figure 17.14
When first imported, the generated table of contents has default tags.

 Tip A quick, easy way to set up a table of contents layout is to use the rulers to drag the indents and tabs to suitable positions on-screen.

5. Highlight each tag in turn and provide the formatting you want for each level of heading. For the sample table of contents, the settings are as follows:

Z_TOC_TITLE. Times, 18pt, Bold, centered, spacing below to 18pt, and inter-line spacing to 18pt.

Z_TOC_LVL1. Times, 12pt, Bold, left, spacing above 18pt, inter-line 18pt, and one tab set at 36 pica with leader enabled.

Z_TOC_LVL2. Times, 12pt, Bold, left, inter-line 18pt, two tabs set at 2,06 pica without leader and 36 pica with leader enabled, and indent set to 0,06 pica.

Z_TOC_LVL3. Times, 12pt, Bold, left, inter-line 18pt, two tabs set at 3,06 pica without leader and 36 pica with leader enabled, and indent 1,00 pica.

Z_TOC_LVL4. Times, 12pt, Bold, left, inter-line 18pt, two tabs set at 5,06 picawithout leaders and 36 pica with leader enabled, and indent 2,00 pica.

Advanced VENTURA Options and Techniques

Figure 17.15 shows the TOC with these settings.

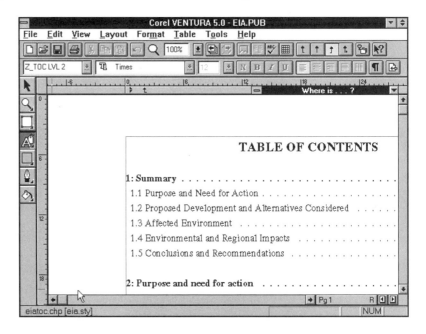

6. Use **F**ile, **S**ave (or Ctrl+S) to save the changes to your publication.

7. Use **F**ile, **P**ublication Manager to access your publication and move the Table of Contents chapter to the start of the publication as described in Chapter 16.

You can use the same style sheet for your table of contents as you use for your other chapters. The tags are automatically generated by VENTURA and do not conflict with any that you have already defined.

If you want your table of contents to have a different column layout than the rest of your document, you need to have a different style sheet because the column layout is stored in the style sheet.

Updating the Table of Contents

As you develop your document, you will need to update the table of contents regularly to reflect the changes you have made. Do not assume that the changes are so small that they will not affect your TOC. It does not take long to generate a new TOC. Updating your table of contents is simple, as long as you follow these simple rules:

1. Save your publication using **F**ile, **S**ave.

2. Renumber your publication using For**m**at, Renumber **P**ublication.

3. Regenerate your table of contents using For**m**at, TOC & Inde**x.**

4. Select the Table of Contents tab, then **G**enerate.

5. When prompted for a file name, select the same file name as the one you used when you originally created the TOC (see fig. 17.16).

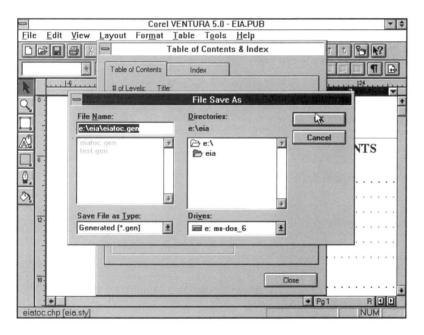

Figure 17.16

Use the file name of the original table of contents GEN file so it gets replaced.

6. When a prompt appears warning you that your actions will overwrite the original TOC, answer Yes (see fig. 17.17).

7. When the generation process is complete, load the Table of Contents chapter and check the entries to make sure it has been updated correctly.

You can build a table of contents using any tags in a document. This means that the table of contents feature can be used for producing lists of figures, tables, diagrams, and so forth, in your document. Simply set up the table of contents entries with different tags for each list you want to produce and give each generated file a different name.

To avoid the need to alter the table of contents entries every time you change a publication, you can create a separate publication using the **F**ile, Save **A**s

Advanced VENTURA Options and Techniques

continues

option. This allows you to create publications that differ only in the tables of contents that they generate. You must, however, be careful that publications used in this way do not get out-of-step with each other.

Figure 17.17
You are warned about overwriting the file with a new table of contents.

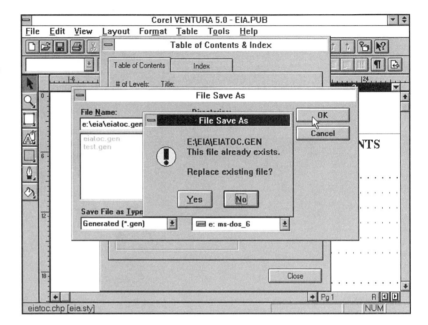

Creating Indexes

An index enables the reader to find a subject anywhere in a document without having to read through the whole document. Indexes are not structured the same way as tables of contents; they do not show the flow and logical development of the document. They do, however, have their own logical structure that highlights how the topics interrelate with each other.

VENTURA enables you to produce indexes containing normal references, as well as entries that refer to other index items in the form of See and See Also entries. With the Index Entries Roll-up, the whole process is easy to master, and a working index can be created easily.

What To Index

What to index is always a problem, even to qualified and experienced indexers. The main problem every indexer faces is knowing how the index will be used by the target audience. In real terms, there is little advice that can be given except the following suggestions.

When producing your index, remember why a reader is referring to it. The reader might be searching for any of the following:

- ✔ A specific item within one of the sections

- ✔ A particular word of phrase he or she is familiar with

- ✔ Other places in the document where a word or phrase is used

- ✔ Something he or she has already read

Remember to think of your target audience when you are developing your index. You are producing an index for the benefit of your reader—not for *your own* benefit. Think of the indexes you have used and how frustrating some of them have been. Look at good indexes and model your index on one from a similar document that you found easy-to-use.

A good index is a work of art and requires careful planning. Before you begin creating an index in VENTURA, sit down with pencil and paper, forget what you know about your document *and* your subject, and repeatedly ask yourself, "Where can I find *x*?"

This is far more difficult to accomplish than you might expect, and it might take some time to understand this concept. How, for example, would you index Nudibranchia? No, they're not rude; they are, in fact, opisthobranchia. "They're what?" you ask. This is a perfectly straightforward description of a subclass of gastropods—snails. So how would you go about it? Nudibranchia typically are referred to by their common name—sea slugs—so this is an obvious entry in the index for a lay person. See how difficult it can be?

Types of Index Entries

Building an index is a balance between entries for every possible method of looking something up and limiting the index to an acceptable level of completeness. Indexes provide their own structure, and it is essential to produce a logical and consistent index for readers to access your document.

The carefully crafted interrelation of index entries is the distinguishing feature of a good index. Not only can you find information about what you are looking for, but you can also find related information, which might not have been apparent from looking at the Table of Contents or reading the whole document. Despite the difficulty of building a practical and useful index, every index is constructed from the following four basic building blocks.

Advanced VENTURA Options and Techniques

Main Entry

Main entries in an index are the most commonly referred to items for any reader. These usually are a word or phrase with an associated page number, or numbers, that points readers to pages for further information on that particular subject. In the index of this book, you will find a main entry for the phrase "table of contents," which will tell you where in the book there are discussions of tables of contents. You won't, however, find *this* page listed in the index because it is not about tables of contents, even though the phrase appears on this page.

Index entries should point to items of interest to the reader and not simply to a phrase that occurs in the document. An index entry for Nudibranchia, for example, will not refer you to every page where the phrase Nudibranchia appears but only to those places where there is useful information. Often this is the initial discussion or introduction of a topic and how it relates to other topics.

Many indexes produced by DTP people are created by simply searching and replacing a set of phrases, but this provides a poor index that is unwieldy. Such indexes are soon ignored by readers because the index is not selective and has too many redundant entries. The technique of search and replace is ideal for starting an index, but the index then needs to be screened and pared down to provide a suitable format for the reader.

The Subentry

Subentries in an index are the next most common part of an index and enable a reader to find a more specific entry from a general entry. The reader might want to find a species of Nudibranchia (sea slug), for example, but might not know its Latin name. To search the whole index would be time-consuming and unproductive. Subentries make it possible for the reader to refer to Nudibranchia and find subentries for *Ancula cristata, Ancula gibbosa, Archidoris Pseudoargus,* and others.

This approach is used extensively in the CorelVENTURA manual and can be seen by looking at the index entries for adding inter-column rules.

This approach of using subentries is used extensively in the Corel VENTURA manual. A good example can be seen by looking at the index entries for adding rule lines between columns. This is a good example of a subentry because the topic is included under both the adding and the ruling lines index headings.

The VENTURA manual illustrates several examples of a poorly constructed index. One of the index entries points the reader to page 44, but the other index entry points to page 45. Which is correct? Are both correct? In addition,

there is no reference to Inter-column rules in the index, although this is the term used in the dialog box when you use it. What will a reader look for if she wants more information on inter-column rules? Great care needs to be taken to avoid this sort of problem.

See

See index entries are used to inform the reader that what he is looking for does not exist in this document but that an alternative does. In the index of this book, you'll find the See entry for "Manage Publication," which refers the user to Publication Manager. This might seem a subtle difference in wording, but the significance of this entry or any other See entry should not be overlooked. In this case, the See entry tells you that the Manage Publication feature in previous versions of VENTURA has been replaced by the Publication Manager feature in VENTURA 5. As a rule of thumb, expect See entries to be one way: they appear with an item that is not in the index and refer to a subject that is in the index.

In the Nudibranchia example, you might have a See entry for sea slugs that refers to Nudibranchia. In this circumstance, you would not provide a See entry in the opposite direction, regardless of the target audience, because Nudibranchia is the correct, internationally recognized name, and sea slug is a generic expression.

See Also

See Also index entries are similar in function to See index entries, except that these entries tell readers what they looked up might be correct, but there are alternatives. In this book, for example, there is a discussion about printing from VENTURA that discusses typesetters and imagesetters. In the index, a See Also index entry appears for Imagesetters under the Typesetter entry—and *vice versa*—to remind readers they should look at the other heading to see if one applies more to their search.

Be careful to avoid circular references when using See and See also references in your indexes. A classic example of a circular reference is contained in the VENTURA manual under kerning, where a See entry refers the reader to kerning. This can be very frustrating and discouraging to the reader who rapidly loses confidence in the index. Remember to check your index by going through each item to ensure it is correct.

See Also entries serve an important function in expanding your readers' ideas of what might be available in the index and should be used consistently. As a rule of thumb, you can expect See Also entries to be two-way; if you encounter a See Also entry, you will find a corresponding See Also entry pointing back to the original.

In the Nudibranchia example, you might have a See Also entry for Turbellaria because these are often confused with Nudibranchia. You would also have a See Also entry for Nudibranchia under the index entry for Turbellaria, creating a cross-reference for the two entries.

Inserting Index Markers with VENTURA

Inserting index entries with VENTURA requires the Tools, Index Entries Roll-up (Alt+F7), which can be used in any screen view. Regardless, the best view for inserting index entries is the Copy Editor view, as shown in figure 17.18. You can see more of the text without being distracted by the formatting, which is irrelevant when generating an index.

Figure 17.18
The Index Entries Roll-up in Copy Editor view.

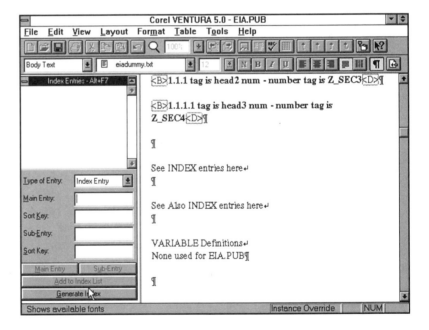

The copy editor is a split screen showing the text on the right and the tags used on the left. Adjust the position of the split so that all the text is visible and the Index Entries Roll-up sits on top of the tags area of the copy editor. This reduces the amount of scrolling required and speeds up the entry of index items.

Adding See Entries

To create a See entry, follow these steps:

1. Select **T**ype of entry and make it See.

2. In the **M**ain entry box type the text you want in your index, such as Sea Slugs, and in the subentry box type the reference you want as the See part of the entry (Nudibranchia).

3. Now click on the **A**dd to Index List and the entry appears in the scroll list at the top of the Index Entries Roll-up, and as an index marker in the form <$ASea slugs;Nudibranchia[]> in the copy editor.

   Although you can see the text of these entries (see fig. 17.19), they cannot be edited directly; you must use the Index Entries Roll-up to edit them.

4. Use **V**iew, **D**raft (Alt+F11) or **V**iew, **P**age layout (Alt+F12) to change to a different view. Make sure that tabs and returns are turned on using To**o**ls, Pre**f**erences, View tab, T**a**bs and Returns or use the Tabs and Return button on the button bar.

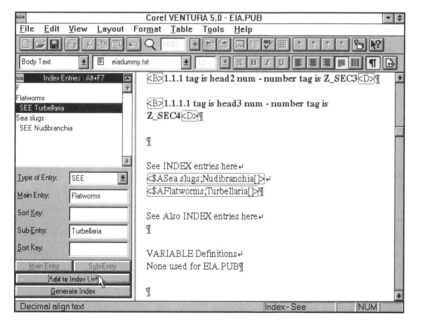

Figure 17.19
A See entry for Nudibranchia and Turbellaria.

You should now see paragraph markers at the end of each paragraph and a degree symbol where you inserted your index marker. If you move the text cursor over the degree symbol, the type of index entry will appear in the bottom right of the screen (see fig. 17.20).

Figure 17.20
The type of index
entry appears in
the bottom right of
the screen.

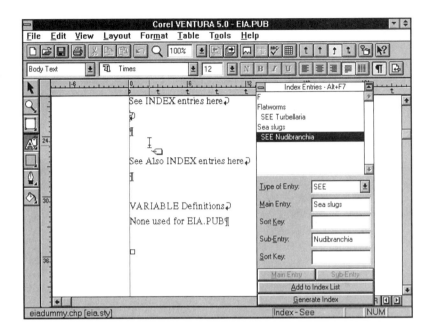

When an index marker is selected in any view, you need to open the Index Entries Roll-up to be able to edit the index marker. If the Index Entries Roll-up is already open, you need to select it before the display in the roll-up reflects the index entry selected.

In the Draft and Page Layout views, index markers appear as degree symbols.

Adding See Also Entries

To create a See Also entry, follow these steps:

1. Select **T**ype of entry and make it See Also.

2. In the **M**ain entry box, type the text you want in your index, such as Nudibranchia. In the subentry box, type the reference you want as the See part of the entry (Turbellaria).

3. Now click on the **A**dd to Index List and the entry appears in the scroll list at the top of the Index Entries Roll-up (see fig. 17.21).

4. Remember to insert the opposite entry so that the reference is two-way.

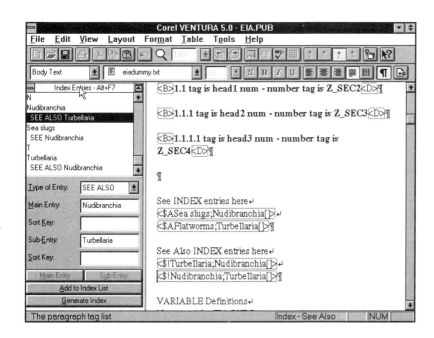

Figure 17.21
See Also entries
for Nudibranchia
and Turbellaria.

The actual text of the See and See Also entries can be changed when you generate the index.

Tip

Create a dummy chapter that contains only the See and See Also index entries in the same way you create a dummy for variable text definitions. With this chapter, all the See and See Also entries are placed in one location. They are easier to find and edit when you need to change them.

Adding Main Entries

Main entries are usually based on text that appears in the body of your document; therefore, the first thing to do is to find the text you want to create a main entry for.

To create a main entry, follow these steps:

1. Select the text by highlighting it with the mouse.

   Notice when you highlight the text with the mouse that the **M**ain Entry and the S**u**b-Entry buttons in the Index Entries Roll-up become available.

2. Select the **M**ain Entry button. The text appears in the Main Entry text box (see fig. 17.22).

3. After the text you want is in the main entry box, proceed in the same way as before and click on **A**dd to Index List. The text you had highlighted is now added as a main index entry.

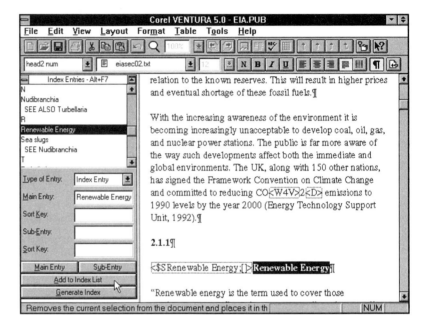

Figure 17.22
Highlighted text can be added to the main entry box by clicking on the Main Entry button.

Tip

Place your index entries close to the text you want to index. It's ideal to place them after the space character but before the first letter of the word or phrase you want to index. This avoids problems of the index marker appearing on one page and the indexed item appearing on another.

Adding Subentries

Subentries are usually based on text that appears in your document. For this reason, creating them is similar to creating main entries.

To create a subentry, follow these steps:

1. Select the text you want for the main entry by highlighting it with the mouse.

2. Select the **M**ain Entry button.

3. Now highlight what you want for your subentry and press the **Su**b-Entry button to add the highlighted text to the Sub-**E**ntry text box.

4. Edit the main and subentry text if necessary, then use the **A**dd to Index List button to add the entry to the scroll box (see fig. 17.23).

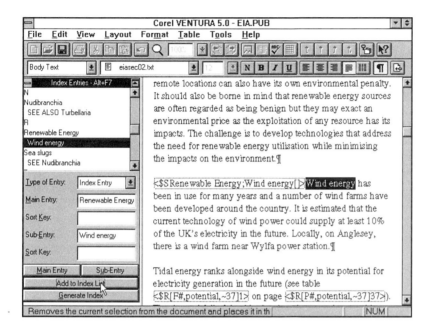

Figure 17.23
Text highlighted with the mouse can be added to both index entry boxes and then edited before adding it to the scroll list of entries.

You will have to type the same index entry several times. It is important to make sure you type it the same way, otherwise it will appear in the index as separate entries. Use the Index Entries Roll-up to make sure you have entered the index text correctly before moving on to the next index entry.

Sorting Index Entries

Index entries are automatically sorted alphabetically when the index is generated. The exact order of sorting is set by the index sort order defined in To**o**ls, Pre**f**erences (Ctrl+J), **I**ndex Sort Order. Non-alphabetic characters, such as exclamation marks, numbers, and special symbols, appear at the start of the index under the heading "exclamation mark."

Occasionally, you might want to override the default sorting for a particular item to ensure it appears in a location where the reader would expect to find it. This is commonly used for items prefixed with numbers and abbreviations, such as 3D and CVU, although the latter is more often handled by See index entries.

III

Advanced VENTURA Options and Techniques

To override the default alphabetical sorting for an index entry, you use the two sort keys **S**ort Key for the subentry and Sort **K**ey for the main entry. Enter the text to be used for the sorting in the appropriate field, and the index marker is added to the scroll box (see fig. 17.24). The sorting does not take effect until the index is generated, when the sort order affects the placement of the index entries in the GEN file. There is no indication in the scroll box of the Index Entries Roll-up that a sort key has been applied until after you have generated the index.

Figure 17.24

Sort entries can override the default alphabetical sort order.

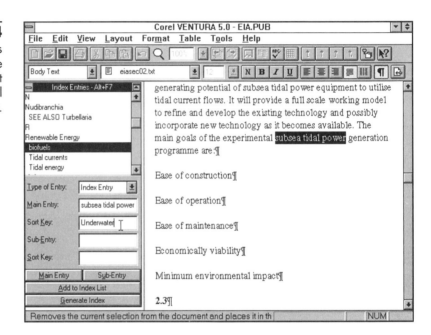

The sort entry can be used to place entries, such as numbers and special items, at the end of the index, instead of the beginning, by making the sort field start with zz to force the entries to the end of the list.

Using a Word Processor

Entering index entries from a word processor is a straightforward process involving the entry of index markers in the same angle bracket form as they appear in the copy editor. Different types of index entries are defined in VENTURA and then used in your favorite word processor, such as Word for Windows 6 (see fig. 17.25).

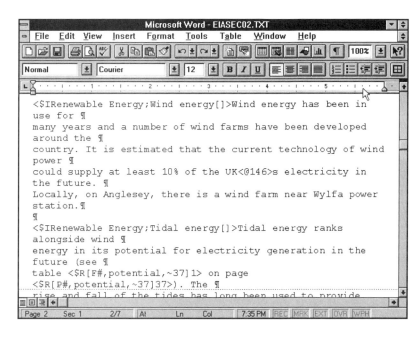

Figure 17.25

Index markers are simply text strings in angle brackets shown here in Word for Windows 6.

Word processors are best used for creating a rough index. The powerful search and replace features of modern day word processor packages can be used to generate an index from every occurrence of a word or phrase. Don't forget what was said earlier: This does not make a good index, but it is a good way to create a rough draft index ready for fine tuning.

> Several utilities, available from groups such as the CorelVENTURA Users group, enable you to search and replace across a range of files using a pre-defined list of options. These utilities can be helpful for the production of quick and dirty indexes that can later be refined.

Generating an Index

After you have finished preparing the index entries, generate the index by clicking on the **G**enerate button at the bottom of the roll-up. The Index Entries Roll-up displays the next dialog box, but you cannot generate an index if you are in Copy Editor view. You need to change to Page Layout view (Alt+F12) or Draft view (Alt+F11) before the generate button in the second dialog box becomes available. For this reason, always change to Page Layout or Draft view before clicking on the roll-up's **G**enerate Index button.

You are prompted to enter details for the generation of the index, such as the text of the title and the See and See Also entries. Choose a D<u>e</u>limiter from the scroll list or add your own delimiter. The delimiter is used to separate non-sequential page numbers in the index from each other. The delimiter for sequential numbers is a dash and cannot be altered by the user.

Sequential page numbers separated by a dash, such as 10–21, appear in the generated index if the same index entry is found on sequential pages. It is not possible to enter index entries in headers and footers directly, but they can be included by using the First Match and Last Match feature discussed in Chapter 14.

Select one of the predefined number formats from the Preset <u>F</u>ormats list (see fig. 17.26). If you want to create your own format, use the buttons to generate any combination you require, including additional text. Use the Index T<u>e</u>xt line to add additional formatting to the index entries. Remember that this text will appear on every index entry. A typical use of this text button is to add bold or italic attributes to the page number.

Figure 17.26
Pre-defined numbering formats used with the text button to make the page number bold.

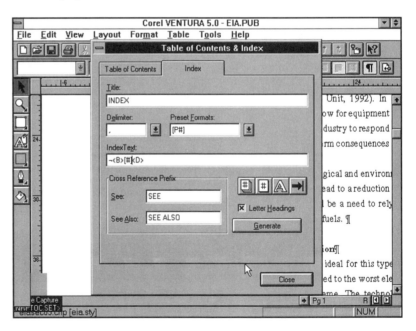

When you click on the generate button, you are prompted for a file name for the entries VENTURA will generate. Enter a suitable directory and file name, but remember to keep the extension (.GEN) for ease-of-identification.

You are prompted to save your publication if there are any changes that have not been saved. VENTURA then creates a GEN file containing index entries you have specified. While VENTURA generates the index, it provides a status report in the bottom left corner of the screen showing the chapter currently being processed.

Formatting an Index

You will need to know about paragraph formatting and tab settings to format your index correctly, and about Publication Manager to place the index in your publication. These skills are covered in detail in earlier chapters, so only the basics are covered here. The following exercise shows you how to format your index:

1. Add a new chapter to the publication using **L**ayout, Add Ne**w** Chapter.

2. Use **F**ile, Save **A**s to save the chapter with a suitable name.

3. Load the generated Index using **F**ile, Load **T**ext option (F9) and select the GEN filter (see fig. 17.27) to locate the file you created.

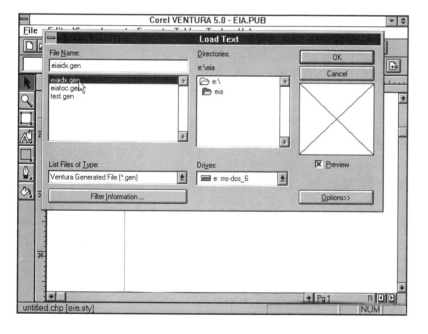

Figure 17.27

Loading the generated index file.

III

Advanced VENTURA Options and Techniques

4. When the index file is imported, the text is already pre-tagged with VENTURA-generated tags. These tags are based on the default body text settings for your document (see fig. 17.28) and need to be modified to format the index.

Figure 17.28

When the generated index is imported, it has default tags.

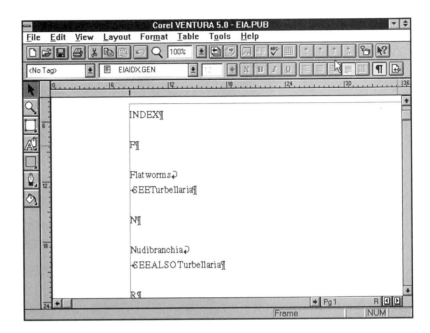

A quick, easy way to set up an index layout is to use the rulers to drag the indents and tabs to suitable positions on-screen.

5. Highlight each tag in turn and specify the formatting you want for each level of heading. The settings used in the example in figure 17.29 are as follows:

   Z_INDEX_TITLE. Times, 18pt, Bold, centred, spacing below to 18pt, and inter-line spacing to 18pt.

   Z_INDEX_LTR. Times, 12pt, Bold, left, spacing above 18pt, and inter-line 18pt.

   Z_INDEX_MAIN. Times, 12pt, left, inter-line 18pt, and two tabs set at 1 pica without leader and 36 pica with leader.

6. Use **F**ile, **S**ave to save the changes to your publication.

7. If you do not want your index at the end of the publication, use the Publication Manager to move it where you want it.

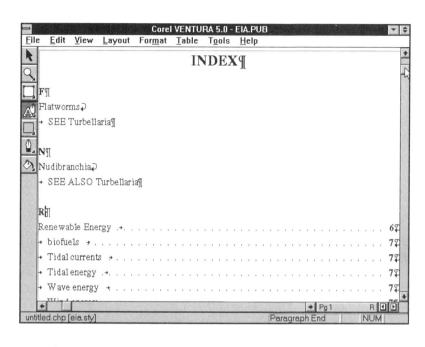

Figure 17.29
The formatted index.

You can use the same style sheet for your index as you used for your other chapters. The tags are automatically generated by VENTURA and do not conflict with any tags you have already defined.

If you want your index to use a different column layout than the rest of your document, you have to use a different style sheet; the column layout is stored in the style sheet.

Updating the Index

As you develop your document, you will need to update your Index to reflect the changes you have made. Do not assume that the changes are so small that they will not affect your Index. It does not take long to generate a new Index and, as you have seen, correct page numbers are essential to the effectiveness of your index and can make all the difference to your final document.

Updating your Index is simple as long as you follow these simple rules:

1. Save your publication using **F**ile, **S**ave (Ctrl+S).

2. Renumber your publication using For**m**at, Renumber **P**ublication.

3. Regenerate your Index using For**m**at, TOC & Inde**x**.

4. Select the Index tab and select **G**enerate.

5. When prompted for a file name in the File Save As dialog box, select the same file name as you used when you originally created the index.

6. When the prompt appears warning you that the index will be overwritten, click on Yes.

7. When the generation process is complete, load the Index and check the entries to make sure the index has been updated correctly.

Chapter Snapshot

As you construct long documents, you might find it necessary or useful to point the reader to another section or chapter of your work. These markers, or cross-references, point the reader to the correct destination. In this chapter, you learn to do the following:

This chapter teaches you how to use cross-references to point to figures, tables, photos, or text on a specific page.

CHAPTER

18

Creating Cross-References and Variables

In a book such as this, in which many figures or examples are mentioned in the instructional text, the reader needs accurate road signs to point from the text to the examples or related information. *Cross-referencing* simply means that strategically placed signs are placed in the document to point to other areas that further explain the concept or procedure being discussed.

These signs might route you to an illustration or to another related section of the book. To ensure that you don't get faulty directions, VENTURA enables you to insert hidden text, called a *marker,* that serves as the destination of your cross-reference. After inserting your marker you can put a sign anywhere in the document that will point to that location. By using VENTURA's text-formatting options, you can even custom format the appearance of your cross-reference road map.

In this chapter, you will learn to insert a marker in a location to which the reader will be directed. You will also create the cross-reference text that will point your reader to this destination. You will see that a cross-reference can point to figures, tables, photos, or text on a specific page.

Advantages of Cross-References

The advantages to using VENTURA's cross-reference tools become evident when editing your document. Cross-references are based on marker locations. Even after you add or delete text or graphics, thereby causing markers to move to another page, VENTURA finds the markers.

You might use cross-references in the following ways:

✔ In a newspaper, magazine, or newsletter in which an article continues on another page

✔ In technical documentation, such as this book, to refer the reader to a graphic that illustrates a point in the text or to further discussion of a concept or instruction

Creating a Cross-Reference

Cross references consist of a marker, a source, and the reference. The reader is pointed to the cross-reference source by a marker. The *source* can be an illustration, continuation of an article, or further information. The *marker* is a key word, consisting of no more than 16 characters. The idea is to link a hidden marker to a source. VENTURA finds the hidden marker, notes its location, and inserts the found information in the reference that points to it.

When working with frames as a source, a frame anchor can also serve as a cross-reference marker.

The *reference* is the formatted text embedded where you want the "road sign" to appear to direct the reader to the source location. This takes on the appearance of text such as "Refer to Table 1-1," "See Figure 23," or "Go to page 42 for further information."

Creating a cross-reference, therefore, consists of the following:

✔ Identifying the source

✔ Inserting a marker (or frame anchor) at the source location

✔ Placing a reference to source in the document

✔ Renumbering the entire publication for VENTURA to find markers and update the embedded references

Sources are fairly easy to identify. Technical documentation can be full of figures and tables; annual reports carry pie and bar charts. Readers can be pointed to any location (source) in your publication with a cross-reference.

Inserting a Marker

VENTURA provides two avenues for working with cross-references. One is to use the Insert Special Ite**m** option found on the **E**dit menu, the other is to use the Cross-Reference Roll-up. To activate the Cross-Reference Roll-up, either pull down the T**o**ols menu and select the Cross-R**e**f Roll-Up or press Alt+F6. The following exercises illustrate the procedure you follow to insert a marker to identify your source.

Using the Cross-Reference Roll-Up

The Cross-Ref Roll-up is the easiest way to insert several markers and references at a time. Because the roll-up can always be displayed, all cross-reference operations are at your fingertips without having to pull down menus and wade through dialog boxes. You can also enter markers through the **E**dit menu by selecting Insert Special Ite**m**. This is discussed later in this chapter.

1. Access the Cross-Ref Roll-up, either through the T**o**ols menu or by pressing Alt+F6 (see fig. 18.1).

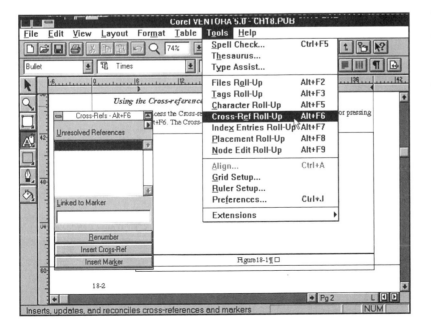

Figure 18.1

The Cross-Reference Roll-up provides quick access to markers and references.

III

Advanced VENTURA Options and Techniques

2. With the Text tool, click on the location at which a marker is to appear. Markers can be placed anywhere. But because editing might cause changes in the page location of referenced information, you should keep the marker as close to the referenced item as possible to ensure that the marker moves with the text and that all cross-references are updated after such renumbering occurs.

3. Select the Insert Marker button on the Cross-Ref Roll-up. In the Marker Name dialog box, type a unique name for the marker; it can be up to 16 characters and can include spaces (see fig. 18.2). Because markers are not case sensitive, "Income," "INCOME," and "income" are considered to be the same. After you click on OK, a small degree symbol (°) appears at the insertion point. When you enter either a marker or reference, VENTURA inserts a degree symbol so that the marker or cross-reference can be found later. Look carefully, though. VENTURA adds the symbol on top of the next character or space.

Figure 18.2

Marker names are added in a dialog box after Insert Marker is selected.

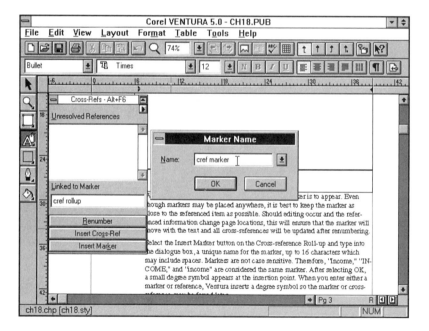

The degree symbol (as seen in fig. 18.3) is visible only when Tabs and Returns are turned on. To turn on Tabs and Returns, either click on the paragraph symbol in the button bar or press Ctrl+H. The symbol does not appear in the printed document.

New Riders Publishing
INSIDE
SERIES

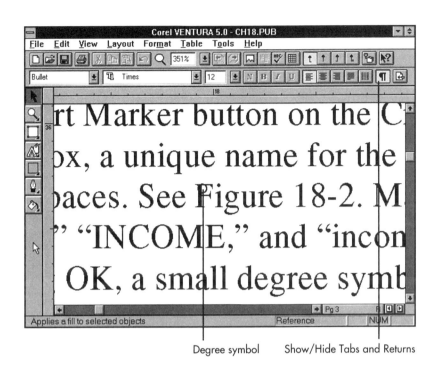

Figure 18.3
The degree symbol is almost hidden behind the 'F' in Figure.

Degree symbol   Show/Hide Tabs and Returns

Having named the marker, you have identified your cross-reference source.

Using the Edit Menu

The following steps show how to use the **E**dit menu:

1. After you have selected the location of your marker, pull down the **E**dit menu and select Insert Special Ite**m**. From the flyout, select **M**arker.

2. Type the name for the marker, as previously explained, and select OK.

You can place markers in the document at anytime. They do not immediately need a cross-reference or a cross-reference source. Imagine, for example, that you have the graphs and illustrations from Accounting for your annual report. The only thing you lack is the revised copy from the Treasurer explaining the graphs. You can assign markers or frame anchors to the graphics and insert the references when you receive the copy. After you insert the references in the text, simply renumber to complete your cross-references. The process of renumbering is discussed in detail later in this chapter.

III

Advanced VENTURA Options and Techniques

Frame Anchors as Markers

Frame anchors can tie a specific frame to a specific location in the text. If the text gets moved to a different page because of editing, the frame moves with it. Frame anchor names can do double duty as a cross-reference marker. When a reference is inserted in the text, the contents of the frame become the source. If the frame moves, the reference is updated after reanchoring frames and renumbering the publication.

A frame does not have to be anchored to text to use an anchor as a cross-reference marker. You have, for example, a full-page photo on page 73 and no text, and you need to reference the photo in the text on page 82. Because there is no text on page 73, the only way to identify the source is by using the frame anchor as a cross-reference marker because you have no place to insert a marker within text.

If your reference is going to be the frame's caption, you can use the frame anchor as your marker. Frame caption text that is entered in the Caption Reference text box found in the General tab of the Frame Settings dialog box cannot be edited on the page. Therefore, you cannot insert a marker on the page layout. You must rely on the frame anchor to be the cross-reference marker. On the other hand, if you have typed the text into the caption box of the frame on the page layout, a marker may be inserted within that text.

The following steps teach you how to use frame anchors to mark references:

1. Select the Pick tool.

2. Select the frame using the left mouse button.

3. Click the right mouse button to view the menu.

4. Select For**m**at from the menu, then select General from the flyout.

5. In the Frame **A**nchor option (see fig. 18.4), insert an anchor name and then click on OK.

6. Determine the position of the frame anchor to be placed in the text, then place the text cursor in this location and click.

A frame anchor in the text is not necessary if you are using the frame anchor as a cross-reference marker (see Chapter 4). When searching for unresolved markers (explained later in this chapter), however, any frame anchor that does not have a corresponding anchor in the document cannot be found.

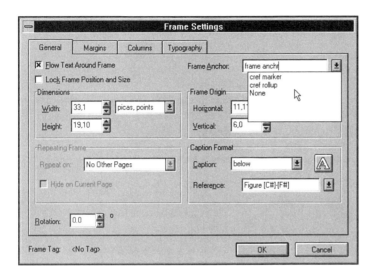

7. Pull down the **E**dit menu and select Insert Special Ite**m**, then Frame **A**nchor.

8. In the dialog box, enter the name of the new anchor or select it from the list of marker names.

9. Choose frame position from the list of options in the dialog box.

10. Click on OK.

Your frame anchor now appears as a marker in the Cross-Reference Roll-up list. If you cannot see your marker names, select the flyout in the upper right corner of the Cross-Reference Roll-up, designated by the triangle, and choose All Markers.

When you use frame anchors as markers, keep their limitations in mind. A frame anchor can be assigned to only one frame. After an anchor name has been assigned to a frame, it cannot be used to name another frame anchor or marker. Even when you copy a frame to another location, the anchor is not copied with it. The duplicate frame calls for a new frame anchor, different from the first.

Keeping Track of Markers

VENTURA keeps a list of the markers and references and indicates those without "mates" with a symbol next to the marker or reference name in the Cross-reference Roll-up list. These are discussed later.

III

Advanced VENTURA Options and Techniques

If there is a pencil icon with a question mark next to it, you have an unresolved marker or reference.

References to markers can be repeated. If you need to refer to the same illustration throughout a document, use the same marker name when you insert a cross-reference. For example, on every third page of the catalog you are producing you need to refer to the order form on page 128. By inserting the same marker name at the cross-reference location, you ensure that the exact page location of the order form is always inserted (very efficient when the order form gets moved to page 64). After you have moved the order form and renumbered the publication, all cross-references will reflect the page change.

Inserting a Cross-Reference

Having identified the item(s) to which you want to refer the reader, you insert the reference in the text. VENTURA provides many options for formatting this text when the cross-reference is complete. This is where you control which information is pulled from the marker location and how it will appear in the text. For example, your reference can say "See chapter 3, page 45 for further discussion," "Refer to Figure 14-7," or "continued on page 12."

When you insert a cross-reference you can use the same options you use when you insert a marker: either use the Cross-Ref Roll-up menu or access the same choices through the **E**dit menu and select Cross-**R**eference.

Using the Cross-Ref Roll-Up

Inserting the reference is a simple procedure. Multiple choice selections are made to control the appearance of the reference. Bear in mind that after you choose a certain style for your cross-reference, it should remain constant throughout your document. If all references are to be capitalized, ensure that your formatting options are always set to be capitalized. To insert a reference in your text, use the following steps:

1. With the Text tool, click on the location at which the cross-reference is to appear.

2. From the Cross-Ref Roll-up menu, select Insert Cross-Ref. The Insert Cross Reference dialog box appears (see fig. 18.5). In this dialog box, you make three major choices about formatting the cross-reference text.

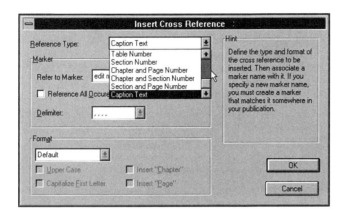

Figure 18.5
The Reference
Type drop-down
list controls which
information is
pulled from the
marker location.

3. Choose the **R**eference Type (Page Number is the default). The reference type should be the information you want extracted from your marker location, to be included in the cross-reference text.

All Reference Type options are available if your marker is a frame anchor. Remember, however, that figures, tables, and section numbers need to be set through the frame caption format in the General Frame Setting menu for numbering. Counters are updated automatically. Remember also that you can set caption text by using the frame caption setting in the frame's General settings. After caption text is set this way, you cannot edit it on the page without opening the frame's General dialog box again. Hence, if your marker is not a frame anchor, you are limited to the choices of Page, Chapter, Section, and combinations thereof. The following is a list of available options:

✔ Page Number

✔ Chapter Number

✔ Figure Number

✔ Table Number

✔ Section Number

✔ Chapter and Page Number

✔ Chapter and Section Number

✔ Section and Page Number

✔ Caption Text

4. After you select the reference type, identify the marker. Browse the markers available in the Refer to Marker drop-down list. At this point, you can also type the name of a new marker.

5. Select Reference All **O**ccurrences if you want VENTURA to cite every page where this marker occurs. Should you not select this option, VENTURA finds and references the first marker location. If you have inserted the same marker in more than one location and have checked this box, VENTURA finds all the locations and includes them in your cross-reference.

6. Select the delimiter format if you want VENTURA to find multiple markers. Following is an explanation of the format:

Choice	Appears as
,,,,	Refer to 1, 2, 3, 4
,,, and	Refer to 1, 2, 3 and 4
,,, or	Refer to 1, 2, 3 or 4
x to z	Refer to 1 to 4
x–z	Refer to 1–4

7. Finally, determine the text format by selecting Default, Alphabetic, Roman Numerals, or Text.

   ✔ **Default.** Text appears as it does at the marker location. If your page numbers are Arabic numerals, the cross-reference will be Arabic numerals.

   ✔ **Alphabetic.** Numbers and Roman Numerals are converted to their alpha character equivalent ("1" becomes "a," "2" becomes "b," and so forth). Note that uppercase formatting is now available. When you select the **U**pper Case option, lowercase letters are converted to capital letters ("a" becomes "A").

   ✔ **Roman Numerals.** All citings are converted to Roman Numerals. Note that uppercase formatting is now available. By choosing the **U**pper Case option, you convert all lowercase Roman numerals to uppercase ("iii" becomes "III").

Formatting options not available for the reference type you select are grayed out. Because Page Number defaults to a numeric format, for example, it cannot be converted to uppercase. If, however, you select Text, the Capitalize First Letter and Upper Case options are available.

Also available are the options Insert "Chapter," and Insert "Page," which insert the word "Chapter" or "Page," respectively, before the cross-reference. The cross-reference "Refer to 8-2," for example, can be changed to "Refer to Chapter 8, Page 2." These options are available only when one of the following reference types is selected: Chapter and Page Number, Chapter and Section Number, or Section and Page Number. When these options are selected, your choice of reference type determines the choices of text to be inserted to further define the reference format. Choosing Upper Case or Capitalize First Letter also affects this generated text.

Should you choose Caption Text as the Reference Type, no formatting is allowed. The frame caption will be repeated as formatted in the caption Reference option on the General tab of the Frame Settings dialog box.

The numbering scheme for the cross-references pointing to Chapters, Pages, Tables, Figures, and Sections are set on the Numbering tab of the Chapter Settings (F5) dialog box.

After a cross-reference is inserted in your document, the marker or reference name is placed in the Cross-Ref Roll-up. Note that a number appears beside the reference. This is the identification number of the reference and does not change, even when other references are inserted and deleted. To track references, this number can be used to identify a reference location by recording it on a printout of the chapter.

Any time you change the format of a cross-reference, you must renumber the publication. After renumbering, VENTURA always returns to page 1 of the current chapter.

Renumbering and Updating Cross-References

When you edit your publication, markers can shift to other pages or be deleted. Therefore, you should always renumber your publication after editing it, to ensure that all cross-references are accurate.

III

Advanced VENTURA Options and Techniques

Before renumbering your publication, always save your current work. If you select Renumber before saving your publication, VENTURA asks if you want to save your current publication. If you choose NOT to save the publication, VENTURA does NOT make any changes to the format of the cross-reference. For example, if you changed from Roman Numerals to Alphanumeric, Roman Numerals are maintained. Renumbering still takes place after the save, but formatting changes are lost. In addition, a bug within the program causes frames with Anchor Names to be sent to the last page of the chapter if the publication is not saved before renumbering.

To update a publication, you can select **R**enumber from the Cross-Ref Roll-up menu or choose Renumber from the For**ma**t menu and then select Renumber **P**ublication. Either selection updates not only your cross-references, but also any figure, table, chapter, section, or page numbering sequence. This feature is essential when tables or figures have been added or deleted.

Unresolved Markers and Cross-References

VENTURA reveals markers with no corresponding cross-references and cross-references with no markers, either of which can easily be overlooked or lost through editing.

You can use the Cross-Ref Roll-up to clean up markers and cross-references. To find all markers and cross-reference entries that have no "mate," select the flyout button in the upper right corner of the Cross-Ref Roll-up and choose either Unresolved References or UnResolved Markers from the flyout (see fig. 18.6). When you select either of these options, VENTURA filters out the "mated" markers and cross-references and enables you to concentrate on the unmatched entries.

Unresolved markers or references are indicated by a pencil with a question mark symbol to the right of its name in the Marker list (see fig. 18.7). After these unresolved markers or references are revealed, you can do one of the following options:

1. Insert a marker for the cross-reference, if none exists. You can create either a new marker or select an existing one.

2. Insert a cross-reference for a specific marker, if none exists.

3. Delete the marker or cross-reference.

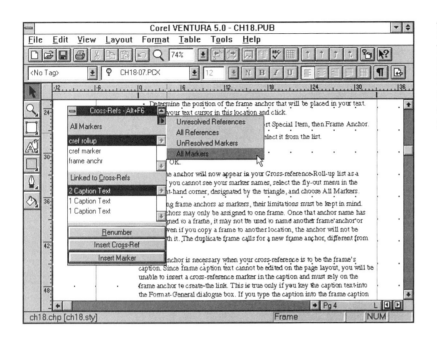

Figure 18.6
The Cross-Refs flyout is accessed by selecting the right-pointing arrow at the top of the roll-up.

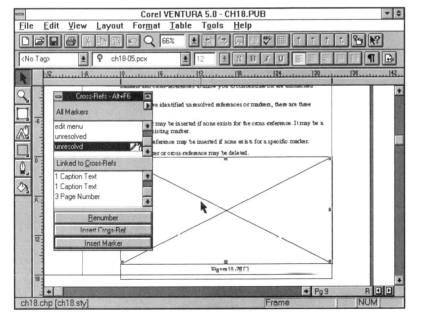

Figure 18.7
Unresolved markers and references are indicated with a pencil and question mark symbol.

III

Advanced VENTURA Options and Techniques

The CorelVENTURA manual cites and illustrates a link and unlink option that does not exist in the current software version.

Locating an Unresolved Marker or Cross-Reference

The only way to locate an unresolved marker or cross-reference is to use the Edit menu's Find and Replace option. Contrary to what is stated in the Corel documentation, you cannot locate a marker or reference name by double-clicking on it in the Cross-Ref Roll-up.

To find a cross-reference, use the procedure described in the following exercise:

1. From the **E**dit menu, select Find and **R**eplace.

2. In the Find and Replace dialog box, select Special Ite**m** (see fig. 18.8).

3. Scroll down the Fi**n**d What list and select Cross-Reference.

4. A list of the cross-references in the publication appears in the **I**tem Name list. Scroll down this list of cross-references until you find the unresolved cross-reference, and select it.

5. Select Find Next. VENTURA goes to the page on which the cross-reference is located, and places the text cursor immediately before the reference.

Figure 18.8
Find and Replace can locate any marker or reference.

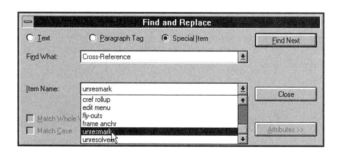

To find a marker, change the Fi**n**d What to Marker Name and repeat the procedure above. If you have more than one occurrence of the same Marker Name in your chapter, use the **F**ind Next button to find subsequent marker locations. Press Close when you have found the marker occurrence you want.

VENTURA does *not* find Frame Anchor names, even if you are using the Frame Anchor as a cross-reference marker. This selection is reserved for cross-reference markers only.

Editing a Cross-Reference

Cross-references are not cast in stone once they are placed. For example, you have formatted all cross-references to be capitalized, and your client now wants them to appear in lowercase. Editing the cross-reference can be done in two ways. The Cross-Ref Roll-up and the **E**dit menu provide access to edit the reference.

To edit a cross-reference, place the text cursor at the degree symbol that indicates the cross-reference location. The word "Reference" appears in the status line. The following steps show how to edit a reference:

1. To edit this reference, pull down the **E**dit menu and select Edi**t** Special Item (see fig. 18.9). The Insert Cross Reference dialog box opens.

2. Make the desired changes and select OK.

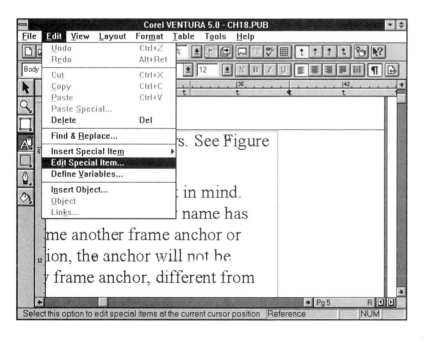

Figure 18.9

Selecting Edit Special item in the Edit menu opens the Insert Cross Reference dialog box.

III

Advanced VENTURA Options and Techniques

Remember that your changes do not take effect until the publication is resaved and renumbered.

Editing a Cross-Reference through the Cross-Reference Roll-Up

If you need to edit several cross-references or markers, you might want to open the Cross-Ref Roll-up. Having the roll-up available on the screen helps you edit more quickly because you do not have to repeatedly access the **E**dit menu and select Ed**i**t Special Item from the list. Especially after using Find and Replace to locate the references, the Cross-Ref Roll-up provides the speediest method to edit the markers. After your cursor is in front of the reference, editing the reference is only one click away instead of the two used to access the **E**dit menu!

Alternatively, the roll-up can cover part of your page layout and could possibly hide a marker or reference for which you might be looking. Whichever way you select is a matter of personal choice.

With the Cross-Ref Roll-up activated, editing markers or references is only a mouse click away. The roll-up can be repositioned anywhere on screen by clicking and dragging in the roll-up's title bar. If desired, reposition the roll-up to an area where it is out of the way, yet easily accessible.

If you choose to use the Cross-Ref Roll-up to edit your references, use the following steps:

1. Use the **E**dit menu's Find & **R**eplace option to locate the reference you want to edit.

2. With the text cursor positioned in front of the reference, select the Insert Cro**s**s-Ref button on the Cross-Ref Roll-up. (Even though the menu says Insert, you will edit the cross-reference.)

3. Edit the reference and select OK.

Remember to resave and renumber your publication so that the changes occur.

Moving and Copying Markers and Cross-References

Once set, markers and cross-references are not permanent. They can be moved or copied like any other text in your publication. The following exercise shows you how to move or copy markers and cross-references:

1. Select the Text tool and highlight the degree symbol for the marker or cross-reference.

2. From the **E**dit menu, select Cu**t** or **C**opy. (Or use the keyboard shortcuts: Ctrl+X for Cut, Ctrl+C for Copy.)

3. Position the text cursor at the new location for the marker or reference, then insert the marker or cross-reference by accessing the **E**dit menu and selecting **P**aste (Ctrl+V).

Remember to resave and renumber your publication to update the marker and cross-reference.

Deleting a Marker or Cross-Reference

Sometimes, an unresolved marker or reference needs to be deleted. For example, the bar chart for the annual report did not get finished but you had already allowed for its placement in your text. You can delete the frame that would have contained the chart, but that would not delete the reference in the text.

Use the following steps to delete a marker or cross-reference:

1. Locate the marker or cross-reference to be deleted.

2. Position the text cursor in front of the degree symbol. Be sure that "Marker" or "Reference" appears in the status line.

3. Press the Del key (or select De**l**ete from the **E**dit menu).

Because cross-references actually become part of the document text, take care to delete all cross-references that point to the deleted marker. Rewrite the text if necessary.

If a marker has been deleted, double check your list of unresolved markers and references. Deleting a marker might generate more unresolved references. If more references need to be deleted, locate them and repeat steps 2 and 3.

Creating Variables

Repeatedly used documents in which only a few items routinely change are tailor-made for VENTURA's variable text feature. By inserting *variable markers* in the text, you can define the marker to be whatever text string you want. This feature is especially useful for form letters, office forms, customized press releases, and legal documents such as contracts, in which a name, date, and address might change.

Variables work somewhat like a mail-merge document, except that you define only one record instead of a list of records. And because you can insert the same marker many times throughout a document, the specified replacement text is repeated at each marker location.

Although the Find and Replace feature does somewhat the same function, consider the following advantages to using variables:

✔ Find and Replace is a one-for-one substitution—you find one item and replace it with another. After you have replaced item #1, you repeat the procedure for item #2, and so on. Variable replacements enable you to enter all replacements in one dialog box so that you can update a document all at once, minimizing the risk of omitting one of the necessary replacements.

✔ With Find and Replace, you might have to select manually which items to replace in the new document and which to leave unchanged. By inserting markers for the variable information, you ensure that only those items you specify are changed.

Some examples of variables you might define are names, addresses, dates, invoice numbers, outstanding balances, legal descriptions, or any specific word or phrase. All can be inserted in the proper location when you use variable definitions.

Inserting Variable Markers

You insert variable markers in much the same way you insert a cross-reference marker. You can place variable markers anywhere on the page—in frame caption text, tables, frames, or in box text.

Because there is no roll-up for variable markers, use the **E**dit menu. To place a variable marker, use the following steps:

1. With the Text tool, position the cursor where the text is to appear.

2. Choose the **E**dit menu, then choose Insert Special Ite**m** (see fig. 18.10).

3. From the flyout, select **V**ariable Marker.

4. A small dialog box appears, in which you can enter the name of the variable marker (see fig. 18.11). This process is similar to the way you name a field in a database. Select a keyword or phrase that identifies the substituted text. You can use any alphanumeric character except curly braces ({}) and brackets ([]).

5. After you enter the variable marker's name, click on OK.

 Variable markers are case sensitive. Therefore, VENTURA recognizes the following as separate variable markers: DEFENDANT, Defendant, and defendant.

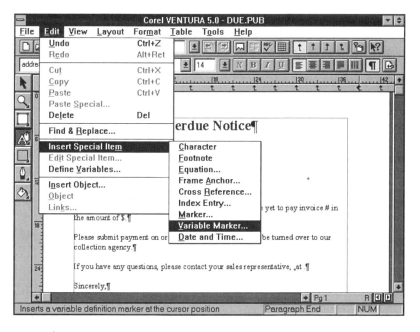

Figure 18.10
Variable markers are special items inserted in the text through the Edit menu.

Figure 18.11
Enter the variable marker name in the dialog box or choose an existing marker from the drop-down list.

Notice that the degree symbol (°) appears in your text, as it does when you enter a cross-reference marker. If you do not see the degree symbol, be sure that paragraph returns and tabs are turned on (press Ctrl+H). Remember, this symbol does not print.

Defining Variable Definitions

After you place the marker you can define the variable. If you wait until all the markers are placed, you can define all variables at the same time.

Use the following exercise to define the variable text for the inserted markers.

1. Choose the **E**dit menu and select Define **V**ariables. The Variable Definitions dialog box appears (see fig. 18.12).

2. To insert a new marker name and define its substituted text, enter the new marker name into the Variable Marker box. Enter the **S**ubstitution Text in the box shown in figure 18.12. Click on **A**dd to add the new marker and definition. It is also possible to enter a new marker name and define the substituted text later.

3. To assign the **S**ubstitution Text to a marker, select a marker in the list by clicking once on it. Enter the variable definition in the Substitution Text: box. This text appears at the variable marker location in the document. Always be sure to click on **A**dd after you enter the Substitution Text so the text is saved with the marker name.

4. To effect the changes throughout the publication, click on Re**n**umber.

Figure 18.12
All variable definitions can be defined by selecting the marker name and entering the substituted text.

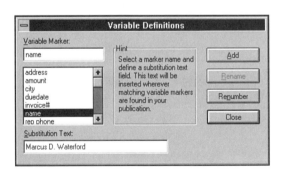

Variable text inserted in a paragraph of text in the document automatically assumes the properties of the current paragraph tag.

Editing Variable Definitions and Markers

Remember that you chose to insert variable markers in a document to customize and reuse it without having to retype it entirely. Therefore, some or all of the substituted text must be changed. To change any variable definitions or marker names, use the following steps:

1. Choose Define **V**ariables from the **E**dit menu.

2. In the Define Variables dialog box, select the marker name you want to edit.

3. Edit the marker name and select **R**ename to keep the current substitution text.

   or

   Place the text cursor in the **S**ubstitution Text box, edit the replacement text, and select **A**dd to save the changes.

4. Select **R**enumber to change the document and to save your changes.

5. Click on Close.

Deleting or Editing Markers

Sometimes, you'll need to get rid of markers that are no longer useful and change others to match your most recent needs.

To delete a marker, follow these steps:

1. With the Text tool, position the cursor in front of the marker symbol. When the cursor is at the marker's location, the word Reference appears in the status line.

2. Press the Del key to remove the marker and delete the marker's substitution text from this location in the document.

To edit a marker, follow these steps:

1. Access the list of markers through the **E**dit menu and choose Ed**i**t Special Item (or press Ctrl+D). The Insert Variable Marker dialog box appears.

III

Advanced VENTURA Options and Techniques

2. Select a new marker name from the list or enter a new marker name. The previous marker name is replaced in the document with the new marker name.

3. Click on OK.

4. After you edit the marker, you can define the variables and renumber your document by using the Define **V**ariables dialog box, accessed from the **E**dit menu.

Renaming Markers

As a document is used and revised, it might be necessary to rename a marker for clarity. For example, your current document does not call for a fax number to be inserted at a marker location. However, you have a marker named "number" to insert an office phone number in your document. Now you want to add the fax number in several locations. Suddenly, your marker name could be confusing and clarity is needed. Renaming the number marker to "phone" and adding a marker called "fax" makes it clear which number is to be inserted in a particular place in the document.

When a marker is renamed in the Define Variables dialog box, it changes throughout the document. If, for example, you were to rename marker number to phone, VENTURA would replace every occurrence of the number marker with a phone marker.

To rename a marker, follow these steps:

1. Select the **E**dit menu, then select Define **V**ariables.

2. Scroll down the list of variable names and choose the one to rename.

3. Enter a new name for the marker. This new name must be different from those already in the list.

4. Select **R**ename.

5. Select Re**n**umber to update the publication (by renaming all marker locations and updating the Substitution Text in the publication).

There is currently no way to delete a variable marker name from the Variable Definitions list.

Currently, there is no way to delete a variable marker name from a publication.

Locating Variable Definitions and Markers

Contrary to Corel documentation, you cannot use VENTURA's Find and Replace option to locate variable definitions or variable marker names. The only way to find all occurrences of the variable marker is to search the document manually. The search might be easier if you switch to Copy Editor mode. This mode shows all VENTURA inserted code. Variable definitions appear in the following format:

```
<$R[V*,marker name,,,0]Substitution Text>
```

Switching to Copy Editor view enables you to find the location of variable markers, but Copy Editor does not enable you to edit inserted VENTURA document format code. You must return to Page Layout view to edit, delete, or rename the variable marker.

III

Advanced VENTURA Options and Techniques

Chapter Snapshot

After you design your VENTURA document, the next step is getting it printed. You may print it on a Laserjet printer or take it to a professional printer. In this chapter, you learn to do the following:

This chapter teaches you VENTURA's powerful printing options. With this knowledge, you can print everything from simple black and white laser copies to four-color documents.

Printing in VENTURA

Whether you are a novice or experienced page designer, printing always promises a little excitement. There's anxious anticipation as a page glides out of the Laserjet or as your latest full-color piece arrives hot off the press. Before you can experience this thrill, however, you have to consider many methods and procedures as you delve into the printing process. For instance, will the printing be done in-house, or are the files being sent to a service bureau or printer for high-resolution output? Are you using spot color or four-color process? If you are using color, how will the colors be separated? All these questions and many more must be considered as you prepare to print your documents.

This chapter focuses on VENTURA's powerful printing features and options. First, you will learn how to select a printer, and print chapter and publication files. Next, you will examine the options for viewing the document, including adding crop marks, registration marks, and calibration bars. And you will read about more advanced printing techniques, such as creating color separations and controlling the line screen frequency.

Know Your Printer

Before you start printing, take time to discover a few things about your printer by reading (or at least thumbing) through the printer manuals. Use the following list to help you get acquainted with your printer:

✔ Is your printer Postscript or non-Postscript? (If this is Greek to you, refer to the following section, "Postscript Versus Non-Postscript.")

✔ What is the maximum page size? Can you print single- and double-sided?

✔ What is the *resolution*—the dots per inch (dpi)? Can the dpi be adjusted? (For more information, refer to "What is DPI?" later in this chapter.)

✔ How much RAM does your printer have?

✔ What printers are installed? (Refer to "Working with Printer Drivers.")

PostScript Versus Non-PostScript

Two main types of printing languages, PostScript and Page Command Language (PCL), are available today. What differentiates PCL and PostScript is their respective page description languages. A page description language is a code that describes page elements such as fonts, and the spatial arrangement of text and graphics into a printed product. PCL printers include the Hewlett Packard printers, and those that emulate them. Postscript printers use the PostScript page description language, developed by Adobe systems.

PostScript printers treat graphics and text elements as lines and curves, whereas PCL printers compose graphics and text from dots. Equally important, PostScript page description language is *device independent*, which means that a graphic or document created as a PostScript file will be printed identically (except for resolution) by any PostScript device. When you switch from one PCL printer to another, the language is the same but the "dialect" differs slightly from one printer to the next. This difference can cause objects to shift just slightly as your document is composed for a printer different from the original target printer.

Postscript is considered the industry standard by most publishing and graphic arts professionals. Its flexibility and sophisticated font handling capabilities give it a clear advantage for the desktop publisher.

What is DPI?

Dpi, or *dots per inch*, is a measure of the output resolution produced by printers and imagesetters. The dpi varies according to printer or output device. Generally, the higher the resolution, the higher the print quality.

Laser printers, such as an Apple Laserwriter or HP Laserjet, print at 300 dpi. Many letters, memos, and in-house newsletters are printed at 300 dpi. Imagesetters, such as a Linotronic 300 or Agfa 9000, can output at 1,270 or 2,540 dpi, providing higher resolution for professional-quality print jobs, such as full-color magazines and posters.

If a commercial printer will print your document, ask for advice on how to select resolution. The printer can provide invaluable tips for determining the appropriate resolution, based on the printing process, paper stock, and cost.

Selecting a Printer

Before you print, always check the printer setup to determine whether the right printer, page orientation, and paper size are selected. VENTURA provides two methods for selecting a printer: either the File menu's Print Setup command or Print command.

Setting Up Your Printer

The following steps illustrate the use of the Print Setup command:

1. Select Print Setup from the File menu. The Print Setup dialog box appears (see fig. 19.1).

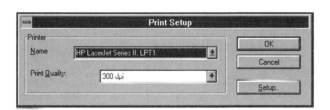

Figure 19.1
The Print Setup dialog box.

2. Click on the down arrow by **N**ame and select the printer you want.

3. For some printers, you can select the print quality, or dpi. With an HP Laserjet II, for example, you can select 300, 150, or 75 dpi. If the black arrow by Printer **Q**uality is black rather than gray, you can click on it and select the dpi from the drop-down list.

4. Click on the **S**etup button to reveal a dialog box with options specific to the chosen printer. The first dialog box in figure 19.2 displays options for setting up an HP Laserjet II (non-Postscript), for example; the second dialog box displays options for an Apple Laserwriter (Postscript). Use the dialog box to specify printing options such as paper size, paper source, and page orientation. After you finish, click on OK to return to the Print Setup dialog box.

5. Click on OK again to return to the document. Now that you have selected a printer and the print options you want to use, you're ready to print.

Figure 19.2
Click on the Setup button to reveal a dialog box with options specific to the chosen printer.

continues...

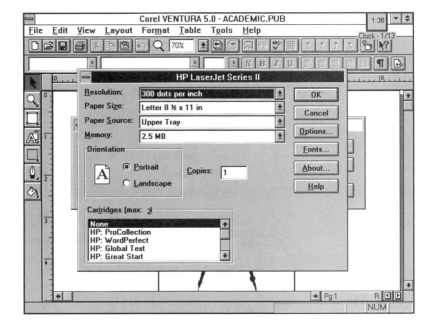

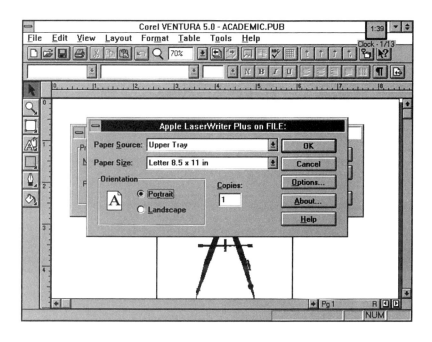

Figure 19.2
...continued

These steps are basically the same as those used for the **P**rint command, which is covered in the next section.

Working with Printer Drivers

In the Windows environment, all applications share the same printing services that are offered by Windows. The only way Windows knows how to send information to a specific printer you have attached to your system is to install a corresponding printer driver for that device. A *printer driver* is a file that includes all the necessary information for controlling the printer, including a list of the built-in fonts available in the printer's memory. Printer driver files have the file name extension .DRV. Refer to your Windows software documentation for information on installing printers. Many printer drivers are provided with the Windows software. If the driver for your specific printer is not included, you will need to contact your printer dealer to obtain a driver.

Make sure that you are using the most current version of the printer driver. To determine which version your system is using, select P**r**int Setup from the **F**ile menu. As described earlier, select the desired printer and click on the **S**etup button to reveal a dialog box with options specific to that printer. Click on the **A**bout button to display a message similar to the one in figure 19.3. At this writing, the Windows Postscript Printer Driver Version 3.57 is the most current. For non-Postscript printers, contact the vendor to determine whether you have the most current printer driver.

Figure 19.3
Click on the About button while setting up a printer to determine the version of the current printer driver.

Printing Files

With VENTURA you can choose to print an entire publication file, an entire chapter file, or specific pages in a chapter file. Initially, the **P**rint command displays a dialog box with simple, straightforward options, such as number of copies and pages to print. As you dig deeper, however, you will find a full range of powerful options for controlling every aspect of printing your documents.

VENTURA makes use of the same powerful printing features found in CorelDRAW. Refer to the printing section of the CorelDRAW software manual for more information about printing in VENTURA.

Printing Publication Files

To print an entire publication, open the publication file. Because all the chapters will print, you can display any chapter in the publication. Select Print Pub**l**ication from the **F**ile menu to display the Print dialog box (see fig. 19.4). Notice that Pu**b**lication is selected as the print range. Other print-range options are unavailable.

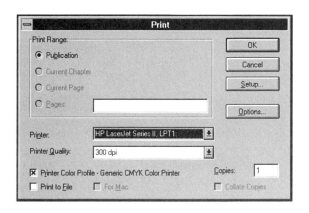

Figure 19.4

When the Print Publication command is selected, Publication is automatically selected as the print range.

Printing Chapter Files or Specific Pages

To print an entire chapter file or specific pages in a chapter, open the publication file and then display the chapter file you want to print. Select **P**rint from the **F**ile menu or click on the Print button in the ribbon bar to display the Print dialog box. As you can see from figure 19.5, the only difference between the options available in this dialog box and those displayed when you selected Print Pub**l**ication is that now the option to print the publication is unavailable.

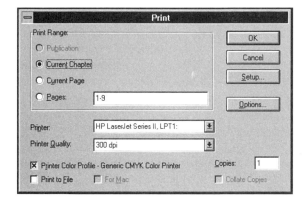

Figure 19.5

When the Print command is selected, you can choose to print the entire chapter or specific pages in the chapter.

To print the entire chapter file, select Curren**t** Chapter. To print the page currently displayed in the document area, select C**u**rrent Page. To print specific pages in the chapter file, select the **P**ages option and enter the page numbers you want to print. To print several single pages, use commas to separate the page numbers (for instance, 2,4,10). To print consecutive pages, use a hyphen to separate the starting and ending pages (for instance, 7–10). You can print single and consecutive pages as well. For instance, you might enter 2,4,7–10. To print all the odd pages in your chapter quickly, enter **1~**. To print all the even pages, enter **2~**.

Selecting a Printer

As mentioned earlier, the Print dialog box provides another way to select a printer. Click on the down arrows next to Printer and Printer Quality to select the desired printer and dpi. Refer to the previous section, "Selecting a Printer," for more information.

By lowering the dpi when you print, you can usually speed up printing—a big time saver when you need to proof a rough draft of your document.

Activating the Color Manager

Click on the Printer Color Profile option in the Print dialog box to turn on the Color Manager, VENTURA's color-calibration feature. The Color Manager creates a System Color Profile by learning about your monitor, scanner, and printers. The profiles help CorelVENTURA to capture, display, and print color more accurately. The defaults built into the Color Manager are pretested settings; use them whenever possible.

For more information about using the Color Manager, refer to the CorelDRAW software documentation or to *Inside CorelDRAW 5*, published by New Riders Publishing.

Printing to File

Select the Print to File option in the Print dialog box to create a file that can be printed from a computer on which VENTURA is not installed. This feature is normally used when you are sending a document to a service bureau for high-resolution output. If you are sending the document to a service bureau that uses Macintosh computers, check the For Mac option. The exact steps for printing to file are covered in this chapter's "Printing a Document to Disk" section.

Specifying the Number of Copies to Print

The Copies box in the Print dialog box enables you to specify the number of copies you want to print. Enter the desired number in the Copies box. You can print as many as 999 copies. If you want the multiple copies to be *collated*, that is, printed in consecutive order, select the Collate Copies option.

Viewing the Document before Printing

Having selected the appropriate settings in the Print dialog box, you can click on OK to print the selected file or pages. Many additional printing options are available in VENTURA, however, including the capability to preview the document before it is printed. Click on the **O**ptions button to open the Print Options dialog box (see fig. 19.6).

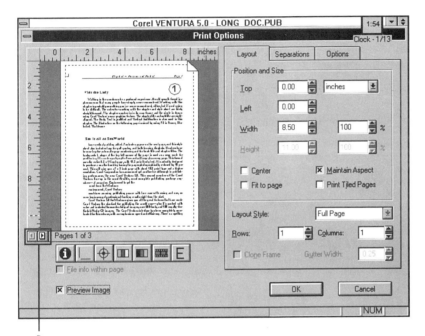

Figure 19.6
The Print Options dialog box.

Page arrows

A page preview area is displayed on the left side of the Print Options dialog box. Click on the Pre**v**iew Image option in the box's lower left corner to view the pages in your publication or chapter file. When the entire publication is selected as the print range, the first page of the first chapter file is previewed. To display another page, click on the left and right page arrows directly below the preview area. (The left page arrow is grayed in figure 19.6.) You can view only the first chapter by using the Print Pub**l**ication command. To view other chapters, you need to open the chapter file you want to preview and use the **P**rint command instead of the Print Pub**l**ication command.

When the current chapter is selected as the print range, the first page of the chapter file is previewed. Use the page arrows to view other pages. When the current page is selected as the print range, only that page is previewed. When specific pages are selected as the print range, you can preview those pages. You might find some hitches here—if the print range is 1,3,5–7, for instance, the preview might display only 1 through 5. In this case, temporarily adjust the print range to print the entire chapter so that you view all the pages. After you preview the pages, return the print range to the actual pages you want to print.

Using the Print Options Button Bar

The button bar below the preview area gives you control over various options essential to outputting film and separating colors. Consult with your service bureau or printer before you select any print options. Their equipment might have special requirements, or they might prefer to enable the options themselves. Table 19.1 provides a brief overview of the function of each button.

Table 19.1
Print Options Button Bar

Button	Description
	The File Information button prints the file name, date, page number, color plate name, screen frequency and color profile.
	The Crop Marks button adds crop marks around the page area to indicate the edges of the page area, should the page need to be trimmed.
	The Registration Marks button adds registration marks or cross hairs necessary on color-separated publications so each color can be properly aligned to the others.
	The Calibration bar button prints a calibration bar, consisting of six basic colors printed outside the page area. The bar is used as a reference for matching colors on your monitor to the actual output colors.
	The Densitometer scale button prints a grid that shows the range of color from 1 to 100 for the current color separation plate. Densitometer readings are helpful in determining the accuracy, quality and consistency of the output.
	The Negative button inverts the image, turning black to white and white to black. Generally, a negative is created when the pages will be output to film.
	The Emulsion button switches between right-reading and wrong-reading film. *Emulsion* is the light-sensitive coating on film.

Understanding Page Area and Printable Page

The *page area* previewed in the Print Options dialog box is the size of the base page frame. As described in Chapter 3, "Creating and Setting Up New Documents," choose Chapter Settings from the Layout menu to control the size of the base frame page. Many preset page sizes, such as legal and tabloid, are available. To create a custom-sized page, select the Custom option and enter the desired width and height for the page.

The *printable page* is the size of the paper on which you are printing. For instance, you could be printing to letter- or legal-size paper on your laser printer. The page area and printable page often vary in size. The preview shows the printable page and the page area. In figure 19.7, for example, the page area is set to 3 inches wide and 2 inches tall. The printable page is set at $8\,^1/_2 \times 11$ inches.

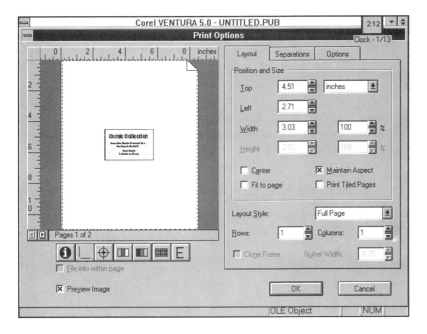

Figure 19.7

The page area is the size of the base page frame. The printable page is the size of the paper on which you are printing.

III

Advanced VENTURA Options and Techniques

File Information, crop marks, and registration marks are not visible unless the page area is smaller than the size of the printable page or the paper being printed on. In figure 19.8, file information, crop marks, and registration marks have been added around the page area.

Figure 19.8

File Information, crop marks, and registration marks are not visible unless the page area is smaller than the printable page.

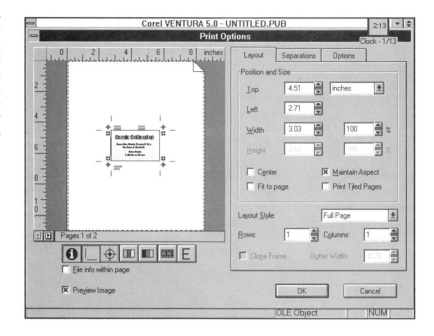

The calibration bar and densitometer scale are not displayed unless the printable page is sufficiently larger than the page area. In figure 19.9, a calibration bar and densitometer scale are added to a 4 × 5 ad printed on letter-size paper.

Figure 19.9

The calibration bar and densitometer scale are not visible unless the printable page is sufficiently larger than the page area.

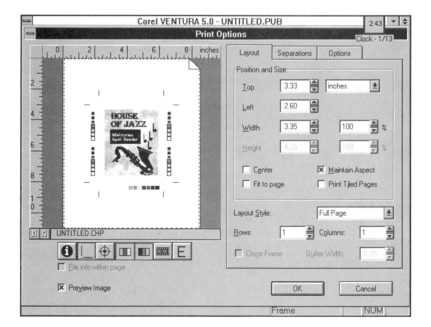

Advanced Print Options

The Print Options dialog box tabs—Layout, Separations, and Options—provide many additional print options. The following sections discuss the options available on each tab.

Layout Print Options

The Layout tab provides options for positioning and sizing the page area (see fig. 19.10). You can also select a Layout style and use the cloning options to repeat a smaller page area on a larger paper size.

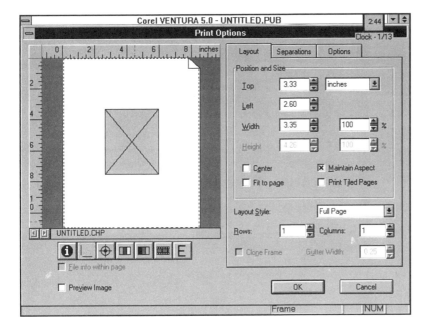

Figure 19.10
The Print Options dialog box with the Layout tab sheet selected.

Positioning the Page Area

Before you print your document, you can enter values in the **T**op and **L**eft boxes to modify the position of the page area on the page. The page area needs to be smaller than the printable page for repositioning to be effective. The first screen in figure 19.11 displays the default position in which a 4×5 ad would print on $8\,^1/_2 \times 11$-inch paper. In the second screen, the page area is moved closer to the upper left corner of the paper.

Figure 19.11
You can reposition the page area when printing.

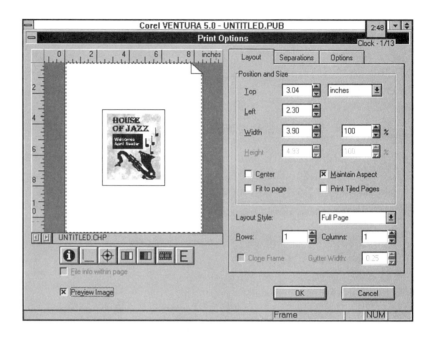

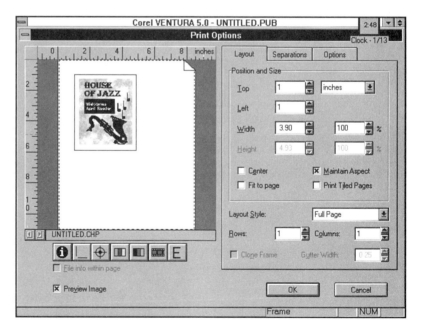

The following steps show how to reposition the page area:

1. Choose **P**rint from the **F**ile menu and click on the **O**ptions button. Click on the Pre**v**iew Image option to view the document (refer to fig. 19.10).

The position of the page area is proportional to its position on the printable page.

2. Increase or decrease the value in the **T**op box to adjust the vertical position of the page area. Increase or decrease the values in the **L**eft box to adjust the horizontal position of the page area.

3. To print the page(s), click on OK to return to the Print dialog box. Click on OK again to begin printing.

It's important to note that adjusting the position of the page area affects only the way it prints; the document itself remains unchanged. In addition, repositioning affects only the current page. You need to adjust the positioning of each page in the document separately.

Sizing the Page Area

When you need to print a document at various sizes, you can adjust the values in the **W**idth and **H**eight boxes in the Layout tab of the Print Options dialog box. The two screens in figure 19.12 illustrate how the page area for an ad was sized. Although manipulation of the sizing may distort the preview, the documents print accurately.

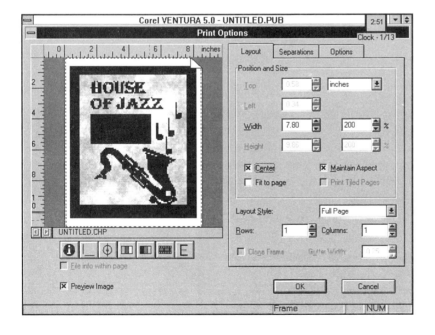

Figure 19.12
Use the Width and Height boxes to adjust the size of the page area.

continues…

Figure 19.12
...continued

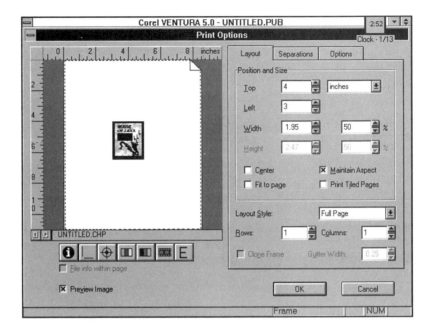

The **M**aintain Aspect option preserves the page area's aspect ratio. When the **M**aintain Aspect option is selected, you can enter a value in the **W**idth boxes only. Changes in the width are reflected proportionally in changes to the height. Turn off the **M**aintain Aspect option to enter values in the **W**idth and **H**eight boxes.

To adjust the size of the page area, do the following:

1. Choose **P**rint from the **F**ile menu and click on the **O**ptions button. Click on the Pre**v**iew Image option to view the document (refer to fig. 19.10). The size of the page area is proportional to its size on the printable page.

2. By **W**idth, use either the inches or percentage boxes to enter an exact value that you want the page area reduced or enlarged. For instance, enter 200% to double the size of the page area. Notice that when the **M**aintain Aspect option is selected, any changes to the **W**idth also affect the values in the **H**eight boxes. To enter values in the **H**eight boxes, turn off the **M**aintain Aspect option.

3. To print the document, click on OK to return to the Print dialog box. Click on OK again to begin printing.

As with positioning, sizing the page area affects only the way it prints; the document itself remains unchanged. In addition, sizing affects only the current page. You need to adjust the size of each page in the document separately.

Centering the Page Area

Click on the Center option to center the page area on the paper. After you adjust the size of the page area, you might want to center it on the printable page. When the Center option is selected, the Top and Left boxes become unavailable, indicating that you cannot reposition the page area until Center is turned off. The Center option is applied to all the pages in a chapter file.

Fitting the Page Area to the Paper Size

Select the Fit to Page option to reduce or enlarge the page area to fit on the size of paper in the printer. For instance, in figure 19.13, the left screen shows the page area at its original size; the screen on the right displays the page area enlarged to fit the printable page. Use the Fit to Page option also to create a smaller proof of a large publication in which the page area exceeds the printer's maximum paper size.

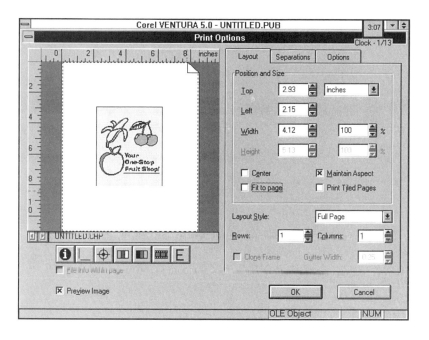

Figure 19.13
The Fit to Page option reduces or enlarges the page area to fit the size of paper in the printer.

continues...

Advanced VENTURA Options and Techniques

Figure 19.13
...continued

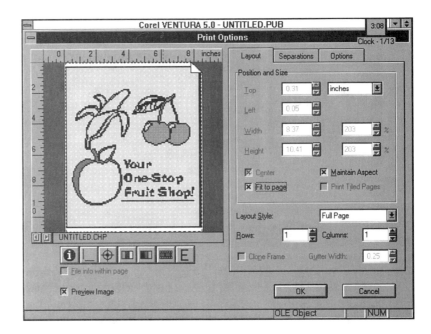

Tiling a Large Document

When the page area is larger than the maximum paper size your printer can output, use the Print Tiled Pages option. This option prints the parts of the page area that fall outside the printable page on additional pages. Suppose, for instance, that you create a poster that measures 24 × 30 inches. By using the Print Tiled Pages option you can create a rough draft of your poster in actual size. Tiling prints different parts of the poster on different pieces of paper. All the pages can then be laid out, or *tiled,* side-by-side to give you a printout of your poster.

In figure 19.14, the Print Tiled Pages option is selected to print a 24 × 30-inch poster on 8 1/2 × 11-inch paper. The preview illustrates the number of pages used to print the entire poster, and which parts of the poster fall on specific pages.

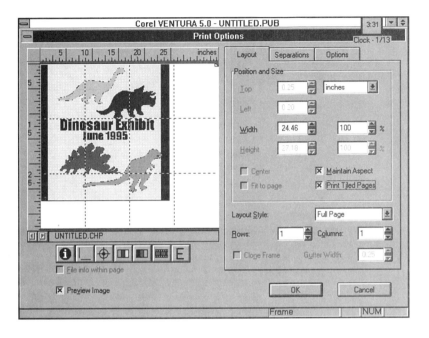

Figure 19.14
The Print Tiled Pages option prints the parts of the page area that fall outside the printable page on additional pages.

Working with the Layout Style

VENTURA provides layout styles for producing booklets, tent cards, and side-fold cards. As discussed in Chapter 3, you select the layout style from the Chapter Settings dialog box and apply it to the base page frame. The selected layout style affects the way the document prints. When you print a booklet, for instance, VENTURA prints the pages in the order they would appear when bound. In a 12-page book, VENTURA prints pages 1 and 12 on one page, 2 and 11 on another, and so on. The printed pages can then be folded into booklet shape.

The Layout Style option in the Print Options dialog box displays the layout style applied to the base page. In figure 19.15, booklet is the selected layout style; the preview displays how the front and back pages of a booklet print on the same page.

Figure 19.15

The Layout Style option in the Print Options dialog box displays the layout style applied to the base page.

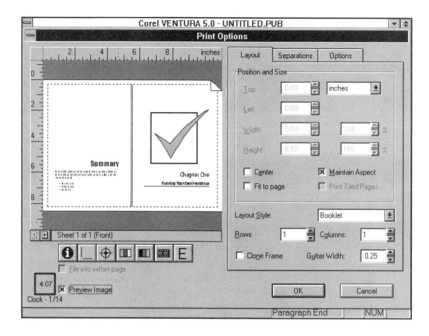

You can click on the down arrow next to Layout **S**tyle to change the way the document prints. For instance, changing the layout style from booklet to full page instructs VENTURA to print every page of the booklet on a separate page.

Cloning the Page Area

In the printing process, multiple copies of smaller documents, such as business cards, are arranged on the page to save paper and increase the number of pieces printed at one time. This process is often referred to as printing "9 up" or "6 up." Instead of arranging multiple copies of the document on the paper yourself, use VENTURA's Clo**n**e Frame feature. You simply specify the number of rows and columns needed to generate the desired number of clones, and turn on the Clo**n**e Frame option. Figure 19.16 illustrates how the page area of a business card was cloned four times on 8 $^1/_2$ × 11-inch paper.

The following steps illustrate cloning a business card on an 8 $^1/_2$ × 11-inch page. You can work with one of your own documents or create a 2 × 3-inch business card for the exercise.

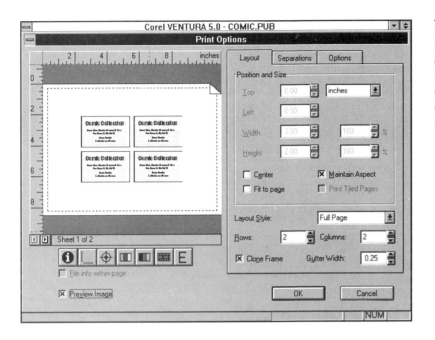

Figure 19.16
Use VENTURA's
Clone Frame
feature to clone or
duplicate the page
area on the
printable page.

To clone a business card, perform the following steps:

1. Display the page layout you want to clone.

2. Select **P**rint from the **F**ile menu or click on the Print button. In the Print dialog box, click on the **O**ptions button.

3. The Print Options dialog box appears (see fig. 19.16). Click on the Pre**v**iew Image option to view the card. In addition, you can click on the Crop Marks button to define the edges of the card.

4. Enter **2** in the **R**ows and C**o**lumns box, and click on the Clo**n**e Frame option. The page area is repeated four times on the printable page (see fig. 19.16). Enter a value in the G**u**tter Width box to adjust the spacing between the cards.

5. To print the page(s), click on OK to return to the Print dialog box. Click on OK again to begin printing.

Note that if you enter too many rows and columns, VENTURA shrinks the page area to fit. Although you can clone 20 rows and 20 columns of the business card, for instance, the size of the card is reduced.

Separations Print Options

The Separations tab provides VENTURA's powerful color separations options (see fig. 19.17). Here, you can specify settings for a variety of color-separation needs.

Figure 19.17
The Print Options dialog box with the Separations tab sheet selected.

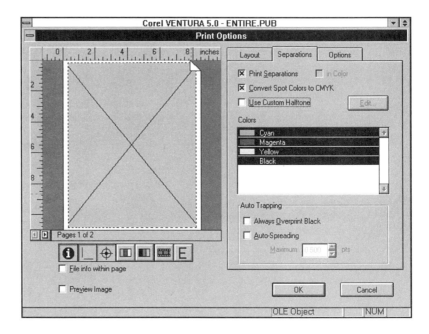

Color separations often are output to film and sent to the printer. Refer to the last section in this chapter, "Printing a Document to Disk," for information about submitting files to a service bureau or printer. If you are unfamiliar with color separations and the printing process, it is essential that you meet with someone from your service bureau or printer. Find out how they want files set up. They might, for instance, prefer to turn on the options for creating separations themselves, rather than have you turn on the options. The following section provides an overview of printing color separations in VENTURA.

Printing Color Separations

The color in documents that will be printed professionally must be separated before the printing process. The term *separated* means that each color used to design the document is printed on a separate piece of paper or film. If you used process colors in the document, four pages are printed—one for each CMYK color used. If you used spot colors, one page is printed for each color.

For more information on selecting colors and working with color models, refer to Chapter 13.

Figure 19.18 provides a basic example of the way four colors used in one page are separated into four pages. Each separation shows where a certain color will be printed on the page. Generally, separations are not printed in color; they are printed in black to create areas designating where the ink color is added in the printing process.

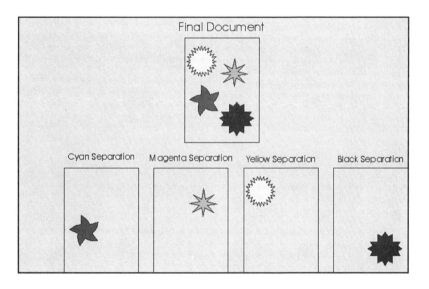

Figure 19.18

Creating color separations enables you to print, on a separate piece of paper or film, each color used to design a document.

III

Advanced VENTURA Options and Techniques

When you turn on the Print **S**eparations feature, crop marks, registration marks, and file information are added automatically to the page. VENTURA assumes that you want to create a color separation for each color in the document. Because black and a Pantone red spot color were used in the document shown in figure 19.19, those colors are highlighted in the Colors box. If all the colors in the document were selected from the CMYK color model, all four of the process colors would be highlighted in the Colors box.

The following steps illustrate how to enable the color separation option for a document, using colors from the CMYK process color model. You can work with one of your own documents or create a document using colors from the CMYK color model.

Figure 19.19
VENTURA
assumes that you
want to create a
color separation
for each color in
the document.

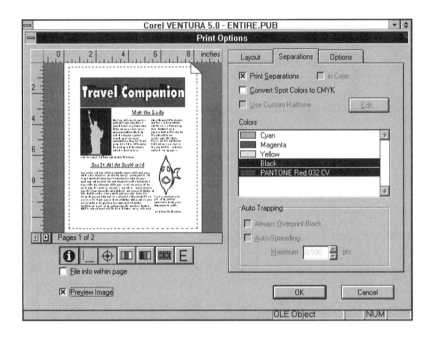

The following steps show how to create color separations:

1. Open the file where you want to work with color separations.

2. Select **P**rint from the **F**ile menu or click on the Print button. In the Print dialog box, click on the **O**ptions button. Click on the Pre**v**iew Image option to view the document.

3. Select the Separations tab in the Print Options dialog box (refer to fig. 19.6). In the Separations tab sheet, click on the Print **S**eparations option. If you do not need a separation for every highlighted color in the Colors box, deselect the color you do not want to print.

4. To print the color separations, click on OK to return to the Print dialog box. Click on OK again to begin printing.

Converting Spot Colors to CMYK

When a document uses colors from both the CMYK process color model and a spot color model, VENTURA creates separations for the four process colors and each spot color used in the document. For instance, if you used the CYMK colors and three Pantone spot colors, you would create seven pages of color separations. VENTURA provides the **C**onvert Spot Colors to CMYK option to convert spot

colors to their CMYK process equivalents. Select this option when you want to print four color separations without printing extra separations for each spot color.

Creating Custom Halftone

The Use Custom Halftone option enables you to manipulate the halftone settings used for printing the document. Click on the Use Custom Halftone option, then click on the Edit button to display the Advanced Screening dialog box shown in figure 19.20.

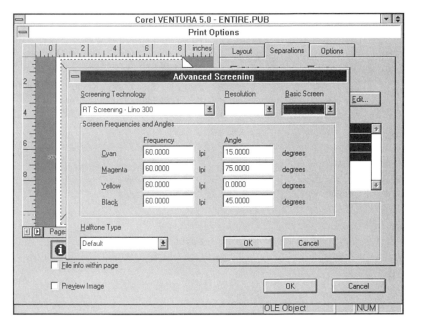

Figure 19.20
The Advanced
Screening
dialog box.

III

Advanced VENTURA Options and Techniques

Use this dialog box to adjust the halftone screen angles and line frequencies for each CMYK color. Click on the down arrow next to Screening Technology to reveal a list of preset specifications for a number of imagesetters, such as a Linotronic. You should not make any changes unless you are familiar with adjusting these settings, or are specifically instructed to do so by your printer or service bureau representative. If no changes are made, your publication prints using Corel's default angle and frequency.

Working with Trapping

Trapping is the process of adding a slight overlap between adjacent areas of color, to avoid gaps caused by registration errors. A *spread* is one type of trap, in which the foreground object is extended into the background object. In another type of trap, a *choke*, the background object is extended into the foreground object. VENTURA's auto-trapping feature creates spreads, not chokes. Notice the white edges around the gray circle on the left in figure 19.21; adding a spread to the second circle eliminated the gap.

Figure 19.21
Trapping adds a slight overlap between adjacent areas of color, to avoid gaps caused by registration errors.

Before you dive in to trapping, you should seek advice from your service bureau or printer. The service bureau might use an application such as Aldus TrapWise to trap your document, for instance, and the printer might want to trap the negative manually to get better results.

VENTURA does offer some trapping functions, however. These trapping options become available when you are printing color separations. Select the Always **O**verprint Black option to print objects that contain at least 95-percent black on top of other printed objects.

Select the **A**uto-Spreading option to add trap (spread) to all objects that have no outline and are filled with a uniform color. In the **M**aximum box, specify the maximum amount of trap you want to add. For instance, entering 1 point spreads the color of the foreground object by 1 point. You can enter a maximum of 10 points.

Additional Print Options

The Options tab of the Print options dialog box provides several features that affect the final output of your file, particularly if you are printing to a high-resolution imagesetter. Click on the Options tab to reveal the features shown in figure 19.22.

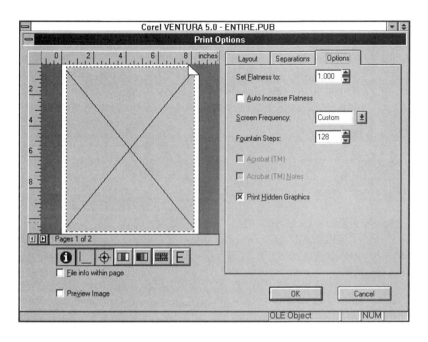

Figure 19.22
The Options tab of
the Print Options
dialog box.

If you are unfamiliar with the printing intricacies of line screen frequency and
PostScript Limitcheck errors, you should discuss these settings with a representative of your service bureau or printing company before you manipulate these
settings.

Screen Frequency

The Screen Frequency option establishes the size of the halftone for the output
device, and the frequency value controls the resolution of the screen. The lower
the screen frequency, the more apparent the screen of dots used to compose the
image will appear when printed. Choosing an appropriate frequency depends on
the resolution of your printer and the printed results you want. In general, you
should choose higher screen frequencies for higher-resolution imagesetters. For
lower-resolution desktop printers, a screen frequency of 60 to 80 *lines per inch*
(lpi) is fine. Screen frequencies below 40 lpi are often used for special effects in
which a coarse screen frequency enhances a particular image.

Unless you designated a new halftone screen in the PostScript Options dialog box
(in the Uniform fill dialog box), all objects print using the screen frequency you
enter here. The ability to enter new halftone screens for individual graphics gives
you the option to assign different line screen frequencies to various portions of
the same image. If you are assigning a special screen effect to one portion of an
image, for example, you can select those portions of the image and assign a line

screen frequency of 40 lpi to them in the PostScript Options dialog box. Then you can assign a more global screen frequency to the rest of the images on the page by entering a figure in the **S**creen Frequency text box. If you intend to print to color separations, you can utilize the Use Custom Halftone feature of the Separations tab to adjust the screen frequency of each CMYK color.

Controlling Flatness

Printing complex images to high-resolution PostScript imagesetters can cause memory problems. These problems often occur because of the number of rasterized dots the imagesetter is required to handle at higher resolutions. These memory problems frequently result in PostScript Limitcheck errors. Basically, the problem stems from the fact that rendering a high number of complex curves bogs down a printer. VENTURA enables you to adjust the flatness or the smoothness of curves to a setting that is easier for the printer to process. These adjustments generally are applied in very small increments, with results that are imperceptible to the naked eye. The higher the flatness setting, the "flatter" the curves; the lower the setting, the smoother the curves. You may not initially notice a problem with a file printed to your 300-dpi desktop printer. At such a comparatively low resolution, the desktop printer will perform beautifully. But when the file is sent to a 2,540-dpi imagesetter, it's a whole different ballgame. To change the flatness, enter a new value in the Set **F**latness to box.

One way to control the flatness, short of experimentation and headache, is with the **A**uto Increase Flatness option. With this option selected, VENTURA's print engine assumes responsibility for adjusting the flatness of curved objects. Each time the print file encounters a PostScript Limitcheck error, VENTURA automatically increases the flatness setting by 2, relative to the initial flatness setting. If the object is still too complex to print after five attempts to increase flatness, the printer will skip the object and move on. If all this sounds like Greek to you, don't worry. A representative from your service bureau can help you work with these selections.

Adjusting Fountain Steps

The Fountain Steps feature controls the number of printed bands used to render a fountain fill. Higher values produce smoother blends but take longer to print. A low setting prints faster, but banding in fountain fills is visible (see fig 19.23). Some older imagesetters have real problems printing large fountain fills with a high number of fountain-fill steps. You should check with your service bureau before sending a file with complex fountain fills. The settings in this dialog box are overridden by the **S**teps setting in the Fountain Fill dialog box and the Preferences dialog box.

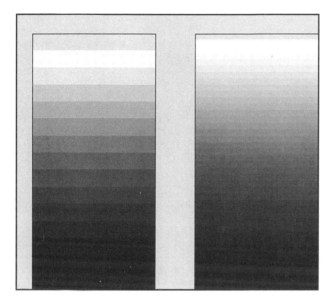

Printing Hidden Graphics

As discussed in Chapter 11, you can hide either all graphics in a chapter, or selected graphics. To hide all graphics, select Draft view from the **V**iew menu. To hide selected graphics only, select the graphic and choose **G**raphic… from the For**m**at menu. When the Frame Setting dialog box appears, select the Graphic tab and turn on the Hide Graphics option.

Hidden graphics will still print, however, unless the Print Hidden Graphics option on the Options tab of the Print Options dialog box is turned off.

Printing a Document to Disk

For documents that will be professionally printed, the publication needs to be output on film. Often, you must print the document to disk so that you can send it to a service bureau or printer for output. When you print a document to disk, one step is to select the device used to output the film. If possible, ask to get a copy of the printer driver file for the device used to output or print your work. For instance, many service bureaus use a Linotronic 300 to output film. Selecting the same printing/output device as your service bureau or printer helps reduce printing errors. With the driver installed, you can select the same printing/output device as that used at the service bureau. Keep in mind that when you print to disk, you do not need the actual output device. You do not, for example, need to be hooked up to a Linotronic to install the printer driver. When you print to disk, you are creating a "print" file set up with information for that particular device.

The printer driver for the AGFA 9000 is a good choice if you don't have access to the PostScript driver used by your service bureau.

The following steps demonstrate how to create a print file:

1. Open the publication file you want to print. Choose **P**rint or Print Publiction from the **F**ile menu. The Print dialog box appears.

2. Select the desired printer/output device and print quality. Click on the Print to **F**ile option. If you are sending the document to a service bureau that uses Macintosh computers, check the For **M**ac check box.

3. Select the other print options you want. For instance, select the Clone Frame or Color Separations option.

4. Click on OK. The Print to File dialog box appears (see fig. 19.24). Enter a file name with the extension .PRN, for the print file. If necessary, change to the drive and directory in which you want to save the print file.

5. Click on OK. A message box appears, displaying the status of the print job. When the printing is finished, your document is printed to disk.

Figure 19.24
The Print to File
dialog box.

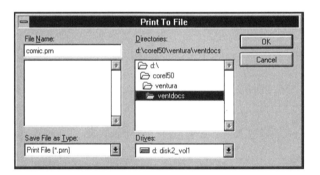

If you have set the printer port connection to FILE in the Windows Control Panel, do not select the Print to **F**ile option in the Print dialog box.

If your document is large (two or more chapters), you might want to create a separate print file for each chapter so that the files are smaller and more manageable. By turning on the Print to Separate File option in the Preferences dialog box, you instruct VENTURA to create a separate print file for each chapter. This feature works only when the Print Publication command is used to create the print file.

III

Advanced VENTURA Options and Techniques

Part IV

Real-World VENTURA Project Exercises

Chapter Snapshot

Although VENTURA is best known for its long document capabilities, it handles short documents with equal ease. In this chapter, you will construct a one-page invitation and learn to do the following:

Setting up a one-page document, such as an invitation, is easy with VENTURA. This holiday invitation will guide you through the process.

Building an Invitation

VENTURA is known for its efficient handling of publishing long, multi-page documents, but this should not stop you from turning to VENTURA when you want to produce a one-page project, such as an invitation. In this chapter, you will discover that VENTURA offers you the tools to design and produce an attractive invitation. These tools enable you to easily set up an appropriate page layout, format the text, and import the graphics needed to produce your invitation.

The exercises in this chapter guide you through creating a holiday card. You can print multiple copies of the card directly from your printer, or you can use the artwork to have the cards printed at your local print shop.

Working with a Style Sheet

Style sheets contain information about documents such as page size, margins, number of columns used, and paragraph tags for formatting text. A new feature for VENTURA is the Quick Format Roll-up, which provides access to a number of predesigned style sheets which simplify the creation of documents such as catalogs, multi-page booklets, newsletters with various column formats, as well as the invitation discussed in this chapter.

The Quick Format Roll-up contains several pre-designed style sheets that can be used to create an invitation. It is best to choose a style sheet that most closely resembles how you want your finished invitation to look. Each of these pre-designed style sheets can be modified to fit your exact needs.

An added benefit of using the style sheets provided in the Quick Format Roll-up is they include empty graphic and text frames on the page. These help to guide you through the design and production of your documents. These elements can be modified to fit your custom design or deleted altogether if they do not meet your requirements.

Using the Quick Format Roll-Up

To display the Quick-Format Roll-up (see fig. 20.1), select the Quick Format Roll-Up option from the For**m**at menu or press Ctrl+Q.

Figure 20.1
The Quick Format
Roll-up.

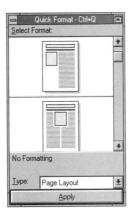

Scroll down until you find the two invitation styles available in the Quick Format Roll-up (see fig. 20.2). One of the invitation styles available is designed as a side-fold card based on an $8\,^1/_2 \times 11$-inch page size. The text is designed to be centered on the inside page in one column. The second invitation style is a top-fold

card also based on an 8 $\frac{1}{2}$ × 11-inch page size. This design includes a graphics frame and a text frame on the base page. The text is formatted as flush left in the text frame.

Figure 20.2
Invitation style
options available
in the Quick
Format Roll-up.

To begin working on this invitation project, select the top-fold card style by clicking on the correct picture. Apply this style to your base page by clicking on the Apply button. The style is displayed as your base page. Notice that a prepositioned graphic frame and text frame are a part of the base page (see fig. 20.3).

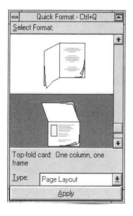

Figure 20.3
The top-fold Quick
Format style.

Saving a Style

When this invitation style is loaded onto your base page, the status bar shows that it is an untitled chapter with an untitled style sheet. To protect your work, it is wise to save your style sheet, chapter, and publication files at this point.

IV

Real-World VENTURA Exercises

Because the styles in the Quick Format Roll-up do not have specific style names, these base styles cannot be overwritten. Thus, you can reuse the Quick Format style for another project or recall a modified invitation style for a future project.

To save the style sheet, select Save Style Sheet As from the **L**ayout menu. By saving the style sheet, you retain the page layout information (such as page size, paragraph tags for formatting text, and page layout characteristics such as margins and columns). Type **holiday.sty** as the name of the style and press Enter.

Select Save Chapter from the **L**ayout menu. Save the chapter as **holiday** and press Enter. The positions of graphics frames and text frames, as well as the actual text files, are saved as part of the chapter information.

VENTURA does not save graphic files or text files as an integrated part of the document. Instead, VENTURA maintains a list of *pointers* that refer to the files' original location so that it can use them when the chapter is opened.

Even though this is a one-page document, select **S**ave from the **F**ile menu. VENTURA saves the publication with the same name as the chapter file, unless you want to specify another name. Although publications usually contain more than one chapter, your invitation project will not.

Setting Up the Page

Before you begin working, you need to check the settings of your base page to make sure that they will work with your design. These settings include page size, margins, and number of columns. You need to check the paragraph tags assigned to your predesigned invitation, as well. These tags assign a type style and type size to elements such as body text and subheadings. VENTURA enables you to change any of these settings to fit your design.

Chapter Settings

To review the chapter settings for this pre-designed invitation style, select the **C**hapter Settings dialog box listed under the **L**ayout menu (see fig. 20.4). The pages are sized 5.5 inches wide and 4.25 inches high and arranged on an $8\,^1/_2 \times 11$-inch sheet size.

The pages are arranged so that the invitation can be printed from a printer and folded into its finished form. The diagram in the lower right corner of the dialog box shows how the individual pages are positioned in the $8\,^1/_2 \times 11$-sheet size. This sketch is important to the design of the invitation as you work in VENTURA.

You will refer to it to determine which page is the inside text page and which is the cover page. This dialog box also shows you that the page is arranged in *landscape* (horizontal) page format.

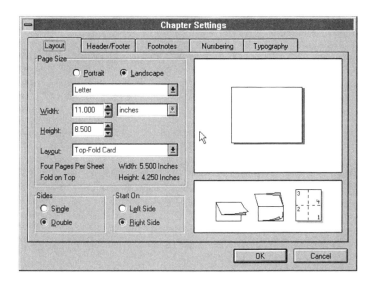

Figure 20.4
Chapter settings for a predesigned Top-Fold invitation style.

Frame Settings

Select **F**rame under the For**m**at heading to review the margins for your invitation base page (see fig. 20.5). The margins have been set to form one small text box to the right side of the page.

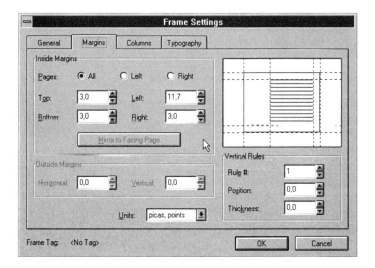

Figure 20.5
Frame format for the invitation style.

Paragraph Formats

Paragraph tags make it easy to format the elements of long documents such as body text and subheadings, but you will also use paragraph tags to design your holiday card. Paragraph tags designate type style, type size, alignment, spacing, and other text features.

This predesigned style sheet has the following five preformatted paragraph tags:

✔ **Body Text.** Times New Roman, 12 point

✔ **Bullet.** Times New Roman, 12 point with Bullet Effect

✔ **Main Heading.** Times New Roman, 24 point, Bold

✔ **Minor Heading.** Times New Roman, 12 point, Bold

✔ **Subheading.** Times New Roman, 16 point, Bold

You can use these paragraph tags to format the text in your invitation, or you can modify them to fit your design. The design of this invitation is fairly simple and does not have many text elements. To add paragraph tags to this style, you select the Manage Tag List option from the Format menu. If you select the Add Tag option, you are given the option of naming your own tag (refer to fig. 20.5). As a starting point for your modifications, you will also select the existing tag that most closely resembles the tag you want to create.

Building Your Invitation Design

When you are ready, begin entering your text into the text frame provided on the base page. Select either Text tool and click on the base page. The insertion point, a blinking cursor, is placed just before the square, hollow box which denotes the end of the text. When you begin to type in any empty frame, VENTURA always positions the insertion point at the beginning of the first line of the frame.

You need not press Enter at the end of a line; VENTURA automatically *wraps* text to the next line. In the sample invitation, though, the Enter key has been pressed to break the lines at specific points in the text (see fig. 20.6).

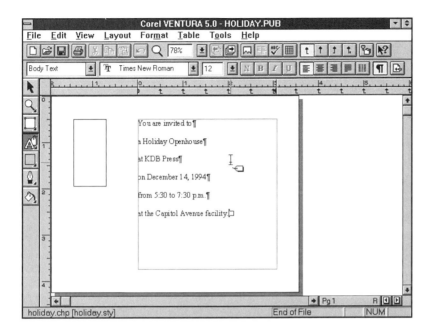

Figure 20.6
Type text into the
text frame on the
base page.

Using Paragraph Tags

As text is typed onto the base page, it is automatically tagged as Body Text and
takes on the attributes of the Body Text paragraph tag. In this example, the text
has the attribute of the font Times New Roman, with a point size of 12 points.
The type is also specified as flush with the left margin.

Modifying a Paragraph Tag's Attributes

The preset paragraph tags are a foundation on which to build your own design.
You need to change the type style to a larger font size for better readability. And
because this is a party invitation, you will want to dress the design with a decorative type style.

To modify the predesigned body text paragraph tag, select the Tagged Text tool
and position it anywhere in the line of text (see fig. 20.7).

Real-World VENTURA Exercises

Figure 20.7
Insert your Tagged
Text tool in a line
of text.

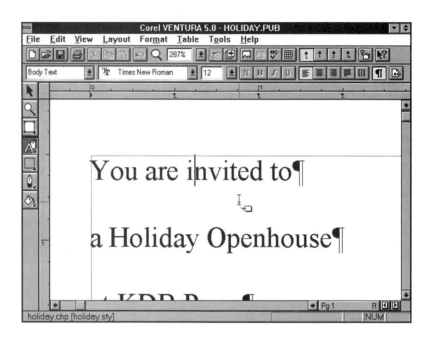

Choose Paragraph from the Format menu. The Paragraph Settings dialog box is displayed (see fig. 20.8). The Character tab lists information relating to the selected paragraph tag such as the fonts, type size, type style, color, and other attributes.

Figure 20.8
The Character tab
in the Para-
graph Settings
dialog box.

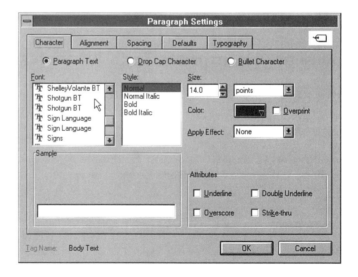

For this sample invitation's holiday theme, a more decorative font seems appropriate. You might select a font such as Shelley Volante. Scroll upward through the list of fonts and select it. The point size of the type in this example is increased to 14 points. To make this change, place the cursor in the size box and type **14**. Figure 20.9 shows the modified text.

 Check that Shelly Volante BT is installed or substitute another font.

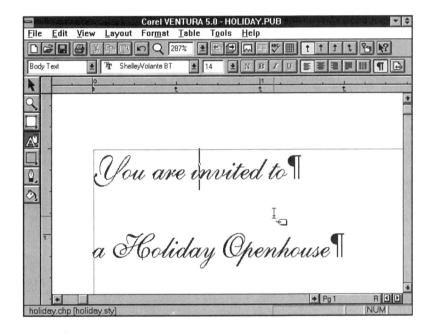

Figure 20.9
Body text is changed to a new font.

In VENTURA, by changing the attributes of a paragraph tag you change all text blocks that have that paragraph tag. In this example, all body text was affected by changing the font to Shelley Volante and type size to 14 point because all text had the Body Text tag.

Modifying an Individual Character of Type

VENTURA enables you to modify individual characters, words, or lines of type. By using the Freeform Text tool, you can alter the font and the size of your selected text without affecting other text on the page.

To add a little flair to your invitation design, you can increase the point size of the initial capital letter. Select the Freeform Text Tool and highlight the *Y* in the word You (see fig. 20.10). Choose Selected Text from the Format menu. In the Selected Text Attributes dialog box, change the type size to 24 point to make a large capital letter (see fig. 20.12).

Figure 20.10
Highlight the
character you
want to modify.

Figure 20.11
The Selected
Text Attributes
dialog box.

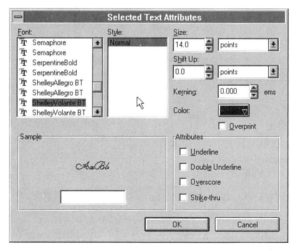

With VENTURA, you can modify not only the font and size of individual characters, but also the spacing between characters, words, or lines of type. In this invitation example, you might want to bring the letters *ou* closer to the large capital letter *Y*. Use the cursor to select the letters *Y* and *o*. On the Format menu,

choose the Selected Text option. Locate the Kerning option in the Selected Text Attributes dialog box. *Kerning* is the term used to describe the spacing between individual characters. A positive number increases the space between letters, and a negative number decreases that space. For this example, type **–0.080** ems in the box. (*Ems* is a typographical unit of measurement the width of the letter *m*.) This value will bring the letters closer together by a fraction of an em. Change this number to produce the look you want for your design.

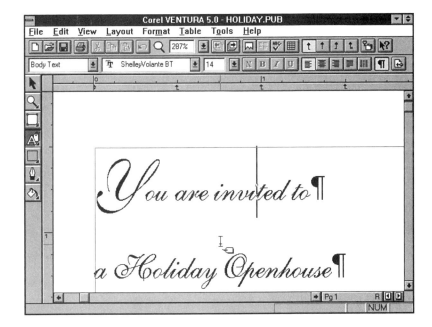

Figure 20.12
Completed text alterations.

Adding a Graphic

Although decorative text and special text effects are very effective design tools, a graphical element, such as a piece of clip art, decorative border, or even a photo, adds visual impact to the design of your invitation.

VENTURA supports a wide range of graphic formats: Corel Draw Graphic (*.cdr), Windows Bitmap (*.bmp), Computer Graphics Metafile (*.cgm), Paint-brush (*.pcx), Encapsulated Postscript (*.eps), and TIFF (*.tif), to name a few.

To place a graphic into the predrawn graphic frame on the base page, select the frame with the Pick tool (see fig. 20.13). From the **F**ile menu, select Load **G**raphic or press F10 to display the Load Graphic dialog box (see fig. 20.14).

Figure 20.13

Selecting the graphic frame.

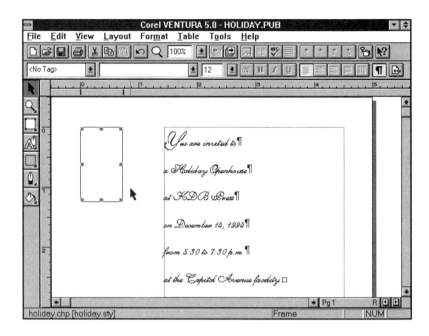

Figure 20.14

The Load Graphic dialog box.

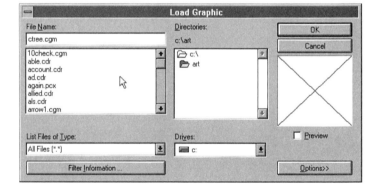

If you are looking for a specific type of graphic file, use the List Files of **T**ype box to display only the files with the correct extension. If you are looking for a file but do not know the correct extension, select All Files (*.*) to display all the files in the directory.

In the File Name box, select the name of the file you want to import, and press Enter. The graphic will appear in the selected graphic frame. Figure 20.15 shows the Christmas tree image (in a Computer Graphics Metafile format) selected for this example.

Figure 20.15
The graphic file is placed in the selected graphic frame on the page.

You might need to resize the graphic to fit your invitation design. To reduce or enlarge the graphic, click on one of the frame's handles and drag it to the correct size. In the example, the lower right handle was dragged downward to make the frame larger (see fig. 20.16). The graphic automatically fills the new frame size.

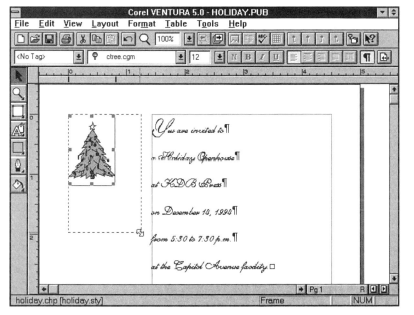

Figure 20.16
The resized graphic frame.

Adding a Front Cover

You have used the invitation format base page to design the inside text portion of your invitation project. An invitation is not complete, though, without a front cover. In this project, the front cover is not designed around the base page. The front cover is a new page added to your chapter, and you build the design from an empty page.

To begin designing a front cover for this invitation, refer to the page layout information provided in the Chapter Settings dialog box shown in figure 20.4. The front cover of the folded invitation corresponds to page 3 in the diagram. When you loaded the Quick Format Roll-up style, only a base page was loaded. To design a page three, you need to add pages to the base page.

To insert two more pages in your design, select the Pick tool. Select the Insert Pages command from the **L**ayout menu and type **2** as the number of pages to enter after the first page (see fig. 20.17). Click on OK to add a blank page for page 2 and the cover page, page 3.

Figure 20.17
The Insert Pages
dialog box.

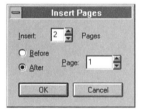

Adding a Frame

To design the cover, page down to the third page. To type text or enter a graphic on this page, you must add a frame. This page is a continuation of the base page, and any new elements must be contained in a free frame.

This page is actually an extension of the first page. If there were more text, it would flow to this page. New text must be entered into a free frame—not just because the attributes are different.

To add a free frame, select the Frame tool and click on the page at the point at which you want your frame to begin. You can draw the frame at any point on the page. For this example, draw a frame the size of the entire base page (see fig. 20.18).

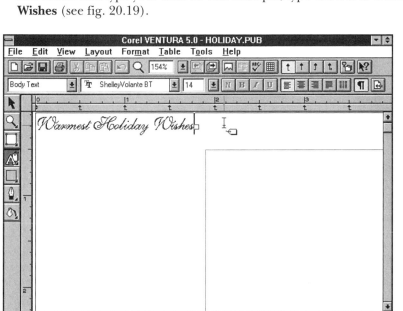

Figure 20.18
Adding a frame.

Adding Text to the Frame

To type text in the frame you have just drawn, select any text tool. Click in the free frame and type your text. In this example, type the words **Warmest Holiday Wishes** (see fig. 20.19).

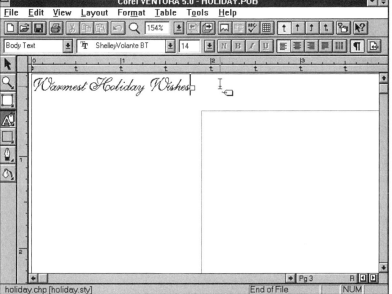

Figure 20.19
Typing new text in the frame.

Formatting the New Text

The design of this invitation calls for the front-cover text to be centered on the page. As you typed this text onto the page, it was designated as Body Text and took on its attributes. The Body Text attributes are flush left. Changing the Body Text attributes to be centered would change the text on the inside page.

To center the cover text, first use the Tagged Text tool to select a point in the newly typed text. Click on the arrow next to the Tag list and select the Main Heading tag (see fig. 20.20).

Figure 20.20
Apply the Main Heading tag to the selected text.

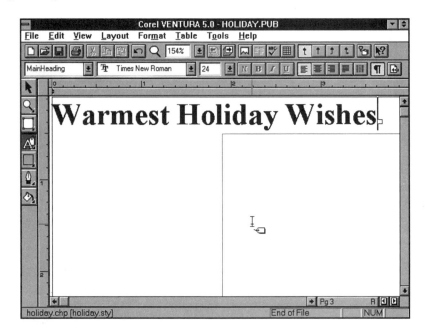

The Main Heading tag changed the point size to 24 points. The next step is to center the text in the frame. To center the text horizontally and vertically in the frame, use the Tagged Text tool and select a point in the text line. Open the Paragraph Settings dialog box from the For**m**at menu. Select the Alignment tab and locate the **H**orizontal and **V**ertical alignment buttons (see fig. 20.21). Press the centered buttons for each alignment option and click on OK. The text is centered in the frame, as shown in figure 20.22.

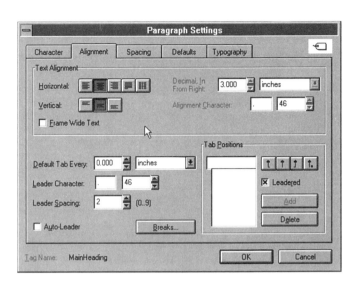

Figure 20.21
The Alignment tab in the Paragraph Settings dialog box.

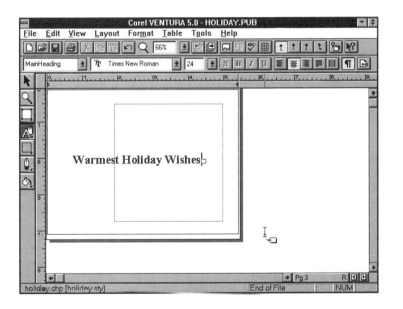

Figure 20.22
Changed text attributes center text vertically and horizontally.

Adding a Ruling Box

A graphic element does not have to be a drawing or a photo. If you do not have access to clip-art files, you can add impact to your design with the tools provided in VENTURA. Any frame in VENTURA can be formatted to have a ruling line above, below, above and below, or completely around the frame. A ruling box does not have to be a single line, but can be a combination of up to three lines with varying thicknesses.

As the invitation's final design element, add a ruling box to the invitation by using the Pick tool to select the frame. Select Ruling **L**ines... from the For**m**at Menu to display the Ruling Lines dialog box (see fig. 20.23).

Figure 20.23
The Ruling Lines
dialog box.

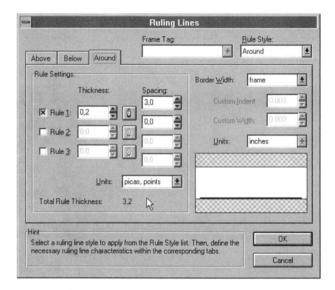

Click the arrow next to the **R**ule Style option and select Around from the drop down list. The Around tab is displayed. Click the Rule **1** radio box and specify the ruling line thickness to be **6** points or 0,6 picas. Enter the value of **4** picas in the top Spacing box. This puts three picas of space between the frame edge and the two-point ruling line. Press Enter to add this ruling box around the frame.

You can change the thickness and color of your ruling box in VENTURA (see Fig. 20.24). To add a more decorative border, look through the clip-art files on your computer and place the appropriate border into its own frame on your page by following the Christmas tree example, discussed earlier.

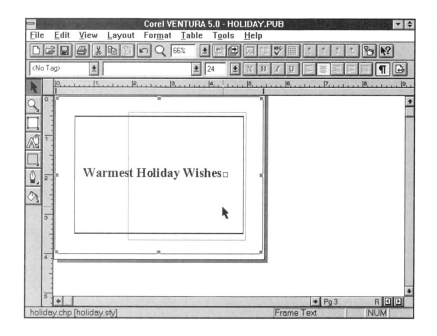

Figure 20.24
A ruling box around the frame.

Printing Your Design

When you have completed your cover design, you can print the finished invitation. Select **P**rint from the **F**ile menu. Press the **O**ptions button, and you will see a preview of your design (see Fig. 21.25).

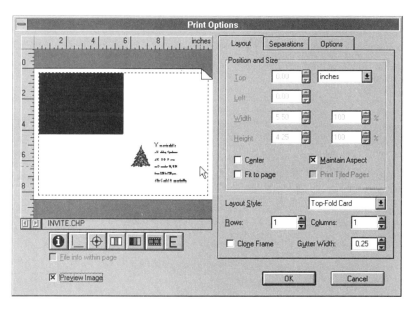

Figure 20.25
Preview your design in the Print Options dialog box.

Real-World VENTURA Exercises

Double-click on OK to print the invitation.

You can print the finished design to your printer and use the invitation straight from the printer. You can also produce the finished artwork from your laser printer or send the file to a service bureau for high-resolution output before taking the artwork to a commercial printer.

Several options in the Print Options box, such as those for adding crop marks, registration marks, and file information to the page, would be helpful to a commercial printer who needs to register the artwork if it is being printed in more than one color. This sample invitation is based on an $8 \frac{1}{2} \times 11$-inch page size, and these informational items appear only when you print to a larger page size or send the file to a service bureau.

Chapter Snapshot

Building a newsletter involves more than just knowing and understanding VENTURA. You will need to understand the entire publishing process. In this chapter, you learn to do the following:

This chapter looks at the entire production process involved when you publish a long document with many contributors, such as a newsletter.

CHAPTER

21

Building a Newsletter

You see newsletters of various sorts every day. They are a cost-effective way to communicate ideas and promote activities to the world at large. Thanks to today's word processor and desktop publishing programs, anyone with a computer can put out a newsletter. Unfortunately, sometimes people seem to be putting out a newsletter without any thought of what they are trying to achieve.

This chapter looks at the production of newsletters and what the process involves. It suggests ways to plan a newsletter—the whos, whats, and whys of production—and shows you how you can use VENTURA to produce your newsletter quickly and effectively.

This chapter does not provide a step-by-step recipe for creating chapters, loading graphics, and so on, as these fundamentals are covered in earlier chapters. It does provide invaluable real-life pointers for the following:

- ✔ How to avoid typical traps and pitfalls

- ✔ How to improve the impression your newsletter makes

- ✔ How to control the production process

- ✔ How to make the most effective use of VENTURA

It also includes a short bibliography for further reference.

The examples used throughout this chapter come from *TAGline!*, which is produced by Data & Documents in the United Kingdom for the CorelVENTURA Users group and distributed worldwide. *TAGline!*, which has been described as a top-of-the-range newsletter, is a 32-page, full-color production mailed 10 times a year to members of user groups all over the world. At the opposite end of the scale are the newsletters produced for a community association or local church—four black-and-white pages issued each spring and fall. No matter what type of newsletter you are producing, this chapter is for you.

Planning and Controlling Your Newsletter

Whether you produce an annual newsletter or a daily news sheet, planning and controlling your newsletter is the most important aspect of newsletter production. Unless you plan what you are trying to achieve and keep close control of it at all stages, you will have more problems than you can imagine.

The first step is to ask yourself the following questions:

✔ What am I trying to communicate?

✔ How often do I need to send out our newsletter?

✔ Who will read our newsletter?

Production Schedule

With clear answers to these questions, you can fairly easily start planning the production of your newsletter. Your answers identify the sections you need to include in your newsletter and how often it must be produced each year. In addition, by asking who will read your newsletter, you identify any special groups that might affect your production schedule. What is the point of producing a newsletter during the school holidays, for example, when its purpose is to describe weekly school events for a Parent Teacher Association?

Holidays can have a dramatic effect on production and must be considered throughout the production cycle of newsletters. Remember personal holidays as well as the public ones. An "ideal" production schedule is pointless if you forget about the holidays of one of the key production people or a major public holiday. Christian holidays are well posted on calendars and diaries. Don't forget to consider the holidays of other religions.

When you have a date for the delivery of your finished newsletter, you are ready to calculate dates for the other stages of production. Work backward from the delivery date until you have all stages of production mapped out for each issue of the newsletter. Some of these stages overlap. You need to provide more time for the overlapping stages than you might originally have planned. You might need to consider the following types of questions:

✔ What method of delivery will I use, and how long will it take?

✔ How much time is needed to prepare for the mailing?

✔ How much time is needed to print and bind the newletter?

✔ How long does preparing original masters for reproduction take (including color separations, if you are using color)?

✔ How long does laying out the pages take?

✔ If my newsletter includes advertising, how is this going to be included? Do you need to allow additional time?

✔ How long does proofreading and editing the pages take?

✔ Do articles need to be typed or written? If so, how long will this take?

✔ How much time do I need to allow for correcting problems?

The answers to these questions will help you establish deadlines for each phase of the production schedule (see fig. 21.1). You can place these deadlines on a wall planner and resolve any conflicts with holidays or other work. Finally, be sure to provide a list of dates to everyone concerned, for reference.

You now have a production schedule that can be used to track the progress of each issue of your newsletter. This is not a static document. It can be modified in light of experience and when things that are beyond your control change. The important thing is that you have a way of monitoring what is happening—this is vital as time progresses.

Be realistic about dates. You will learn how to estimate the time required with more accuracy as time goes by, but start by erring on the side of caution. Things usually take longer than expected. And remember—when you miss one date, all the other dates tend to move as well.

IV

Real-World VENTURA Exercises

Figure 21.1
By producing a set of deadlines, you ensure that each stage of the production cycle can be monitored.

Outline flatplan issue date
February issue 31 - 30 November
March issue 32 - 30 November
April issue 33 - 31 December
May issue 34 - 31 January
June issue 35 - 28 February
July/August issue 36 - 31 March
September issue 37 - 31 May
October issue 38 - 30 June
November issue 39 - 31 July
December/Jan issue 40 - 31 August

Last advertising notification date
Final flatplan within one week of this date
February issue 31 - 31 December
March issue 32 - 31 January
April issue 33 - 28 February
May issue 34 - 31 March
June issue 35 - 30 April
July/August issue 36 - 31 May
September issue 37 - 31 July
October issue 38 - 31 August
November issue 39 - 30 September
December/Jan issue 40 - 31 October

Last Advertising artwork delivery date
Last date for confirmation of an insert
11 January for Feb issue 31
8 February for March issue 32
8 March for April issue 33
12 April for May issue 34
10 May for June issue 35
7 June for July/August issue 36
9 August for September issue 37
6 September for October issue 38
11 October for the November issue 39
8 November for the December/Jan issue 40

Last possible insert delivery date
Note inserts include agendas, letters, and other material sent out by the CVU as well as advertising inserts that have to be mailed with TAGline!
February issue 31 - 27 January
March issue 32 - 24 February
April issue 33 - 24 March
May issue 34 - 28 April
June issue 35 - 26 May
July/August issue 36 - 23 June
September issue 37 - 25 August
October issue 38 - 22 September
November issue 39 - 27 October
December/Jan issue 40 - 24 November

Building a Team

Seldom is a newsletter an individual effort, with one person writing, designing, laying out, editing, proofing, printing, and distributing the newsletter. Ordinarily, several people are involved, and molding these individuals into an effective team is one of the greatest challenges of effectively producing a newsletter.

This is not the time or place to provide you with great screeds of information on how to best utilize the people available to you. The plan you have produced has already laid the foundations for this team approach, however, as everyone understands the direction in which you are heading. Your challenge, and it remains your challenge, is to use the available people to the best advantage.

You should concentrate on the following key areas:

✔ Production of initial copy for the newsletter

✔ Copy editing and proofreading

✔ Reproducing the newsletter

✔ Distributing the newsletter

These apparently obvious divisions of labor are not always as straightforward as they seem, especially in a voluntary environment in which you rely on the good-will of others to get things done.

Production of Initial Copy for the Newsletter

Getting your initial copy is often the most difficult stage, as many people will volunteer but quite often fail to deliver on time or to deliver anything at all. Use your production plan to assist you when talking to people about writing copy, so that you can agree to realistic deadlines and then monitor their progress.

Organizing more copy than you need for each issue of your newsletter is advisable as protection against the possibility that some of the copy will not arrive. Keeping some copy for a future newsletter is much easier to do than getting additional copy written at short notice.

You might want to consider having some ready-made articles written—articles you can use in any issue of your newsletter. Keep them in reserve for times when you are short of copy. Keep a record of what you expect to receive, and when you expect to receive it. You can do this with a simple VENTURA document like the one shown in figure 21.2, which is used for tracking *TAGline!* articles.

Commissioned Articles (Updated 22 September 94)

Title	From	Commissioned	Due	Submitted	Notes
Simplify Tech Docs	Rick Altman	1/8/93	30/8/93	21/8/93	
Creating a three level index	Byron Canfield	30/8/93	9/9/93	9/9/93	
Turning the Tables	Byron Canfield	30/8/93	9/9/93	9/9/93	
Frame Anchoring Pt1	Byron Canfield	30/8/93	9/9/93	9/9/93	
Frame anchoring pt2	Byron Canfield	30/8/93	9/9/93	9/9/93	
For the record	Byron Canfield	30/8/93	9/9/93	9/9/93	
VPWIN Macro recorder	Byron Canfield	30/8/93	9/9/93	9/9/93	
Type matters - leaflets	David Woodward	1/8/93	14/3/94		
Face to Face - Souvenir	David Woodward	1/8/93	1/4/94		
Type matters - Books	David Woodward	1/8/93	1/5/94		
Face to Face - Stone series	David Woodward	1/8/93	1/6/94		
Type matters – History and design	David Woodward	1/11/93	1/7/94		
Face to Face - Galliard	David Woodward	1/8/93	1/8/94		
Face to Face - Lucida	David Woodward	1/8/93	1/9/94		
House style analysis of TAGline	Lesley Ward	10/12/92	31/12/94		Chased 3/10/94
Commonly confused words/phrases	Lesley Ward	10/12/92	31/10/94		Chased 3/10/94
Utilities	Kathy Lang	1/9/93	1/10/93		
Wish List	Alex Gray	YES	1/11/94		Next one to be published following release of VP5 to show what they missed and what they didn't
Beginners Series	Kathy Lang	8/2/94	18/2/94		Start in March issue if we can find space; include some beginners' Q&A anyway
TAGline Production	Edward Brown	1/8/93	1/10/93		
Making a CD	Mark Langley	26/1/94	15/3/94		Chased 23/5/94
Committee members' profiles	Anne Gray to chase	26/1/94	1/2/94		Six published, more to follow Issues 26 and 28
The future of printing	Bob Kent	31/3/94	1/4/94	28/6/94	Received and to be published Issue 30
Beginners Q&A	Bob Kent	yes	regular		First batch received and in issue 22
Beginners Hints & Tips	Bob Kent	yes	regular		
Offcuts from the Printers floor	Bernard Harrison	yes	regular		First one received - more to follow Issue 26 received, issue 27 onwards probably one page each
Shipboard Publishing	Kevin Slater	1/2/94	15/3/94		Seems to have gone back to the ship without sending us the article still chasing
Word definitions	Phil Benjamin	yes	regular		First batch received 1/3/94 - more to follow
Hints and Tips	Alex Gray	1/2/94	15/3/94		
TrueType article	Ian Chivers	3/3/94	10/3/94	10/6/94	
Adobe Acrobat	Ian Chivers	3/3/94	31/5/94		Ian writing this at the moment
Something on typesetters	Ian Chivers	??/6/94	30/7/94		Ian writing this at the moment
Common Phrases	Ian Chivers	3/3/94	ongoing		ALL committee members to send their words to Ian ASAP
Imposition Software	Bob Kent				Need to arrange software and what is to be done and let Bob know
Document production	Tracey Palmer		20/6/94		May make two articles starting Issue 27
DTP in Colour	Gary Brown		1/7/94		Interesting tech item on automation
Q&A images inc screen shots	Ed Brown	3/9/94	7/9/94		For issue 28
362 review	Richard Bater	23/8/94	6/9/94		
Puzzles	Michael Mepham	23/8/94	28/9/94		Christmas issue - puzzles plus description of how VP is used to produce them
User Story	Patrick Dawson	23/8/94	10/10/94		Christmas issue - How VP is used for travel guides - some colourful pictures
Adobe Illustrator	Bernard Harrison	23/8/94	10/10/94		Software and book sent
Stylewriter	Fiona Vincent/Peter Isaac	23/8/94		10/10/94	
Lexmark 4039R Plus printer	Ed Brown	1/9/94	7/9/94		Issue 28 - from Susannah Bourne at Lexmark
Unimatriser 2	Various				Issue29 - From Contemporary software Robert Humphrey
Logitech colour scanner	Jeff Tang	1/9/94	13/10/94		Issue29 - from Logi UK Victoria Thoroughgood
Slide making and output	Paul Marchant	23/8/94	27/9/94		Paul is at Proteus Designs
Glossary and printing article	Prof Isaac	1/9/94		15/9/94	
Corel Flow	Brian Rees	6/9/94	1/10/94	3/10/94	Issue 30
Draw Plus from Serif					Serif Simon Rudkin

Figure 21.2

Keeping track of expected articles is essential.

A very effective tactic, especially in a voluntary environment, is to get the person submitting the copy to set his or her own deadline for submission. Agreeing on a date before the deadline, when you will talk to them to check that everything is OK, is also useful.

When you use this approach, the person writing the copy has a greater incentive to meet the self-imposed deadline because he or she knows that you are relying on him or her. This approach also gives you the opportunity to check on progress before the deadline and, if a problem exists, to make alternative arrangements.

Copy Editing and Proofreading

If you look closely enough, every example of printed matter seems to have mistakes. The mistakes often go unnoticed, but sometimes they are glaringly obvious. Another fact of life is that we rarely notice our own mistakes until it is too late to correct them.

Copy editing and proofreading are designed to eliminate the errors and to improve the quality of what is printed. In essence, the copy editor makes sure that the text conforms to correct language usage and is technically accurate, whereas the proofreader attempts to spot errors, such as references to pictures that do not exist.

By the very nature of the job, especially when you use DTP, these two roles overlap and are difficult to distinguish. You should not worry if you cannot tell the two roles apart, as it is the process of checking, and more importantly correcting, that needs to be instilled into your production process. House style, discussed later in this chapter, is a fundamental tool that can assist you in the copy editing process.

Do not try to proofread your own writing or editing. If you made a mistake in the first place, you probably won't spot it when you are proofreading. You will have the same mental blind spot the second time around. This is particularly true of spelling and misuse of language, which one rarely ever spots.

Reproducing the Newsletter

Unless you are going to print every copy of your newsletter on your laser printer, you need to consider how the newsletter will be reproduced. You thought about this when you considered the production schedule because the method of reproduction affects both the time and resources required.

Many successful newsletters are simply photocopies, folded and stapled, but even for these newsetters, you need to consider whether to do the job yourself or get someone else to do it for you. The decision is strongly influenced by whether you have the equipment and time necessary to carry out the task. The important thing is to discuss the reproduction method with whomever is going to do the work for you. This allows you to decide who will do what so you can use your time and money efficiently when reproducing your newsletter.

Do not assume, simply because you can do something with VENTURA, that this is the only way—or the best way—to do it. Often, an experienced printer can achieve the same thing with ease and save you a great deal of time, effort, and money.

Efficient use of time and money is particularly important when the newsletter is going to be printed rather than photocopied. The printing process—with its imagesetting, platemaking, and impositions—adds an additional level of complexity with which many DTP users are not familiar. By talking with your printer, you can to understand the process and provide what is needed to ease the production process.

Distributing the Newsletter

The final stage—distributing the newsletter—hardly seems to need a mention in its own right. Consideration does need to be given to this stage early in the production phase, however, because it can dramatically influence schedules and reproduction.

If your newsletter is to be delivered by hand, few considerations are necessary because almost any page size is acceptable. Indeed, one benefit of distributing newsletters in this way is that they do not have to conform to a particular format. Nevertheless, you might need to ensure that the newsletter is stapled, not folded, so that nothing is lost.

If you are going to mail your newsletter, you need to consider such things as the weight of the paper, bulk mailing (to minimize postage costs), the size of the newsletter (so that it fits a standard envelope), and whether to include additional inserts. If inserts are included in a newsletter that is being mailed, placing the inserts in the newsletter before you put the newsletter in the envelope makes the job easier.

Examine postal rates carefully. You can often get dramatic savings on postage by selecting the correct way to mail the newsletter. In some countries, for example, you can halve postage costs by sending newsletters as *printed papers*, a method requiring only that the envelope remain unsealed.

With this method, you not only save on postage but you also save time because you don't have to seal each envelope. Remember that this method is not acceptable if the contents fall out and get lost.

The Flatplan

A *flatplan* is a visualization of the way your newsletter will appear. As you can see from figure 21.3, a flatpan shows every page in the newsletter, what is on the page, and the state of production for each section of the newsletter.

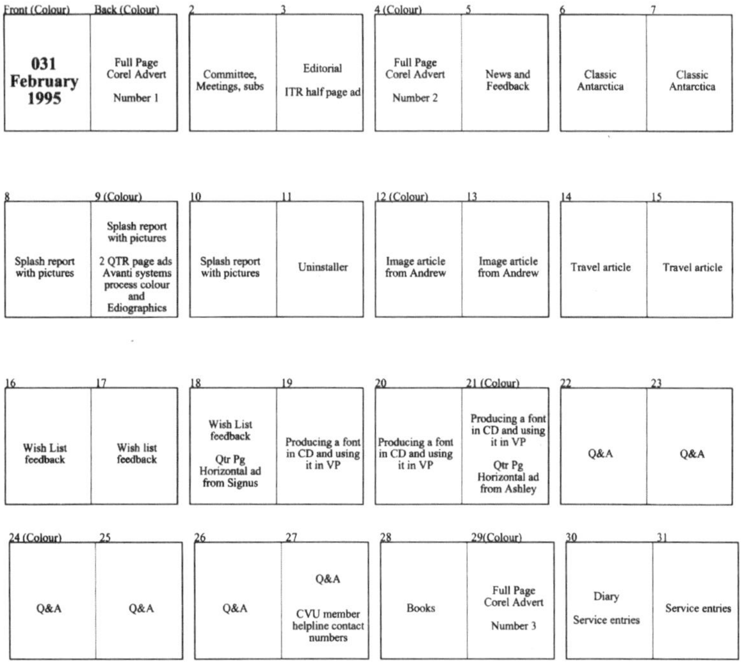

Figure 21.3
A flatplan provides a visual idea of your newsletter and includes brief tracking details.

continues...

Front (Colour)	Back (Colour)	2	3	4 (Colour)	5	6	7
031 February 1995	Full Page Corel Advert Number 1	Committee, Meetings, subs	Editorial ITR half page ad	Full Page Corel Advert Number 2	News and Feedback	Classic Antarctica	Classic Antarctica

8	9 (Colour)	10	11	12 (Colour)	13	14	15
Splash report with pictures	Splash report with pictures 2 QTR page ads Avanti systems process colour and Ediographics	Splash report with pictures	Uninstaller	Image article from Andrew	Image article from Andrew	Travel article	Travel article

16	17	18	19	20	21 (Colour)	22	23
Wish List feedback	Wish list feedback	Wish List feedback Qtr Pg Horizontal ad from Signus	Producing a font in CD and using it in VP	Producing a font in CD and using it in VP	Producing a font in CD and using it in VP Qtr Pg Horizontal ad from Ashley	Q&A	Q&A

24 (Colour)	25	26	27	28	29(Colour)	30	31
Q&A	Q&A	Q&A	Q&A CVU member helpline contact numbers	Books	Full Page Corel Advert Number 3	Diary Service entries	Service entries

New Riders Publishing
INSIDE SERIES

Figure 21.3
...continued

STATUS
Issue 31 February 1995
Updated 28 December 94

Page	Title	From	Rcvd	Layout	Check1	Check2	Proof	Seps	Date	Filename	Notes
1	front								28/11/94	31FRONT	
2	VPUINFO	EB	EB	EB		N/A			28/11/94	31INFO	
3	Editorial	EB	EB	EB					28/11/94	31EDIT	
4	Corel Ad	Corel	Border	N/A	N/A	N/A	N/A	N/A	28/11/94	31CRL1AD	
5	News and Feedback	EB	EB	EB		N/A			28/11/94	31NEWS	
6-7	Classic Antarctica	PN	KL						28/11/94	31PCD	
8-10	Splash report	KL	KL						28/11/94	31SPLASH	
11	Uninstaller	JT							28/11/94	31UNINST	
12-13	Images article	AndG	KL						29/11/94	31IMAGE	
14-15	Travel guides	PD	KL						28/11/94	31TRAVEL	
16-18	Wish List feedback	MJ							28/11/94	31WISHL	
19-21	Producing a font in CD for VP	JS	KL						28/11/94	31CD2VP	
24-27	Q&A	EB	EB	EB					28/11/94	QUERY31	
28	Books	Various							28/11/94	31BOOKS	Video review and DTP manual update
29	Corel Ad	Corel	Border	N/A	N/A	N/A	N/A	N/A	28/11/94	31CRL2AD	
30	Diary	EB	EB	EB					28/11/94	31DIARY	
31	Service ads	LF	EB	EB		N/A			28/11/94	31SENTRY	
32	Corel Ad	Corel	Border	N/A	N/A	N/A	N/A	N/A	28/11/94	31CRL3AD	

GENERAL NOTES
Advertising opportunities for CD/VP add on manufacturers, font producers, and image editing and image libraries

Creating a Flatplan

The process of creating a flatplan with VENTURA is straightforward. Create a frame and make it a two-column layout with a ruling line between the columns to simulate a two-page spread (see fig. 21.4).

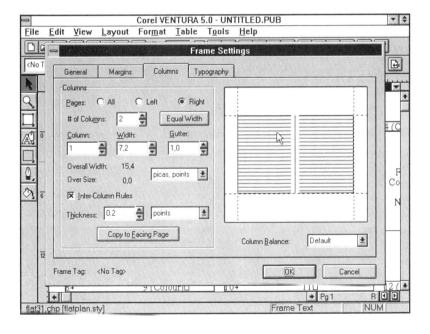

Figure 21.4
Create a small frame to represent facing pages.

Now, add above the frame a caption in which you can put the page numbers and any other information relevant to the specific page, such as whether color is used on that page (see fig. 21.5).

Figure 21.5
Use captions for information such as the page number and whether the page is a color page.

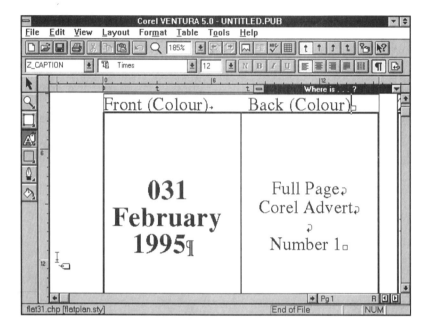

Duplicate the frame to create as many two-page spreads as you need for your newsletter. On the last page of your flatplan, create another frame and add a section for tracking the progress of each section of the newsletter. Use the ruler bar to help you set up the tab settings for the different entries (see fig. 21.6).

The final stage is to fill each frame with details from the corresponding page of the newsletter. Make sure that the first two "pages" are the front and back cover (refer to fig. 21.3) and that the other pages continue in sequence from page two. By using this technique, you can easily see what is on facing pages and how each section fits into the overall newsletter.

Create your newsletter in multiples of four pages (4, 8, 12, 16, and so on). In this way, you can print on both sides of the paper and then fold it before you staple the newsletter. If you plan to have a commercial outfit print the newsletter, ask them how to lay out your pages to maximize the available press and binding options, such as spot color and folding. Printing might be cheaper if your newsletter contains additional pages, as adding those pages might maximize the way the printer operates.

The position of the color pages in the flatplan shown in figure 21.3 is dictated by the way the pages are folded, ready for stapling. By talking to your commercial printer, you are able to distribute the color pages throughout the newsletter and not have them bunched together as they had previously been. This greatly enhances the appeal of the newsletter and gives the impression of more color, without additional cost.

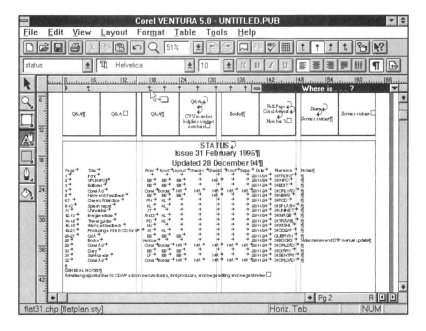

Figure 21.6

Use the ruler to set tabs for the tracking section on the flatplan.

Defining and Using Your House Style

As mentioned earlier, house style is a fundamental tool that must be mastered by anyone who is producing a newsletter. During the production process, you are responsible for ensuring that the newsletter reaches the necessary level of quality. By creating, maintaining, and conscientiously applying a house style, you can achieve the desired effect. Your house style dictates the appearance and consistency of your newsletters from month to month. But why use a house style at all?

Some mistakes are transparent and pass unnoticed unless you have a way of checking and correcting them. Your house style makes sure that the mistakes are checked and corrected. Having read this far, you have already passed over a problem with house style (deliberately introduced, I should add). You probably noticed the mistake, but only subconsciously. It didn't leap out at you, but had a negative affect on your understanding and appreciation of what was written. Look back at the third paragraph of Copy Editing and Proofreading on page 560 and read it again. Notice the incorrect use of the word *importantly.*

In the normal copy editing and proofreading process for a New Riders Publishing book, one of the editors would have spotted and corrected the mistake. This is one example of the type of thing a house style enables you to monitor and correct. Admittedly, the mistake is fairly subtle, but the same principle applies to spelling errors, titles, references, and so on. You can't check them and correct them if you don't know the rules that should be applied.

Your house style provides the rules by which your document is formatted, but it is not set in stone, never to be altered. House style changes over time, developing into a more comprehensive document than you originally envisaged. As you produce your newsletter, what has been overlooked in the house style document becomes obvious. You can make additions and changes to deal with new cases and exceptions to the existing rules. You need to start somewhere, however, because without a house style, all will be chaos.

Creating a House Style

House style has two main aspects. The first is the layout and the appearance of the text and graphics on the page. The second is the way in which text and graphics are edited so they are consistent within an issue and from one issue to the next.

The first aspect is effectively handled by VENTURA when you set up a style sheet. As discussed in Chapter 1, a VENTURA style sheet controls the overall appearance of your document. By using the same style sheets from issue to issue, you can produce a consistent appearance with ease.

Tip Remember to use the Next **T**ag feature in For**m**at, Pa**r**agraph (Ctrl+T) to help ensure a sequence to the way your tags are applied.

The second aspect is more difficult to implement and requires the production of a house-style manual. Although producing a manual might seem to require a major investment of time and resources, you can start with a simple manual and add to it over time. The important thing is to make sure that when you decide how a word is spelled or a phrase is formatted, you add that information to your style manual. At a minimum, your style manual should contain sections for the following topics:

✔ Spelling

✔ Punctuation and capitalization

✔ Grammar

✔ Abbreviations

✔ Formatted words and phrases, such as product names, book titles, and foreign words

✔ Dates, times, numerals, mathematics, and units

✔ Quotations, references, and titles

✔ Reference works to be consulted

Other things that might be appropriate for your particular newsletter include guidelines for sexist and racist language, legal aspects, or the use of extracts. Your manual should contain sections for all relevant topics.

Spelling

Consistency in spelling is important. Are you going to use standard British English? American? Australian? Specify which dictionary to use to check spelling, and specify whether words should end with *-ise* or *-ize*. Document your rules for foreign words that have been Anglicized.

Punctuation and Capitalization

Although lowercase is commonly used for such terms as type 2, Newton's laws, and so on, you should make a conscious decision about whether to follow this convention or use uppercase initial letters.

How will you capitalize headings? Will only the first word be capitalized, as in "The first and last?" Will all important words be capitalized, as in "The First and Last?" Or will all words be capitalized, as in "The First And Last?" If you capitalize all important words, how do you define the important words? What happens when punctuation is introduced into a heading, as in "Sunday: A day of rest?" When do you use uppercase letters for phrases, such as The Church or the Government? What about product names, titles, and so on?

What about punctuation? Will you use commas, like this, for subordinate clauses? When are commas to be used at the beginning of a sentence, such as sentences that start with phrases like "However,…?" What about commas in lists? Do they precede *and*, *but*, and so on? Or are they omitted?

What about *nested punctuation*, such as quotation marks, brackets, dashes, and the like? Do they remain the same or do they change from single to double quotation marks, round to square brackets, and so on?

What about the use of semicolons and colons? Where should they be used, and where should they be avoided?

Grammar

Grammar is the use of words and the order in which they are applied to construct sentences. One example of which word to use is the use of *important* and *importantly*. Other examples are the correct uses of *that* and *which*, *since* and *because*, and *while* and *although*.

Include guidelines for the use of plural verbs with group nouns such as *the orchestra*, and with words such as *none* and *any*.

Beware of words that are often confused, such as *militate* and *mitigate* or *alternate* and *alternative*.

Abbreviations

Which words will be abbreviated, and what are the acceptable forms of abbreviation? Should abbreviations end in a period or not (USA or U.S.A., for example)?

Should abbreviations be upper- or lowercase, or should they vary depending on the type of abbreviation? Are there any precedents for the way abbreviations are applied, such as those for *Système International* (SI) units and numbers discussed later.

Many abbreviations are widely used and need no explanation (examples include etc., e.g., nb., and the like). Others will have to be introduced and defined. You must decide whether having an abbreviation for words or phrases is justified. Do not assume that your reader will know an abbreviation simply because you commonly use it.

You should also decide whether to treat contractions that include the last letter (such as St.) in the same way you treat abbreviations.

What do you do about several consecutive abbreviations, such as "Co. Ltd."? Do you include the periods or do you avoid abbreviation?

Most publications contain a limited number of abbreviations and contractions. Often the best approach is simply to make a list of those that are acceptable and keep it up to date, adding new ones as they occur.

Formatted Words and Phrases (Product Names, Book Titles, Foreign Words)

Are product names formatted as they appear in the product literature, together with copyright and trademark symbols on every occurrence? Is a full acknowledgement made, or are generic terms used? Is a single uppercase letter enough to distinguish a proprietary name, or do you use italics? What do you do about names such as Hoover and Xerox, which have become generic descriptors?

Do you put foreign phrases in italics, quotations marks, or leave them unformatted? If you put them in italics, what do you do about words already in italics? Are commonly used foreign phrases treated the same way?

Do you abbreviate titles such as Doctor? What do you do about the difference between MD, PhD, DD? Do they all get the prefix *Dr*?

Dates, Time, Numbers, Mathematics, and Units

Should dates and time be in full or abbreviated? Should dates be abbreviated to 12/6, 6/12, 12/6/95, 6/12/95? Or should you use an unambiguous abbreviation, such as 12 Jun 95. Should the clock be in 24-hour format or have an a.m. and p.m. suffix? If a suffix, must the suffix always be present? How are the hours, minutes, and seconds separated from each other?

With numbers, when do you use numerals, such as 23, and when do you use words, such as twenty-three? Are numerals permissible at the end of a sentence? How are numbers represented: 10000, 10,000, or 10 000? Do you use scientific notation, such as 3.14×10^6?

Avoid using vague expressions like a billion. In the USA, this means a thousand million (1,000,000,000), but in the UK, France, and Germany, it means a million million (1,000,000,000,000), and the potential for confusion is readily apparent.

Should mathematical expressions be in the main body of the text—a/b—or on a separate line:

$$\frac{a}{b}$$

If in the main body of the text, should they be allowed to alter the line spacing or must they conform to the existing line spacing?

Traditionally, variables in equations are in italic type and constants are in normal type. Will you use these conventions or do you have reasons to adopt a different approach?

Will you use internationally accepted SI units or local units, such as pounds and ounces, feet and inches? If you use SI units, all abbreviations and contractions for different measurements are dictated by ISO (International Standards Organization) standards and you must use the abbreviations defined in these standards.

Decide when abbreviations are to be used and when they are to be avoided. Remember not to abbreviate phrases such as "the sample was then weighed in grams." When you use abbreviations for units, should the abbreviations follow directly after the numerals, as in 30ml, or should a space follow, as in 30 ml?

 Avoid using vague measurements like "a cup." State the volume to be used in units that are consistent with others used in the same article. Instead of "a cup," use a measurement such as 25 ml or 3 fl. Oz.

Quotations, References, and Titles

When quoting from other works, do you quote literally or do you make quotations conform to your house style? Are quotations enclosed in quotation marks or are they set in a different typeface, italics, or simply distinguished from the general text by context.

What form do any references you quote follow? Do they use a particular system, such as that provided by *Hart's Rules for Compositors and Readers,* or do you produce your own system of references? How are referenced items referred to in the text, and how are they presented at the end of the article? Do you use a number, letter, or phrase to link the references?

A similar consideration needs to be given to titles of books, films, newspapers, and other titled material. Do you make them conform to your house style? Are they formatted in italics? How do you reference them?

Reference Works To Be Consulted

However comprehensive your style manual, questions always arise. The style manual should state which reference books to consult, and the order of precedence for these books because they can provide conflicting information.

For English, use easily available works such as *Hart's Rules for Compositors and Readers*, the *Oxford English Dictionary*, and *A Dictionary of Modern English Usage* or American equivalents, such as the *Chicago Manual of Style* and *The Elements of Style*. You might want to include specialist works for different fields, such as journal abbreviations and medical terms.

Remember your target audience as you produce your style manual and select reference works. The style of English used throughout the world varies considerably. Documents produced in English are generally acceptable worldwide. American English is gaining wider acceptance, especially in the computer and technology fields.

Pay particular attention to detail if you are working in a language that is not your first language, as the customary use is often different. Beware of common pitfalls, such as referring to something as English when it is, in fact, British or American.

Anatomy of a Newsletter

Newsletters have the following readily apparent, common structure:

✔ Cover page with some sort of masthead

✔ Distinguishable sections, such as News, Letters, Diary, and so on

✔ Short articles (in relation to the length of the newsletter)

✔ Multiple columns (rarely single columns)

From the discussion of *TAGline!* and how it is produced, you can select the parts that interest you and incorporate them into the production of your own newsletter. At the same time, you can gain valuable insight into how you might be able to improve your own newsletter.

Now you will walk through the *TAGline!* newsletter, highlighting the relevant features and providing pointers as to how you might implement things in your own newsletter to get the maximum impact. After an overview of the general procedures for producing each issue of a newsletter, you will look at each section in *TAGline!* so that you can see how the whole thing fits together.

From Month to Month

After you produce your first newsletter, you will have a VENTURA publication that contains several different chapters for each section of the newsletter. You will

Real-World VENTURA Exercises

probably want to use some of these sections again for the next issue of the newsletter. You will want to copy forward the files that are of use to you, leaving behind those that are out-of-date.

VENTURA provides the ideal tool for doing this—its support for templates. Templates are covered in detail in Chapter 3, "Creating and Setting Up New Documents." To prepare for the issue of your newsletter, you should first archive your current issue by using Publication Manager, as described in Chapter 16, "Assembling Publications." Then use File, New (Ctrl+N) to open the New Publication dialog box, shown in figure 21.7.

Figure 21.7
The New
Publication
dialog box.

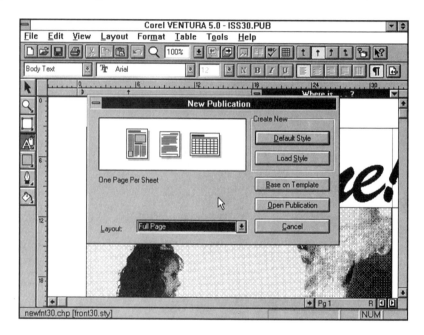

Select **B**ase on Template to display the Select Source Publication dialog box (see fig. 21.8).

Select the publication for the issue you have just archived and click on OK. You will see the Base on Template dialog box (see fig. 21.9).

Select the chapters and files you want to use for the next issue by double-clicking on the files you want included. A check mark appears alongside them. For those files that you do not want, make sure there is no check mark.

Choose a File **N**ame and a **D**irectory for the new publication, check the **C**opy all files box (see fig. 21.10), then click on OK.

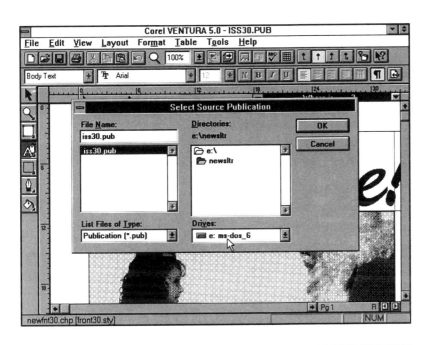

Figure 21.8
The Select Source Publication dialog box.

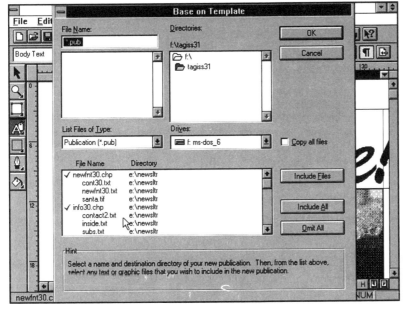

Figure 21.9
The Base on Template dialog box.

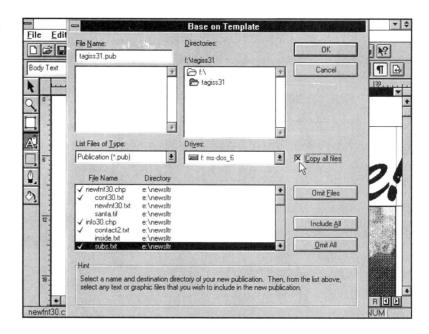

The files you have selected are copied to the new directory. If you do not check the **C**opy all files check box, the component files are not copied; instead, a new document is created with pointers to the original files. VENTURA's system of pointers is described in Chapter 1, "Introducing CorelVENTURA."

Some sections of the newsletter will not change from month to month, and you can safely leave pointers to the original files. An example of this is committee lists and contact details, which rarely change. You need only one copy of a chapter with these details.

Use the template facility to copy across chapters whose parts will change, and the **L**ayout, Add **N**ew Chapter option to add chapters that do not change. Placing the chapters that do not change in a different subdirectory is convenient, so that they can easily be found.

After you have copied across the files that you want, use the **F**ile, Pu**b**lication Manager to add any additional chapters and arrange them in the proper sequence.

Make sure that all the style sheets you need are stored in a separate subdirectory. Some months you will not use every style sheet. If they are not stored somewhere safe, you will find yourself searching your archives to find missing style sheets.

From Page to Page

Because the front cover of your newsletter is the first thing people see, it should make an immediate impact by combined use of text and graphics. Your masthead, which should be short and punchy, acts as a visual cue to your readers and identifies your newsletter (see fig. 21.11). You do not want to create an unwieldy or complicated title. The masthead is there primarily for identification, not communication.

Figure 21.11
The *TAGline!* masthead gives the newsletter a visual identity that readers come to recognize instantly.

The *TAGline!* masthead is deliberately linked to the table of contents by overlapping the exclamation mark with the Pantone Reflex Blue frame for the table of contents and issue details (see fig. 21.12). As a rule of thumb, you do best to left-align the masthead and use a heavy, condensed font with white space (no text or graphics) to the right of the masthead. This technique gives the masthead a feeling of openness.

Include the issue details only if they are likely to be referred to in the future. Remember that readers will interpret your issue details—Fall '94 becomes four issues a year, whereas Spring/Summer becomes two issues a year. If you don't need to reference issue details, leave them out. In the case of *TAGline!* and its forerunner, *VPU News*, six years of reference material are stored on VENTURA and CorelDRAW, and the ability to identify individual issues is important.

Figure 21.12

The exclamation mark overlaps the issue and table of contents panel.

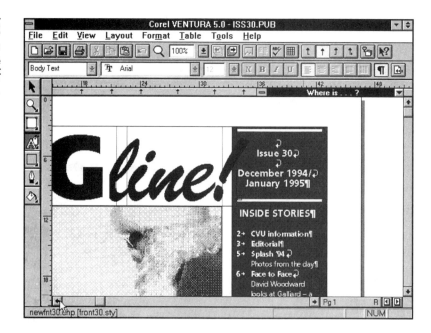

A table of contents is very useful for long newsletters but probably unnecessary for a short newsletter, which probably will be scanned. If you do include a table of contents, placing it on the front cover is customary. Make sure that the pages referenced are correct, and do not include articles that are on the same page as the table of contents (see fig. 21.13) because this is redundant information that only leads to confusion.

The use of color greatly enhances the appeal of a newsletter, but even two-color production can increase the cost dramatically. You might be able to have pages printed in bulk with one color and then have each issue of your newsletter overprinted. This is particularly applicable to repeating pages whose overall layout does not change. For the front cover, for example, you should be able to use preprinted pages containing the masthead and other repeating items.

With community-based projects, talking to your local printer is often worthwhile. He or she might be able to preprint some pages for you, at little or no cost, on the back of a job done for someone else.

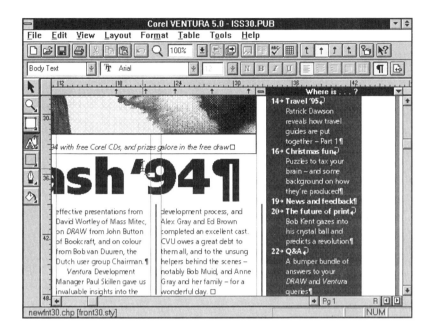

Figure 21.13
The table of contents should provide a teaser to the articles inside, to encourage people to read further.

If you are unable to use color printing, you might try varying the newsletter's appearance by using colored paper. Don't forget that with VENTURA you can have tints that add variation to the appearance of a black-and-white newsletter.

Adding an *International Standard Serial Number* (ISSN) to your newsletter gives it an authority that might otherwise be lacking and allows people to obtain it through libraries. To use an ISSN, however, you must first get permission from your local standard numbering agency.

After you have obtained the ISSN, you must deposit several copies of the newsletter with your national library to retain the right to use the ISSN. In addition, penalties for noncompliance exist. (The penalties vary from country to country.)

Inside the front cover is the traditional place for general information such as the ISSN, production details, committee lists, and so on. If the front cover does not include a table of contents, readers will expect to find one here. In figure 21.14, notice the use of tinted boxes to separate information and the use of a smaller typeface so more information can be included on the page.

Figure 21.14
Tinted boxes help to highlight different sections of information.

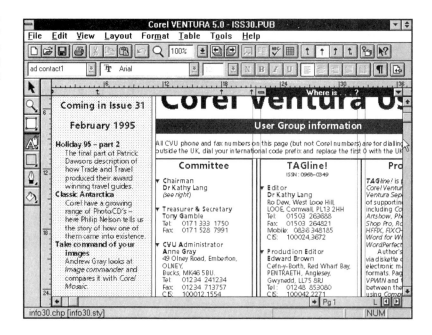

Smaller point sizes can be used in reference material; because readers look at this information only if they need to find something, they will accept the smaller point size. Choose a point size that does not strain the reader's eyesight but is noticeably smaller than the general text size.

Tables are often a way to present complex information quickly and easily, as shown in figure 21.15. Again, the use of tints helps the reader follow along the line of the table to find the item of interest and helps compensate for the smaller typeface.

Finally, a footer contains the page number and information about the newsletter. In the case of *TAGline!*, the issue and copyright details are included so they are always available to the reader. If your newsletter is not bound together, a numbering scheme, such as "1 of 6," tells readers how many pages they should have. To add your footer, use VENTURA's footer capabilities, discussed in Chapter 14, "Advanced Options for Chapter Formatting."

Try to put your page numbers on the outside edge of the page so they can be seen when you flick through the newsletter. Remember that you must have different settings for the right and left footers. Use the Mirror to Facing Pages option in the Header/Footer tab of the Chapter Setting dialog box (see fig. 21.16). Page numbers that are centered on the page make it difficult to find (quickly) the page you want.

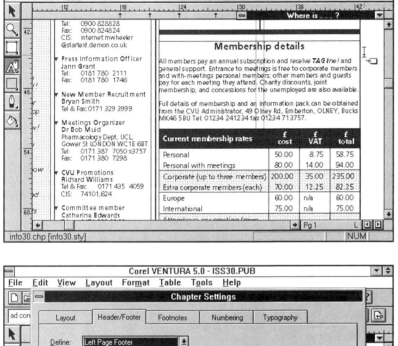

Figure 21.15
Tables are a
useful way to
present complex
information
in an easy-to-
understand
format.

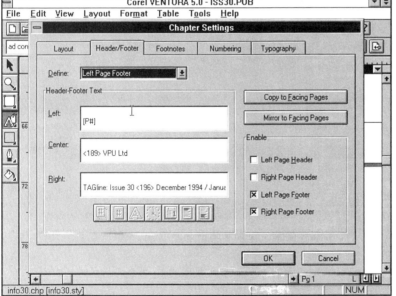

Figure 21.16
Include reference
information and
page numbers in
your footer,
mirroring them on
left and right.

Tip

You can place page numbers anywhere on the page by using VENTURA's cross-reference feature.

Right pages, the first pages people see as they turn through a newsletter, are therefore best for attention-grabbing items such as editorials. If you include advertising, right pages are also prime locations for ads. You should be charging a premium for "hot spots," such as the space below the editorial in figure 21.17 which appears on page three (the first page anyone sees after the front cover).

Figure 21.17

Make good use of page three, probably the most viewed page of any newsletter, after the front cover.

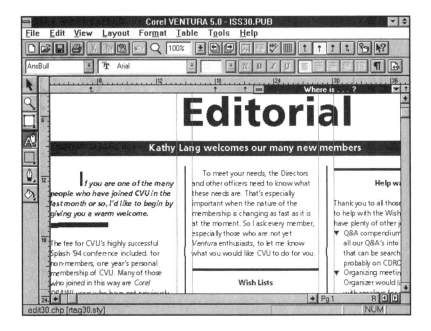

Headings do not have to be simply text. They can be logos, such as the one in figure 21.18, which introduces an article about typeface. What is important is that the device you use imparts meaning to the reader. Like the masthead, it does not have to say everything—with regular use, it becomes an icon that readers understand.

As you produce your newsletter, remember that readers will see it as a two-page spread, not as individual pages. You should aim for a balance across the facing pages. Remember to use VENTURA's facing page view (see fig. 21.19) to do an initial check of the spread's appearance. Do not rely solely on this view, however. Be sure to print the pages and look at them spread out in front of you.

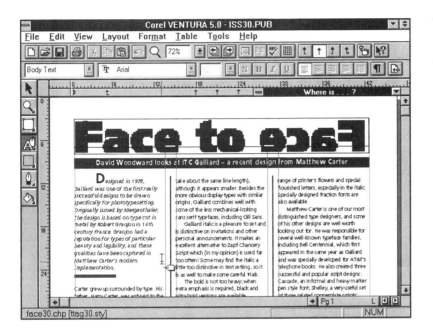

Figure 21.18
Logos or graphics can be used as headings for sections.

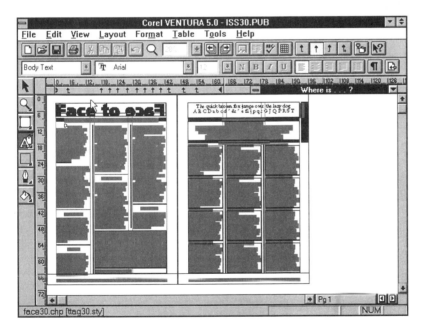

Figure 21.19
Use VENTURA's facing page view for an initial check of the appearance of a two-page spread.

Remember that readers might want to keep articles for future reference (especially from technical newsletters). Do your best to help the reader make the best use of the articles you provide. In figure 21.20, a blue tab bleeding off the edge of the page and containing the typeface name was used. The reader can photocopy the page and saved it in a folder for future reference. Over time, readers can collect these pages and build a comprehensive typeface reference library. This typeface library is then useful in its own right, as well as being part of the newsletter.

Figure 21.20
To help readers access information in the newsletter, provide appropriate keys, such as the reference tab on the right.

Block, or *pull*, quotes are a good way to attract attention to an article and draw the casual browser into reading the entire article. Make then stand out from your text by using a variety of emphasis (see fig. 21.21). In this example, color, size, and italics are combined with generous white space to attract attention. Try to place pull quotes in the body of a paragraph, not between paragraphs, to avoid the possibility that readers will mistake them for subheadings that introduce a new topic.

Tip

Too many pull quotes detract from any article, however, and make it difficult to read. Try to limit your pull quotes to one or, at most, two per page. Keep pull quotes short.

Don't forget to include examples and illustrations. The old saying that a picture is worth a thousand words should always be in the back of your mind. Whether you use a photograph or some other device, such as clip art or a cartoon, make sure

that the text does not get too close to the illustration. If the illustration includes a great deal of text, consider adding a ruling line to help emphasize the division, as shown in figure 21.22, which shows the distinction of the screen capture from the body of the article.

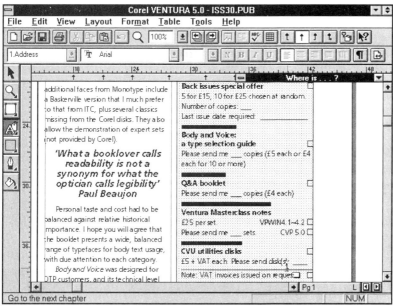

Figure 21.21
A pull quote should attract the browser's attention and encourage him or her to read the entire article.

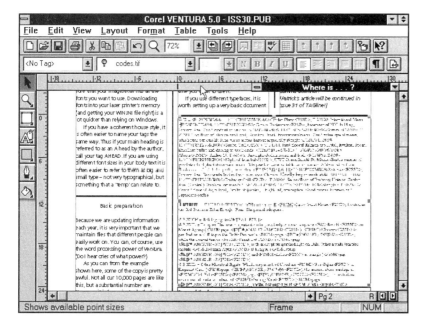

Figure 21.22
You sometimes need to add ruling lines to distinguish the screen capture from the body of the article.

IV

Real-World VENTURA Exercises

Use CorelMOSAIC to build a complete library of the files you use for illustration. These files can then be accessed easily from the Mosaic Roll-up in VENTURA so that you can preview all the graphics you might want to use.

Because readers get a sense of ownership and a feeling of well-being if they are included in your newsletter, make sure that your readership is involved. Earlier, you saw that putting the editorial, if you have one, on the third page is a good idea because this is one of the first pages read. Another way to involve your readers is to get them to contribute, through a feedback or letters page. Here, your readers can communicate directly with you and you can talk back, while still remaining in control of the newsletter's content.

If you include a feedback or letters page, remember to treat your readers with respect. This means including both good and bad responses together with polite correction, when necessary. Readers will not accept that everything is good but are quick to leap to your defense if criticism gets too strong. When in doubt, err on the side of caution and print a good and bad letter side-by-side.

Don't be afraid to leave space at the end of articles and columns (see fig. 21.23). If you pack every last centimeter of every column with text, your newsletter will start to resemble wallpaper and become intimidating and oppressive. By leaving space throughout the newsletter, you allow the text and graphics to breathe and make your publication attractive and easy-to-read.

One of the best books you can obtain for hints and tips on improving your documents is *One Minute Designer*, by Roger Parker. If you buy only one book on design, this has to be the one.

Regular features, such as diaries, should always appear in the same position in the newsletter. The two inside back pages of the newsletter are ideal for this sort of material because they are easy to find. With pages such as diary pages, events can easily get lost (see fig. 21.24). Try to emphasize those that are of current interest, while providing sufficient advance notice of forthcoming events. Use a different typeface for your own events or pull the events out into a separate tinted box to draw attention to them.

If you are not using the back page of your newsletter for advertising, this is an ideal place for your diary information. It is also an ideal place for mailing information, if you are going to use one of the newsprint mailing options available in

many countries. With these options, you can often get cheaper mailing rates, provided that the newsletter is not sent in an envelope; the newsletter must be folded and have space for mailing details, and the back page is ideal for this information.

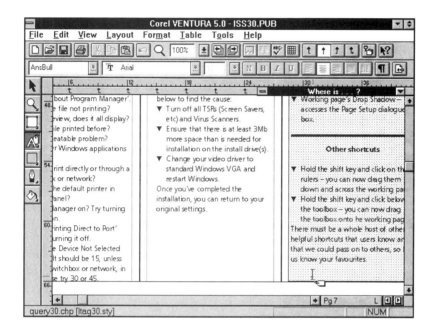

Figure 21.23
Don't be afraid to leave white space.

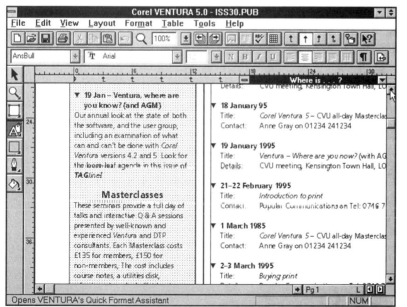

Figure 21.24
Use emphasis to make sure that events of current interest don't get lost.

Bibliography

Chambers Pocket Guide to Good English, George W. Davidson, W & R Chambers, ISBN 0-550-18029-x

The Chicago Manual of Style, University of Chicago Press, ISBN 0-226-10390-0

A Dictionary of Modern English Usage, H. W. Fowler, Oxford University Press, ISBN 019-281-3897

The Elements of Style, Strunk and White, ISBN 0-02-418190-0

Hart's Rules for Compositors and Readers, Oxford University Press, ISBN 0-19-212983-x

One Minute Designer, Roger C. Parker, Que, ISBN 1-56529-216-2

Oxford English Dictionary, Oxford University Press, ISBN 019-86-11862

The Oxford Writer's Dictionary, R. E. Allen, Oxford University Press, ISBN 0-19-282669-7

Webster's Collegiate Dictionary, Merriam Webster, Inc., ISBN 0-87779-508-8

Special offer: Readers interested in subscribing to *TAGline!*—the newsletter of the CorelVENTURA Users group—can take advantage of the special offer given near the back of the book. Simply return the ad with your payment, and *TAGline!* will be on its way.

For further information about *TAGline!* in the USA and Canada, call 802-244-7820 or contact through CompuServe at 70602,1215 or 100042,2771. For information about *TAGline!* and the CVU outside of the USA and Canada, contact the following address:

Anne Gray
CorelVENTURA Users Group
49 Olney Road
Emberton, OLNEY
Bucks, MK46 5BU, Great Britain

Tel: +44 1234 241234
Fax: +44 1234 713757
CompuServe: 100012,1554

Building a Book

Books are part of our everyday life—from the cradle to the grave. A quick visit to your local library will show the vast range of publications that are called books. Everything from children's picture books to multi-volume encyclopedias. Over recent years, the spread of computer technology has lead to an explosive rise in the availability of books because they allow more people to handle more aspects of book production than ever before. This chapter looks at what is involved in the creation of books and suggests ways you can plan your book: the whos, whats, and whys of production. Pointers are provided to help you tie together techniques you've learned from the rest of this book to use VENTURA in an efficient and effective way.

This chapter does not provide a step-by-step recipe on how to create chapters, load graphics, and so forth, because these fundamentals were covered in the previous chapters. It does, however, provide real-life advice to help you in producing a book from the initial planning stage through to final output. It does show you how to avoid many of the typical traps and pitfalls, and gives pointers to which of VENTURA's features are of most use to you for producing books.

Books generally have a single column layout with multiple columns being reserved for "dictionary" type reference works. They have a common structure that is readily apparent to the reader. A book typically contains some, or all, of the following sections:

✔ Cover page with some sort of masthead

✔ Front matter, including copyright and production information

✔ Acknowledgments

✔ Preface

✔ Table of Contents

✔ Main text

✔ Appendices

✔ Bibliography

✔ Index

✔ Advertising

Planning and Controlling Your Book

As with newsletters, planning is the most important aspect of book production, whether you are producing a novel, a multi-volume reference work, or an annual guide book. Unless you plan what you want to achieve and keep close control at all stages, you will have more problems than you can imagine. It is essential to track production and keep all parties informed of what is happening at every stage. What can seem a minor change in one step can dramatically affect other steps, and keeping everyone informed helps to reduce problems.

The first step to good planning is to ask the following questions:

✔ What am I trying to communicate?

✔ When do I need to publish my book?

✔ Who will read my book?

Production Schedule

With the answers to these questions it is fairly easy to start planning the production of your book. By knowing what you are trying to communicate, you are able

to identify the sections required for your book. By identifying when you need to publish your book, you can establish the final deadline. And by identifying who will read your book, you are able to decide how to treat the text and graphics in your book. A child's alphabet book, for example, does not need to be ready on a certain date (children are born all year round), but would need to be produced with bright, colorful pictures and large san serif letters to communicate the simple ABCs. In such a situation, you are considering that children respond better to bright, primary colors and find it easier to read letters in a typeface such as Avant Garde.

Other books, such as an annual reference book, must be produced for a specific date, such as the start of the financial year. Reference books often do not require any pictures at all and are probably okay with small typeface because people will be looking for information, not graphics or pretty colors.

After you have a date for the delivery of your finished book, you can calculate dates for the other stages of your production. Work backward from the delivery date until you have all stages of the production mapped out for each book you are producing. Some of these stages will overlap, and you will need to provide more time for the overlapping stages than you might have originally planned. The types of things you need to consider are as follows:

✔ *What is the method and timetable for the distribution of my book?* Most books are distributed by large publishing houses, and talking to whoever is going to distribute your book provides the details required to plan this section. If you are going to distribute the book yourself, you will need to find out about warehousing and the different ways of dispatching your book from the warehouse.

✔ *How long does it take to print and bind?* Talk to the company you have selected to do the printing and binding of your book. Find out how long they expect it to take from the receipt of your final pages to the delivery of your completed book.

✔ *How long does it take to prepare the initial pages ready for printing, including color separations if I use color?* This depends a great deal on how you are going to prepare the pages for the printing company and what they contain. If you are going straight to your own laser printer to output the final pages, you will have a good idea of how long it takes to output the pages by the work you already carry out. If you are using an external laser printer or imagesetter, you will need to carry out some tests for compatibility at an early stage, and these tests can be used to get an idea of turnaround for your pages when they are finally ready for output.

✔ *How long does it take to lay out the pages?* Again, your initial tests will have given you some idea of how long it will take to format a page. Remember that there will be a range of pages of varying complexity that you will need to produce, so don't base your timing on pages that are easy to format. You may get faster as you become more experienced, but do not rely on this happening. It is better to err on the side of caution and assume that you won't get any faster—and might even get slower.

✔ *If I have advertising, how is it going to be included? Do I need to allow additional time?* The main effect that advertising has on the production schedule is when the artwork for advertisements does not turn up on time. The impact this can have can be minimized by ensuring that you have a range of "house" ads that can be substituted if a paid advertisement does not arrive on time.

✔ *How long does it take to proofread and edit the pages?* For proofreading and copy editing, allow yourself a lot more time than you think is necessary. It is not simply a matter of reading through the text, but involves many checks to ensure the quality of what you produce. Copy editing and the use of a house style are covered in Chapter 21, but a rule of thumb is to allow yourself time to read the book from cover to cover six or seven times. You won't actually read it from cover to cover this often, but you will read it several times and need enough time to edit and check facts.

✔ *Does the text need typing or writing, and, if yes, how long will it take?* The text for your book will usually be produced by authors in a word processor format, and you will not need to have it typed. You might need to allocate time to review what has been submitted. Remember when setting deadlines with authors that they are remarkably optimistic of their own abilities and often grossly underestimate the time it takes to produce their words. Plan accordingly and allow yourself at least twice the time an author quotes in your schedule.

✔ *How much time do I need to allow for slippage?* There will always be times when things do not proceed as planned, and you need to allow more time for unforeseen problems. Don't wait until a deadline arrives, but rather check on progress in advance to give yourself more flexibility to modify your plans to account for any changes in the time scale. Initially, allow for a ten percent slippage over the whole project, in addition to what has been discussed above. As you become more experienced, you will find that you are able to predict the time needed more accurately, and the planning and control will become easier.

After you have answered these questions, you will be able to come up with deadlines for each phase of the production schedule, as demonstrated in figure A.1 by a segment of the "tracking log" used for this book. Deadlines can then be placed on a wall planner, or the like, and any conflicts with holidays or other work resolved. Remember that there are some people and equipment for which there is limited availability, and you need to plan for their use. Finally, issue a reference list of dates to everyone involved.

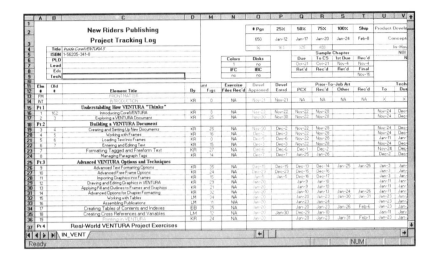

Figure A.1

A segment of the Excel spreadsheet used to track the progress of *Inside CorelVENTURA 5*.

You now have a production schedule to use for tracking the progress of your book. Yours is not a static document. It will be modified as you gain experience and as things change that are beyond your control. The important thing is that you have a way to monitor what is happening, and this is vital as time progresses.

Be realistic about dates. You will learn how to estimate the time required with more accuracy as time goes by, but start by erring on the side of caution. Things usually take longer than expected, and missing one date tends to make all the other dates move as well. Beware of factors on time that are not obvious, such as a computer disk or illustration not being in the correct format. Although this sort of thing can be corrected, it can add days or weeks to the production schedule.

Building a Team

Most fiction is written by individual authors, but the vast majority of reference works are written by multiple authors. This book, for example, had five separate authors who wrote different chapters. It is unusual, though not unknown, for the production of a book to be an individual effort with one person writing, designing, laying out, editing, proofing, printing, and distributing the book. More often, the authors are just one small link in the production process, although they would hate to admit it.

The plan you have produced has already laid the foundations for this team approach because everyone can understand the direction you are heading. Your challenge—and it remains your challenge—is to use your available people to your best advantage.

The whole process becomes dramatically more complicated as more people— with their diverse interests—become involved. Working toward a common goal takes effort and commitment from all those concerned, and good communication is essential to the success of all projects.

Update everyone involved regularly. People work best by praise and encouragement, and keeping them informed of progress with regular feedback works wonders. Make the feedback a regular feature of your production process, but keep the production feedback brief and to the point. Try to strike a suitable balance between the carrot and the stick.

You should concentrate on the following key areas, although the division of labor is not always as straightforward as it might seem. Most of these topics are covered in detail in Chapter 21, and they are briefly summarized here with some additional comments where books are notably different.

✔ Production of initial copy for the book

✔ Copy editing and proofreading

✔ Reproducing the book

✔ Distributing the book

Production of Initial Copy for the Book

Getting the initial copy is often the toughest stage. With novels, it is often easiest to wait for the complete text, but with other books, especially those produced by multiple authors, it is usually best to have the text arrive at different times to stagger the production workload—each worker can only do one thing at a time. Start with an initial outline and a sample chapter or two so that you can see the outline and some detail of what is to be provided. This is discussed later in more detail under the heading "Creating a Book Plan."

If the subject matter is not familiar to you, have the outline and sample chapter reviewed by one or two experts. Ask them their opinion about whether the subject is covered well and get them to highlight any omissions or errors.

Don't fall into the trap of looking at two general chapters. Make sure that one sample chapter you have is general and the other is a specific chapter from later in the book, allowing you to judge both the overall appeal and the specific detail of the book.

Refer to your production plan when talking to authors about writing copy so you can agree on realistic deadlines. Keep a record of what you are expecting to receive and when. Talk to the authors on a regular basis and provide feedback on their progress. Remember that you are relying on the author to produce quality work that meets your house style. Give them quick and positive feedback to encourage them to write what you require—when you require it.

It is effective to get the person submitting the copy to set his own deadline for submission, and linking the delivery of the written word to staged payment can provide an additional incentive. Remember that many authors are remarkably ambitious about their ability to write and meet deadlines. Provide regular feedback, keep authors informed of progress, and provide help and assistance whenever necessary to enable them to submit their work on time.

Using this people friendly approach means that the person writing the copy has a greater incentive to meet the deadline, knowing you are relying on him. It also gives you the opportunity to check on his progress before the deadline and make other arrangements if there is a problem. Remember that you are working together toward a common goal, and your support and feedback are far more effective that threats and pressure. But if worse comes to worst, you can assess a financial penalty to add weight to your gentler persuasions.

Copy Editing and Proofreading

Copy editing and proofreading exist to eliminate the errors and to improve the quality of what is printed. In essence, the copy editor ensures the text conforms to standard language usage and is technically accurate, and the proof reader attempts to find errors, such as references to pictures that do not exist.

By the very nature of the job, especially when using DTP, these two roles overlap and are difficult to distinguish. You should not worry if you cannot tell the two roles apart because it is the process of checking, and more importantly correcting, that needs to be instilled into your production process. A well defined house style, as discussed in Chapter 21, will help you in this process.

Do not try to proofread your own writing or editing. If you made a mistake in the first place, it's unlikely that you will spot it when you proofread. You will have the same mental blind spot the second time around. This is especially true of spelling and language usage mistakes, which one rarely ever catches.

Reproducing the Book

Unless you're going to print every copy of your book on your laser printer, you will need to consider how the book will be reproduced. Many successful books are simply photocopies, folded and stapled, but even here you need to consider whether you do this yourself or get someone else to do it for you. The decision is strongly influenced by whether you have the equipment and time to complete the task. The important thing is to discuss the reproduction method with other members of your team.

Do not assume that because you can do something with VENTURA that this is the only or best way to do it. A good, experienced printer can achieve the same thing with ease and save you a lot of time, effort, and money. One example is this book which would be ideal for VENTURA, but, due to the production set-up at New Riders Publishing, it is easier and cheaper to produce the book using different methods.

Discussing your reproduction options allows you to decide who will do what and how to make the most efficient use of your time and money when reproducing your book, particularly important when the book is going to be printed rather than photocopied. The printing process, with its imagesetting, platemaking, and impositions, adds an additional level of complexity that many DTP users are unfamiliar with. Talking with your printer allows you to understand the process and provides what is needed to ease the production process.

Talk to your printer about the most economical way to reproduce your book and maximize the available press options such as color. Unlike laser printers, a printing press will print several of your book pages onto each side of a sheet of press paper. These large sheets are then folded, trimmed, and bound together to form your book. The way the sheet of paper is folded will make a difference to how the pages are initially laid out and where color, if you are using it, will appear.

You can use the information provided by the commercial printer to help in planning your book. If, for example, the commercial printer says you will get 16 pages of your book to each side of a printed press sheet, you know that each sheet will contain 32 book pages. You can then plan your book accordingly in multiples of 32, 64, 96, 128, and so on.

The way your book pages are laid out on the printer's press sheet is called an *imposition*. Producing an imposition is best left to the commercial printer because it is a specialized process where mistakes are costly.

Distributing the Book

At first glance, it might seem strange to consider distribution as part of the production process of books, but distribution can have a dramatic effect on other stages of production. For example, in the United Kingdom, books are not taxed, but disks and CDs are, which means that a book that includes a CD or disk is taxed for the disk part of the package. This leads to complicated pricing and a reluctance for booksellers to stock the book. The size and weight also need to be considered for shipping and onward distribution because most shipping companies calculate their rates based on a weight-to-volume ratio; making your book a suitable size and weight or packaging them differently can make a big difference in the cost of distribution.

The types of illustrations need to be considered. Illustrations that are acceptable in some countries are not acceptable in others. In some countries, showing the face of a woman or mentioning Christianity is enough to have your book banned.

Creating the Book Plan

The very nature of books means that you have a ready made outline in the table of contents (TOC). The TOC will be referred to by your reader and reflects the headings used throughout your book. It provides an indication of how the book is structured and the logical development of ideas from chapter to chapter and within each chapter. It is because of this that a TOC can be used as an overall guide to planning the content of your book. It is, however, not sufficient in its own right and, as discussed earlier, you will need to get sample chapters written and reviewed before the project starts.

Remember that this initial outline in the form of a table of contents is a working document that can change over time as the book develops. This is especially the case where several authors are involved. For example, this chapter changed from the initial outline shown in the following TOC form:

Exercise: Building a Book

Using VENTURA Style Sheets

Importing Text onto the Base Page

Adding Frames

Headers and Footers

Tagging Text

Adding Chapters into Publications

Such an order is quite different from the chapter as it actually appears in the book. During development of the book, it became apparent that the original outline was merely a repeat of previous chapters. It was decided that a discussion of the production process would be more valuable to people trying to produce books.

Use your word processor's outline facility to produce an outline for each chapter using the different levels of heading you expect to use in the book. These headings can be expanded and filled as the book develops. Use the table of contents features of VENTURA to generate a TOC from the chapters that comprise your book.

Understanding the Anatomy of a Book

This section gives a look at the typical features of a book, highlighting and providing pointers to how you might implement things in your own book for maximum impact. It begins with an overview of the general procedures for producing each edition of your book and moves on to looking at how the whole thing fits together.

Using Your Book as a Template

After your first book is produced, you will have a VENTURA publication containing several different chapters for each section of your book. You will probably want to use some of these sections again for the next edition of your book. You will want to copy the useful files and leave behind those that are out-of-date.

VENTURA provides the ideal tool for saving appropriate files in its support for templates. The procedure for using templates is identical to that described in the newsletter chapter. First, archive your existing book using Publication Manager's Smart Copy feature. Then start a new publication using the Base on Template option to copy over the files you want to retain for the new edition.

Remember that if you are using shared chapters that are used by many different books, these should not be copied. Shared chapters should be added to the publication using the **L**ayout, Add E**x**isting Chapter option, which adds a pointer to the shared chapter, rather than copy the files across to a new subdirectory.

If you are producing several books on a common theme, you might find that they can share common chapters, such as reference tables and bibliographies. It is worth including material in a chapter that is not directly relevant to the current book you are publishing if it allows you to maintain one common set of chapters for use throughout a series of books.

For example, you might have one common chapter on "Useful Information" that is included in all books, even though all the information in this chapter might not be used in every book. The benefit is that you only need to track changes in one chapter, and these changes are automatically reflected in all books that use this chapter.

After you have copied the files that you want, use the **F**ile, Pu**b**lication Manager to add any additional chapters and arrange them in the right sequence.

Make sure that you have all the style sheets you need stored in a separate subdirectory. You will not always use every style sheet. If they are not stored somewhere safe, you will find yourself in the future searching your archives to find missing style sheets.

From Page to Page

The front cover of your book is the first thing that people see, and it should make an immediate impact through the combined use of text and graphics. You should have a short, punchy visual title, or *masthead*, to act as a visual cue to your readers to identify a book as yours. You do not want to create a title that is unwieldy or complicated because the masthead is there primarily for identification, not communication. Because of the graphical nature of most book covers, you probably want to produce the cover in CorelDRAW or PHOTO-PAINT, not VENTURA.

The first few pages of any published book host a range of "front matter" pages, covering such things as copyright notices, library cataloging information, production information, acknowledgments, and introductions. For books that are generally available from booksellers and libraries, the essential information is the library cataloging information and the *International Standard Book Number* (ISBN) number.

Adding an ISBN to your book gives it an authority that might otherwise be lacking and allows people to obtain it through libraries. Many booksellers do not handle books that do not have ISBNs. The ISBN should appear on the

continues

cover of the book and in the front matter, along with the library cataloging information. For examples of both, look at how it is done in this book.

You first have to get permission to use an ISBN from your local standard numbering agency. After you have obtained the ISBN, you must submit several copies of the book to your national library to retain the right to use the ISBN. In addition, there are penalties for non-compliance that vary from country to country.

In most books, the table of contents is the next thing most readers come across. Works of fiction are the most likely exception to this rule, but even these usually have a table of contents. As described in Chapter 17, the Table of Contents should show the logical and structured way the book is put together. Although the final Table of Contents might not resemble the originally planned Table of Contents, it should still have a logical structure and be complete.

Page numbers and chapter and section headers should be included throughout the book. Try to put your page numbers on the outside edge of the page so they can be seen when flipping through the book. Remember that there are different settings for the right and left footers. Use the Mirror to Facing Pages option in the Header/Footer tab of the Chapter Setting dialog box. If page numbers are in the center, it is difficult to find the page you want quickly.

It is also possible to place page numbers anywhere on the page using the cross reference feature.

New chapters traditionally start on right pages, and this might mean that you have to insert blank pages at the end of preceding chapters.

Remember when producing your book that your reader sees it as a two-page spread and not as individual pages. You should aim to strike a balance across the facing pages. Remember to use VENTURA's facing page view to do an initial check of the appearance. Do not rely on this and make sure you print the pages and look at them spread in front of you before committing to full-blown print. It is always worth making a *dummy* copy of your book that is as close as possible to what your reader will see to check that everything is all right. Print every page with all the illustrations in place so you can see what they will look like. Next, trim the pages to the correct size if necessary and place them back-to-back so they appear as they would in the final printed book. Now look through the whole book, checking for any problems.

Remember that novels and reference books are structured differently to reflect their different purposes. With reference books, readers want to know how chapters interrelate, and you should provide as much help to them as possible.

Cross-references are an ideal way to provide pointers to readers of where further information can be found.

Consider adding an index entry wherever you have a cross-reference because it is likely that if a reader needs to follow the cross-reference, she'll also want to look the topic up in an index.

Don't forget to include examples and illustrations. The old saying that a picture is worth a thousand words should always be in the back of your mind. Whether it is a photograph, line art, clip art, or a cartoon, make sure that the text does not get too close to the illustration. If the illustration includes a lot of text, make sure it is adequately distinguished from the surrounding body text.

Use CorelMOSAIC to build a complete library of the files you use for illustration. These can then be accessed easily from the Mosaic Roll-up in VENTURA, which enables you to see a preview of all the graphics you might want to use. See *Inside CorelDRAW! 5*, published by New Riders, which discusses MOSAIC in more detail.

Don't be afraid to leave blanks pages at the end of chapters; every last page does not have to be filled. If you pack every last centimeter of every page with text, your book will start to resemble wallpaper and become intimidating and oppressive. Leaving *white space* throughout the book allows the text and graphics to breath and, in turn, provides a more attractive and easy-to-read publication.

Creating Print Files

Creating print files for sending to an outside commercial printer is covered in Chapter 19, "Printing in VENTURA." When preparing print files, make sure you send a proof print out of your book with the disks so the commercial printer knows what should be printed. The best way to do this is to first create the print files. Copy them to the disk to send to your commercial printer, then send the print files to your local laser printer using a utility such as PCSEND, which comes with Adobe fonts. Check these pages carefully; it is these pages that should go to the commercial printer. Make sure the commercial printer knows what fonts are used in your book or, better still, embed the fonts in the print file.

If you are producing the book for someone else, it is a good idea to send them these proof pages and get them to initial every page to indicate their satisfaction so the book can be produced. Keep a copy of these pages in case there are any queries to be resolved.

Bibliography

In addition to the books given in Chapter 21, the following slim volumes provide some useful pointers to those producing their own books. Both are written for the UK market.

Preparing for Publication, King Edward's Hospital Fund for London, ISBN 0 900889 62 4

Why Not Start Your own Printing Business?, Alan Robinson, Kirkfield Publications, ISBN 0 946353 03 4

INDEX

INDEX

INDEX

INDEX

INDEX

INDEX

INDEX

INDEX

INDEX

INDEX

INDEX

INDEX

INDEX

N

INDEX

INDEX

INDEX

INDEX

INDEX

INDEX

INDEX

INDEX

INDEX

INDEX

INDEX

INDEX

TAGline!

News — Up to the minute news on all that concerns *Ventura*, *CorelDraw* and *PhotoPaint* users

Reviews — Hardware, software, typefaces, utilities, books, videos, and CDs that can help you in your everyday work.

User Stories — *How to* articles written by users - for users. See how *Ventura*, *CorelDraw*, *PhotoPaint* and other packages are used by others for their work.

Hints & Tips — Hints and tips that can save hours of effort and save you money.

Q&A — Your questions answered in plain English. Practical and straightforward explanations of how to get round the limitations of the software. If it's a bug we call it a bug.

In the USA/Canada TAGline! (not CVU membership) is available at $49.95 for 10 issues from:
John R. Faunce,
RR1 Box 6020,
Waterbury Center,
Vermont 05677
Tel: (802) 244 7820
CompuServe 70502,1215

Send check, Visa, or Mastercard details without delay

In the UK annual membership of CVU (with TAGline!) is available at £58.75 (inc. VAT) from:
Anne Gray (CVU),
49 Olney Road,
Emberton, Olney,
Bucks, MK46 5BU
Tel: 01234 241234
CompuServe 100012,1554

Send cheque, Visa, or Mastercard details without delay

PLUG YOURSELF INTO...

THE MACMILLAN INFORMATION SUPERLIBRARY™

Free information and vast computer resources from the world's leading computer book publisher—online!

FIND THE BOOKS THAT ARE RIGHT FOR YOU!

A complete online catalog, plus sample chapters and tables of contents give you an in-depth look at *all* of our books, including hard-to-find titles. It's the best way to find the books you need!

- **STAY INFORMED** with the latest computer industry news through our online newsletter, press releases, and customized Information SuperLibrary Reports.

- **GET FAST ANSWERS** to your questions about MCP books and software.

- **VISIT** our online bookstore for the latest information and editions!

- **COMMUNICATE** with our expert authors through e-mail and conferences.

- **DOWNLOAD SOFTWARE** from the immense MCP library:
    - Source code and files from MCP books
    - The best shareware, freeware, and demos

- **DISCOVER HOT SPOTS** on other parts of the Internet.

- **WIN BOOKS** in ongoing contests and giveaways!

TO PLUG INTO MCP: →

GOPHER: gopher.mcp.com
FTP: ftp.mcp.com

WORLD WIDE WEB: http://www.mcp.com

WANT MORE INFORMATION?

CHECK OUT THESE RELATED TOPICS OR SEE YOUR LOCAL BOOKSTORE

CAD and 3D Studio

As the number one CAD publisher in the world, and as a Registered Publisher of Autodesk, New Riders Publishing provides unequaled content on this complex topic. Industry-leading products include AutoCAD and 3D Studio.

Networking

As the leading Novell NetWare publisher, New Riders Publishing delivers cutting-edge products for network professionals. We publish books for all levels of users, from those wanting to gain NetWare Certification, to those administering or installing a network. Leading books in this category include *Inside NetWare 3.12, CNE Training Guide: Managing NetWare Systems, Inside TCP/IP,* and *NetWare: The Professional Reference.*

Graphics

New Riders provides readers with the most comprehensive product tutorials and references available for the graphics market. Best-sellers include *Inside CorelDRAW! 5, Inside Photoshop 3,* and *Adobe Photoshop NOW!*

Internet and Communications

As one of the fastest growing publishers in the communications market, New Riders provides unparalleled information and detail on this ever-changing topic area. We publish international best-sellers such as *New Riders' Official Internet Yellow Pages, 2nd Edition,* a directory of over 10,000 listings of Internet sites and resources from around the world, and *Riding the Internet Highway, Deluxe Edition.*

Operating Systems

Expanding off our expertise in technical markets, and driven by the needs of the computing and business professional, New Riders offers comprehensive references for experienced and advanced users of today's most popular operating systems, including *Understanding Windows 95, Inside Unix, Inside Windows 3.11 Platinum Edition, Inside OS/2 Warp Version 3,* and *Inside MS-DOS 6.22.*

Other Markets

Professionals looking to increase productivity and maxmize the potential of their software and hardware should spend time discovering our line of products for Word, Excel, and Lotus 1-2-3. These titles include *Inside Word 6 for Windows, Inside Excel 5 for Windows, Inside 1-2-3 Release 5,* and *Inside WordPerfect for Windows.*

Orders/Customer Service **1-800-653-6156**   Source Code **NRP95**

New Riders Publishing   201 West 103rd Street ◆ Indianapolis, Indiana 46290 USA

REGISTRATION CARD

Inside CorelVENTURA 5

Name _____ Title _____

Company _____ Type of business _____

Address _____

City/State/ZIP _____

Have you used these types of books before? ☐ yes ☐ no

If yes, which ones? _____

_____

How many computer books do you purchase each year? ☐ 1–5 ☐ 6 or more

How did you learn about this book? _____

Where did you purchase this book? _____

Which applications do you currently use? _____

_____

Which computer magazines do you subscribe to? _____

_____

What trade shows do you attend? _____

_____

Comments: _____

_____

_____

Would you like to be placed on our preferred mailing list? ☐ yes ☐ no

☐ **I would like to see my name in print!** You may use my name and quote me in future New Riders products and promotions. My daytime phone number is: _____

New Riders Publishing 201 West 103rd Street ◆ Indianapolis, Indiana 46290 USA

Fax to **317-581-4670** Orders/Customer Service **1-800-653-6156** Source Code **NRP95**

Fold Here

BUSINESS REPLY MAIL
FIRST-CLASS MAIL PERMIT NO. 9918 INDIANAPOLIS IN

POSTAGE WILL BE PAID BY THE ADDRESSEE

NEW RIDERS PUBLISHING
201 W 103RD ST
INDIANAPOLIS IN 46290-9058